FIRE FORCE

01

ATSUSHI
OHKUBO

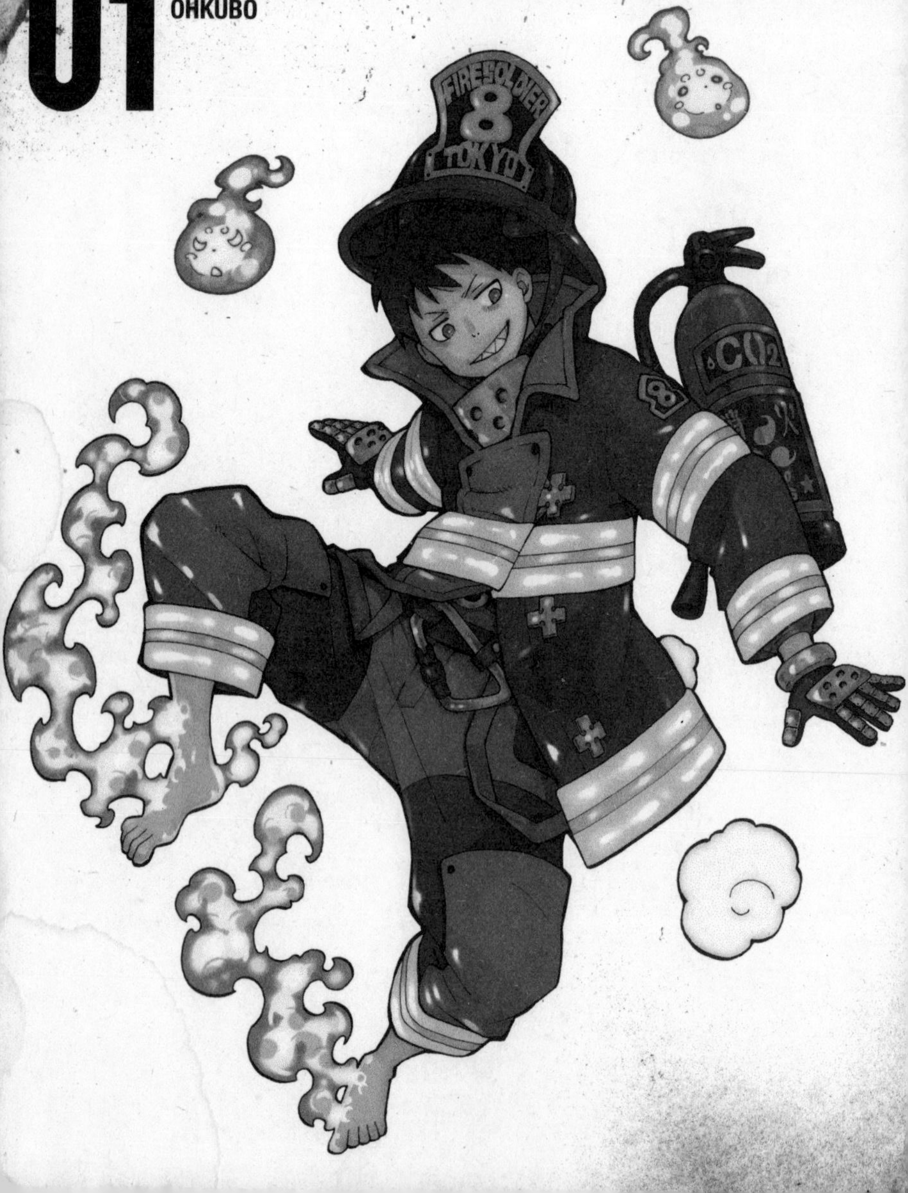
FIRESOLDIER
8
TOKYO

FIRE FORCE

CONTENTS 01

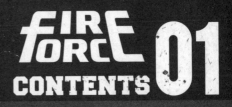

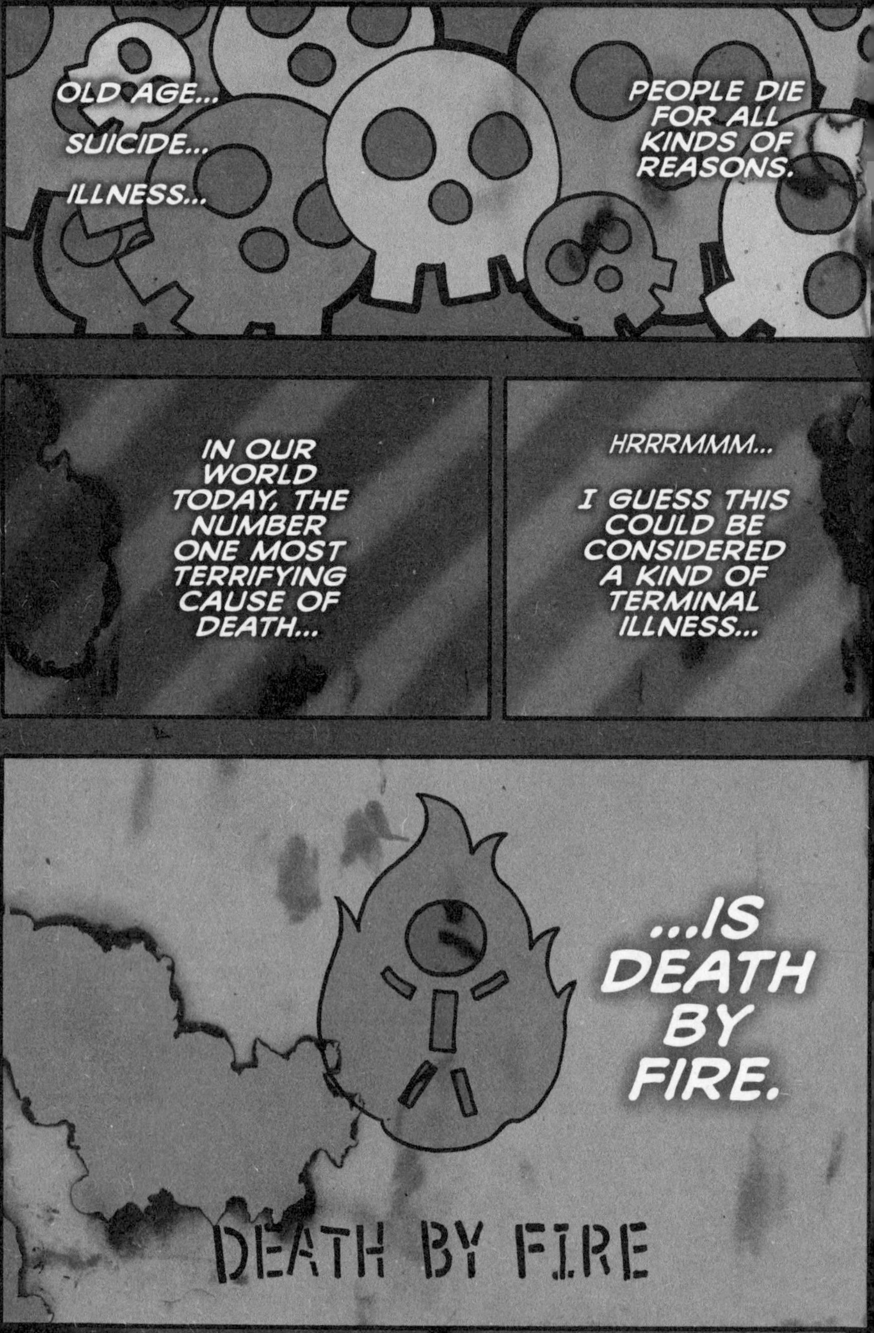
PEOPLE DIE FOR ALL KINDS OF REASONS.
OLD AGE...
SUICIDE...
ILLNESS...
HRRRMMM...
I GUESS THIS COULD BE CONSIDERED A KIND OF TERMINAL ILLNESS...
IN OUR WORLD TODAY, THE NUMBER ONE MOST TERRIFYING CAUSE OF DEATH...
...IS DEATH BY FIRE.
DEATH BY FIRE

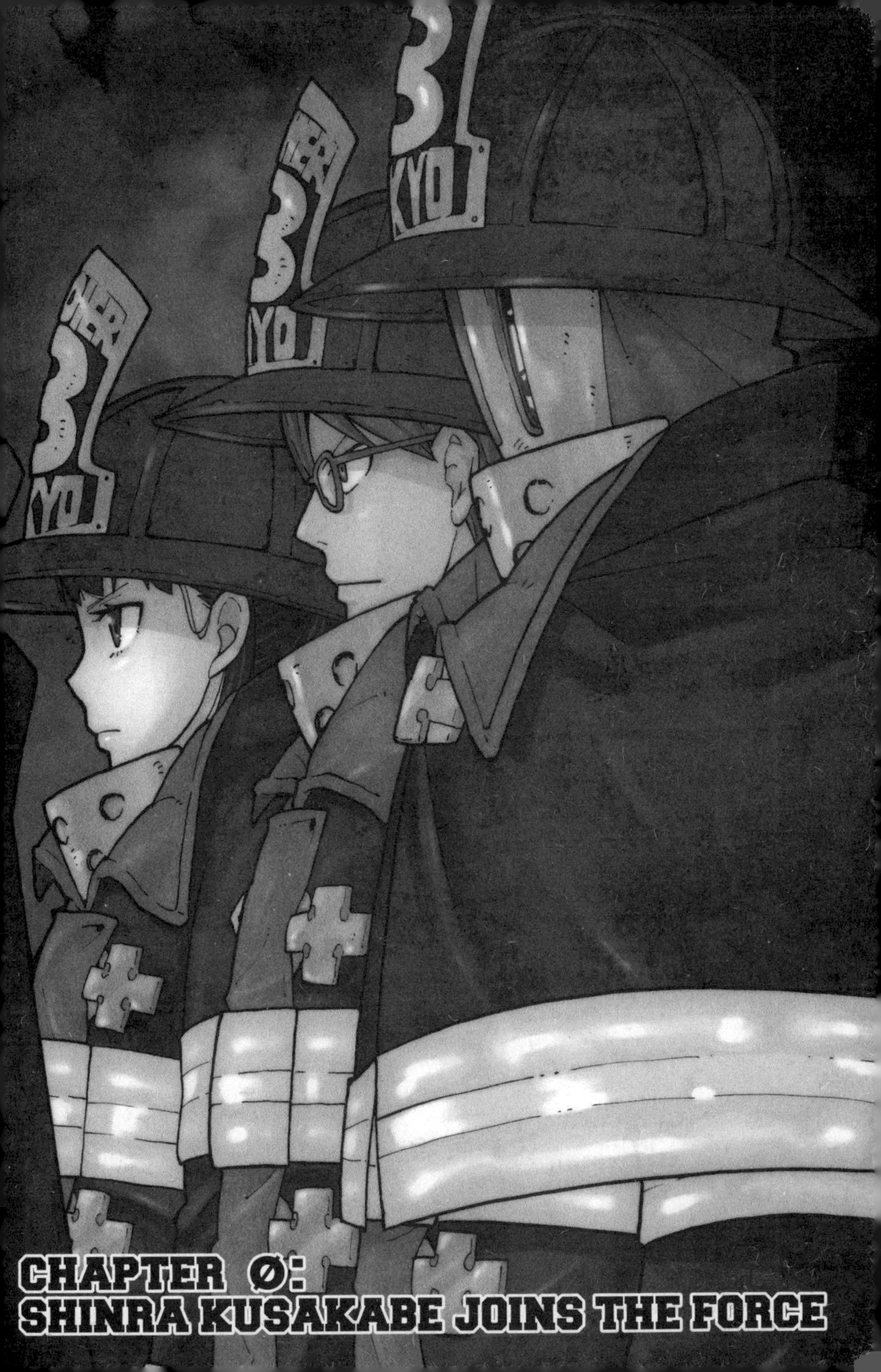

CHAPTER Ø: SHINRA KUSAKABE JOINS THE FORCE

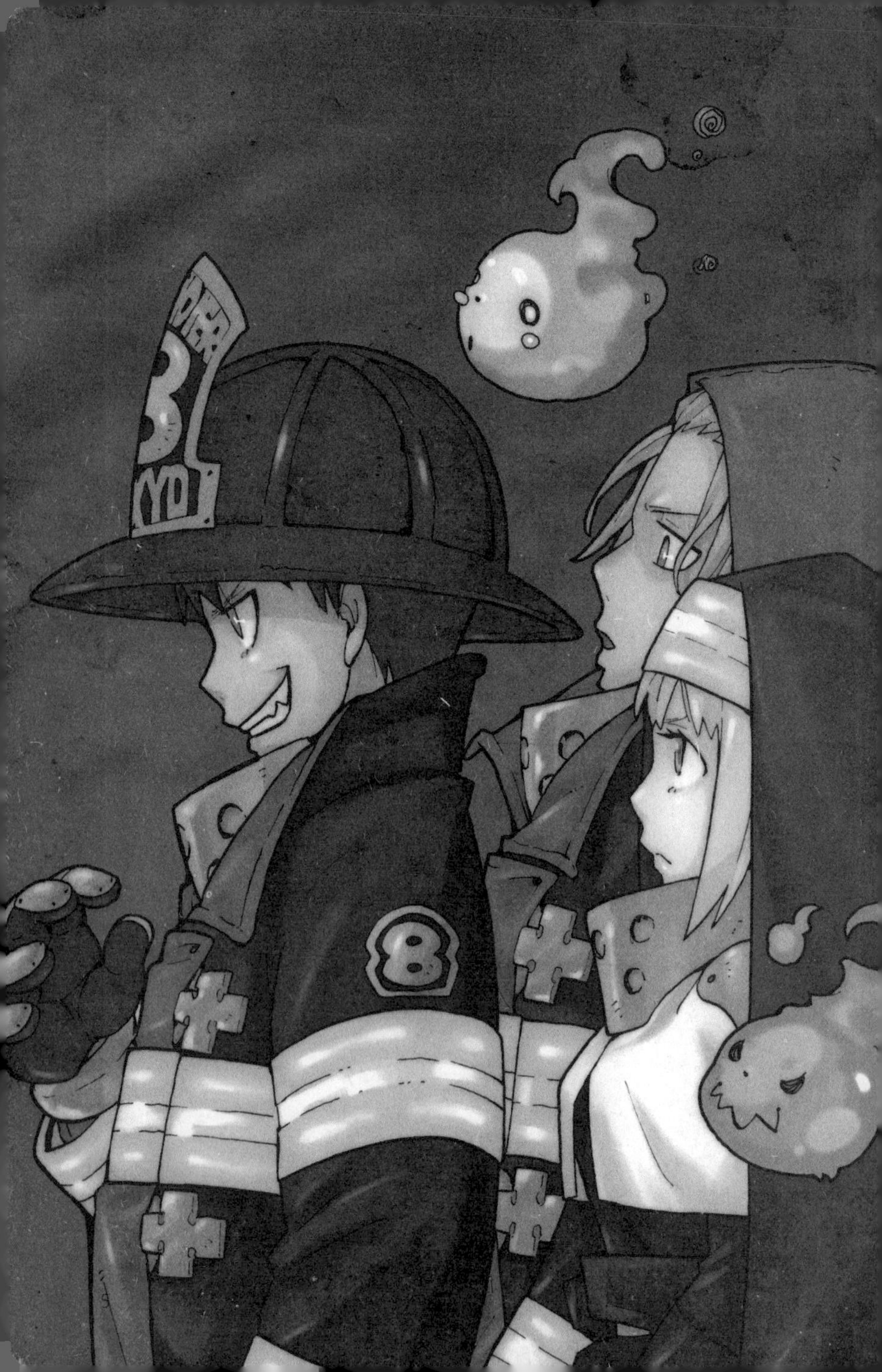

FIRE FORCE

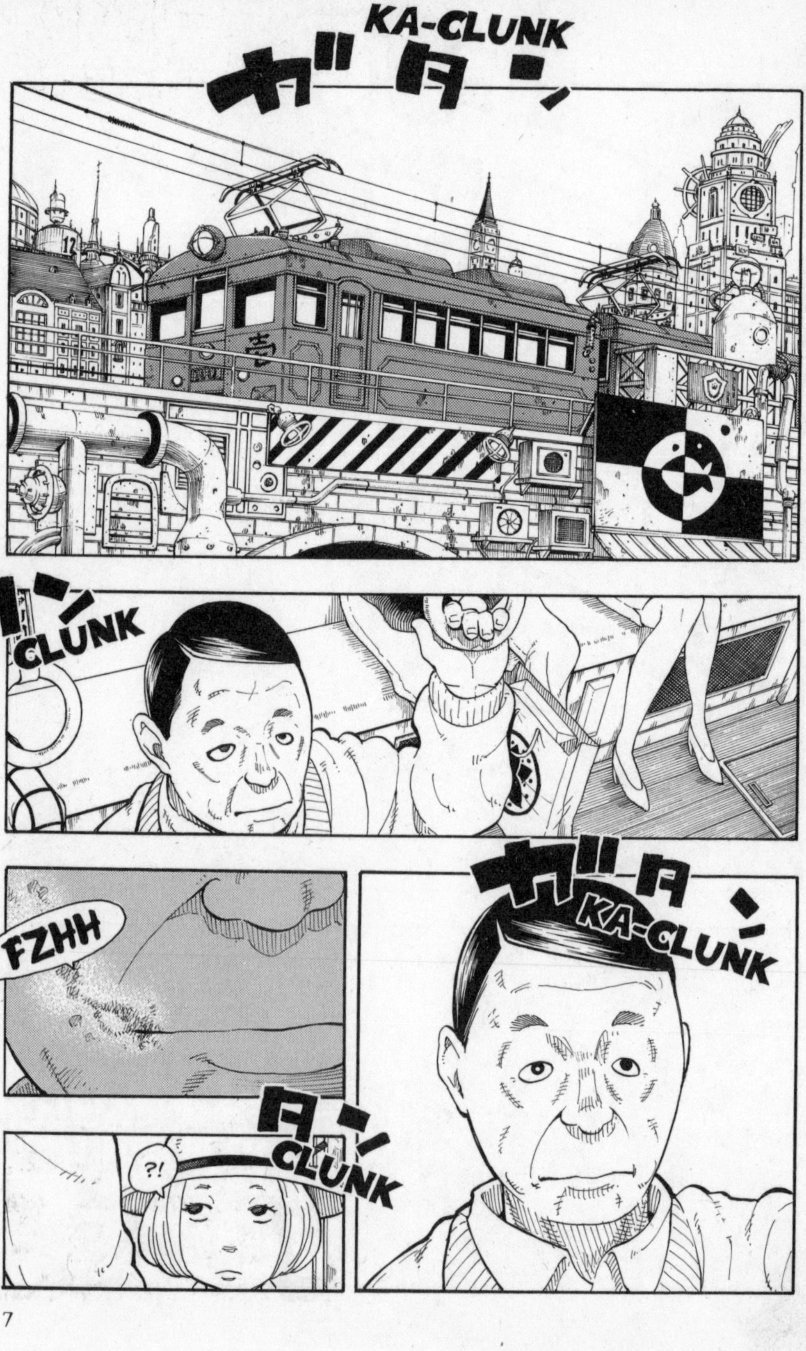
ガタン
KA-CLUNK
タン
CLUNK
ガタン
KA-CLUNK
FZHH
タン
CLUNK
?!

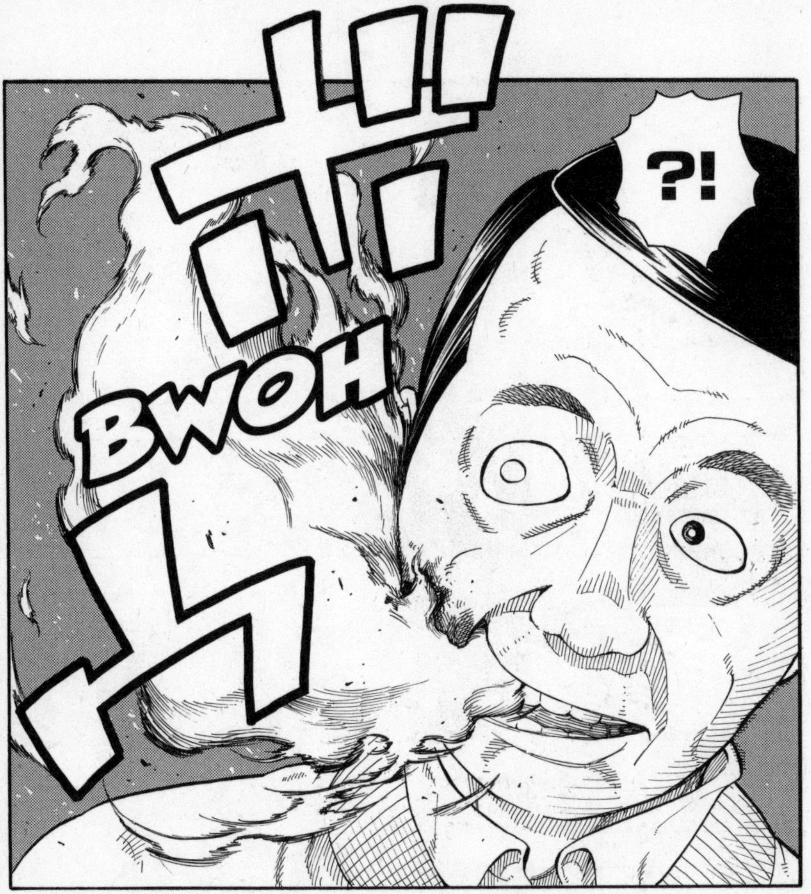
?!
BWOH

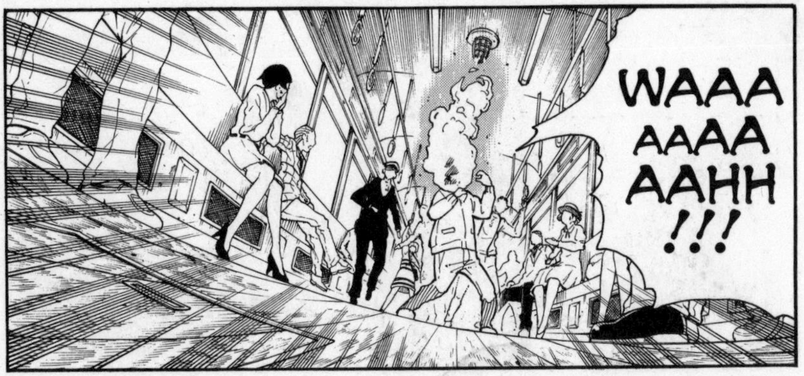
WAAAAAAAAAHH!!!

TEP
TEP
HUFF HUFF
DANG, IT'S ALREADY HERE!
Z-Z-ZOOM
SIZZLE SIZZLE
OOPS!
DIDN'T MEAN TO–
BUMP
EEK!

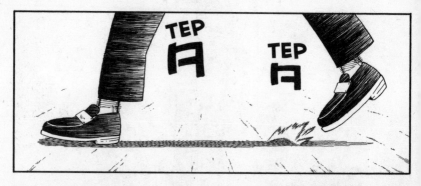

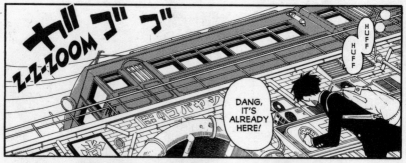

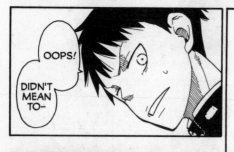

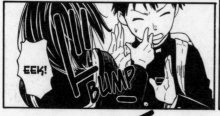

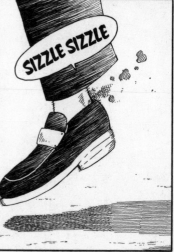

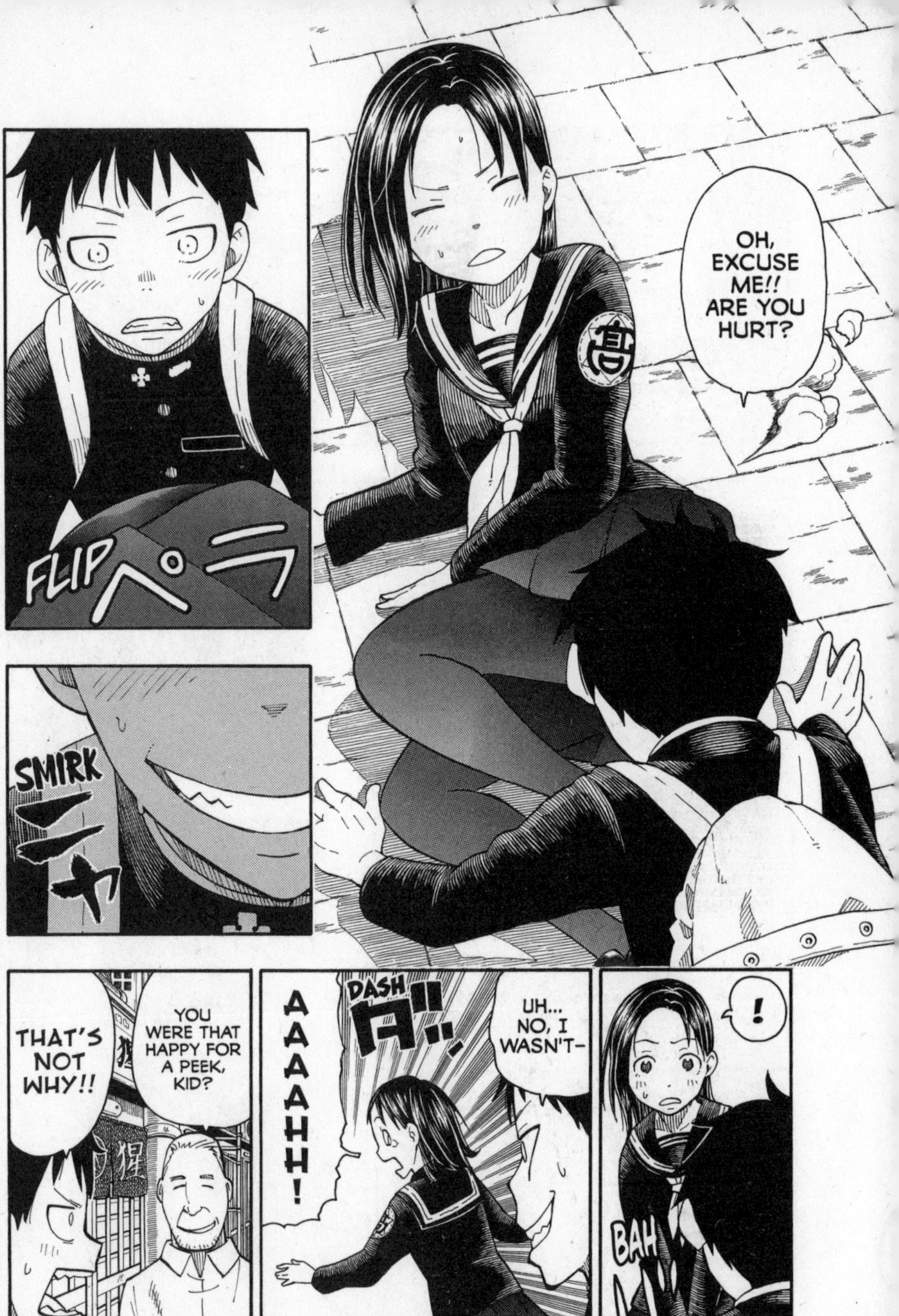
OH, EXCUSE ME!! ARE YOU HURT?
FLIP
ペラ
SMIRK
!
BAH
UH... NO, I WASN'T-
DASH
ダッ
AAAAAHH!
YOU WERE THAT HAPPY FOR A PEEK, KID?
THAT'S NOT WHY!!

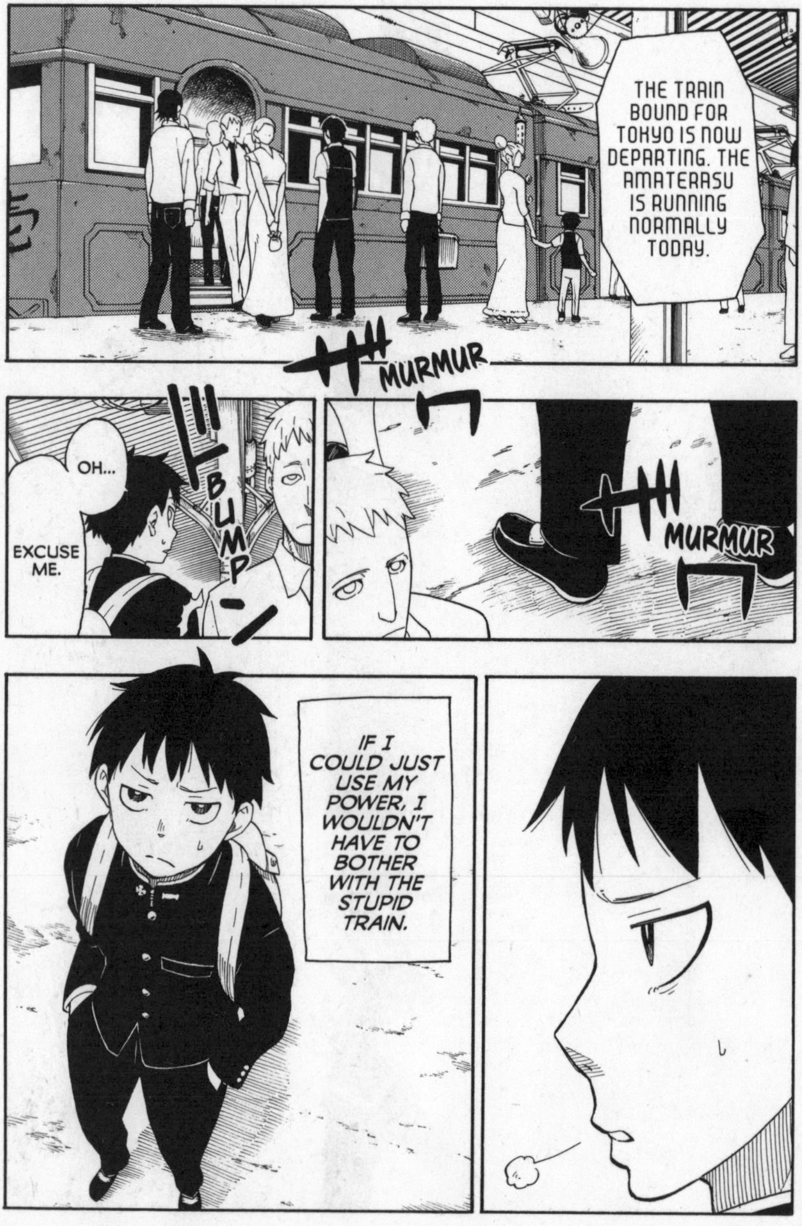
THE TRAIN BOUND FOR TOKYO IS NOW DEPARTING. THE AMATERASU IS RUNNING NORMALLY TODAY.
MURMUR
MURMUR
BUMP
OH...
EXCUSE ME.
IF I COULD JUST USE MY POWER, I WOULDN'T HAVE TO BOTHER WITH THE STUPID TRAIN.

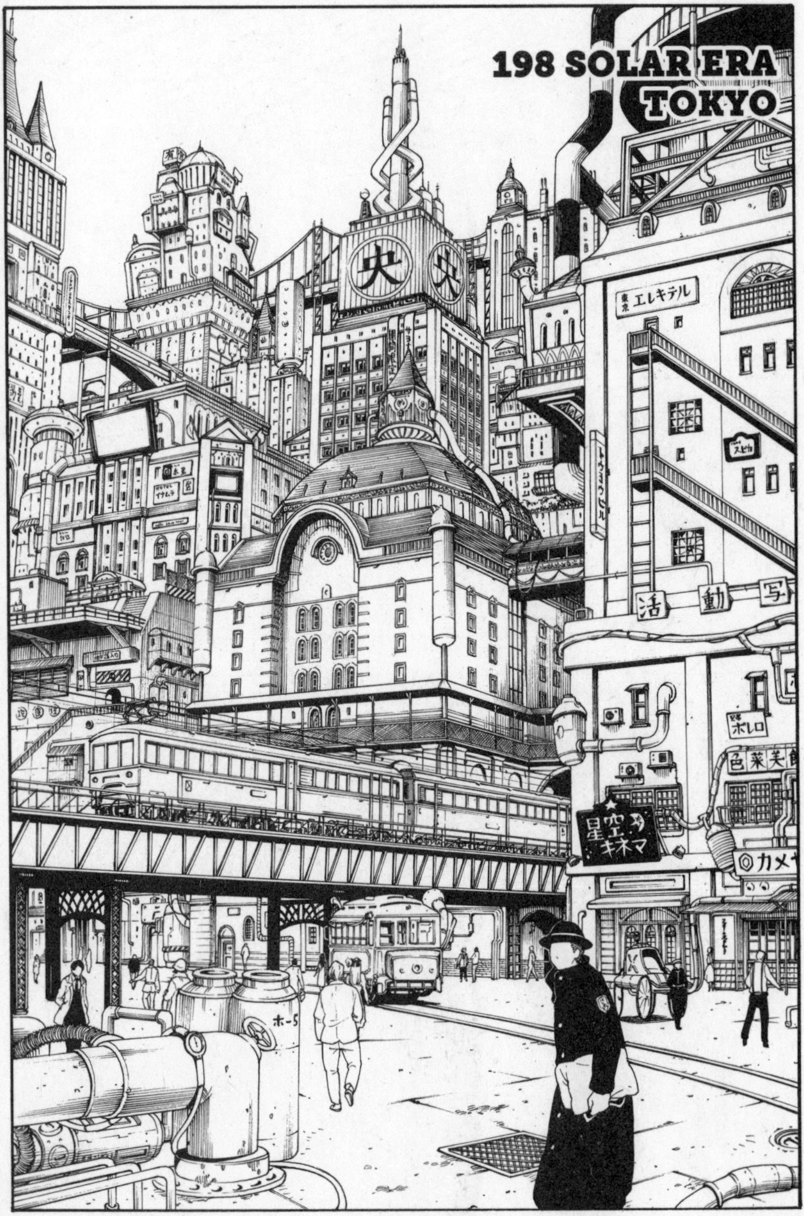
198 SOLAR ERA
TOKYO
東京 エレキテル
活 動 写
星空 キネマ
ボレロ

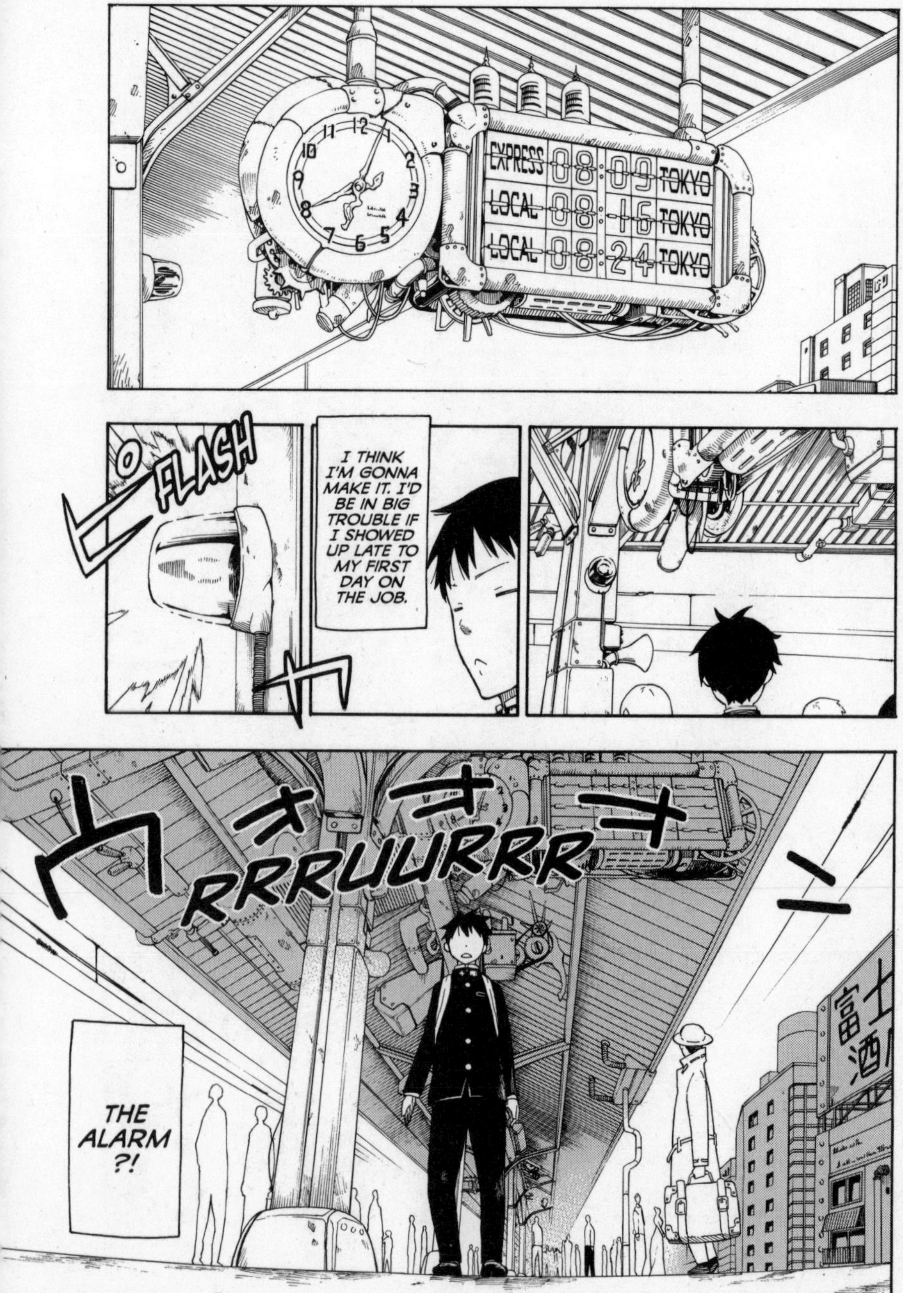
EXPRESS 08:09 TOKYO
LOCAL 08:16 TOKYO
LOCAL 08:24 TOKYO
I THINK I'M GONNA MAKE IT. I'D BE IN BIG TROUBLE IF I SHOWED UP LATE TO MY FIRST DAY ON THE JOB.
FLASH
RRRUURRR
THE ALARM ?!

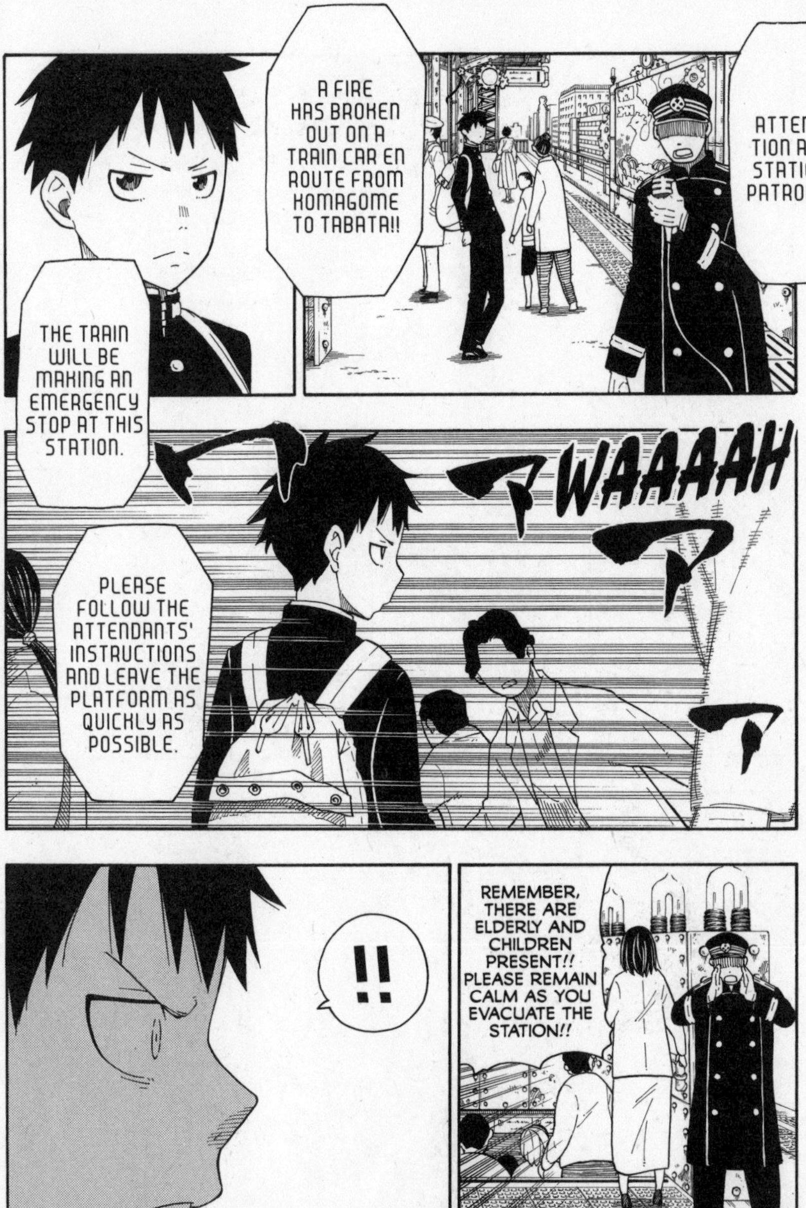
ATTEN-TION ALL STATION PATRONS.
A FIRE HAS BROKEN OUT ON A TRAIN CAR EN ROUTE FROM KOMAGOME TO TABATA!!
THE TRAIN WILL BE MAKING AN EMERGENCY STOP AT THIS STATION.
WAAAAH
PLEASE FOLLOW THE ATTENDANTS' INSTRUCTIONS AND LEAVE THE PLATFORM AS QUICKLY AS POSSIBLE.
REMEMBER, THERE ARE ELDERLY AND CHILDREN PRESENT!! PLEASE REMAIN CALM AS YOU EVACUATE THE STATION!!
!!

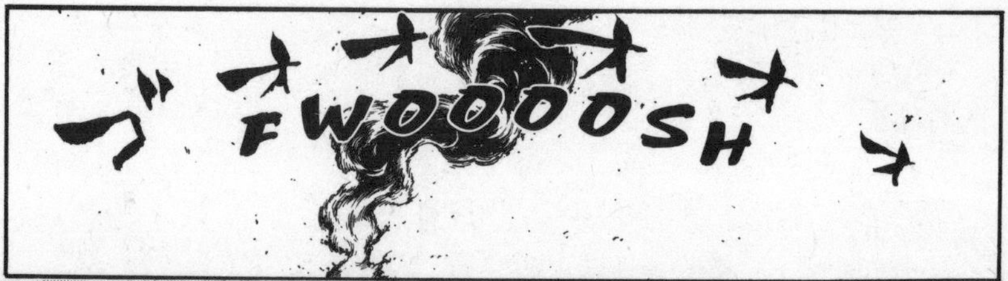
ゴオオオオオ
FWOOOOOSH

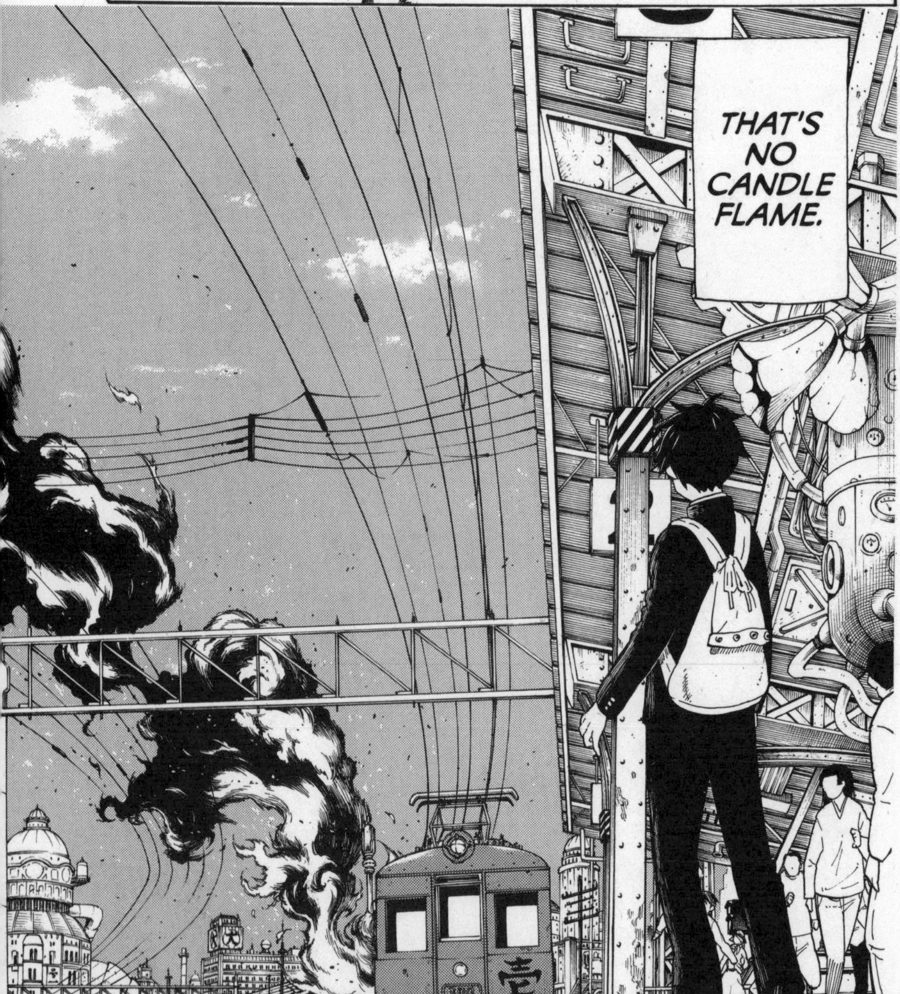
THAT'S NO CANDLE FLAME.

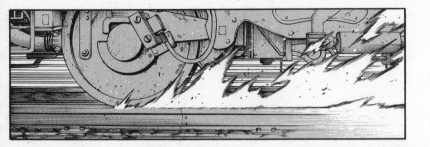

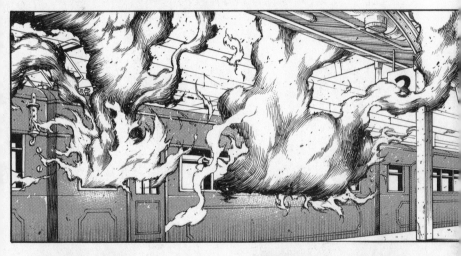

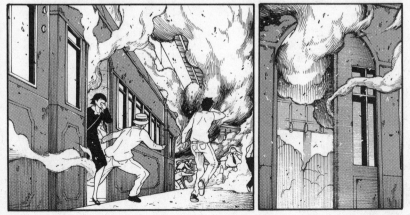

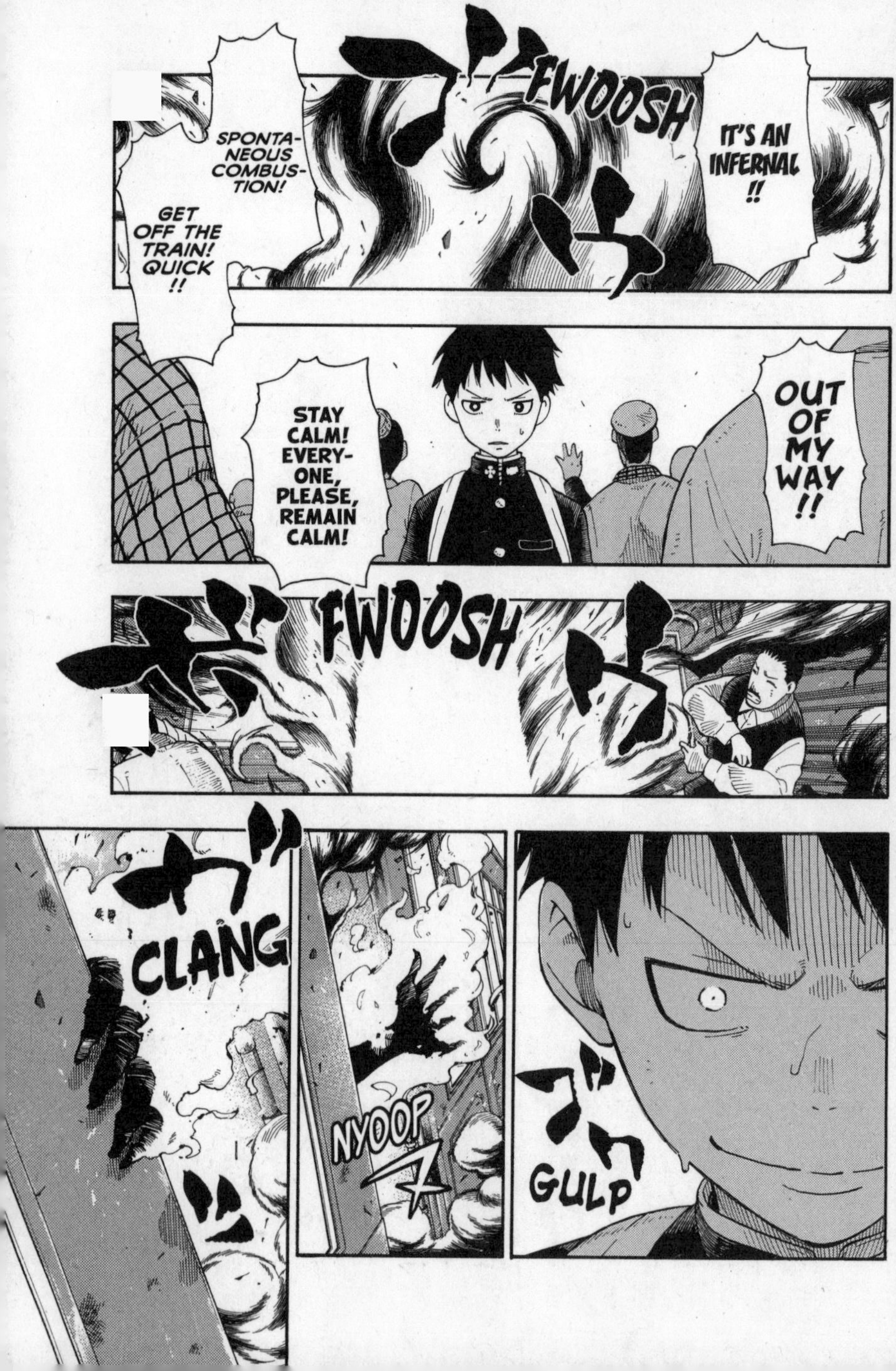
IT'S AN INFERNAL !!
FWOOSH
SPONTANEOUS COMBUSTION!
GET OFF THE TRAIN! QUICK !!
OUT OF MY WAY !!
STAY CALM! EVERYONE, PLEASE, REMAIN CALM!
FWOOSH
GULP
NYOOP
CLANG

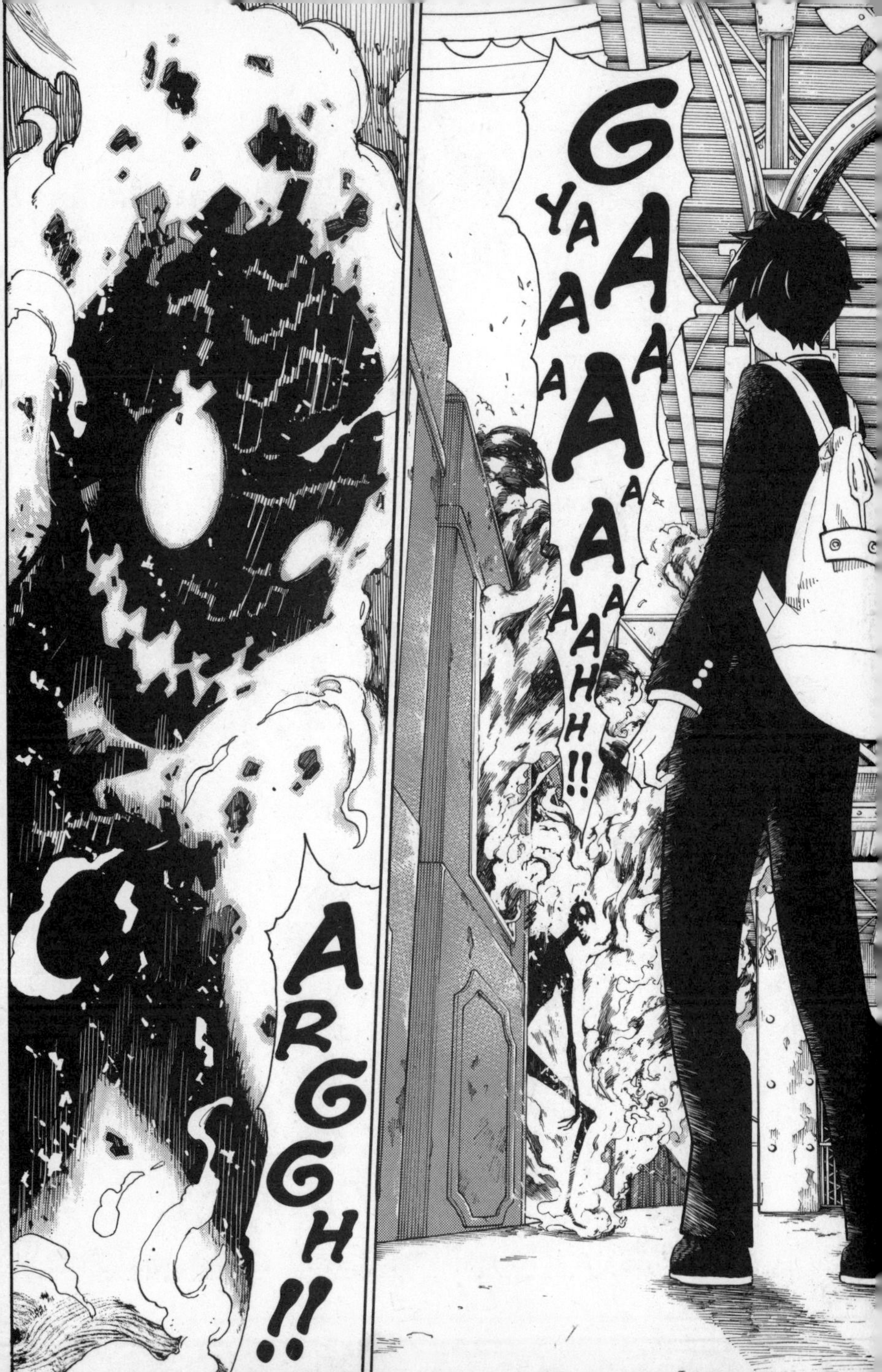
GYAAAAAAAAAAAAHH!!
ARGGH!!

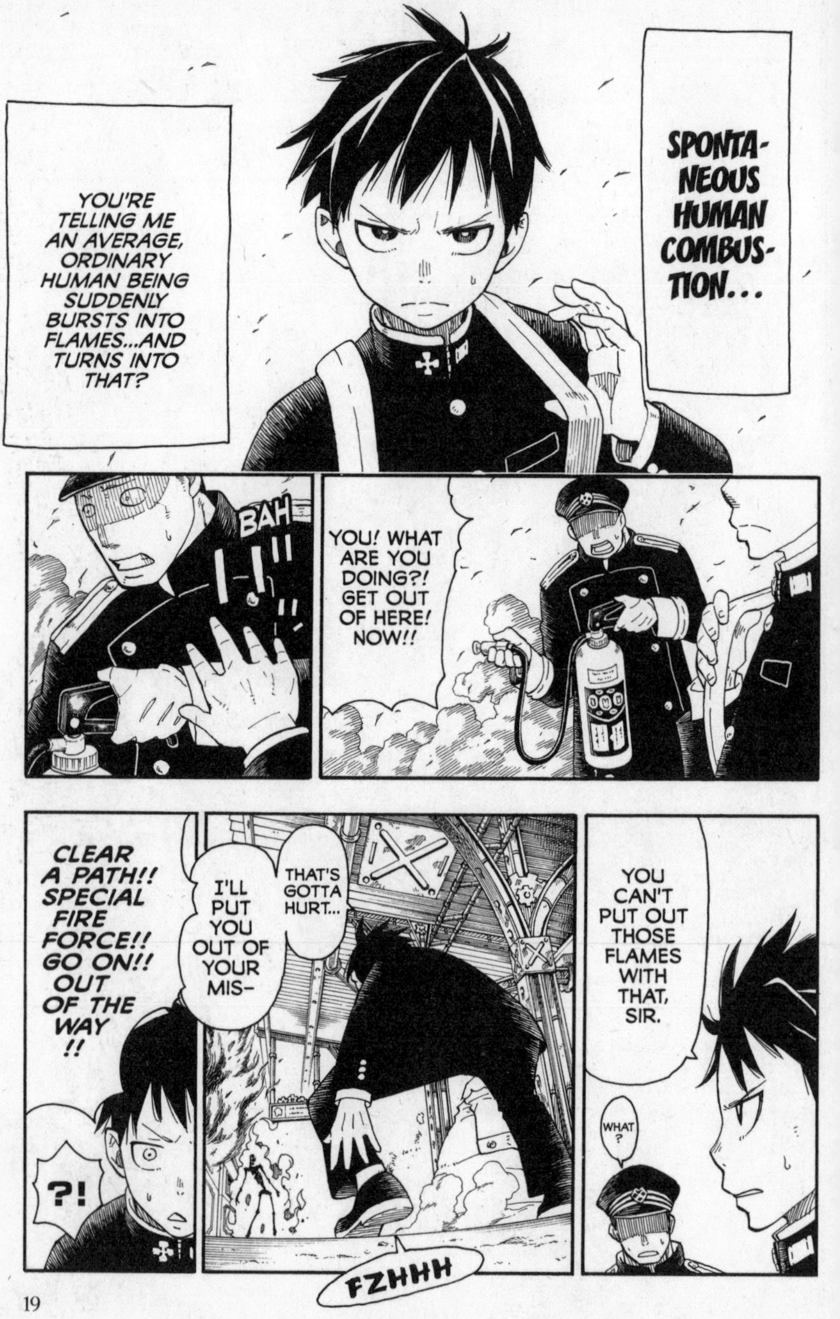
SPONTANEOUS HUMAN COMBUSTION...
YOU'RE TELLING ME AN AVERAGE, ORDINARY HUMAN BEING SUDDENLY BURSTS INTO FLAMES...AND TURNS INTO THAT?
YOU! WHAT ARE YOU DOING?! GET OUT OF HERE! NOW!!
BAH!!
YOU CAN'T PUT OUT THOSE FLAMES WITH THAT, SIR.
WHAT?
THAT'S GOTTA HURT...
I'LL PUT YOU OUT OF YOUR MIS-
FZHHH
CLEAR A PATH!! SPECIAL FIRE FORCE!! GO ON!! OUT OF THE WAY!!
?!

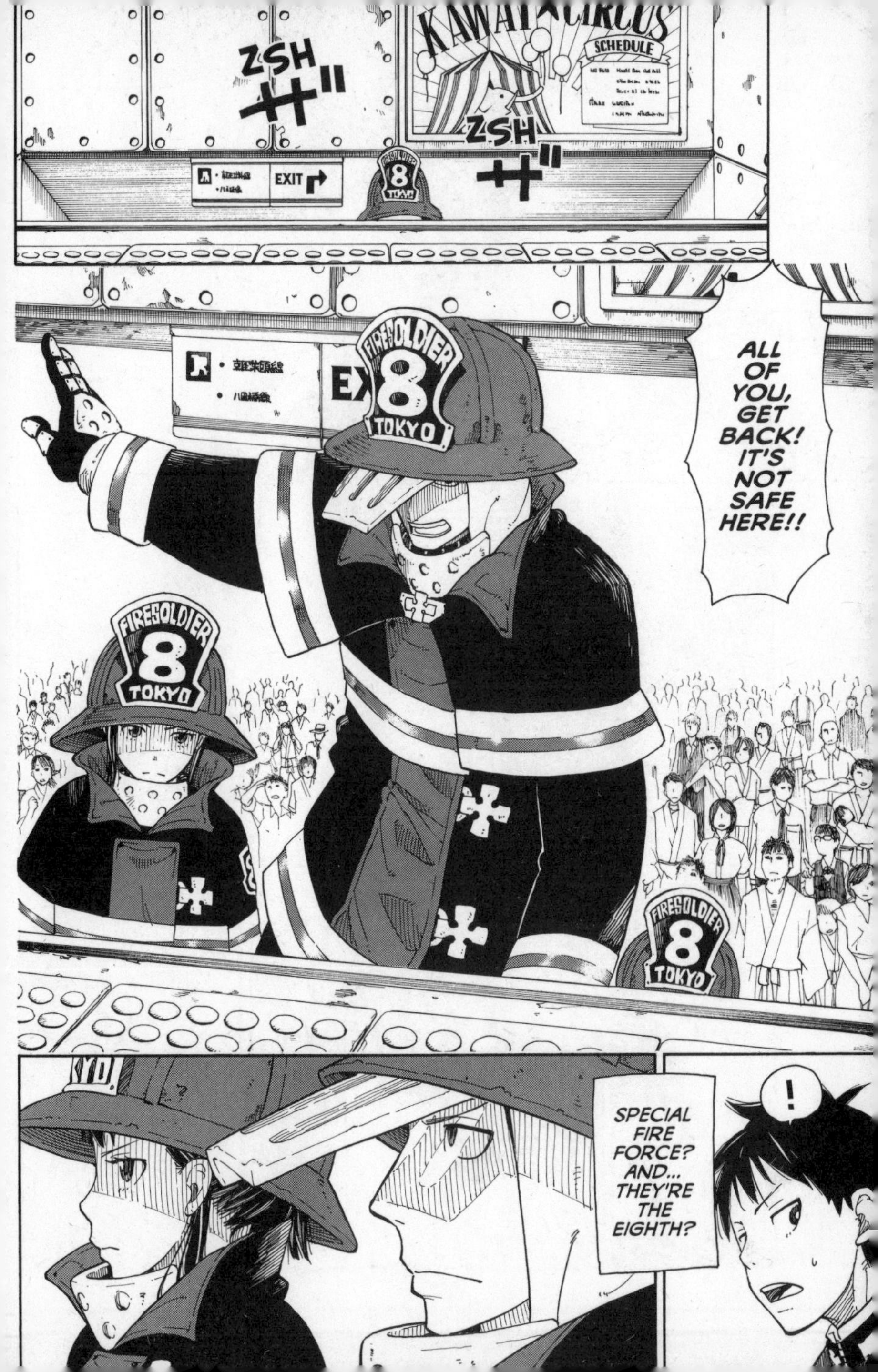

SCHEDULE
ZSH
ZSH
EXIT
ALL OF YOU, GET BACK! IT'S NOT SAFE HERE!!
FIRESOLDIER 8 TOKYO
!
SPECIAL FIRE FORCE? AND... THEY'RE THE EIGHTH?

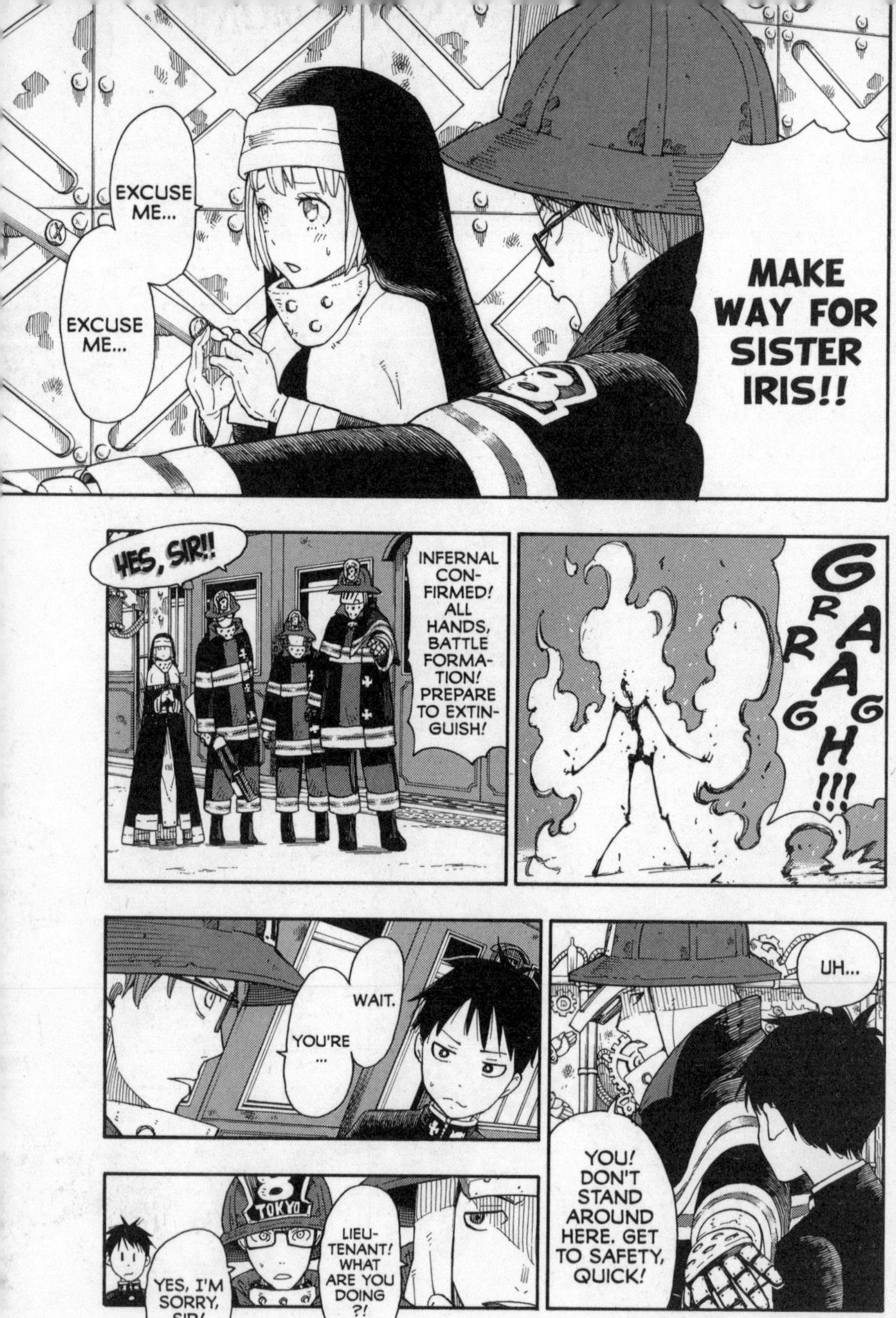
MAKE WAY FOR SISTER IRIS!!
EXCUSE ME...
EXCUSE ME...
GRRAAGGH!!!
INFERNAL CONFIRMED! ALL HANDS, BATTLE FORMATION! PREPARE TO EXTINGUISH!
YES, SIR!!
UH...
YOU! DON'T STAND AROUND HERE. GET TO SAFETY, QUICK!
WAIT.
YOU'RE ...
LIEUTENANT! WHAT ARE YOU DOING?!
YES, I'M SORRY, SIR!

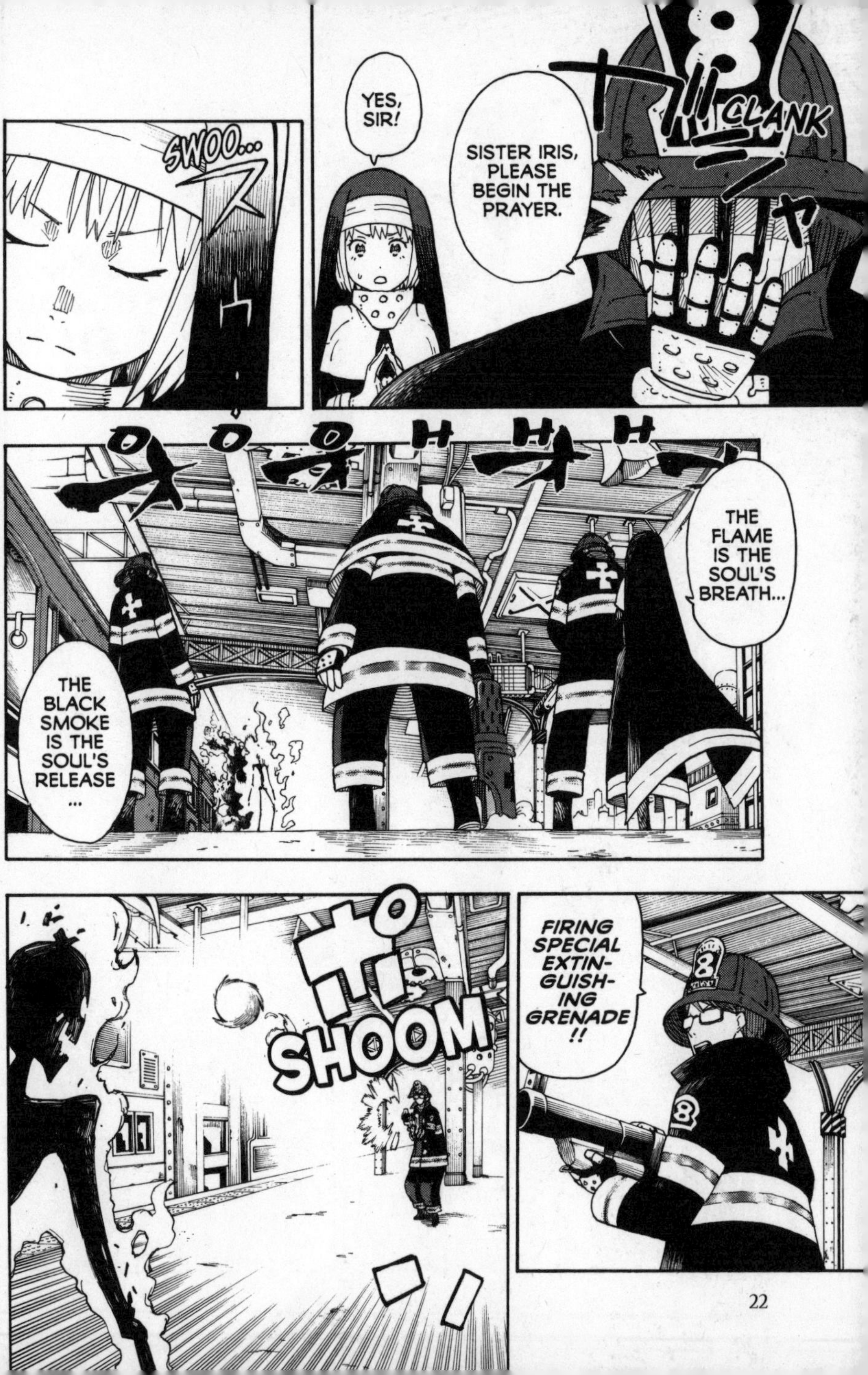
CLANK
SISTER IRIS, PLEASE BEGIN THE PRAYER.
YES, SIR!
SWOO...
OOOHHH
THE FLAME IS THE SOUL'S BREATH...
THE BLACK SMOKE IS THE SOUL'S RELEASE ...
FIRING SPECIAL EXTIN-GUISH-ING GRENADE !!
SHOOM

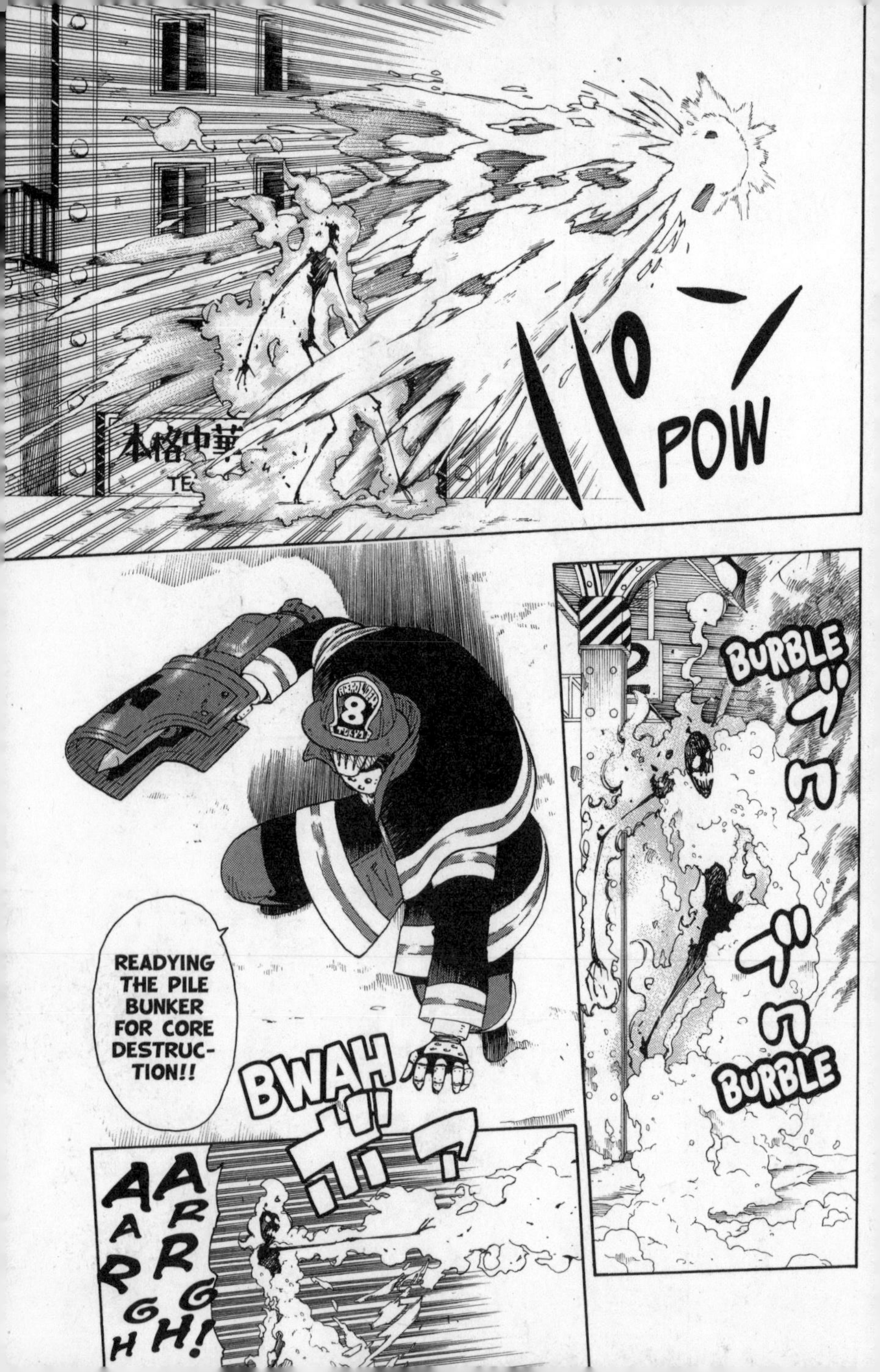
本格中華
TE
POW
BURBLE
BURBLE
READYING THE PILE BUNKER FOR CORE DESTRUCTION!!
BWAH
AAARRGGHH!

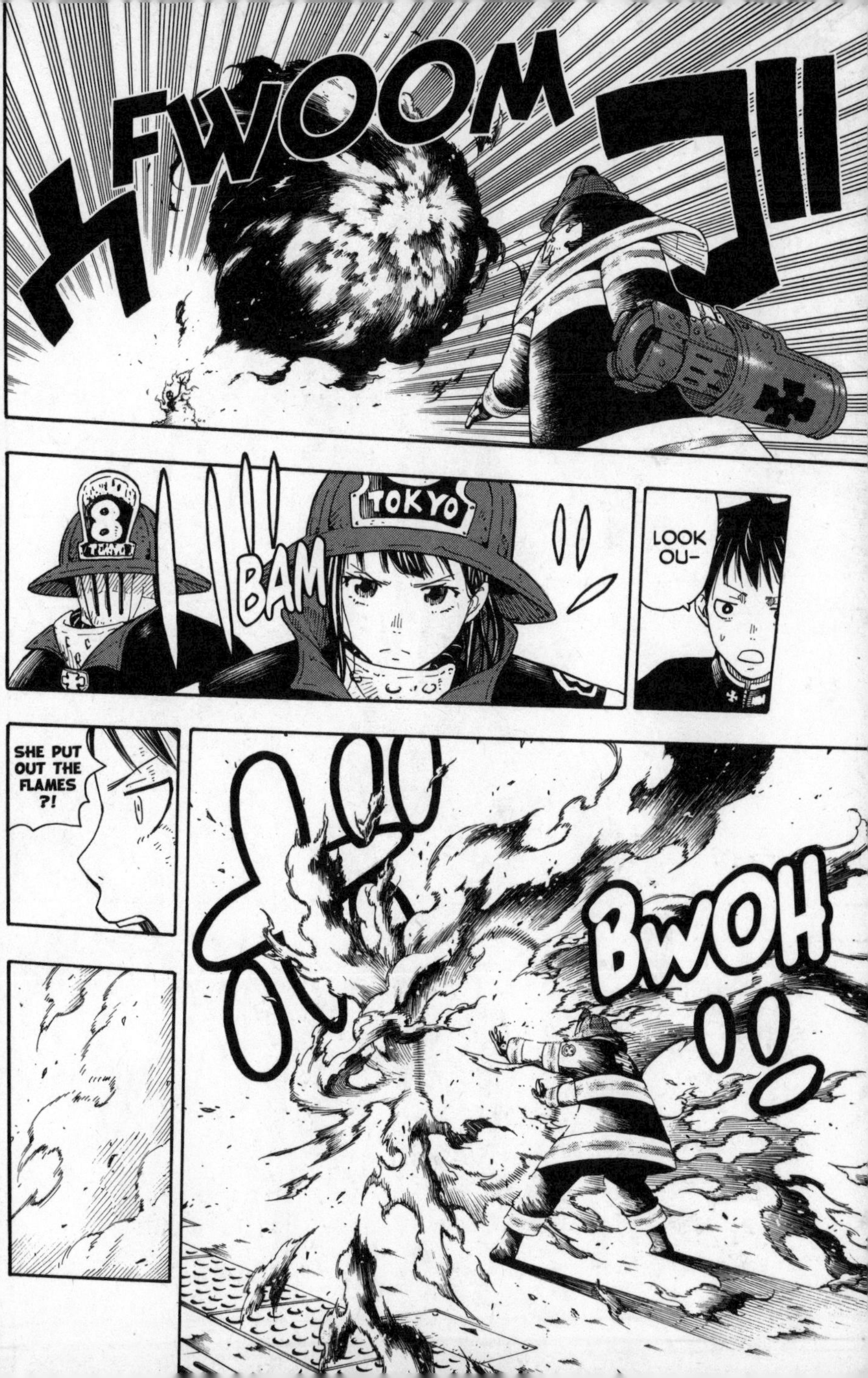
FWOOM
LOOK OU-
BAM
TOKYO
8
BWOH
SHE PUT OUT THE FLAMES ?!

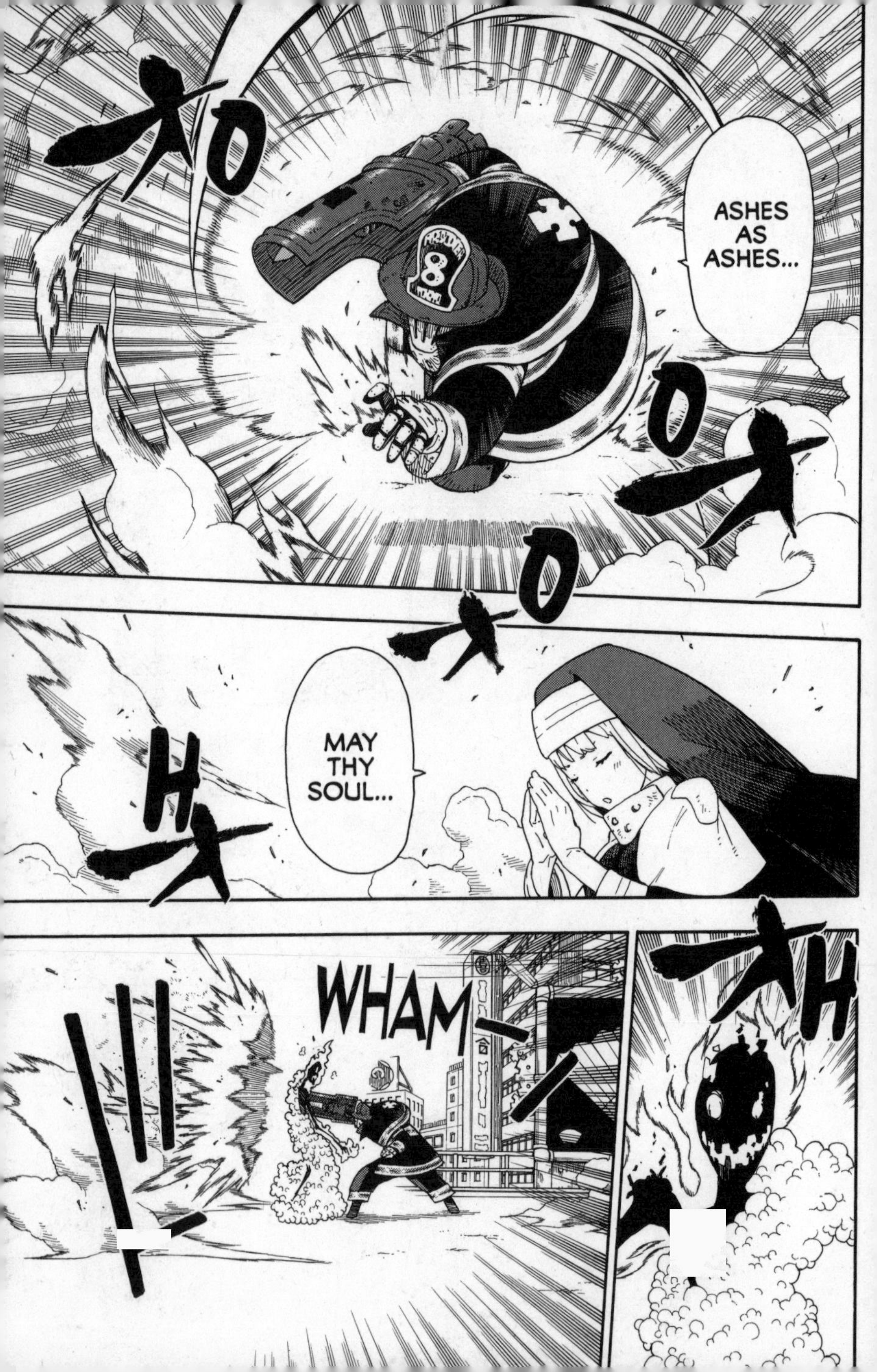
ASHES AS ASHES...
MAY THY SOUL...
WHAM

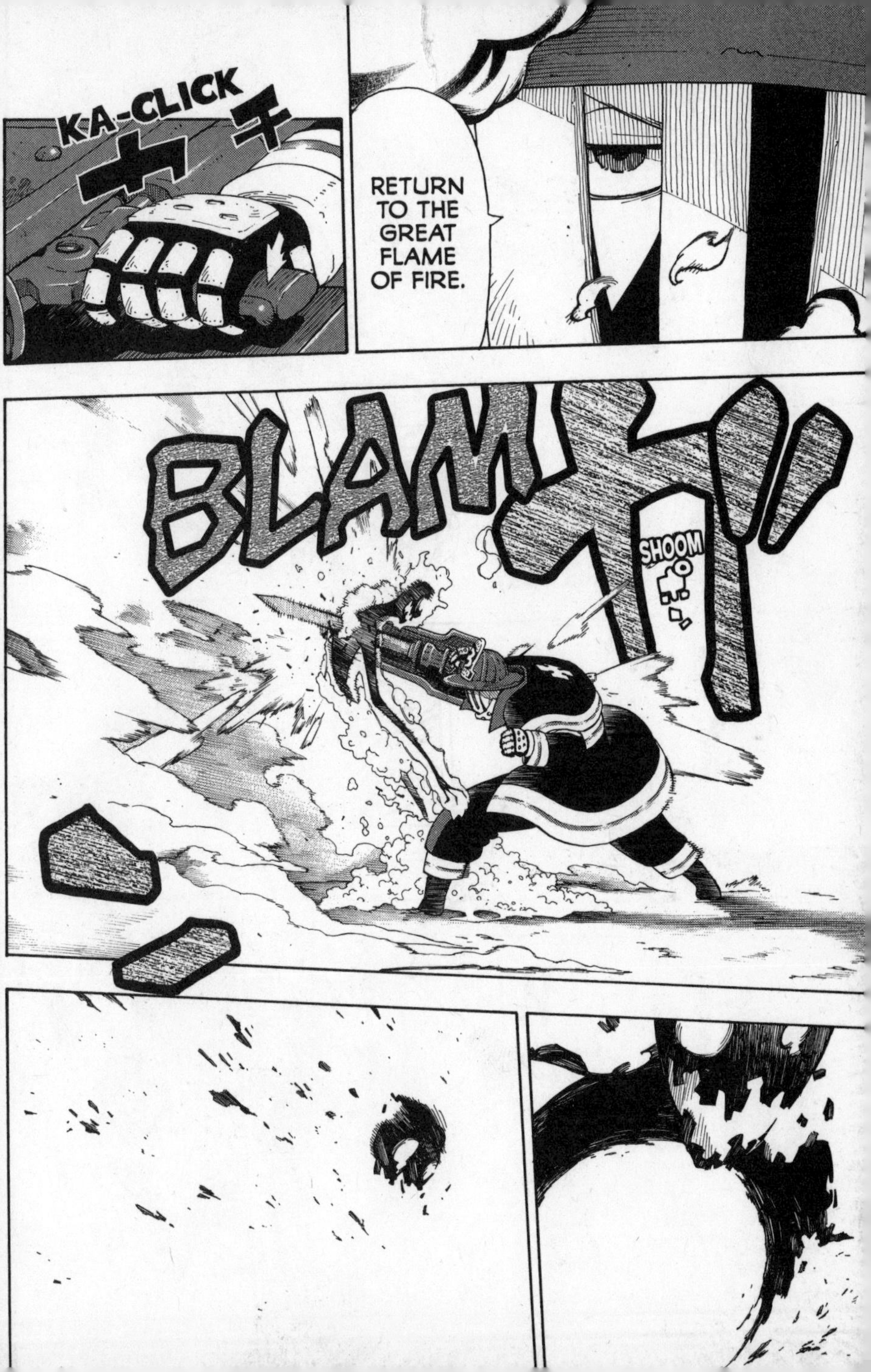
RETURN TO THE GREAT FLAME OF FIRE.
KA-CLICK
BLAM
SHOOM

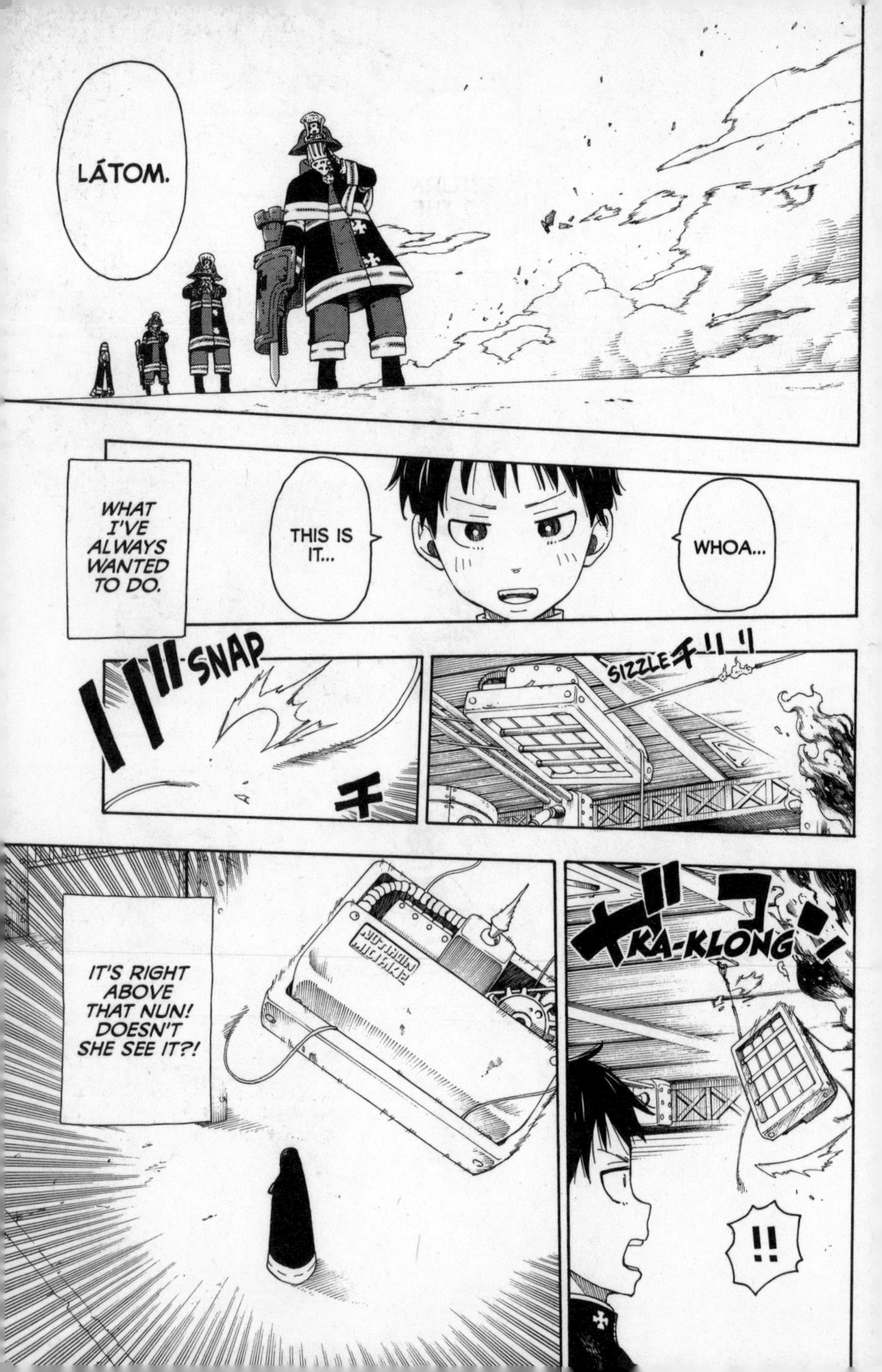
LÁTOM.
WHOA...
THIS IS IT...
WHAT I'VE ALWAYS WANTED TO DO.
SIZZLE チリリ
SNAP
チ
KA-KLONG
!!
IT'S RIGHT ABOVE THAT NUN! DOESN'T SHE SEE IT?!

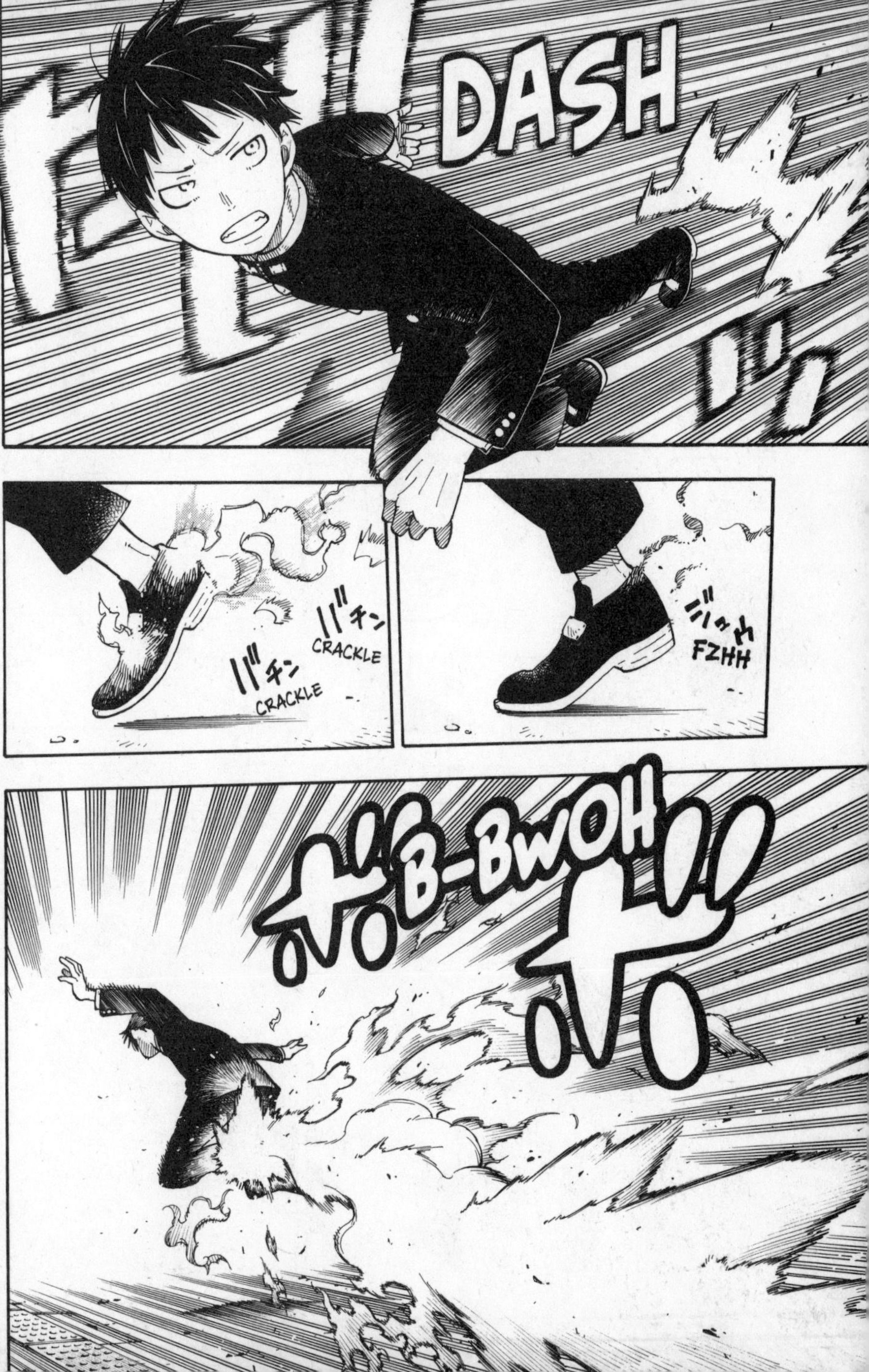
DASH
FZHH
バチン
CRACKLE
バチン
CRACKLE
B-BWOH

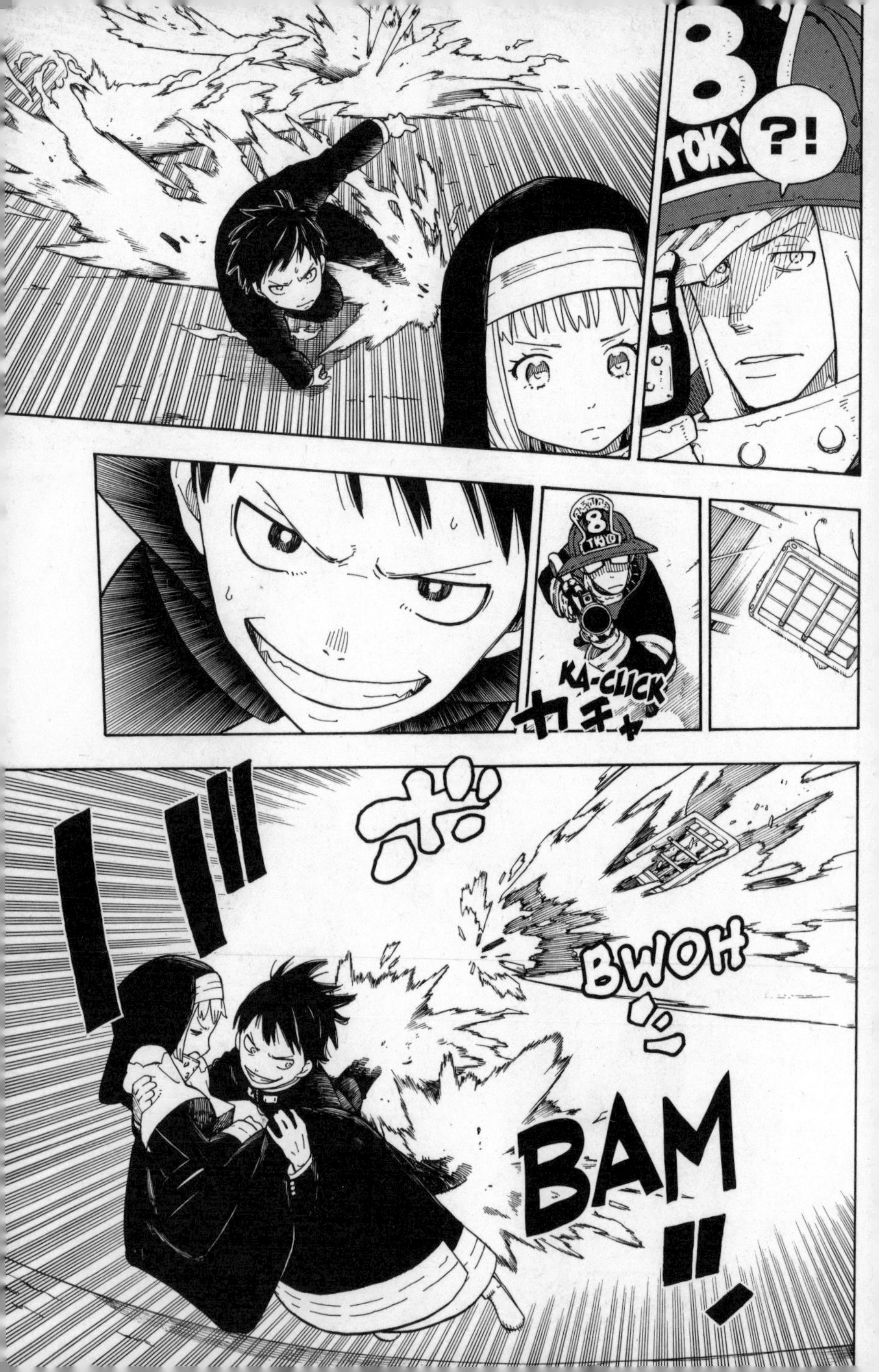
?!
KA-CLICK
カチャ
BWOH
BAM

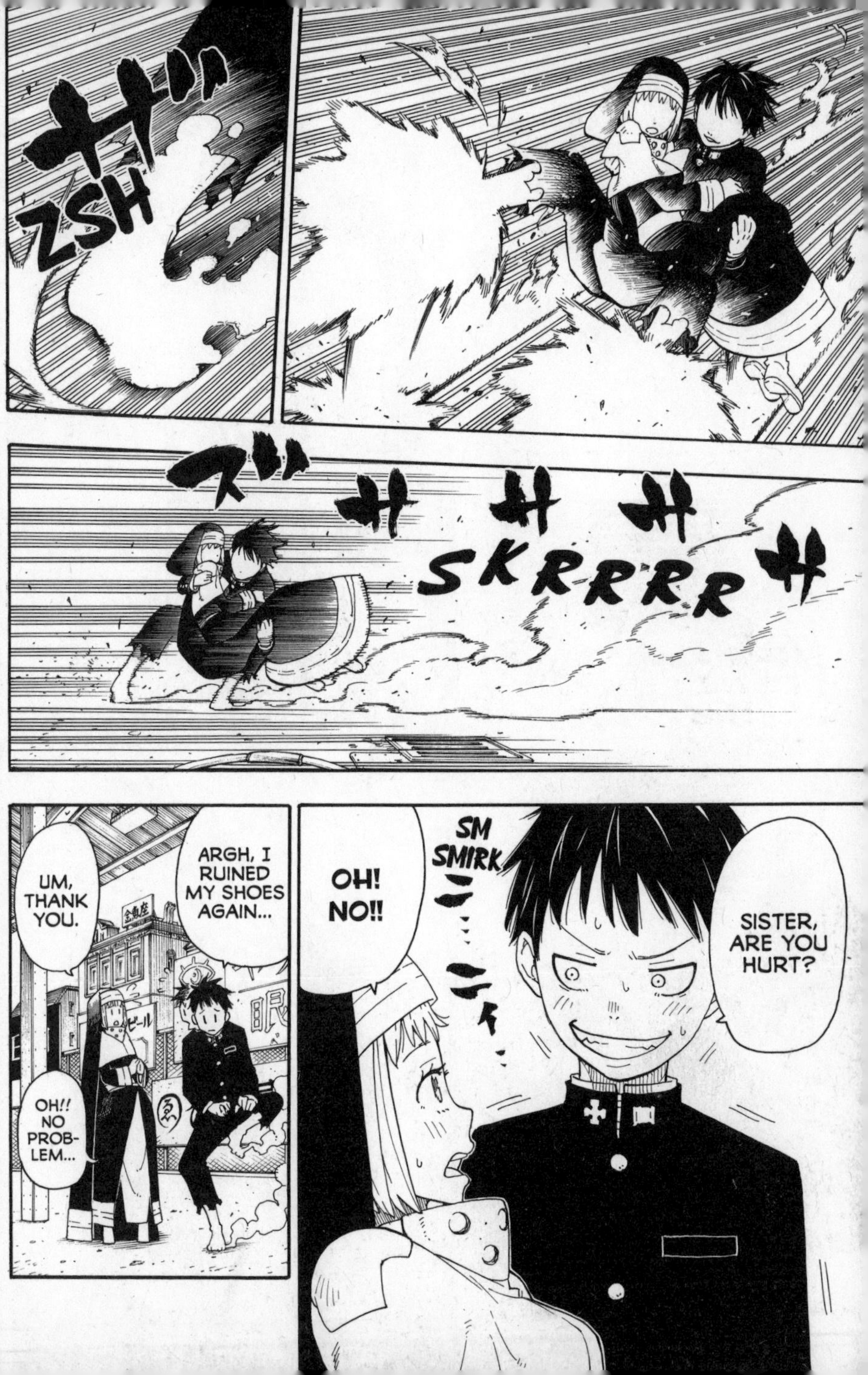
ZSH
SKRRRR
SISTER, ARE YOU HURT?
SM SMIRK
OH! NO!!
ARGH, I RUINED MY SHOES AGAIN...
UM, THANK YOU.
OH!! NO PROBLEM...

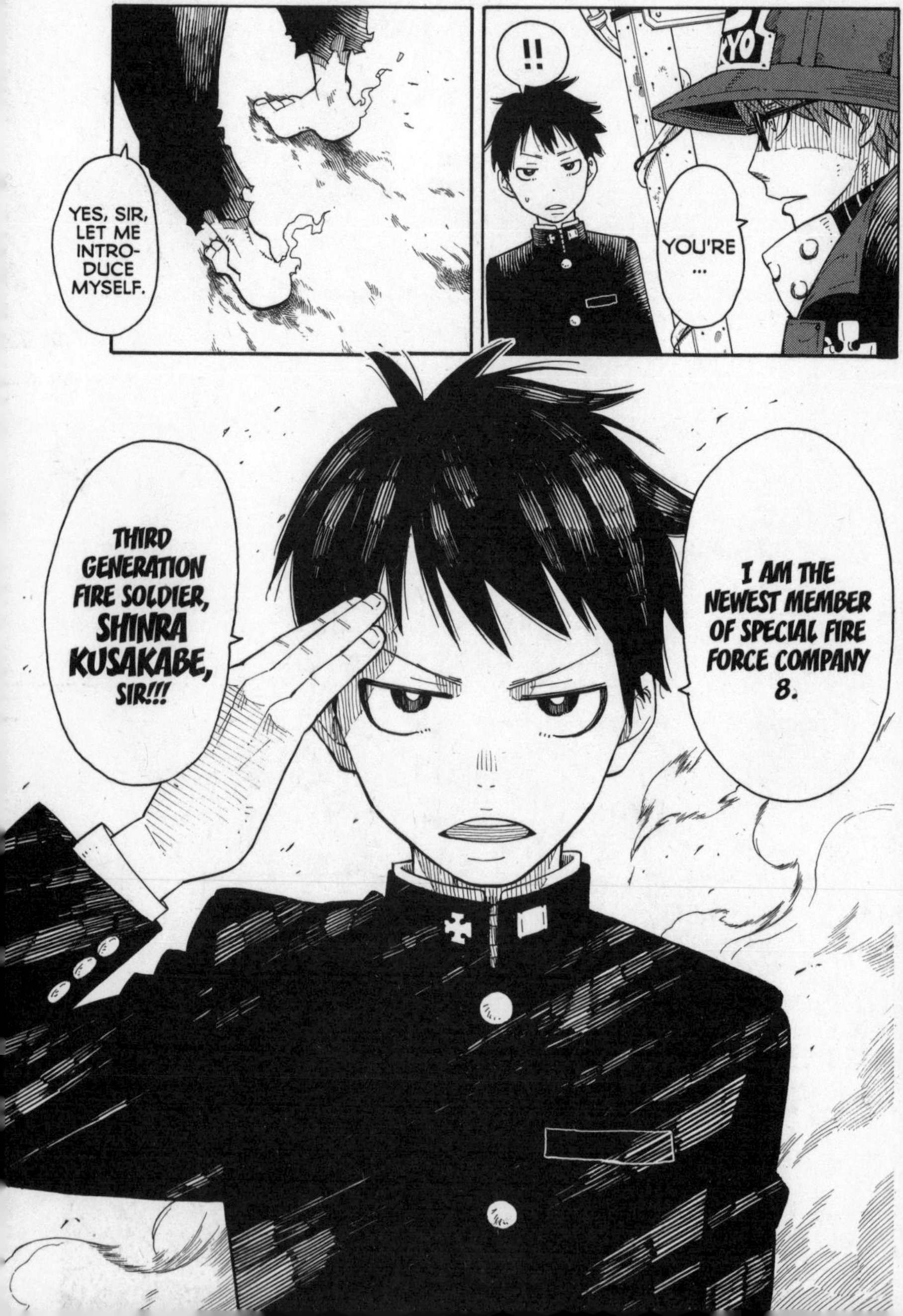
!!
YOU'RE ...
YES, SIR, LET ME INTRO-DUCE MYSELF.
I AM THE NEWEST MEMBER OF SPECIAL FIRE FORCE COMPANY 8.
THIRD GENERATION FIRE SOLDIER, SHINRA KUSAKABE, SIR!!!

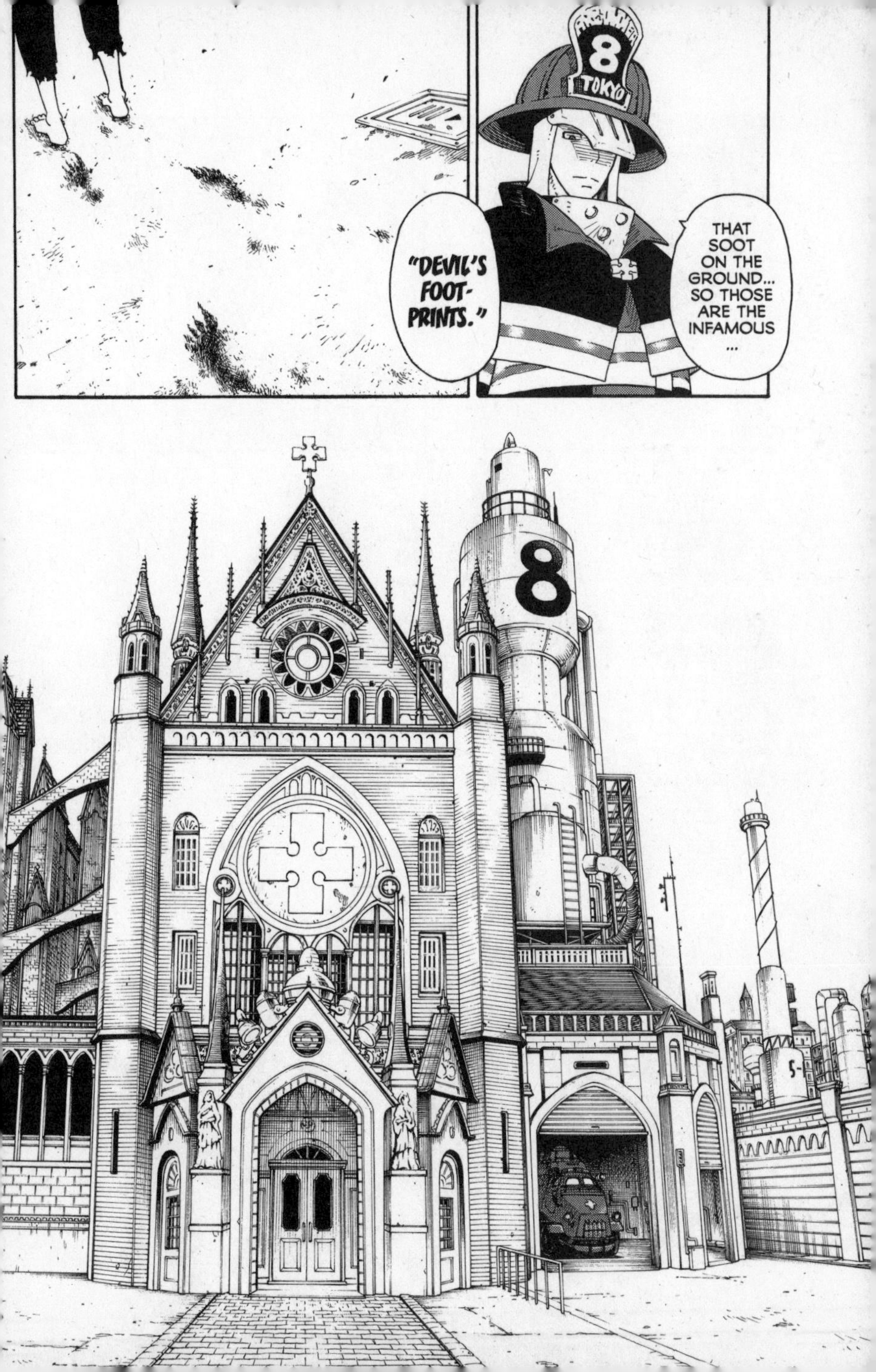
THAT SOOT ON THE GROUND... SO THOSE ARE THE INFAMOUS ...
"DEVIL'S FOOT-PRINTS."

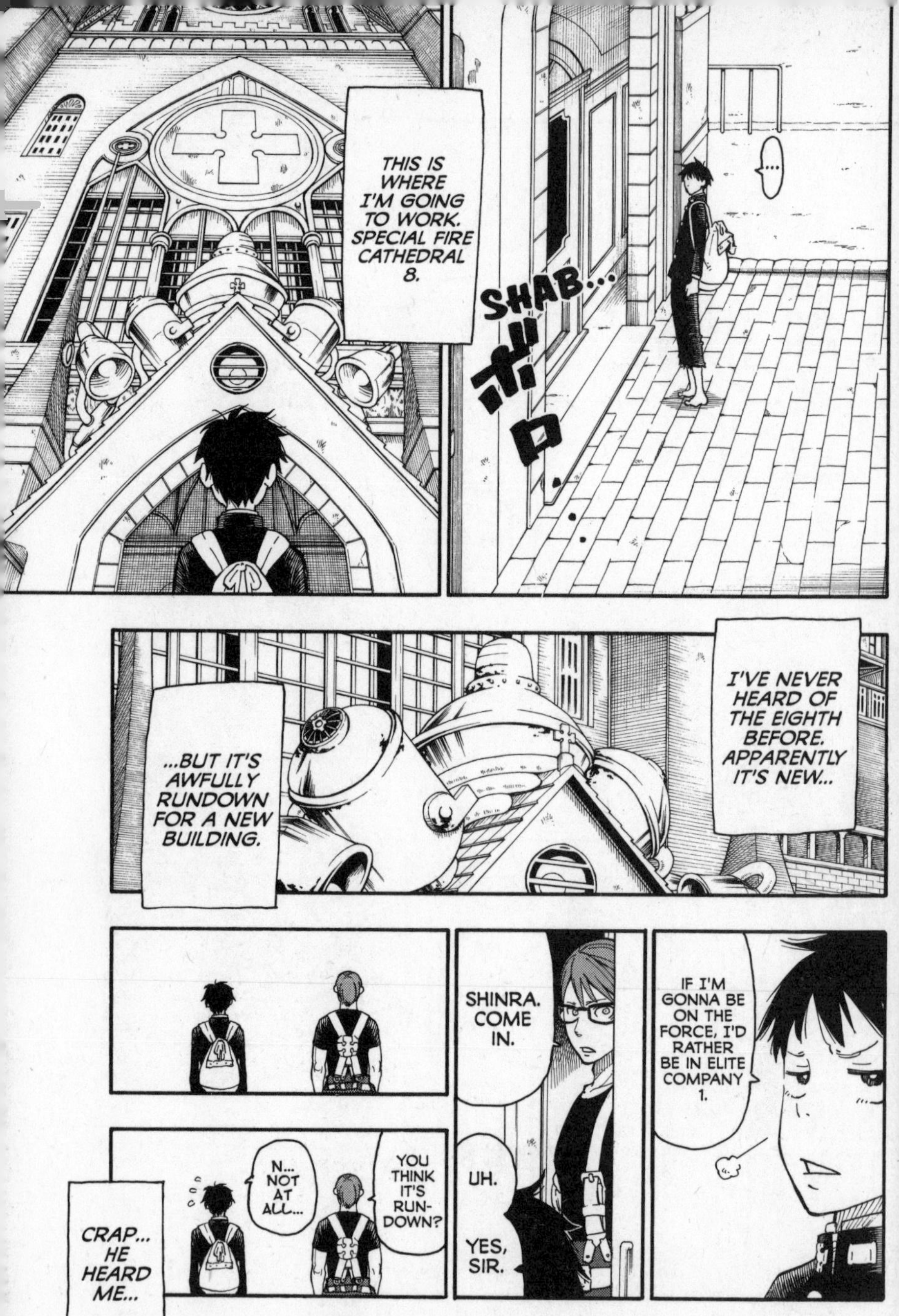
...
SHAB...
ボロ
THIS IS WHERE I'M GOING TO WORK. SPECIAL FIRE CATHEDRAL 8.
I'VE NEVER HEARD OF THE EIGHTH BEFORE. APPARENTLY IT'S NEW...
...BUT IT'S AWFULLY RUNDOWN FOR A NEW BUILDING.
IF I'M GONNA BE ON THE FORCE, I'D RATHER BE IN ELITE COMPANY 1.
SHINRA. COME IN.
UH.
YES, SIR.
YOU THINK IT'S RUN-DOWN?
N... NOT AT ALL...
CRAP... HE HEARD ME...

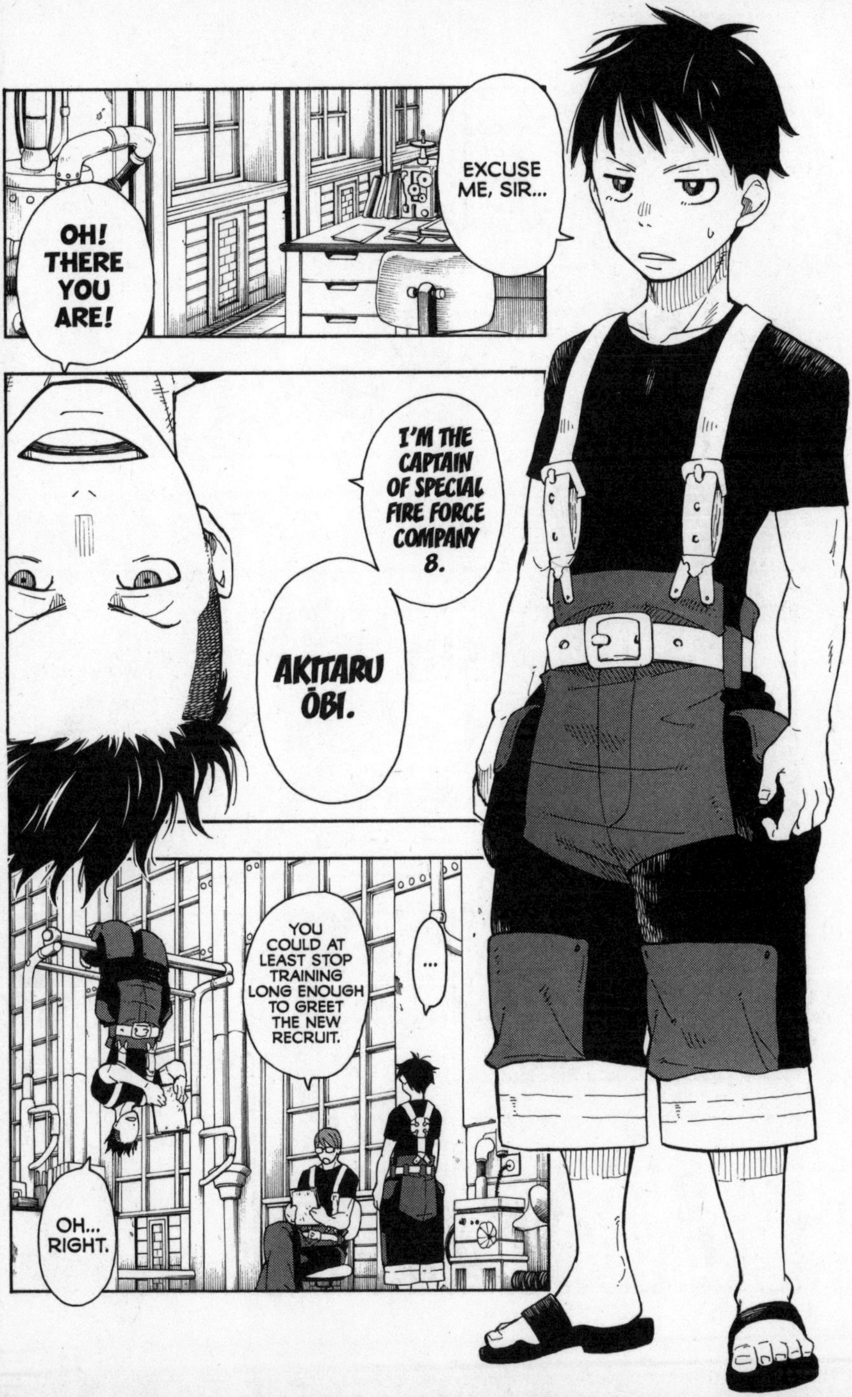
EXCUSE ME, SIR...
OH! THERE YOU ARE!
I'M THE CAPTAIN OF SPECIAL FIRE FORCE COMPANY 8.
AKITARU ŌBI.
...
YOU COULD AT LEAST STOP TRAINING LONG ENOUGH TO GREET THE NEW RECRUIT.
OH... RIGHT.

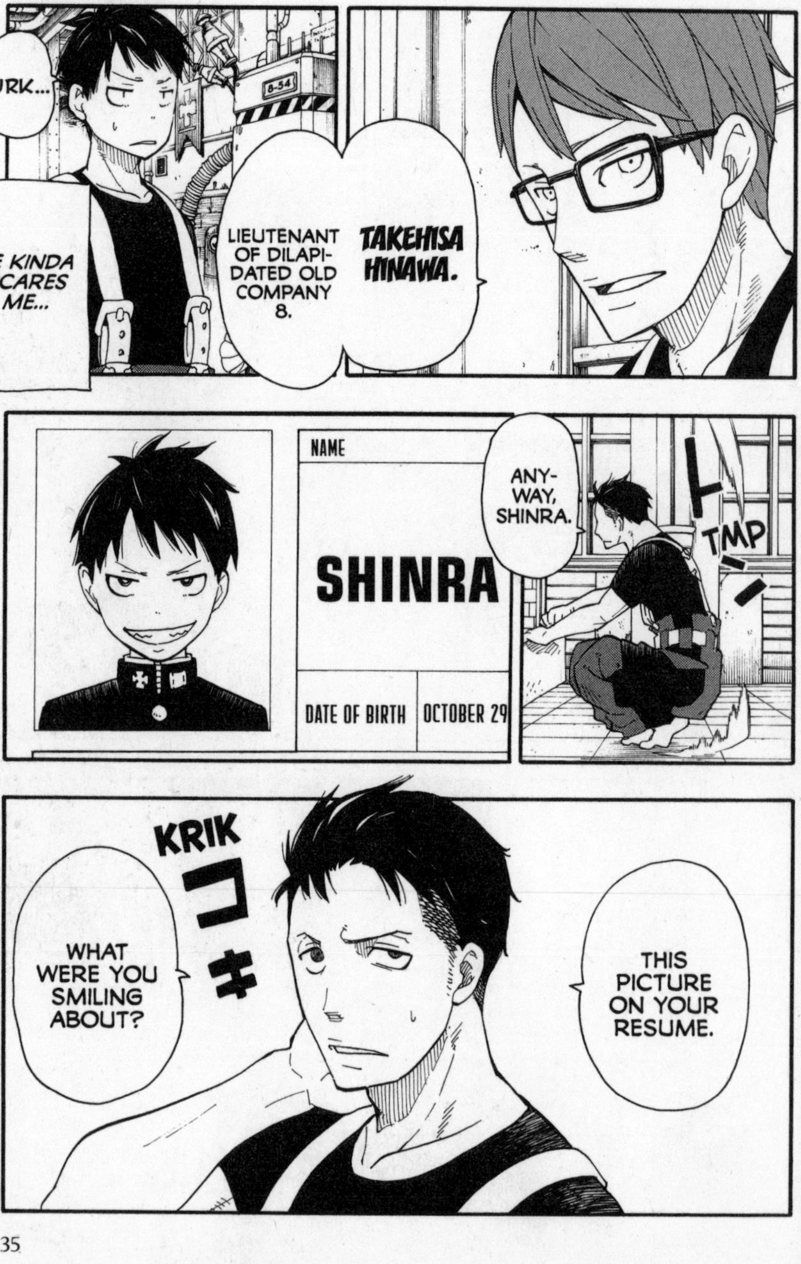
TAKEHISA HINAWA.
LIEUTENANT OF DILAPI-DATED OLD COMPANY 8.
URK...
HE KINDA SCARES ME...
ANY-WAY, SHINRA.
TMP
NAME
SHINRA
DATE OF BIRTH
OCTOBER 29
THIS PICTURE ON YOUR RESUME.
KRIK
WHAT WERE YOU SMILING ABOUT?

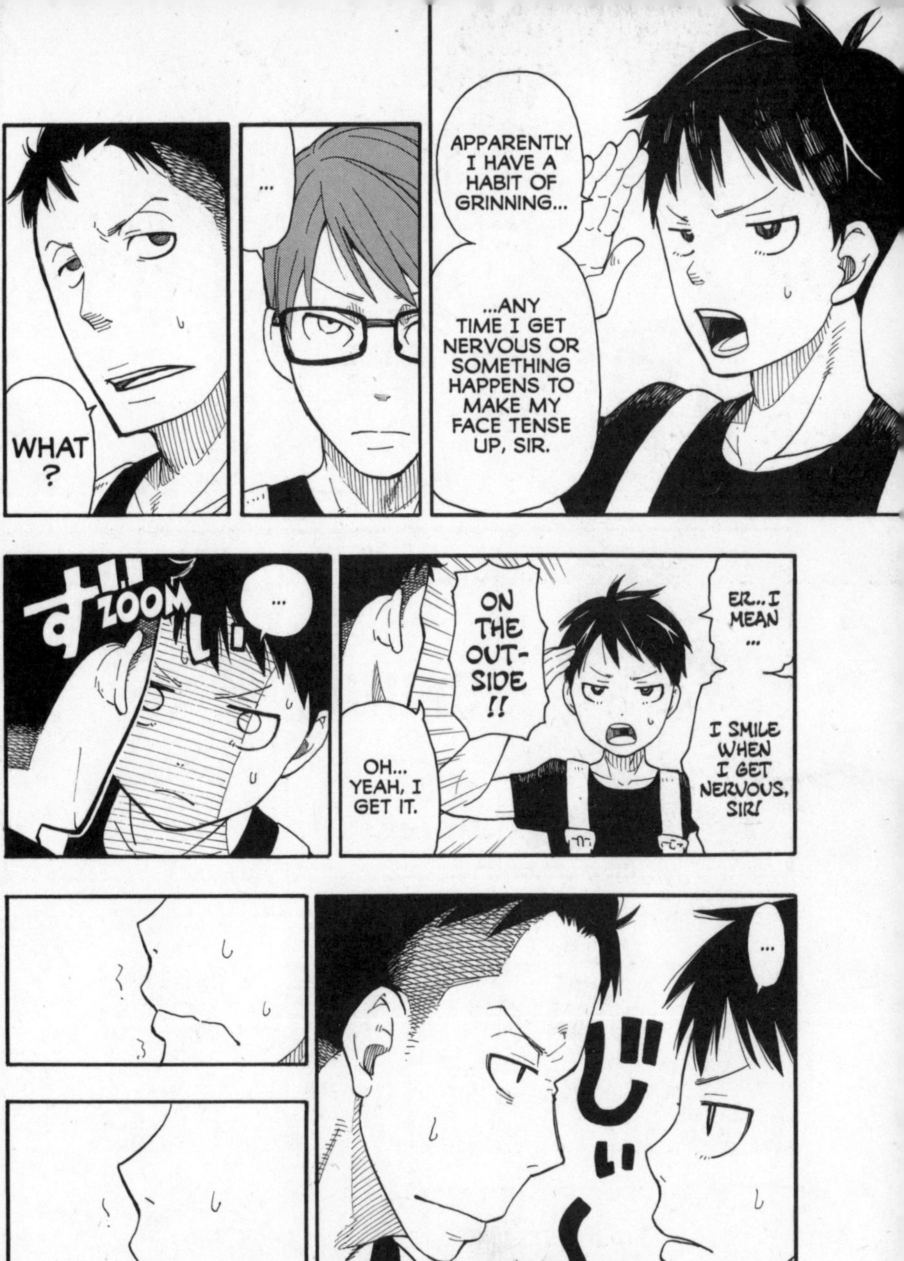
APPARENTLY I HAVE A HABIT OF GRINNING...
...ANY TIME I GET NERVOUS OR SOMETHING HAPPENS TO MAKE MY FACE TENSE UP, SIR.
...
WHAT ?
ER... I MEAN ...
ON THE OUT-SIDE !!
I SMILE WHEN I GET NERVOUS, SIR!
OH... YEAH, I GET IT.
ZOOM
...
...
STAAAARE

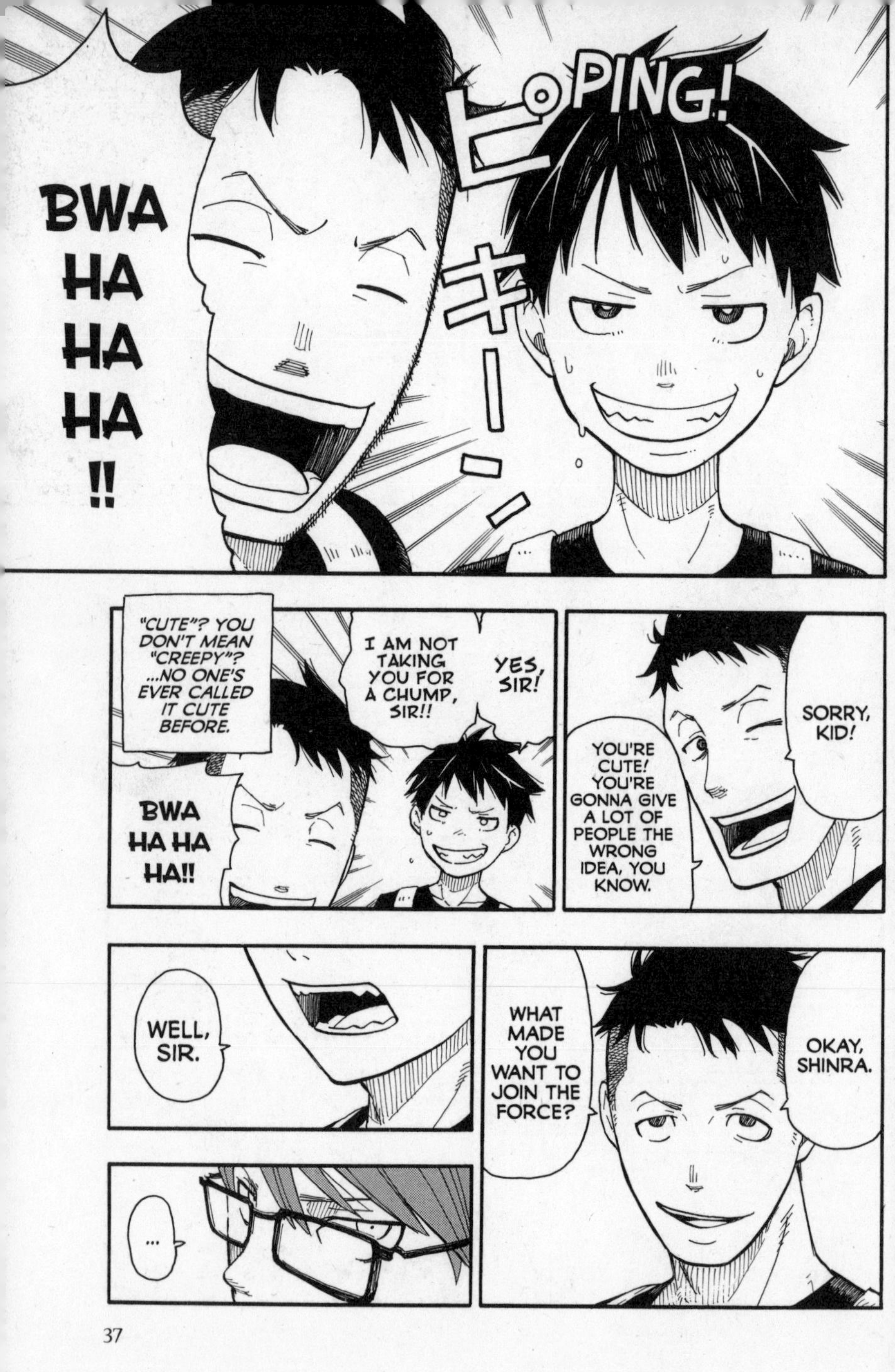
PING!
BWA HA HA HA HA!!
SORRY, KID!
YOU'RE CUTE! YOU'RE GONNA GIVE A LOT OF PEOPLE THE WRONG IDEA, YOU KNOW.
YES, SIR!
I AM NOT TAKING YOU FOR A CHUMP, SIR!!
"CUTE"? YOU DON'T MEAN "CREEPY"? ...NO ONE'S EVER CALLED IT CUTE BEFORE.
BWA HA HA HA!!
OKAY, SHINRA.
WHAT MADE YOU WANT TO JOIN THE FORCE?
WELL, SIR.
...

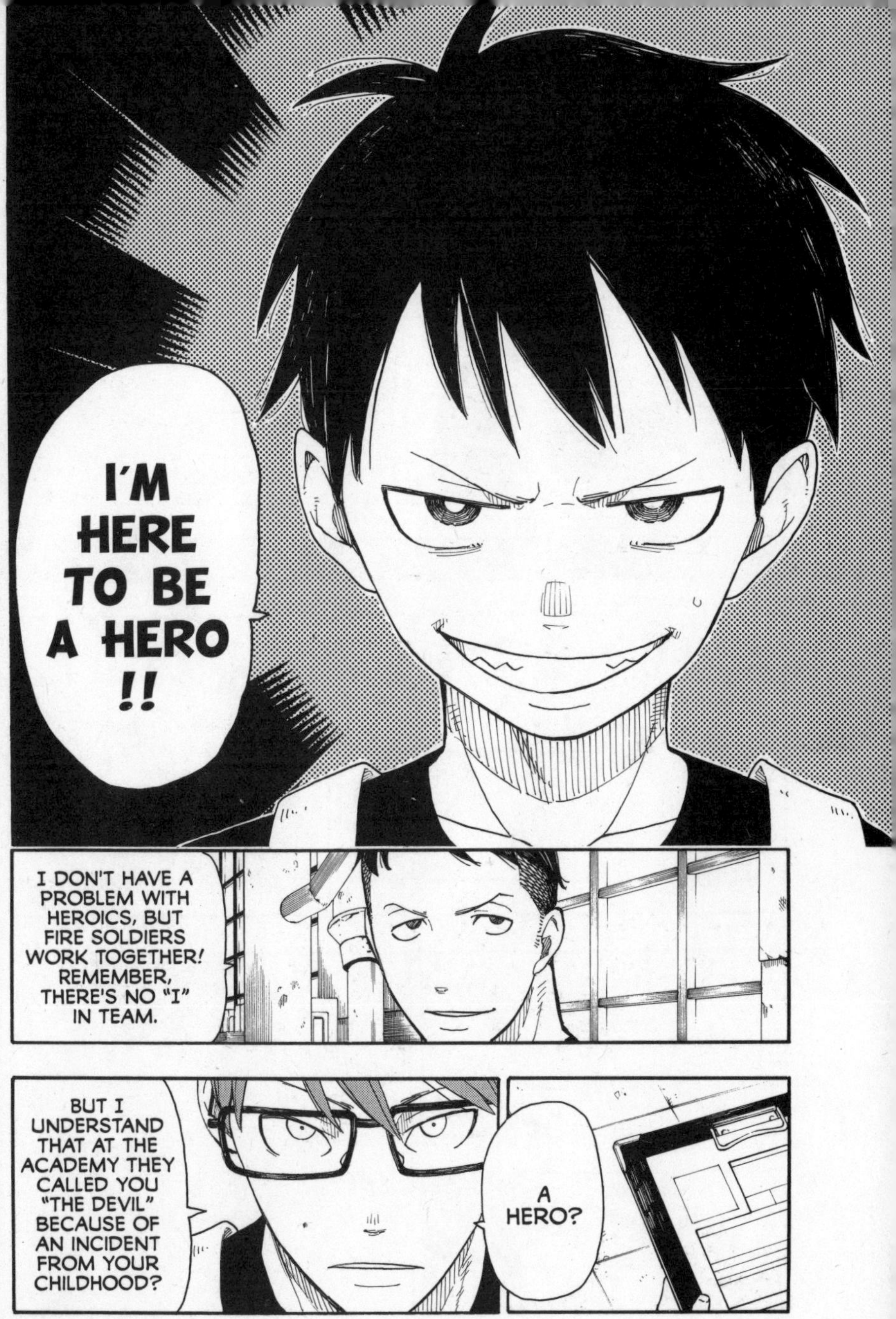
I'M HERE TO BE A HERO !!
I DON'T HAVE A PROBLEM WITH HEROICS, BUT FIRE SOLDIERS WORK TOGETHER! REMEMBER, THERE'S NO "I" IN TEAM.
A HERO?
BUT I UNDERSTAND THAT AT THE ACADEMY THEY CALLED YOU "THE DEVIL" BECAUSE OF AN INCIDENT FROM YOUR CHILDHOOD?

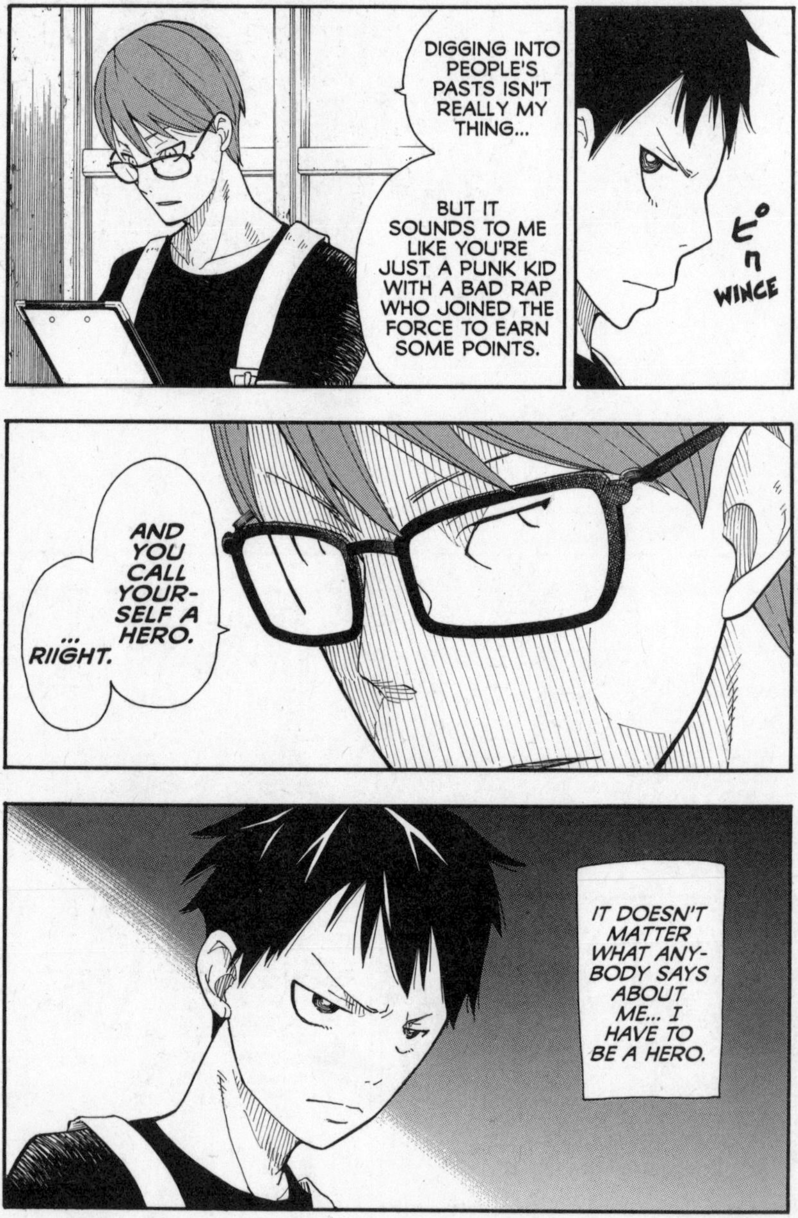
ピク
WINCE
DIGGING INTO PEOPLE'S PASTS ISN'T REALLY MY THING...
BUT IT SOUNDS TO ME LIKE YOU'RE JUST A PUNK KID WITH A BAD RAP WHO JOINED THE FORCE TO EARN SOME POINTS.
AND YOU CALL YOURSELF A HERO. ...RIIGHT.
IT DOESN'T MATTER WHAT ANYBODY SAYS ABOUT ME... I HAVE TO BE A HERO.

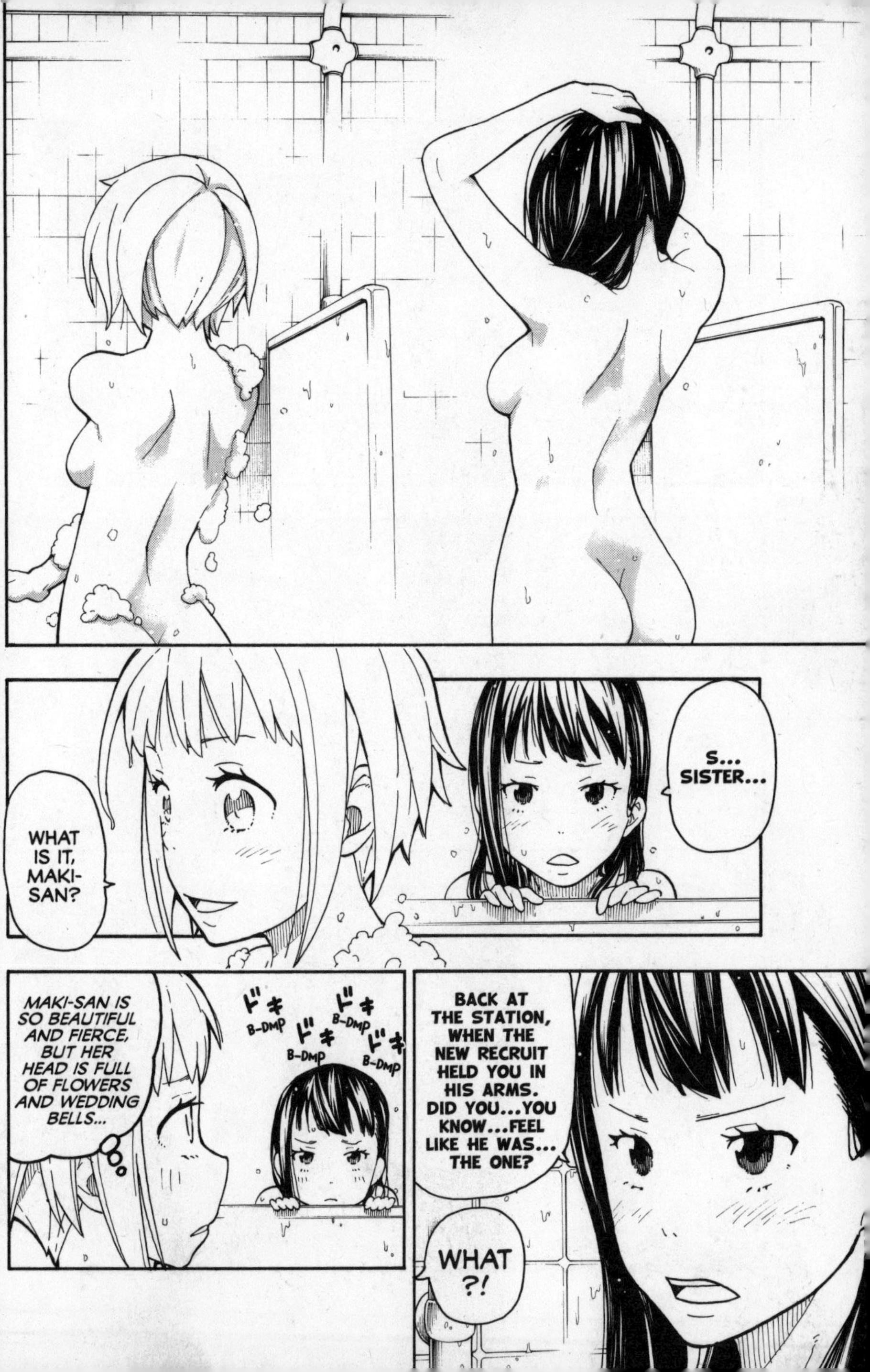
S... SISTER...
WHAT IS IT, MAKI-SAN?
BACK AT THE STATION, WHEN THE NEW RECRUIT HELD YOU IN HIS ARMS. DID YOU...YOU KNOW...FEEL LIKE HE WAS... THE ONE?
WHAT ?!
ドキ B-DMP
ドキ B-DMP
ドキ B-DMP
ドキ B-DMP
MAKI-SAN IS SO BEAUTIFUL AND FIERCE, BUT HER HEAD IS FULL OF FLOWERS AND WEDDING BELLS...

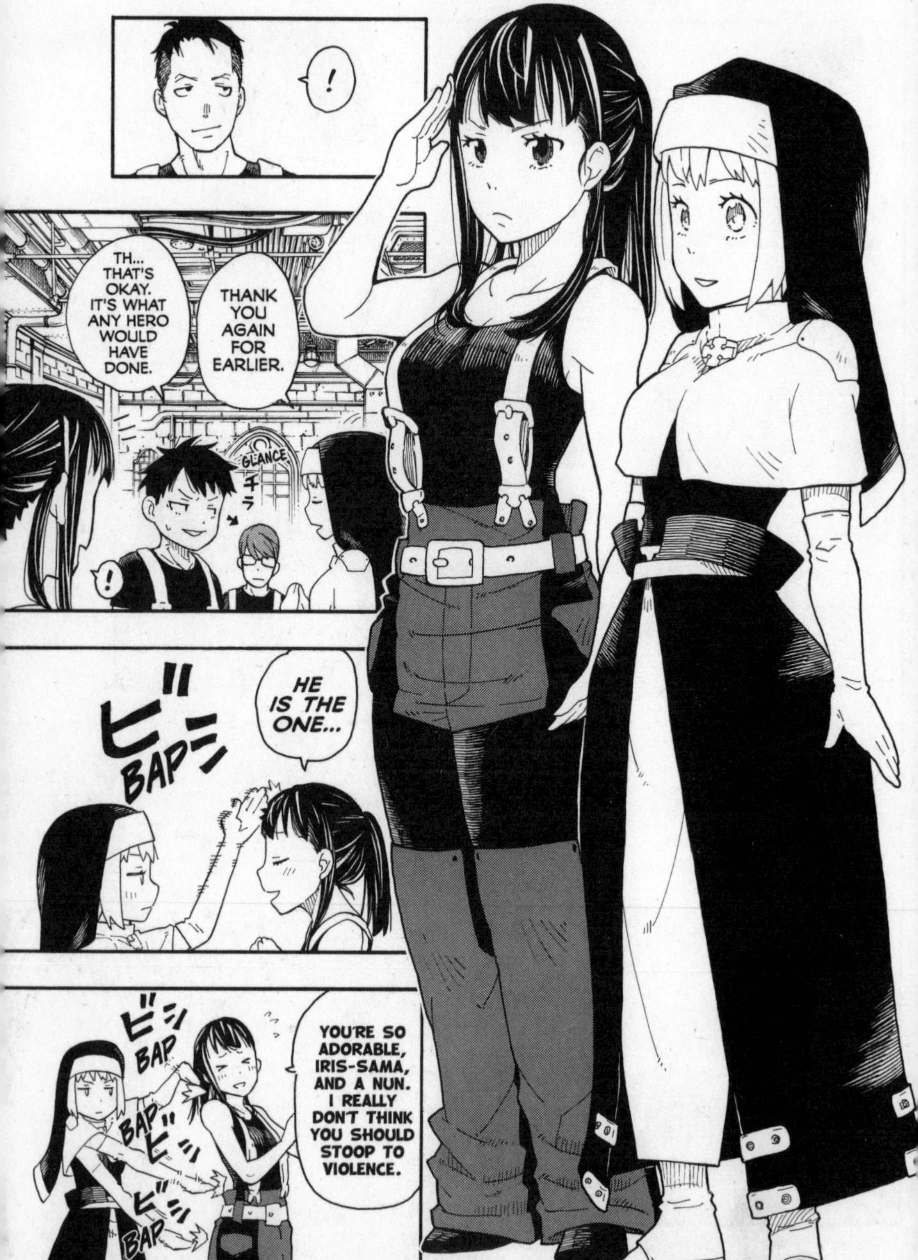
!
THANK YOU AGAIN FOR EARLIER.
TH... THAT'S OKAY. IT'S WHAT ANY HERO WOULD HAVE DONE.
GLANCE
!
HE IS THE ONE...
BAP
YOU'RE SO ADORABLE, IRIS-SAMA, AND A NUN. I REALLY DON'T THINK YOU SHOULD STOOP TO VIOLENCE.
BAP
BAP
BAP

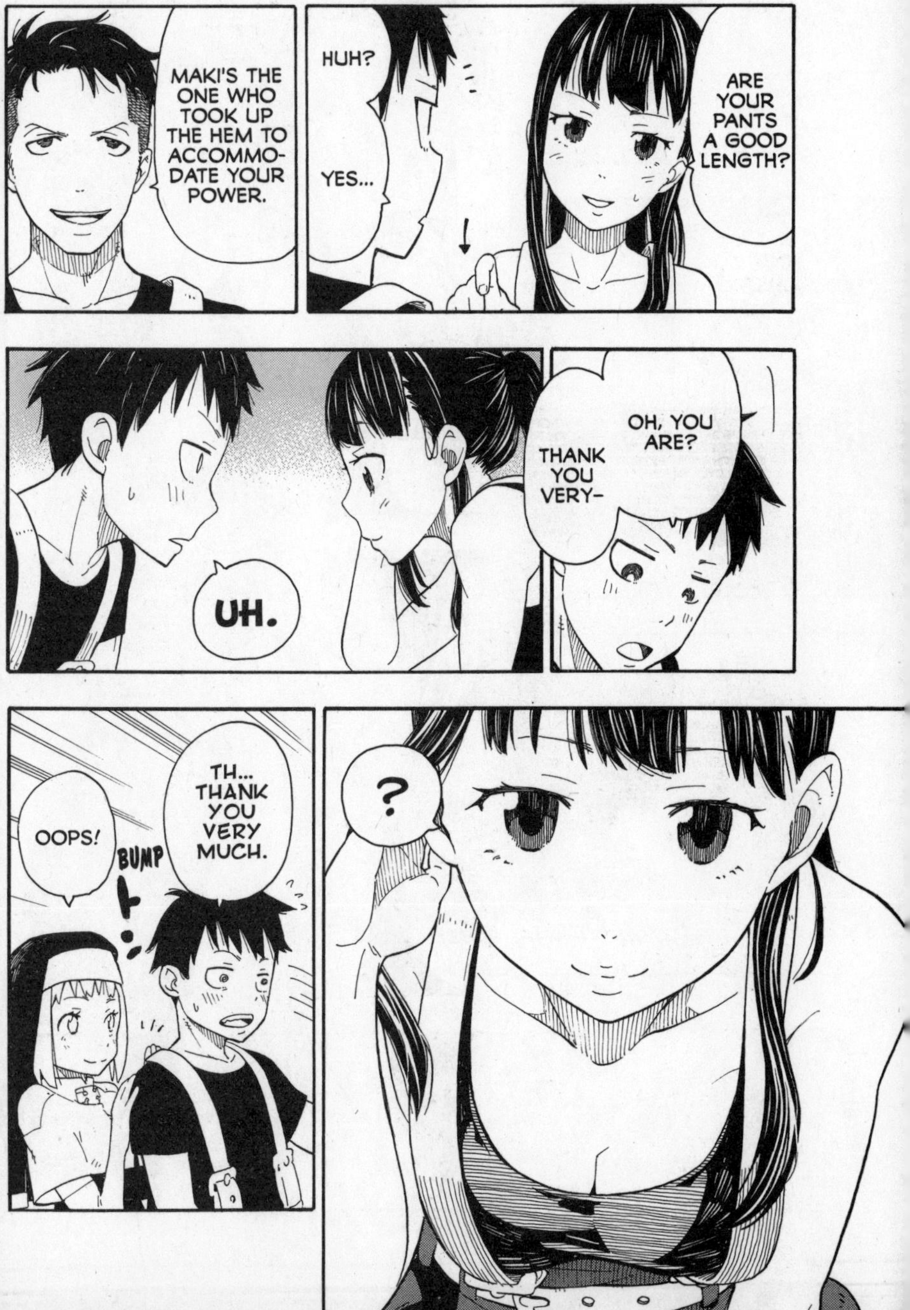
ARE YOUR PANTS A GOOD LENGTH?
HUH?
YES...
MAKI'S THE ONE WHO TOOK UP THE HEM TO ACCOMMODATE YOUR POWER.
OH, YOU ARE?
THANK YOU VERY-
UH.
?
TH... THANK YOU VERY MUCH.
BUMP
OOPS!

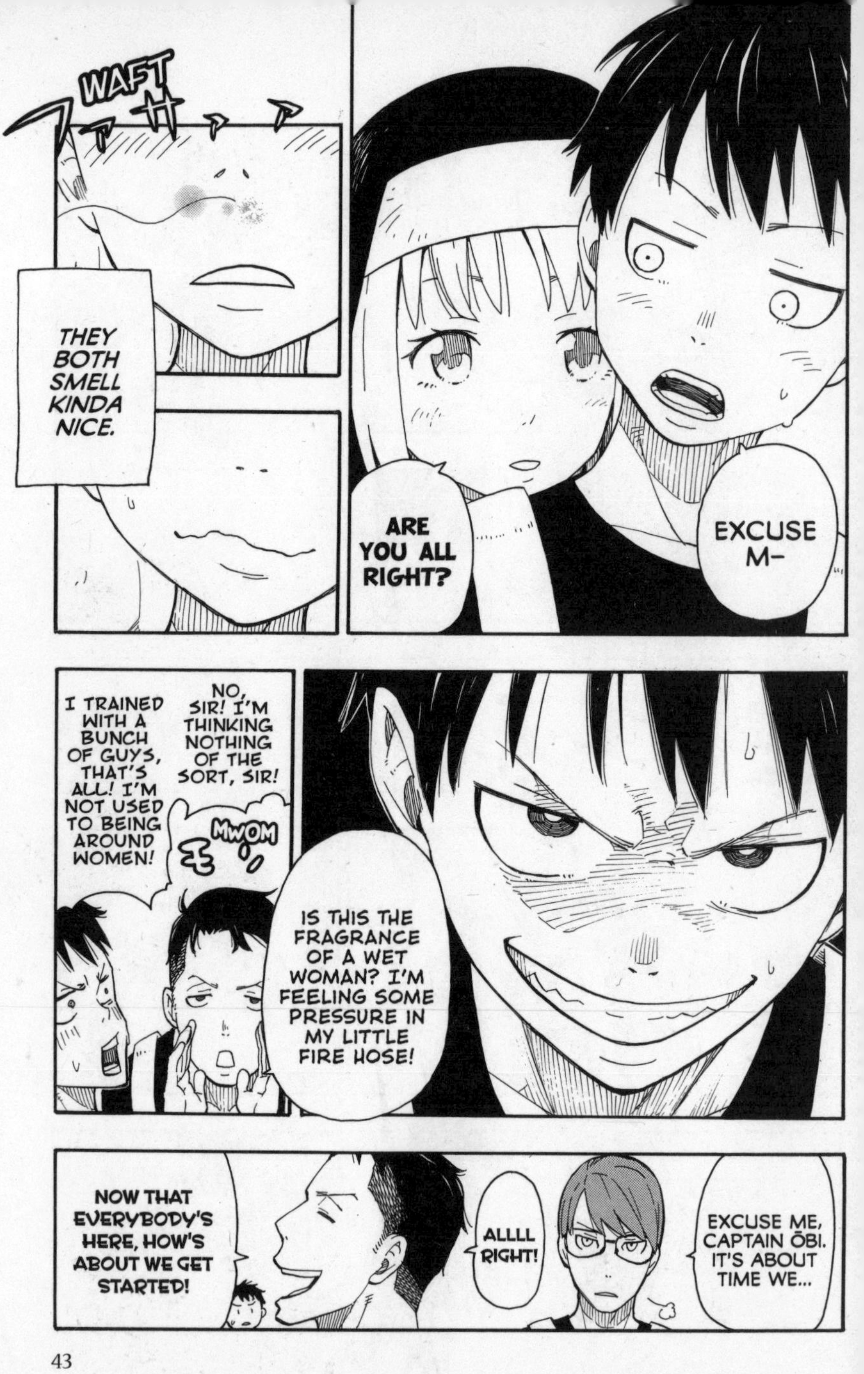
EXCUSE M–
ARE YOU ALL RIGHT?
WAFT
THEY BOTH SMELL KINDA NICE.
IS THIS THE FRAGRANCE OF A WET WOMAN? I'M FEELING SOME PRESSURE IN MY LITTLE FIRE HOSE!
NO, SIR! I'M THINKING NOTHING OF THE SORT, SIR!
I TRAINED WITH A BUNCH OF GUYS, THAT'S ALL! I'M NOT USED TO BEING AROUND WOMEN!
MWOM
EXCUSE ME, CAPTAIN ŌBI. IT'S ABOUT TIME WE...
ALLLL RIGHT!
NOW THAT EVERYBODY'S HERE, HOW'S ABOUT WE GET STARTED!

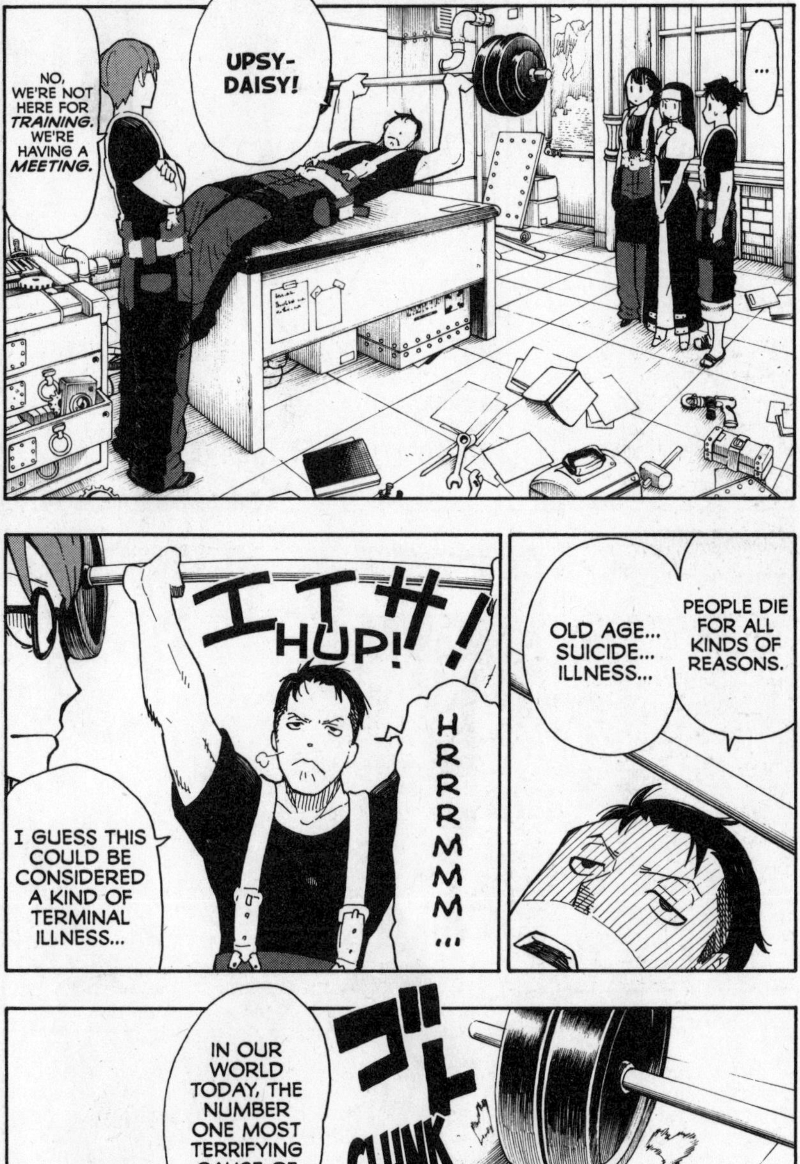
...
UPSY-DAISY!
NO, WE'RE NOT HERE FOR *TRAINING*. WE'RE HAVING A *MEETING*.
PEOPLE DIE FOR ALL KINDS OF REASONS.
OLD AGE... SUICIDE... ILLNESS...
エイサ!
HUP!
HRRRMMM...
I GUESS THIS COULD BE CONSIDERED A KIND OF TERMINAL ILLNESS...
ゴト
CLINK
IN OUR WORLD TODAY, THE NUMBER ONE MOST TERRIFYING CAUSE OF DEATH....

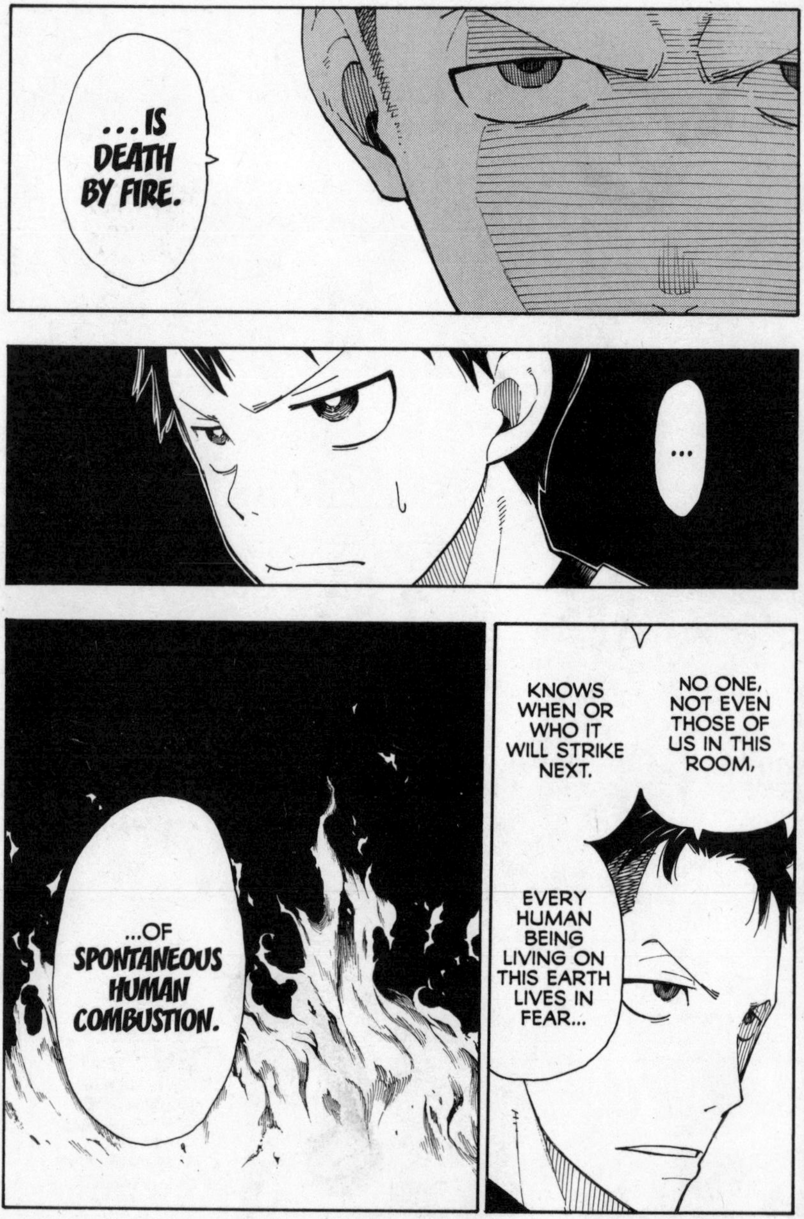
...IS DEATH BY FIRE.
...
NO ONE, NOT EVEN THOSE OF US IN THIS ROOM,
KNOWS WHEN OR WHO IT WILL STRIKE NEXT.
EVERY HUMAN BEING LIVING ON THIS EARTH LIVES IN FEAR...
...OF SPONTANEOUS HUMAN COMBUSTION.

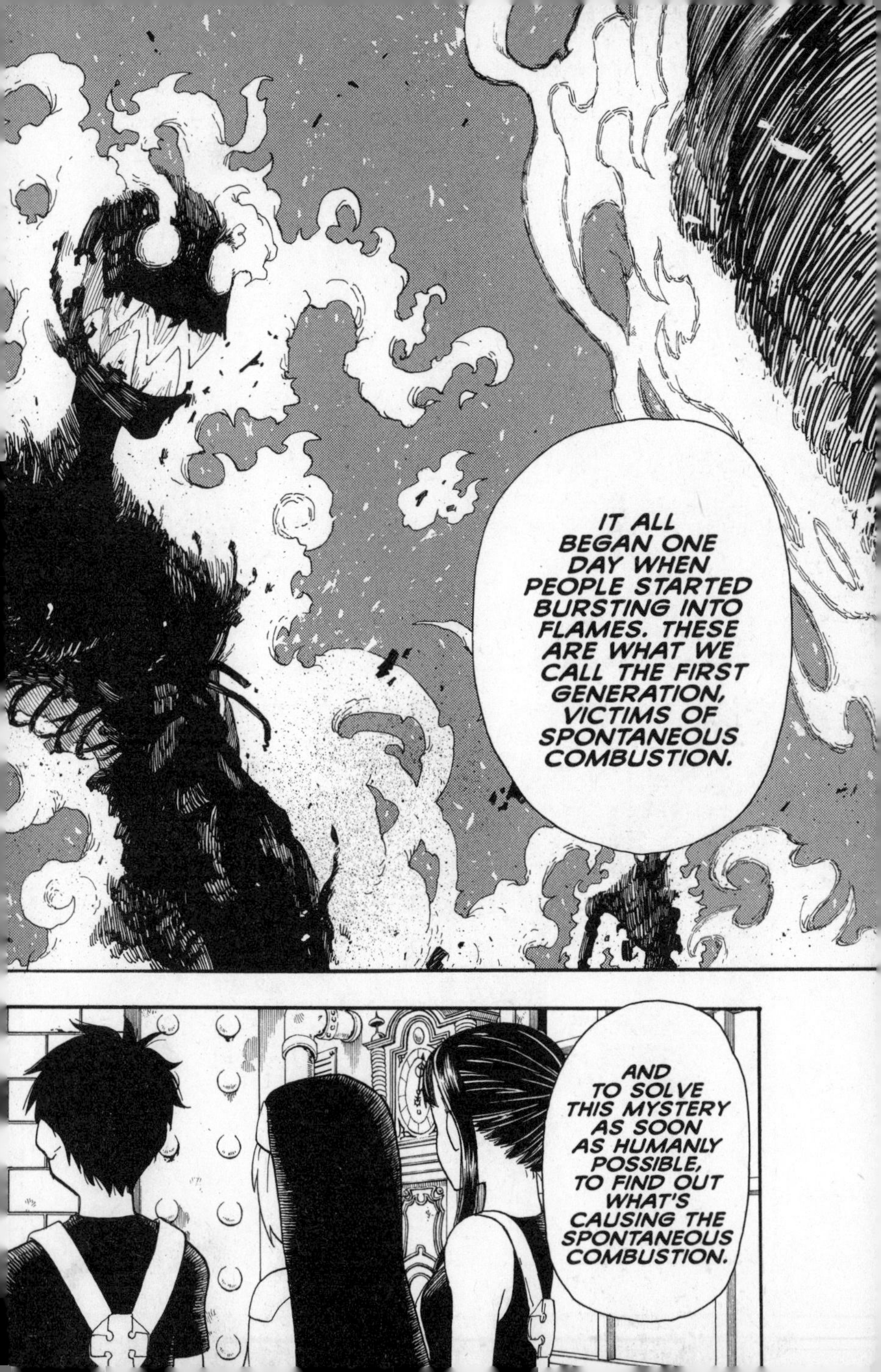
IT ALL BEGAN ONE DAY WHEN PEOPLE STARTED BURSTING INTO FLAMES. THESE ARE WHAT WE CALL THE FIRST GENERATION, VICTIMS OF SPONTANEOUS COMBUSTION.
AND TO SOLVE THIS MYSTERY AS SOON AS HUMANLY POSSIBLE, TO FIND OUT WHAT'S CAUSING THE SPONTANEOUS COMBUSTION.

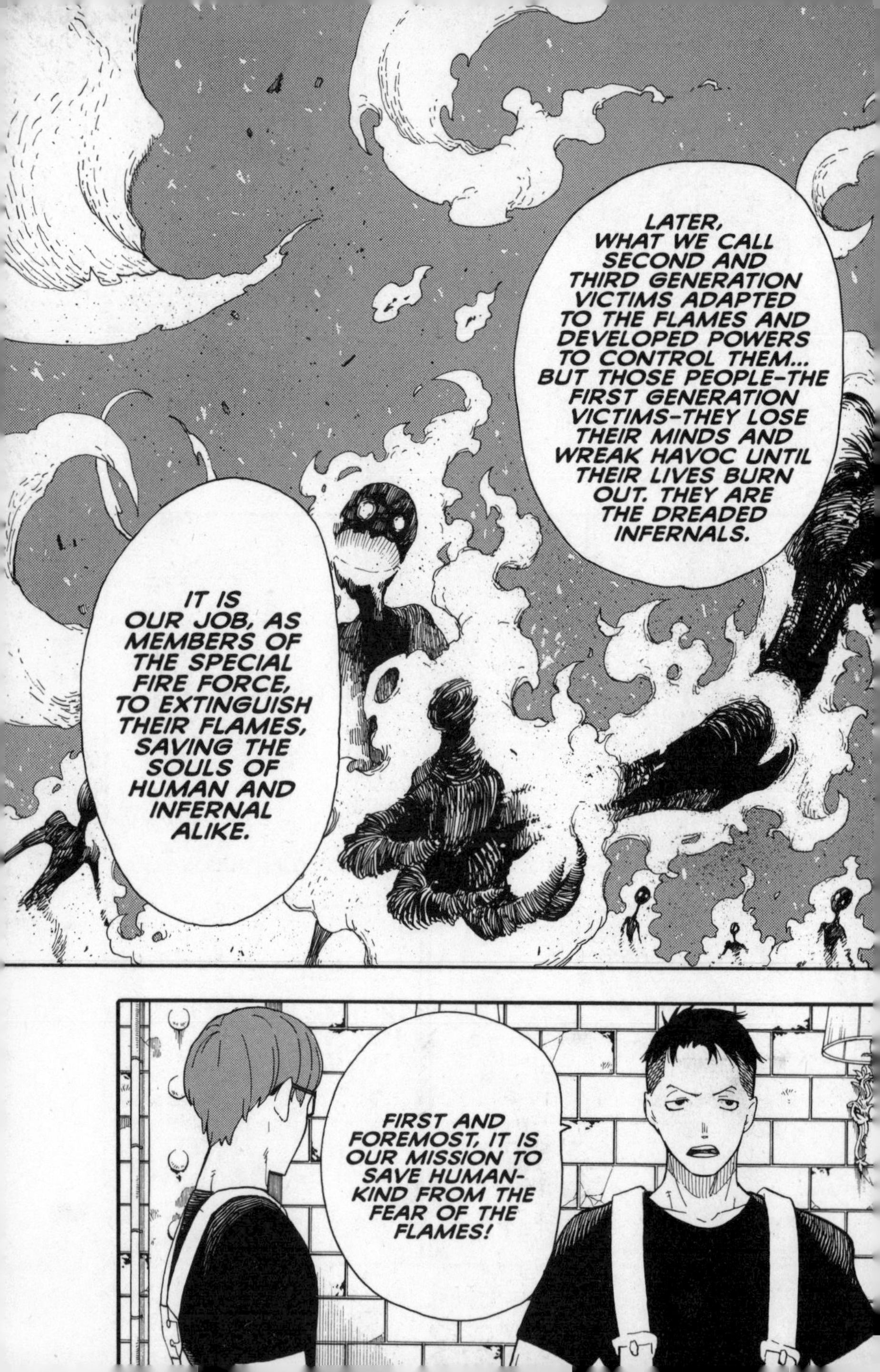
LATER, WHAT WE CALL SECOND AND THIRD GENERATION VICTIMS ADAPTED TO THE FLAMES AND DEVELOPED POWERS TO CONTROL THEM... BUT THOSE PEOPLE–THE FIRST GENERATION VICTIMS–THEY LOSE THEIR MINDS AND WREAK HAVOC UNTIL THEIR LIVES BURN OUT. THEY ARE THE DREADED INFERNALS.
IT IS OUR JOB, AS MEMBERS OF THE SPECIAL FIRE FORCE, TO EXTINGUISH THEIR FLAMES, SAVING THE SOULS OF HUMAN AND INFERNAL ALIKE.
FIRST AND FOREMOST, IT IS OUR MISSION TO SAVE HUMAN-KIND FROM THE FEAR OF THE FLAMES!

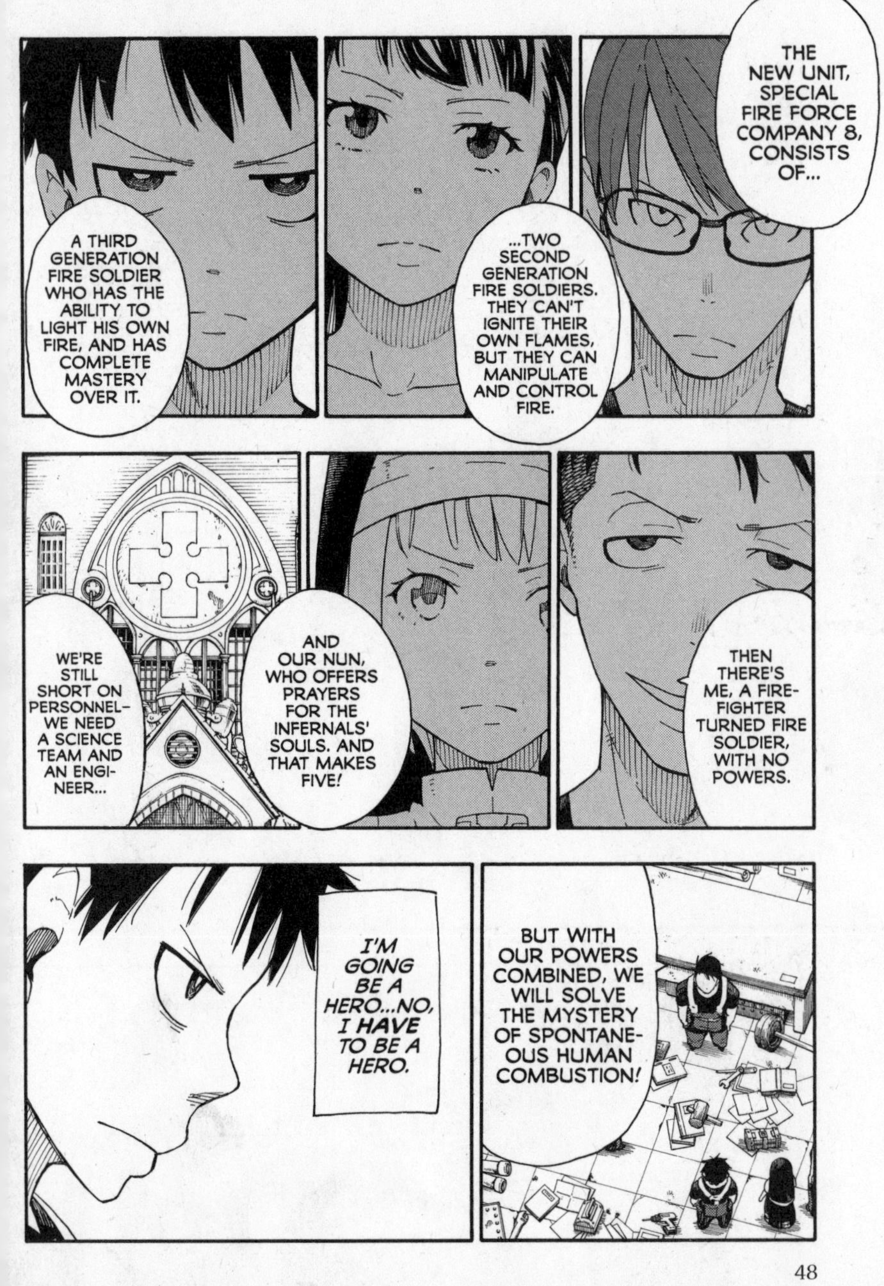
THE NEW UNIT, SPECIAL FIRE FORCE COMPANY 8, CONSISTS OF...
...TWO SECOND GENERATION FIRE SOLDIERS. THEY CAN'T IGNITE THEIR OWN FLAMES, BUT THEY CAN MANIPULATE AND CONTROL FIRE.
A THIRD GENERATION FIRE SOLDIER WHO HAS THE ABILITY TO LIGHT HIS OWN FIRE, AND HAS COMPLETE MASTERY OVER IT.
THEN THERE'S ME, A FIRE-FIGHTER TURNED FIRE SOLDIER, WITH NO POWERS.
AND OUR NUN, WHO OFFERS PRAYERS FOR THE INFERNALS' SOULS. AND THAT MAKES FIVE!
WE'RE STILL SHORT ON PERSONNEL- WE NEED A SCIENCE TEAM AND AN ENGI-NEER...
BUT WITH OUR POWERS COMBINED, WE WILL SOLVE THE MYSTERY OF SPONTANE-OUS HUMAN COMBUSTION!
I'M GOING BE A HERO...NO, I HAVE TO BE A HERO.

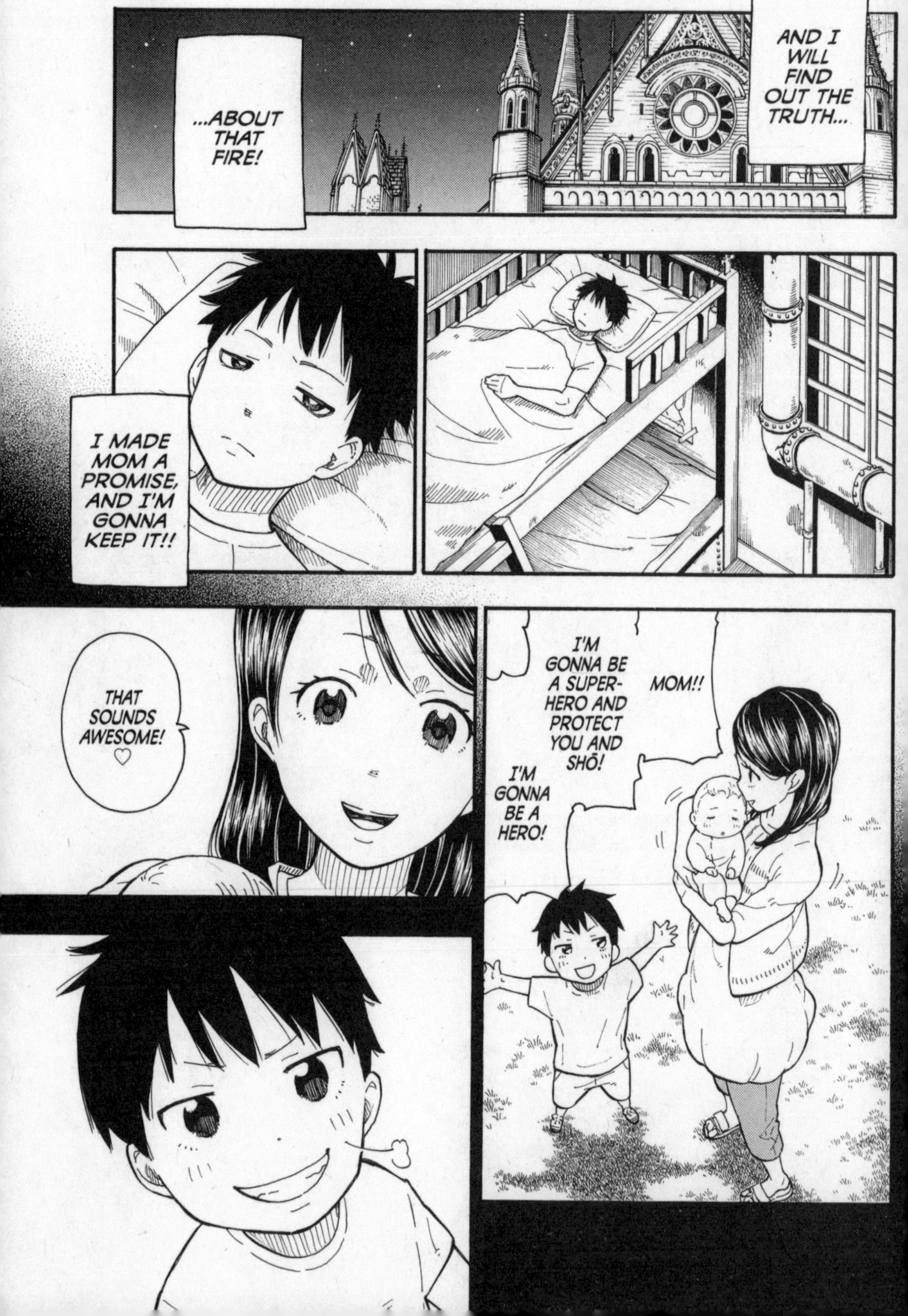
AND I WILL FIND OUT THE TRUTH...
...ABOUT THAT FIRE!
I MADE MOM A PROMISE, AND I'M GONNA KEEP IT!!
MOM!!
I'M GONNA BE A SUPER-HERO AND PROTECT YOU AND SHŌ!
I'M GONNA BE A HERO!
THAT SOUNDS AWESOME! ♡

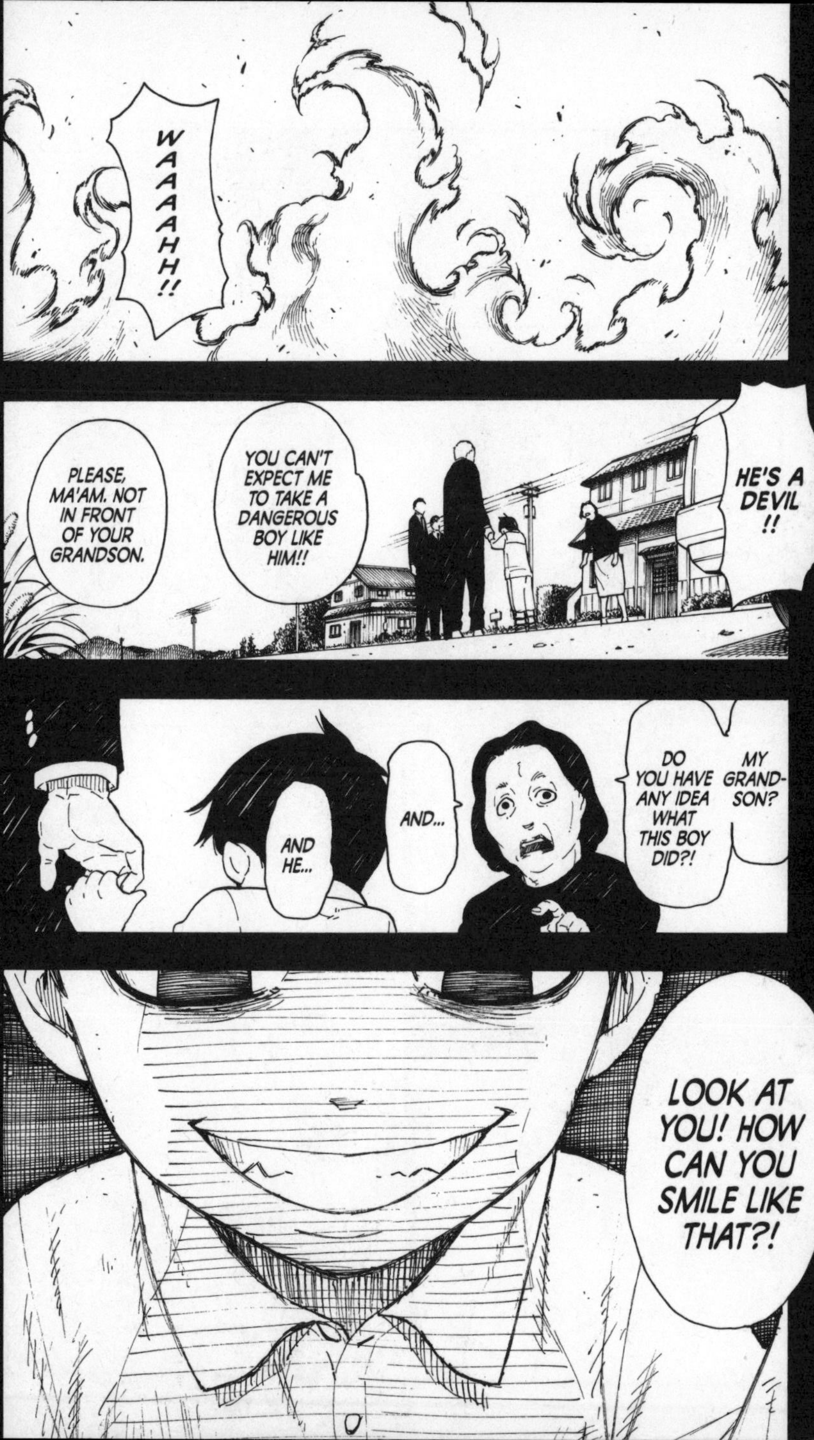
WAAAAAHH!!
HE'S A DEVIL!!
YOU CAN'T EXPECT ME TO TAKE A DANGEROUS BOY LIKE HIM!!
PLEASE, MA'AM. NOT IN FRONT OF YOUR GRANDSON.
MY GRANDSON?
DO YOU HAVE ANY IDEA WHAT THIS BOY DID?!
AND...
AND HE...
LOOK AT YOU! HOW CAN YOU SMILE LIKE THAT?!

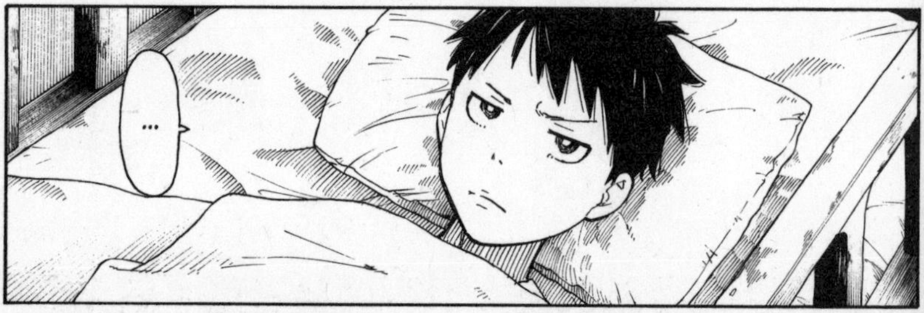
...

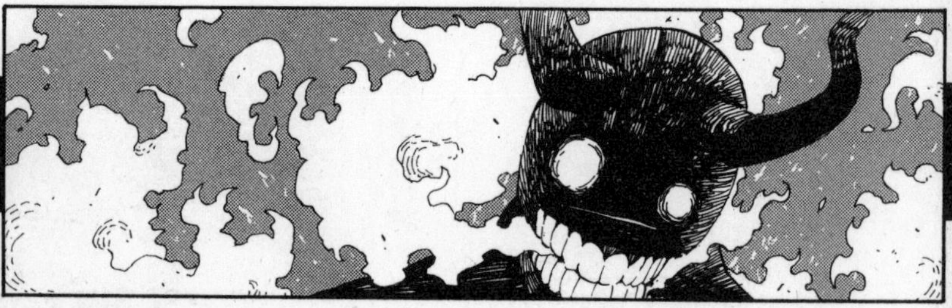

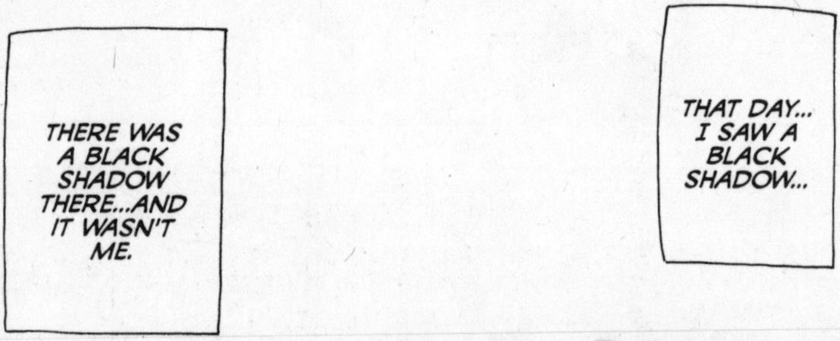
THAT DAY... I SAW A BLACK SHADOW...
THERE WAS A BLACK SHADOW THERE...AND IT WASN'T ME.

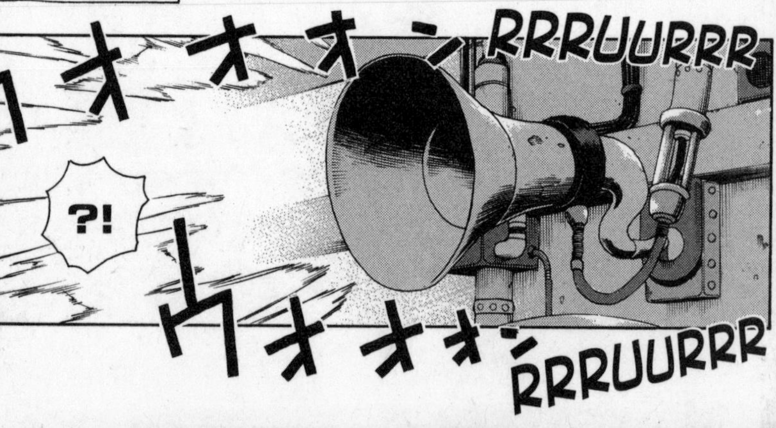
ウオオオン RRRUURRR
?!
ウオオオン RRRUURRR

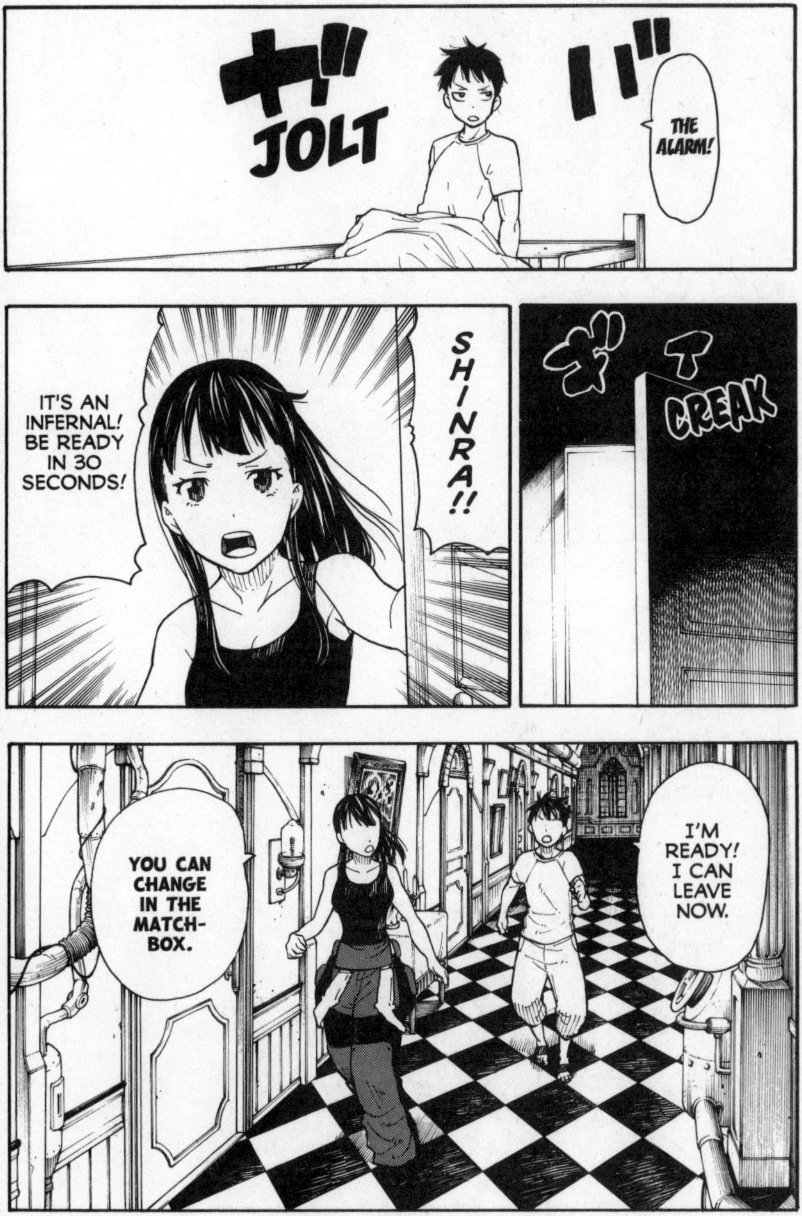
JOLT
THE ALARM!
CREAK
SHINRA!!
IT'S AN INFERNAL! BE READY IN 30 SECONDS!
I'M READY! I CAN LEAVE NOW.
YOU CAN CHANGE IN THE MATCH-BOX.

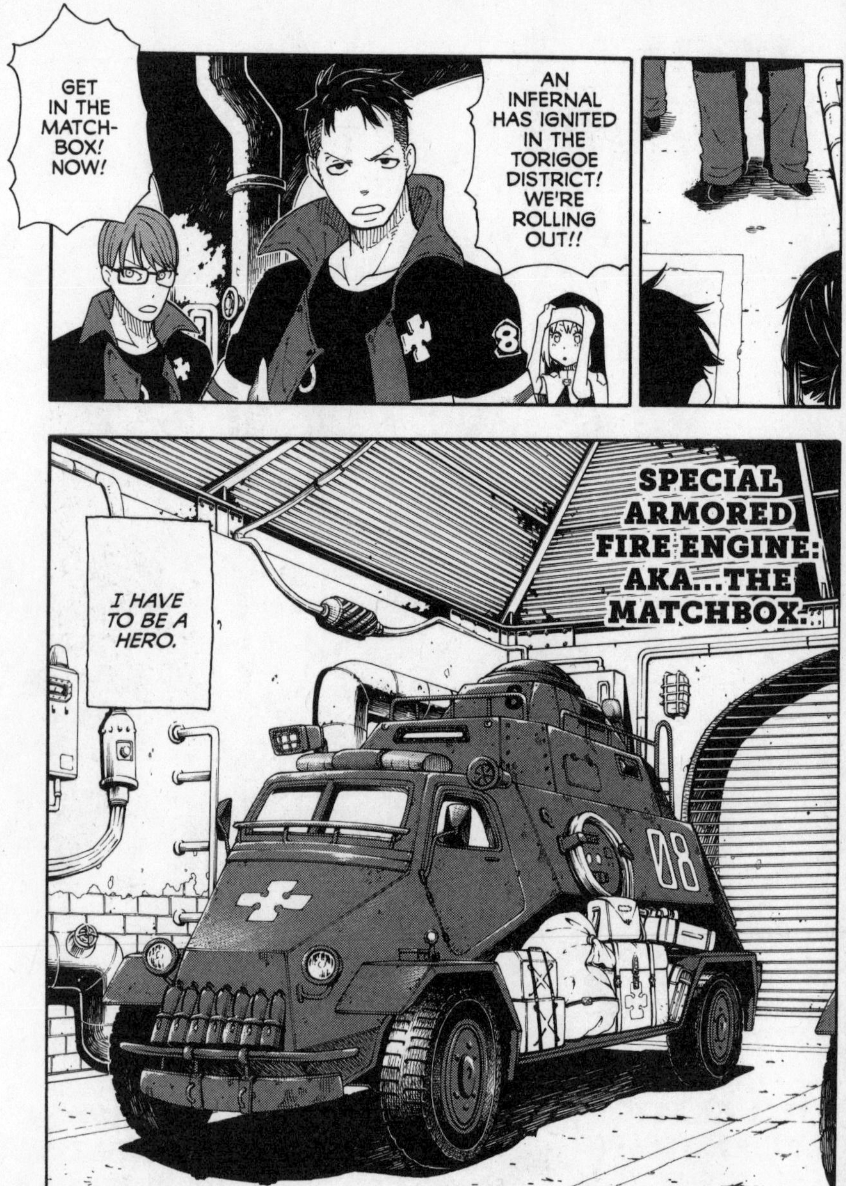
AN INFERNAL HAS IGNITED IN THE TORIGOE DISTRICT! WE'RE ROLLING OUT!!
GET IN THE MATCH-BOX! NOW!
SPECIAL ARMORED FIRE ENGINE: AKA...THE MATCHBOX.
I HAVE TO BE A HERO.

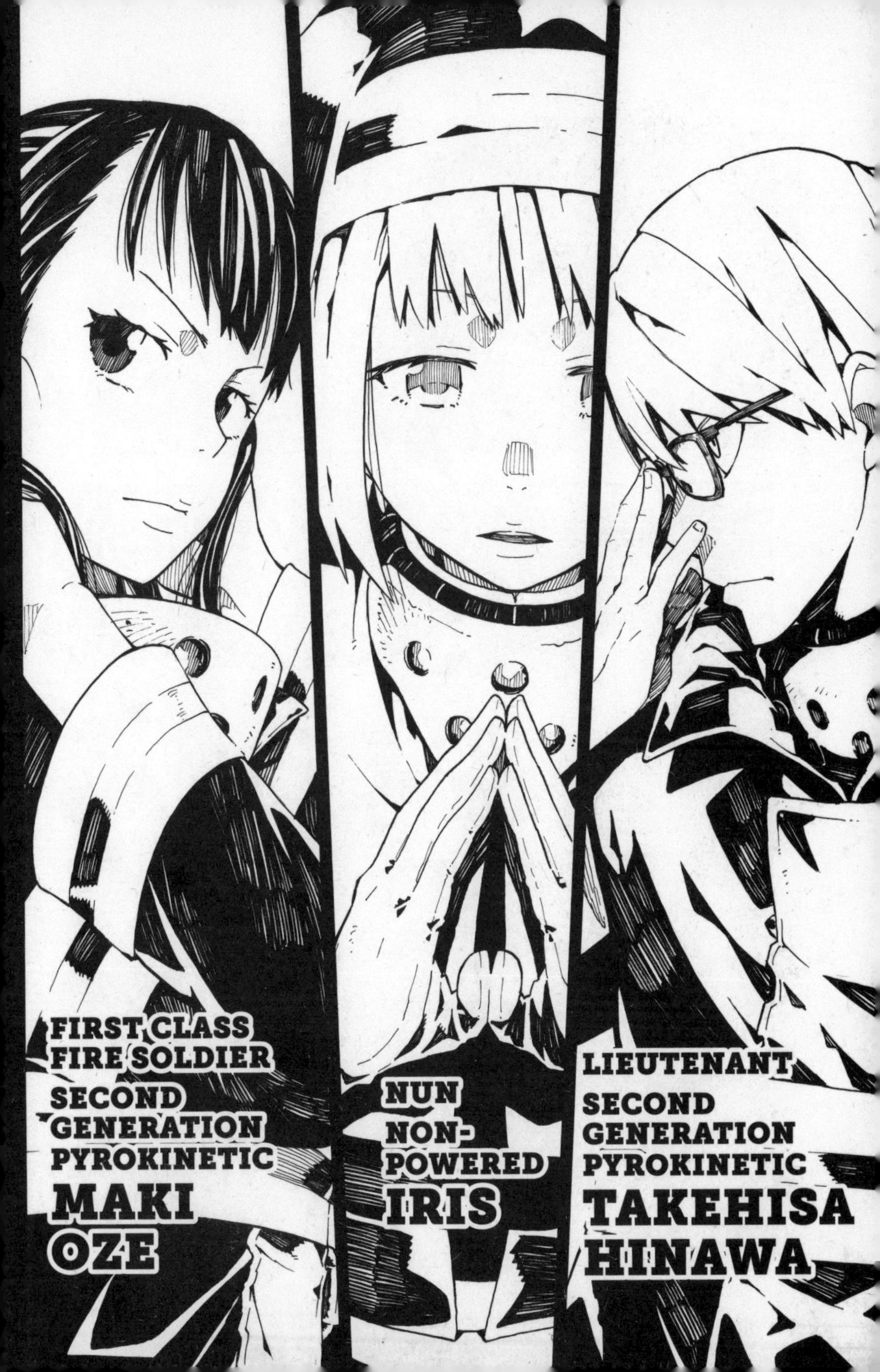

LIEUTENANT
SECOND GENERATION PYROKINETIC
TAKEHISA HINAWA
NUN
NON-POWERED
IRIS
FIRST CLASS FIRE SOLDIER
SECOND GENERATION PYROKINETIC
MAKI OZE

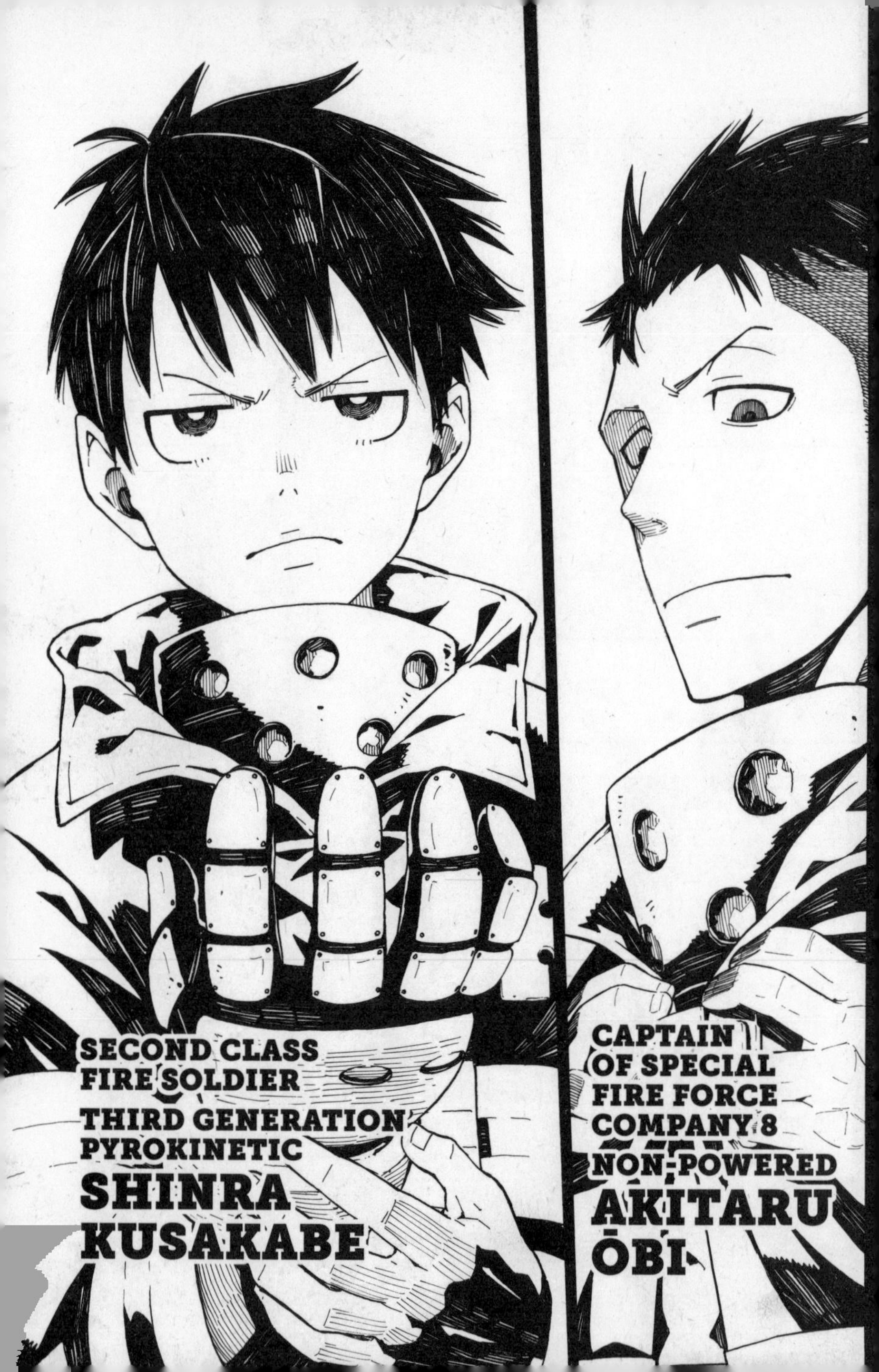
CAPTAIN OF SPECIAL FIRE FORCE COMPANY 8
NON-POWERED
AKITARU ŌBI
SECOND CLASS FIRE SOLDIER
THIRD GENERATION PYROKINETIC
SHINRA KUSAKABE

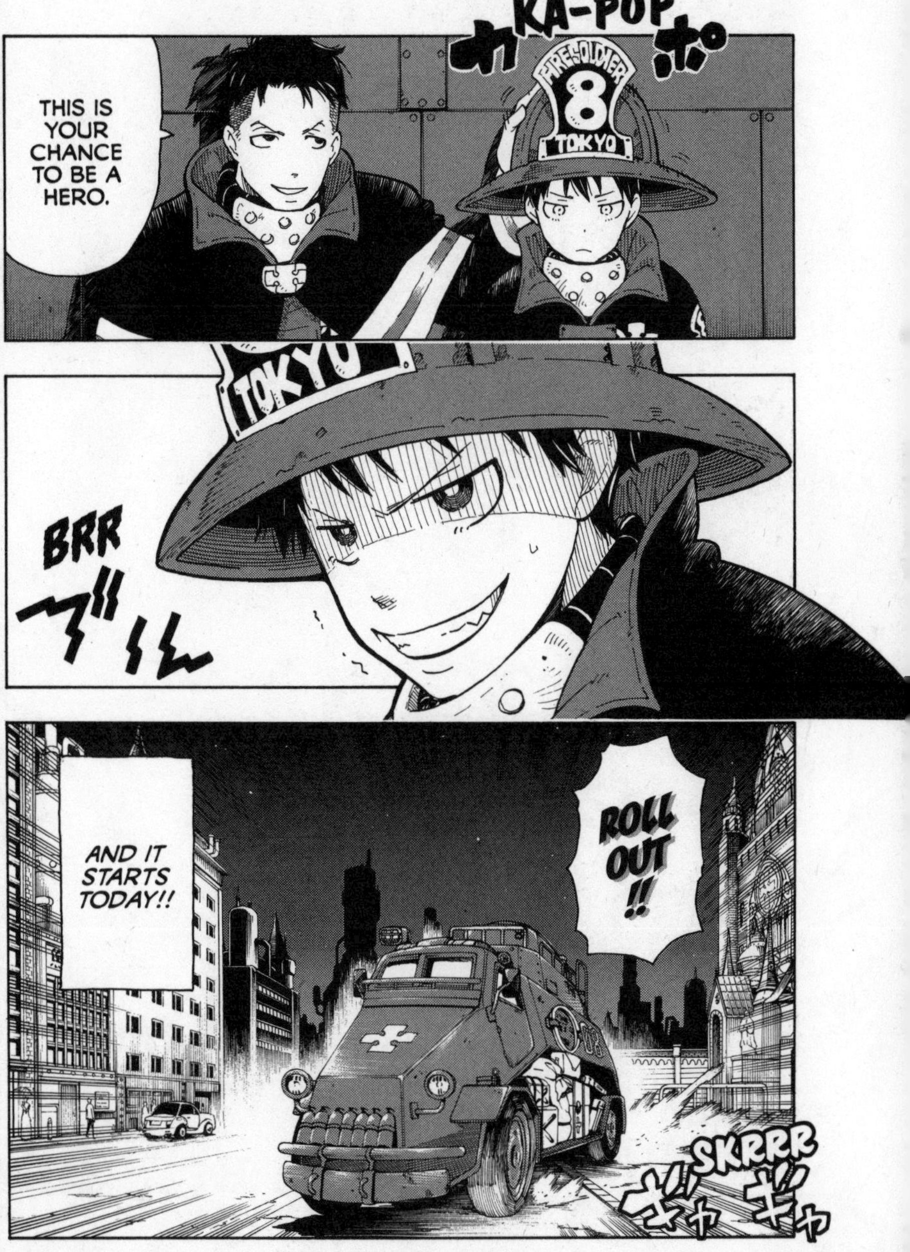
KA-POP
THIS IS YOUR CHANCE TO BE A HERO.
FIRE SOLDIER 8 TOKYO
TOKYO
BRR
ROLL OUT!!
AND IT STARTS TODAY!!
SKRRR

CHAPTER 1: FIRST RUN

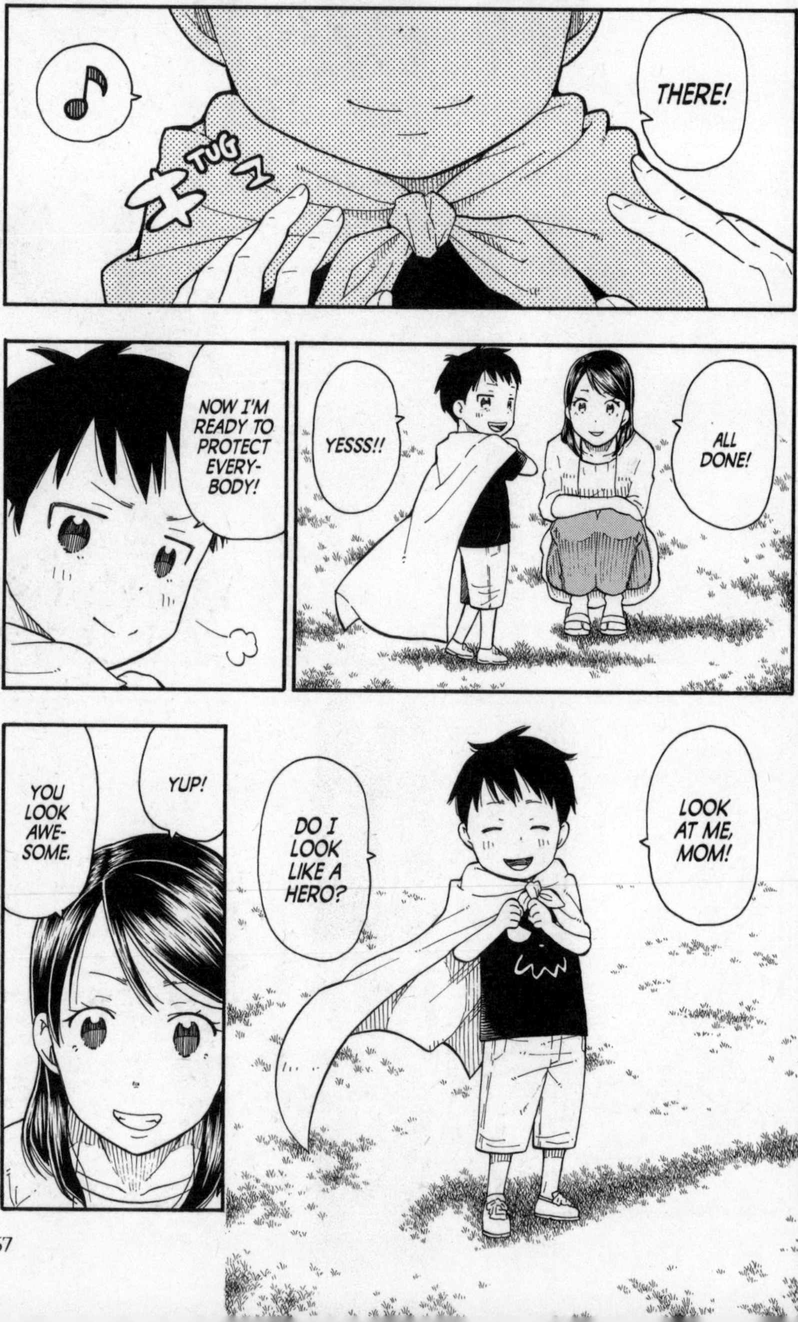

THERE!
♪
TUG
ALL DONE!
YESSS!!
NOW I'M READY TO PROTECT EVERY-BODY!
LOOK AT ME, MOM!
DO I LOOK LIKE A HERO?
YUP!
YOU LOOK AWE-SOME.

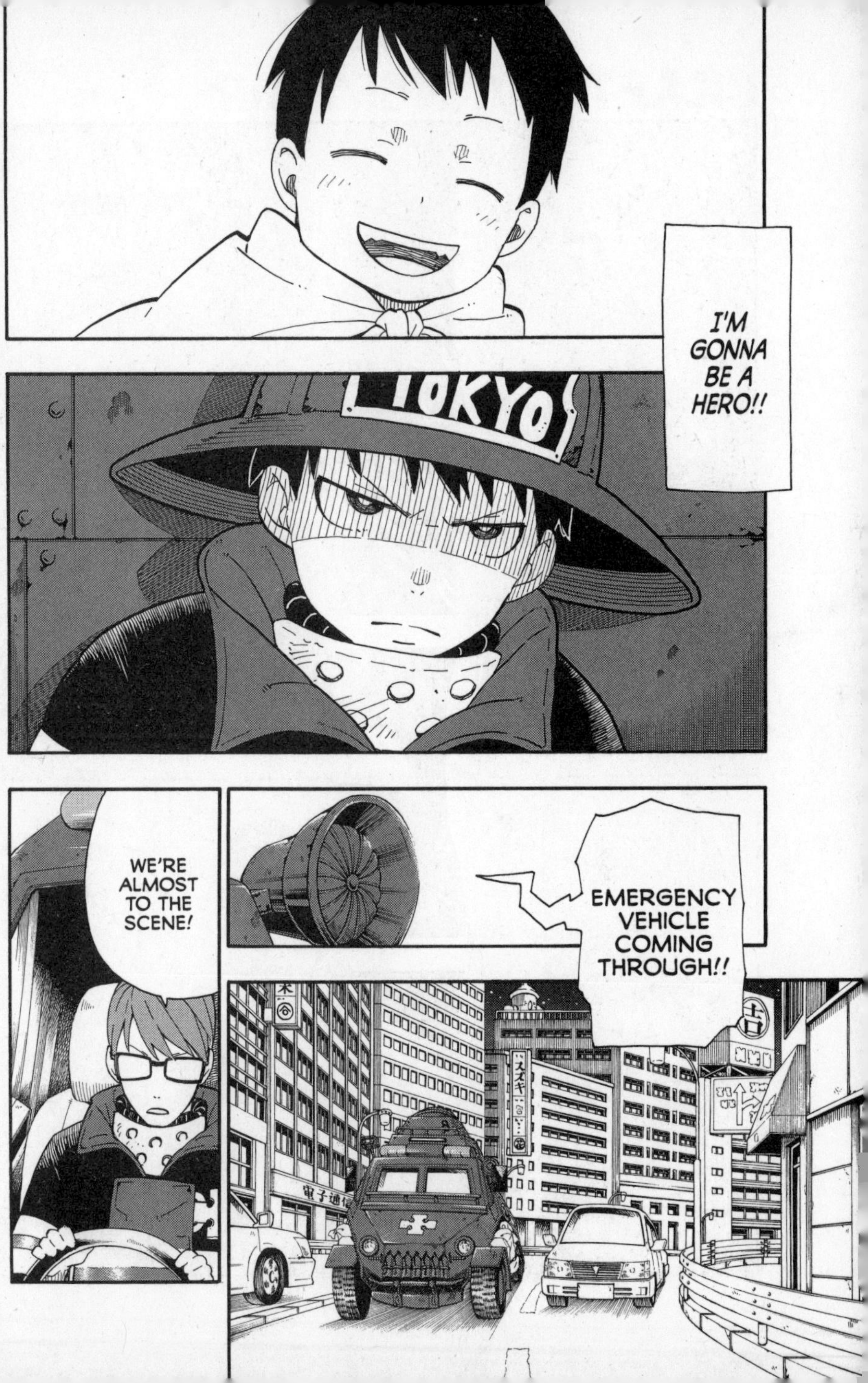
I'M GONNA BE A HERO!!
TOKYO
EMERGENCY VEHICLE COMING THROUGH!!
WE'RE ALMOST TO THE SCENE!

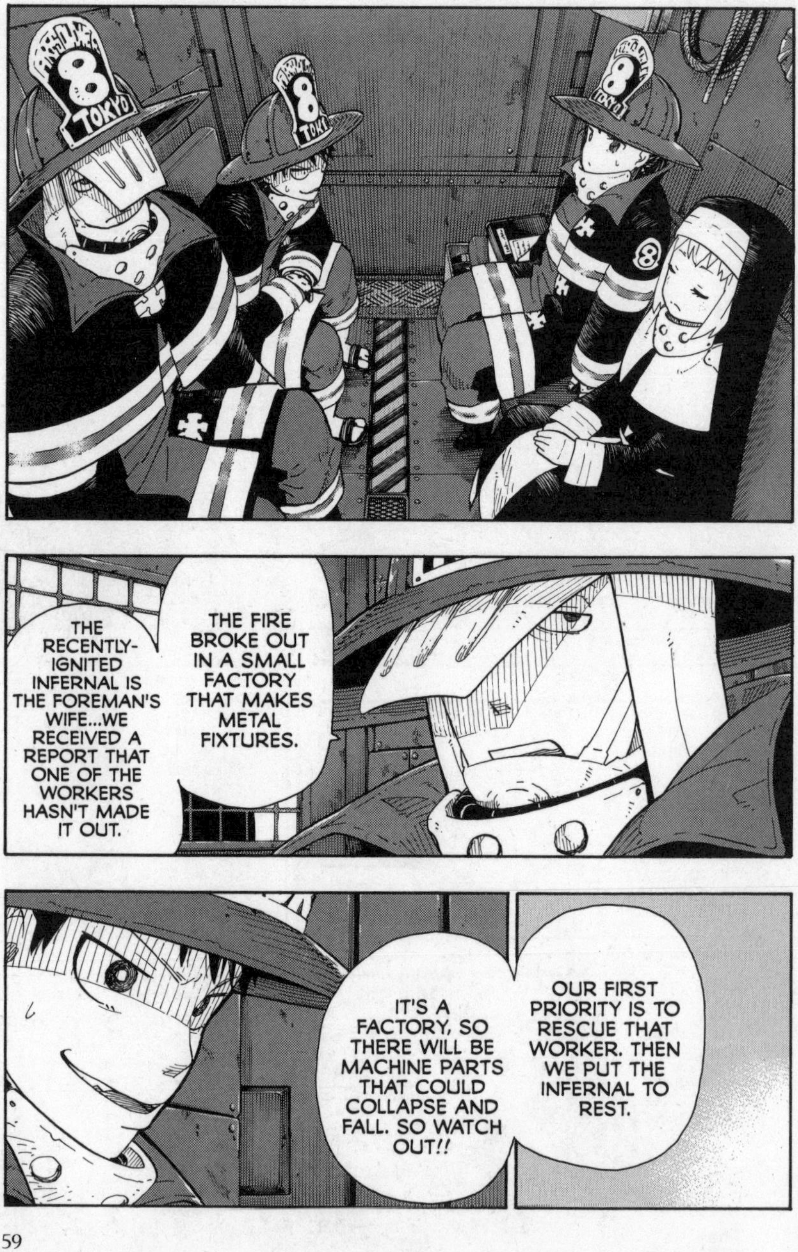
8 TOKYO
THE FIRE BROKE OUT IN A SMALL FACTORY THAT MAKES METAL FIXTURES.
THE RECENTLY-IGNITED INFERNAL IS THE FOREMAN'S WIFE...WE RECEIVED A REPORT THAT ONE OF THE WORKERS HASN'T MADE IT OUT.
OUR FIRST PRIORITY IS TO RESCUE THAT WORKER. THEN WE PUT THE INFERNAL TO REST.
IT'S A FACTORY, SO THERE WILL BE MACHINE PARTS THAT COULD COLLAPSE AND FALL. SO WATCH OUT!!

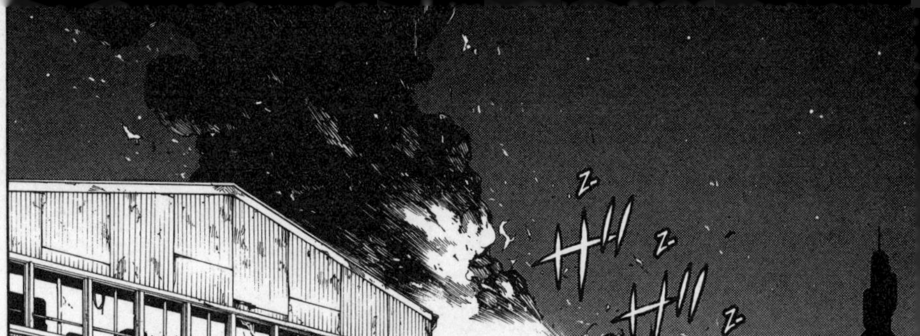
Z-
Z-
Z-
ZSH
川口金具 株式会社
Sign: Kawaguchi Fixtures, Inc.

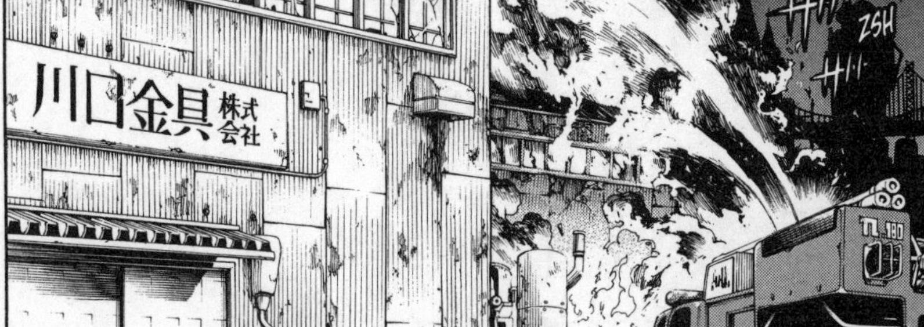
LOOKS LIKE THE FIREFIGHTERS HAVE STARTED PUTTING OUT THE FLAMES.
THE STEAM'S GONNA LOWER VISIBILITY...
WE'RE SPECIAL FIRE FORCE COMPANY 8.
OH, YOU'RE HERE, BLUE STRIPES.
THAT INFERNAL IN THERE... SHE'S PRETTY AGGRESSIVE.
WE'RE DOING WHAT WE CAN TO KEEP THE FIRE FROM SPREADING, BUT IF WE CAN'T PUT OUT THE INFERNAL...
Jumpsuit: Kawaguchi Fixtures

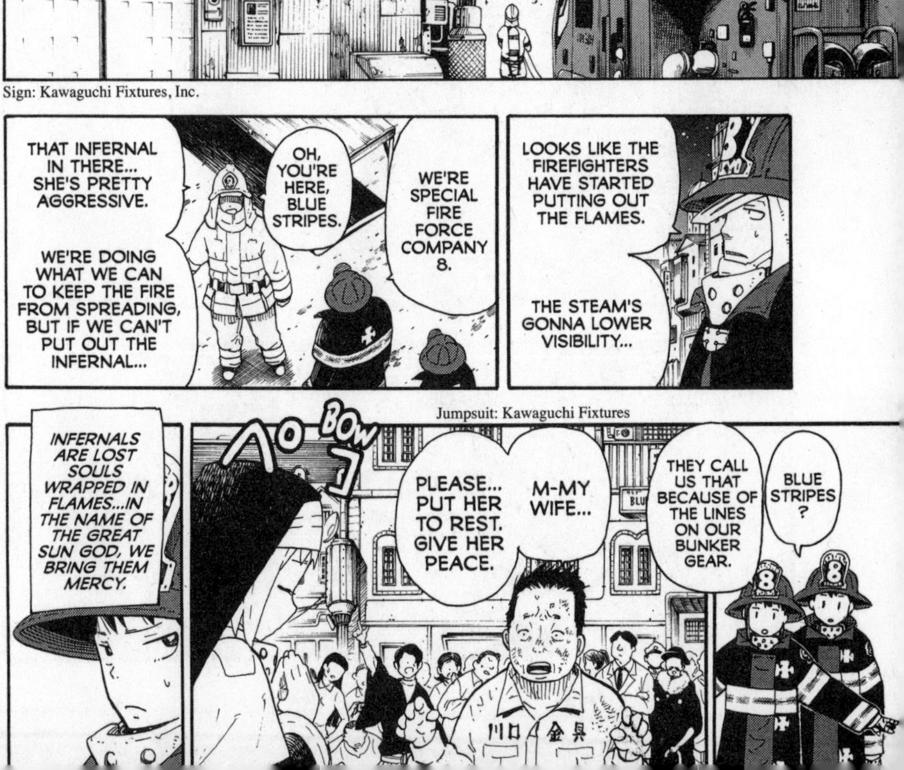
BLUE STRIPES?
THEY CALL US THAT BECAUSE OF THE LINES ON OUR BUNKER GEAR.
M-MY WIFE...
PLEASE... PUT HER TO REST. GIVE HER PEACE.
BOW
川口 金具
INFERNALS ARE LOST SOULS WRAPPED IN FLAMES...IN THE NAME OF THE GREAT SUN GOD, WE BRING THEM MERCY.

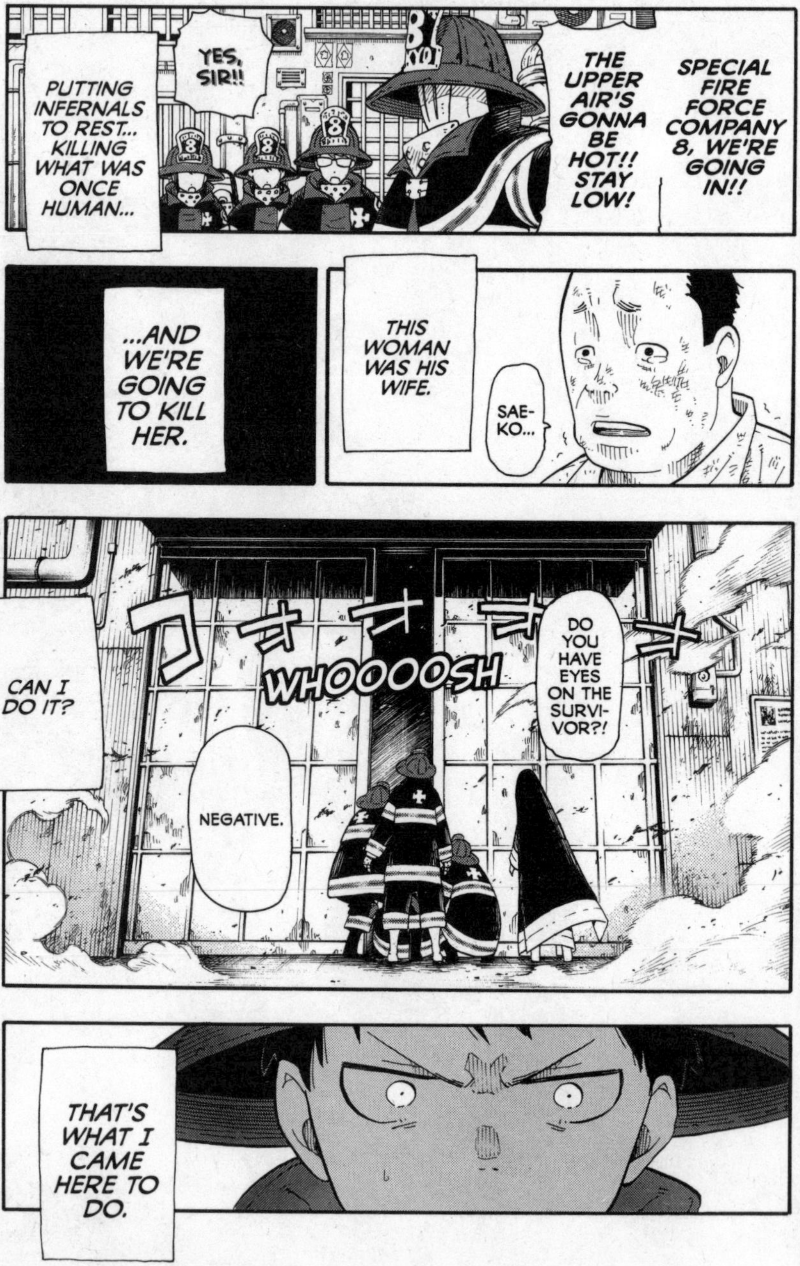
SPECIAL FIRE FORCE COMPANY 8, WE'RE GOING IN!!
THE UPPER AIR'S GONNA BE HOT!! STAY LOW!
YES, SIR!!
PUTTING INFERNALS TO REST... KILLING WHAT WAS ONCE HUMAN...
SAE-KO...
THIS WOMAN WAS HIS WIFE.
...AND WE'RE GOING TO KILL HER.
WHOOOOSH
DO YOU HAVE EYES ON THE SURVIVOR?!
NEGATIVE.
CAN I DO IT?
THAT'S WHAT I CAME HERE TO DO.

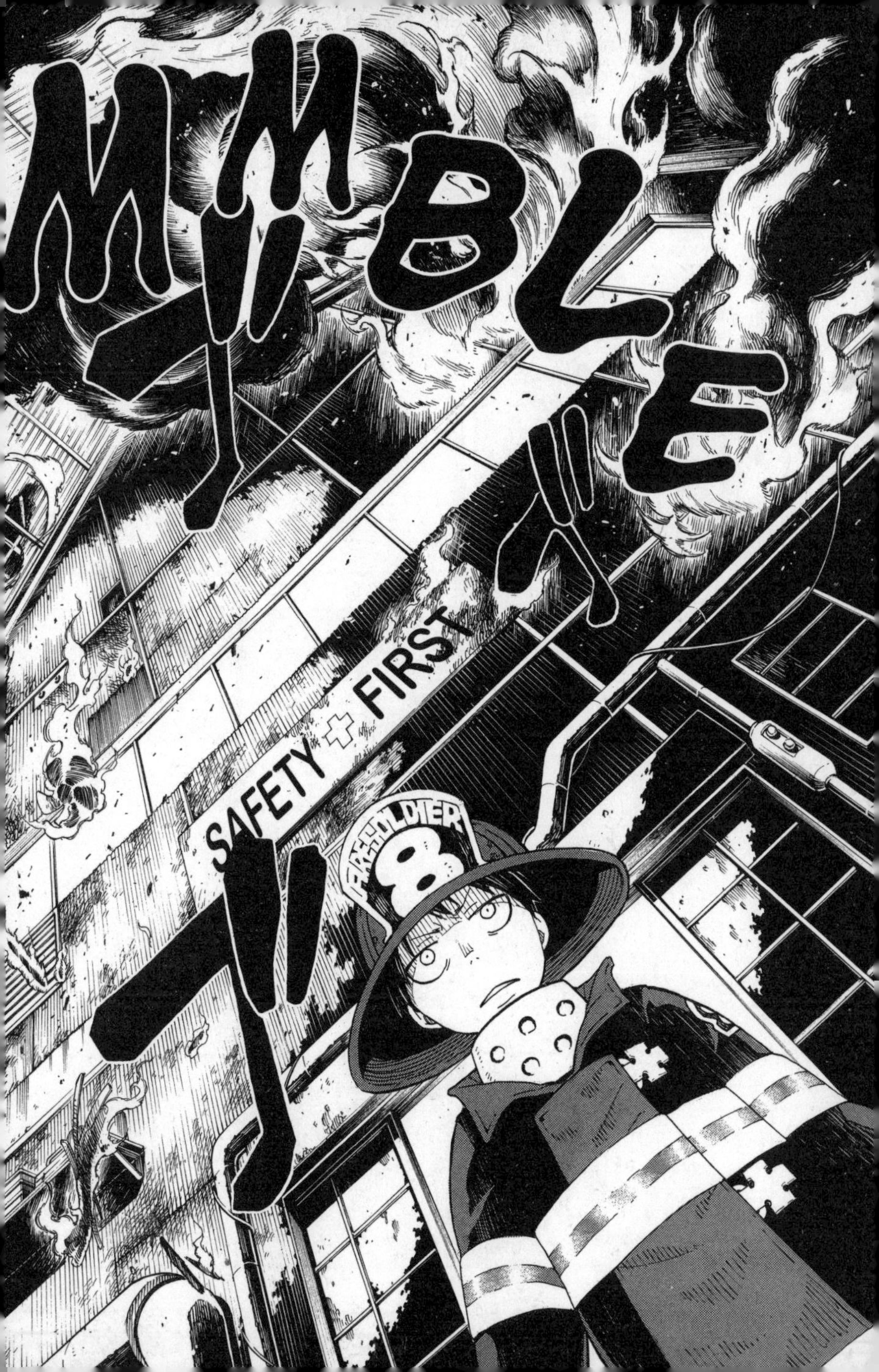
SAFETY FIRST
FIRE SOLDIER
8

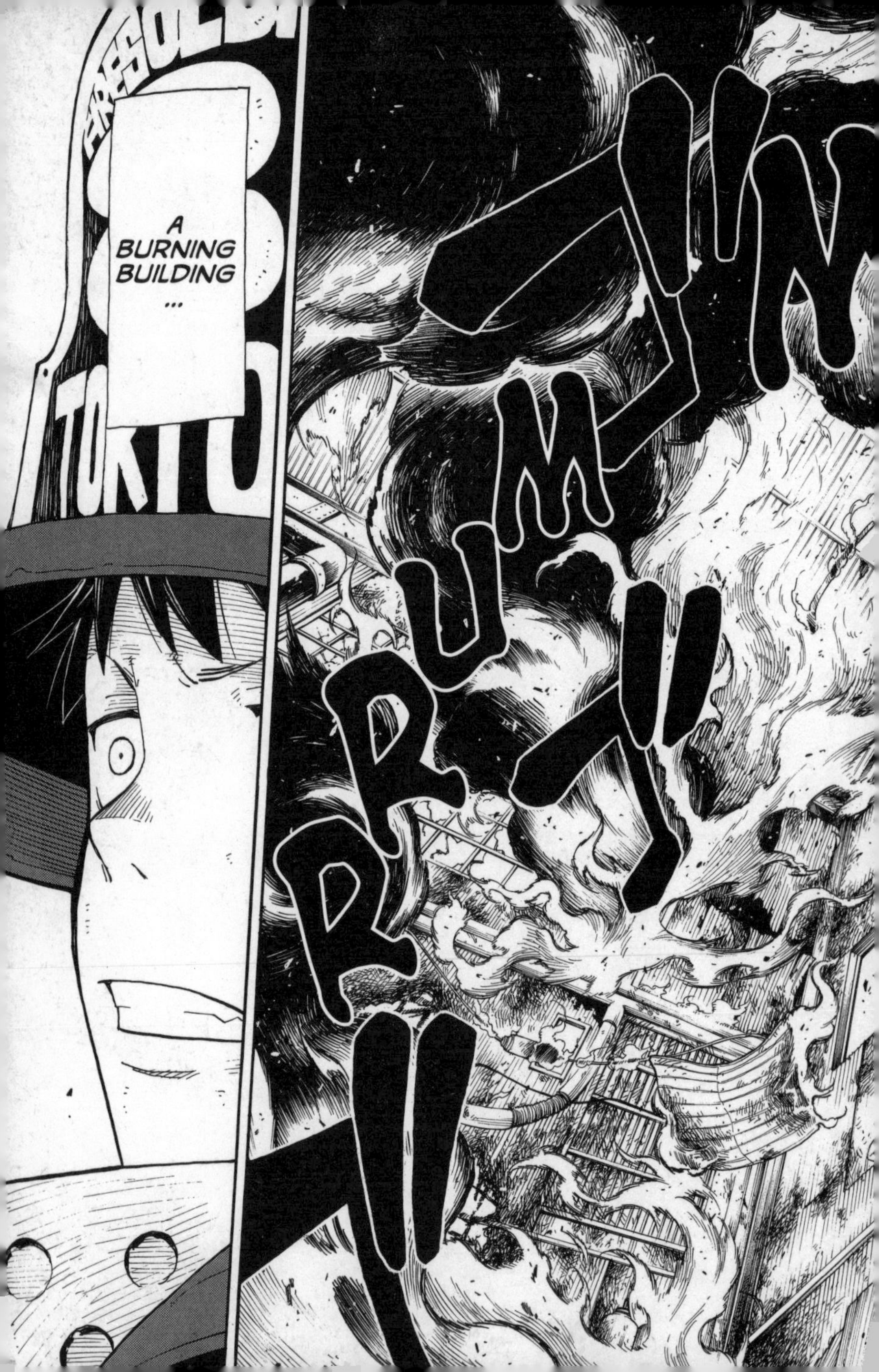
A BURNING BUILDING ...

OH!
RIGHT, STAY LOW.
ZSH
!!
CLUNK
IS THIS...
A PERSON ?!
A DEAD BODY ?!

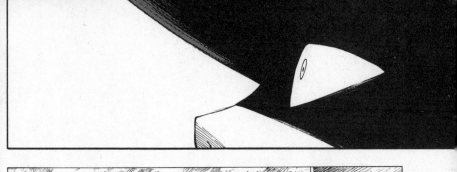

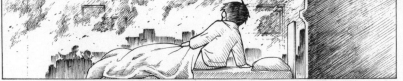

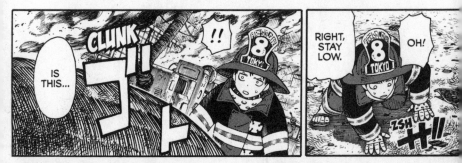

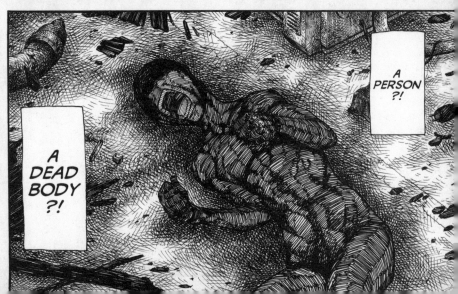

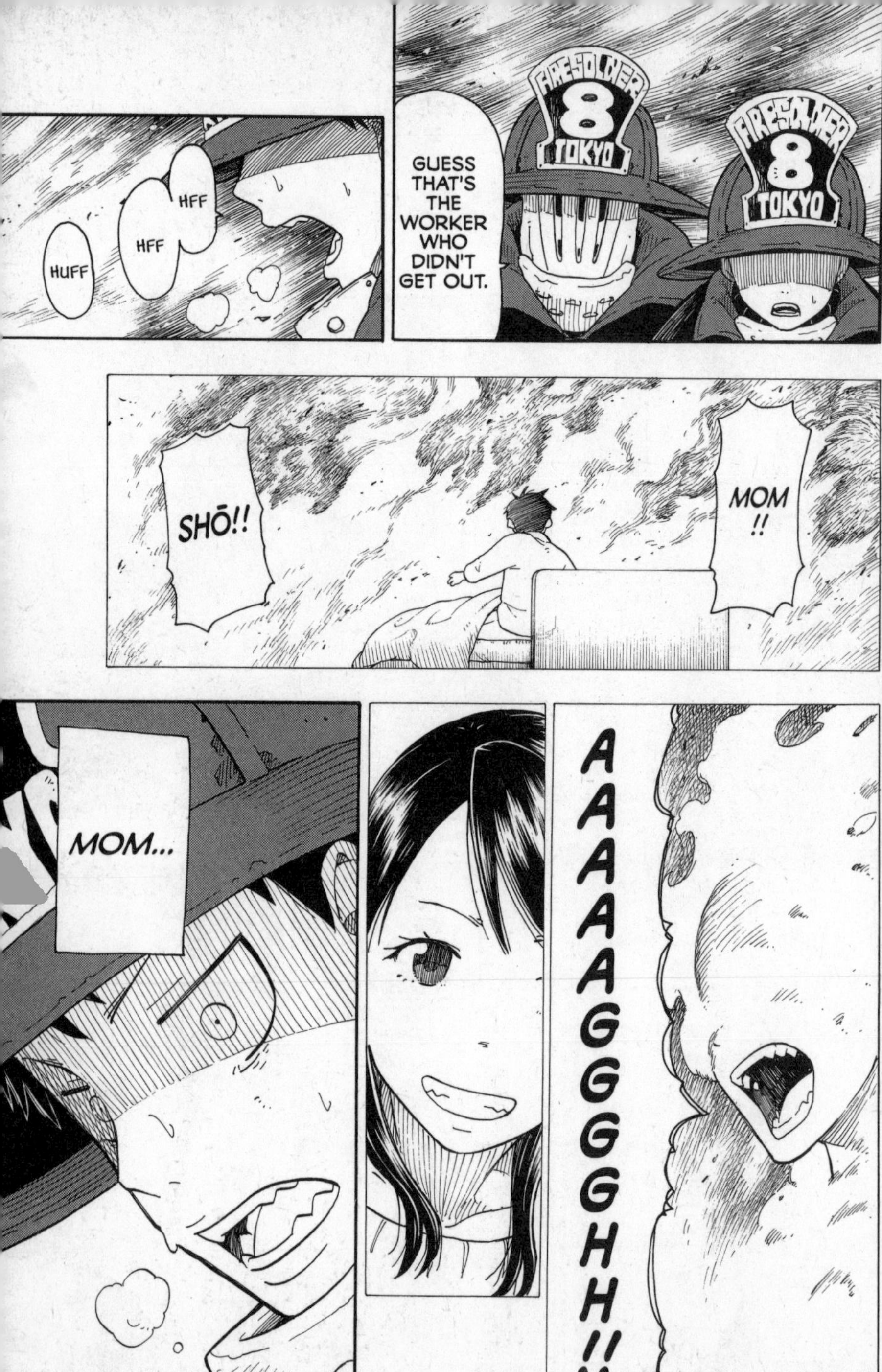
GUESS THAT'S THE WORKER WHO DIDN'T GET OUT.
HFF
HFF
HUFF
MOM !!
SHŌ!!
AAAAAAGGGGHH!!
MOM...

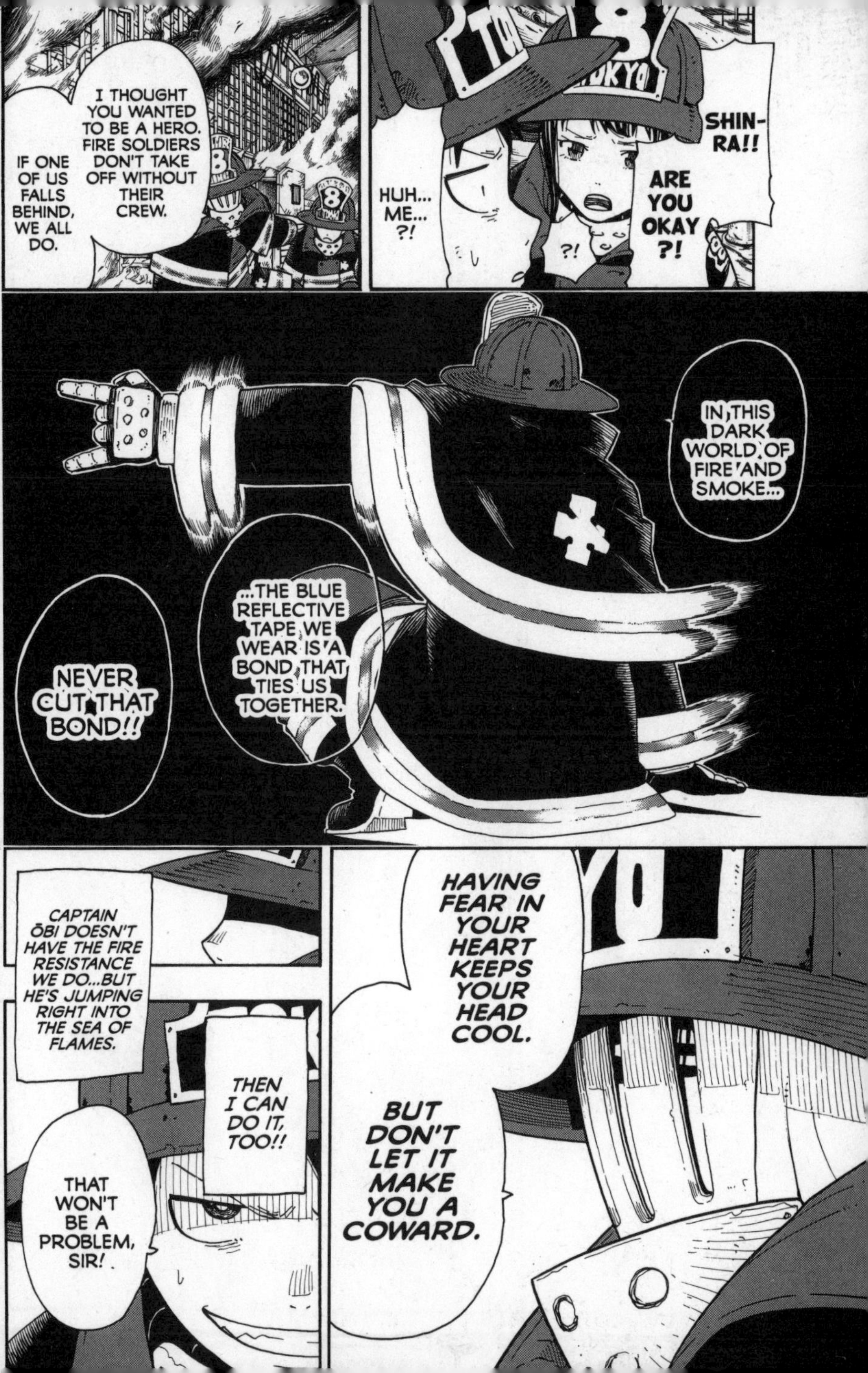
SHIN-RA!!
ARE YOU OKAY?!
HUH... ME... ?!
?!
I THOUGHT YOU WANTED TO BE A HERO. FIRE SOLDIERS DON'T TAKE OFF WITHOUT THEIR CREW.
IF ONE OF US FALLS BEHIND, WE ALL DO.
IN THIS DARK WORLD OF FIRE AND SMOKE...
...THE BLUE REFLECTIVE TAPE WE WEAR IS A BOND THAT TIES US TOGETHER.
NEVER CUT THAT BOND!!
HAVING FEAR IN YOUR HEART KEEPS YOUR HEAD COOL.
BUT DON'T LET IT MAKE YOU A COWARD.
CAPTAIN ŌBI DOESN'T HAVE THE FIRE RESISTANCE WE DO...BUT HE'S JUMPING RIGHT INTO THE SEA OF FLAMES.
THEN I CAN DO IT, TOO!!
THAT WON'T BE A PROBLEM, SIR!

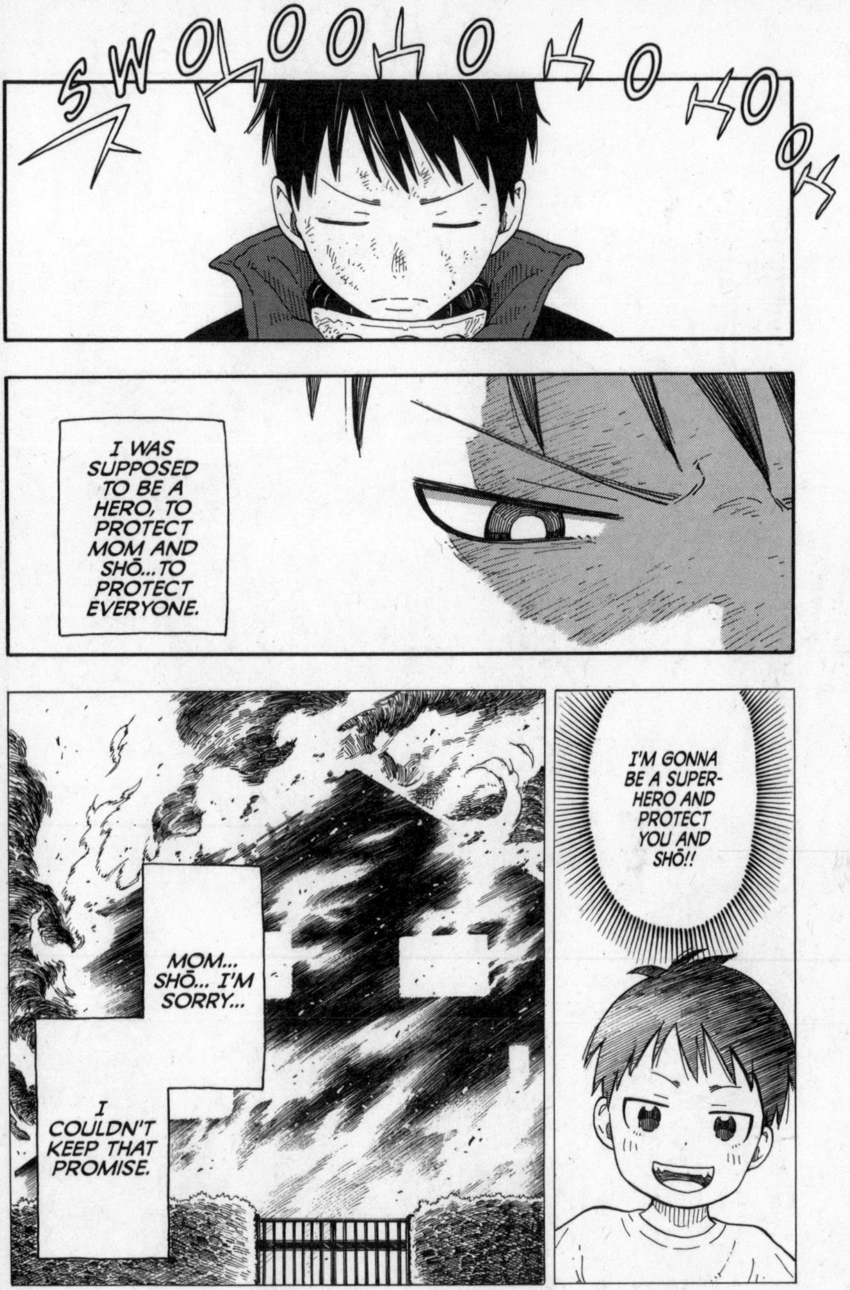
I WAS SUPPOSED TO BE A HERO, TO PROTECT MOM AND SHŌ...TO PROTECT EVERYONE.
I'M GONNA BE A SUPER-HERO AND PROTECT YOU AND SHŌ!!
MOM... SHŌ... I'M SORRY...
I COULDN'T KEEP THAT PROMISE.

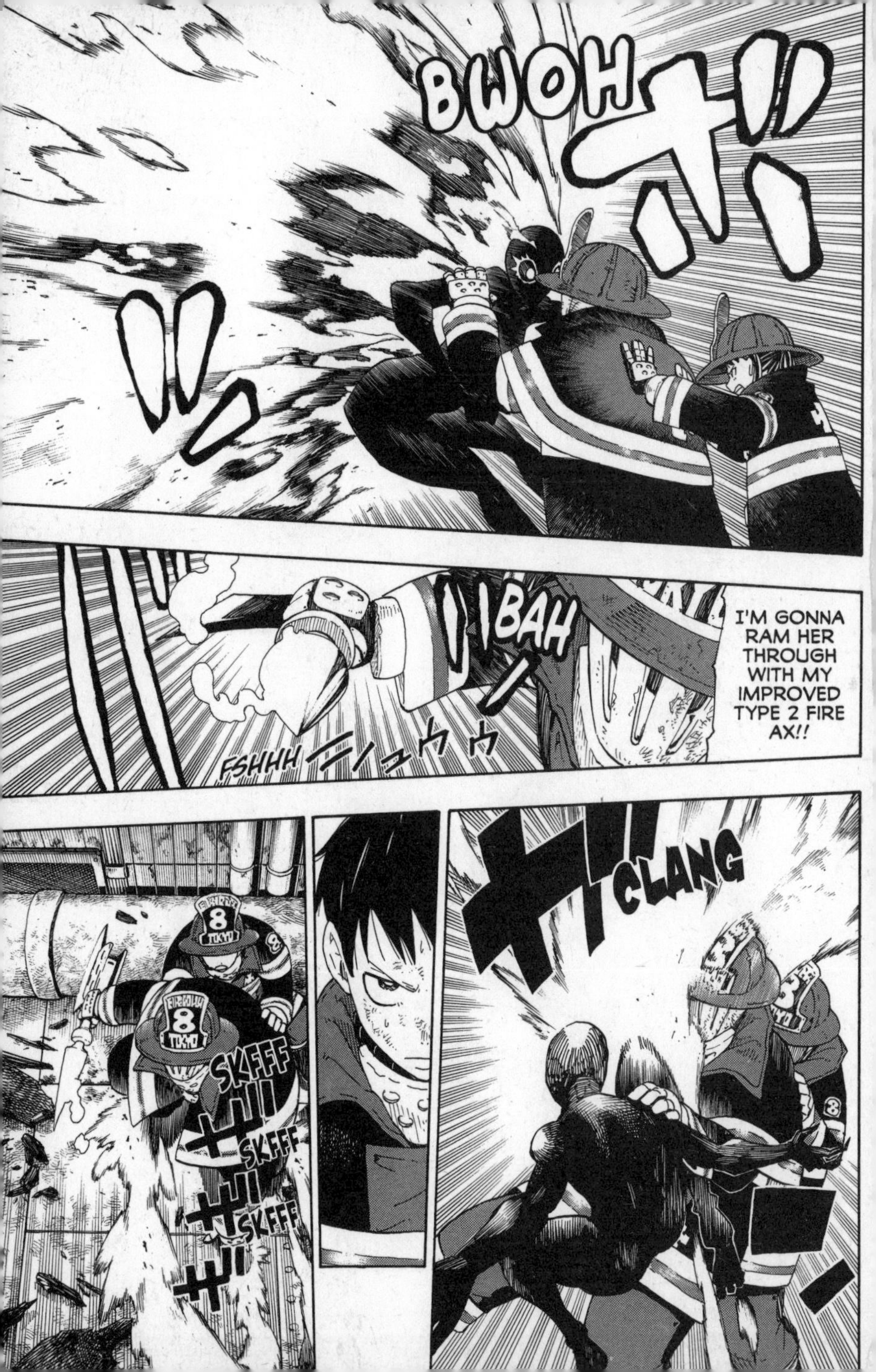
BWOH
I'M GONNA RAM HER THROUGH WITH MY IMPROVED TYPE 2 FIRE AX!!
BAH
FSHHH
CLANG
SKFFF
SKFFF
SKFFF

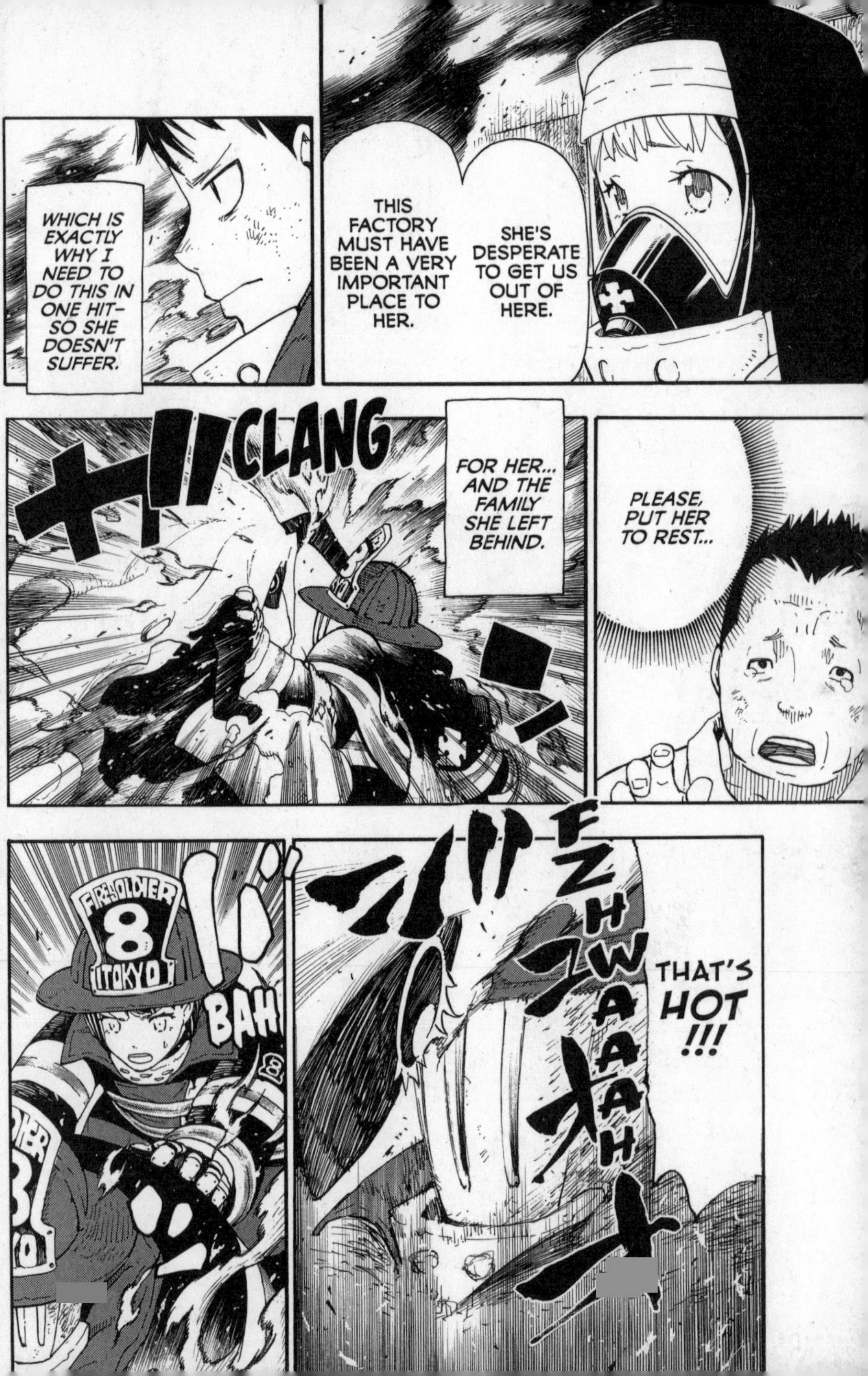
SHE'S DESPERATE TO GET US OUT OF HERE.
THIS FACTORY MUST HAVE BEEN A VERY IMPORTANT PLACE TO HER.
WHICH IS EXACTLY WHY I NEED TO DO THIS IN ONE HIT– SO SHE DOESN'T SUFFER.
PLEASE, PUT HER TO REST...
FOR HER... AND THE FAMILY SHE LEFT BEHIND.
CLANG
FZHWAAAAH
THAT'S HOT !!!
BAH

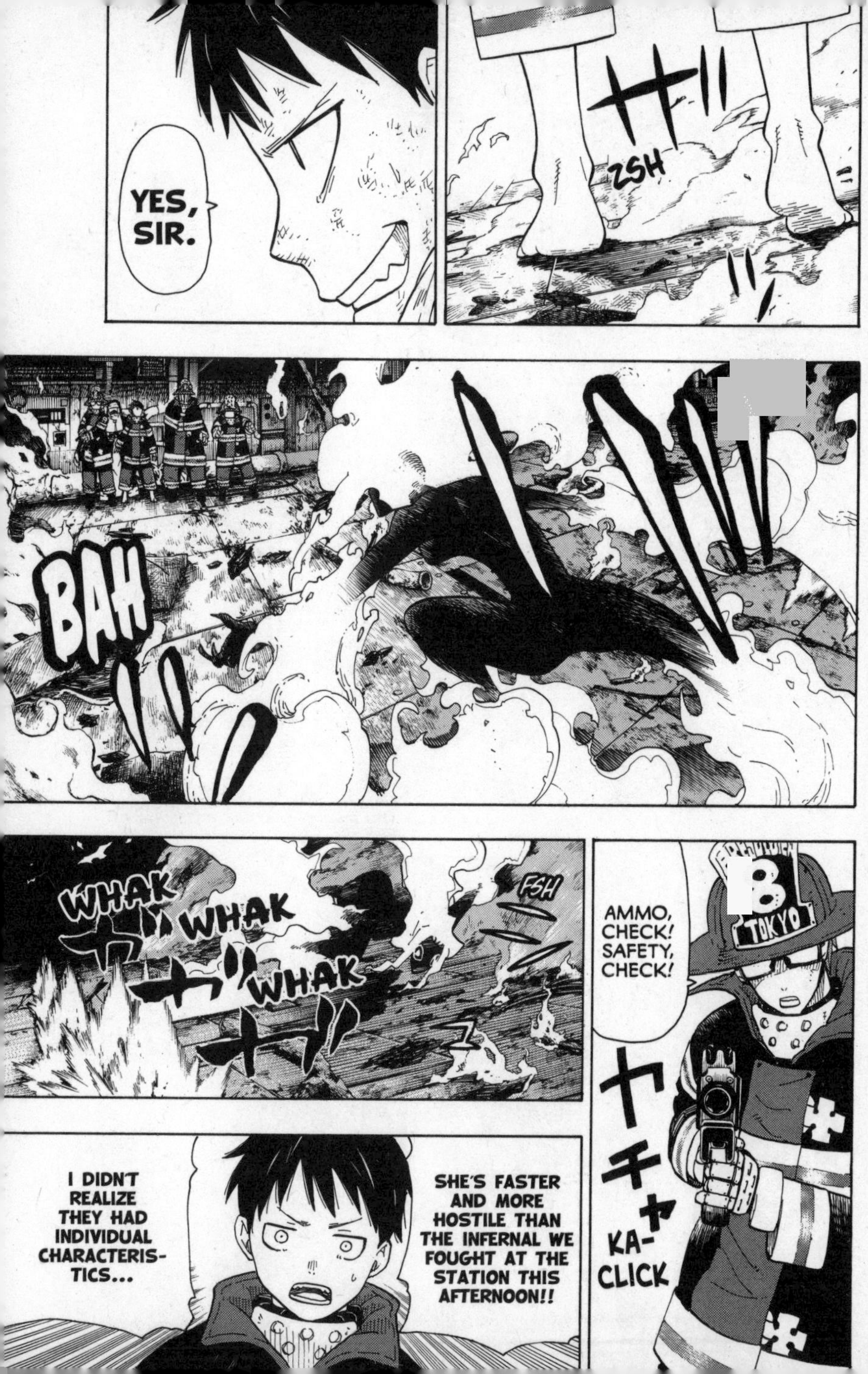
ZSH
YES, SIR.
BAH
AMMO, CHECK! SAFETY, CHECK!
TOKYO
KA-CLICK
WHAK
WHAK
WHAK
FSH
SHE'S FASTER AND MORE HOSTILE THAN THE INFERNAL WE FOUGHT AT THE STATION THIS AFTERNOON!!
I DIDN'T REALIZE THEY HAD INDIVIDUAL CHARACTERIS-TICS...

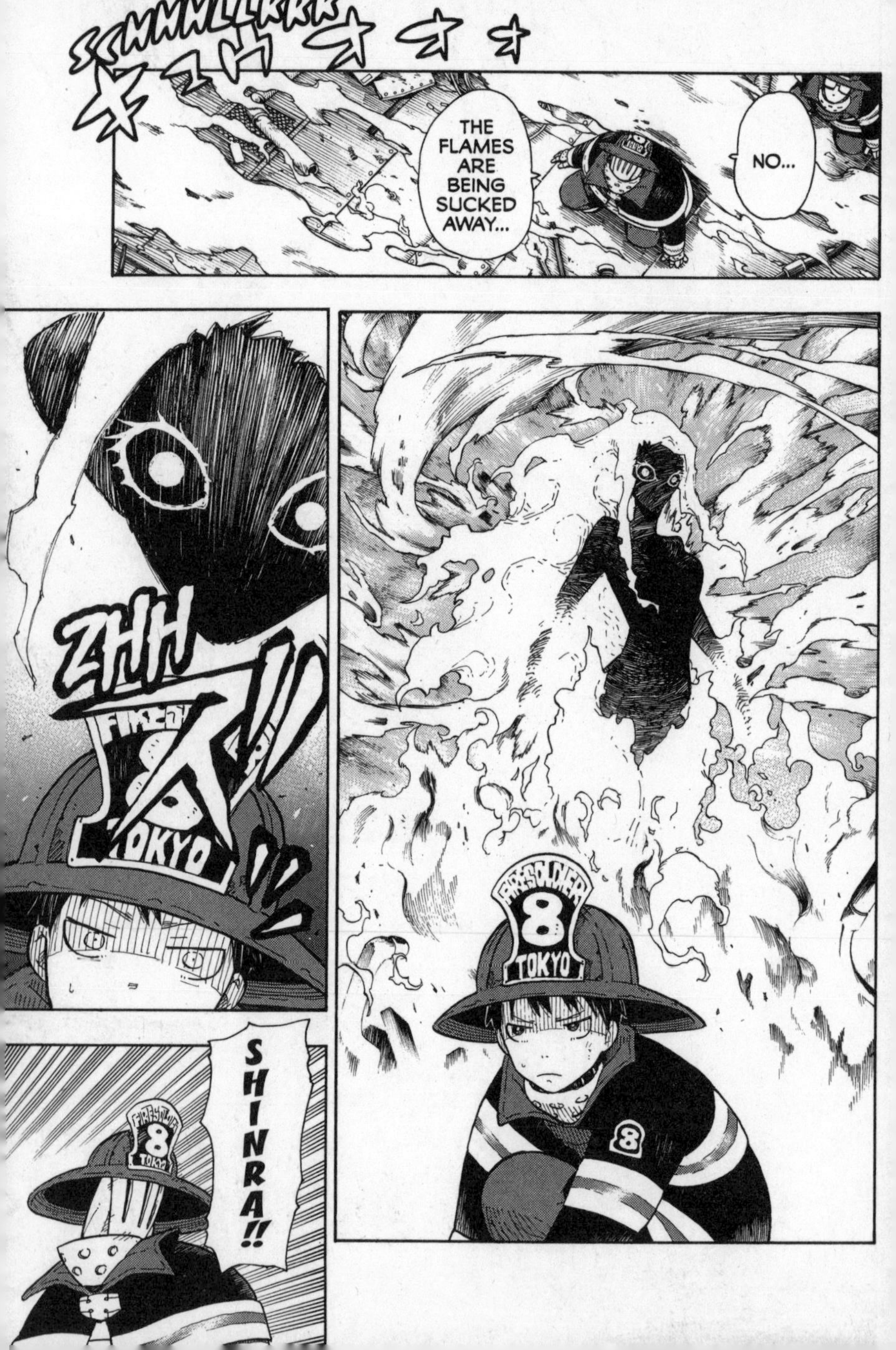
SCHHWLLRRR
NO...
THE FLAMES ARE BEING SUCKED AWAY...
ZHH
SHINRA!!

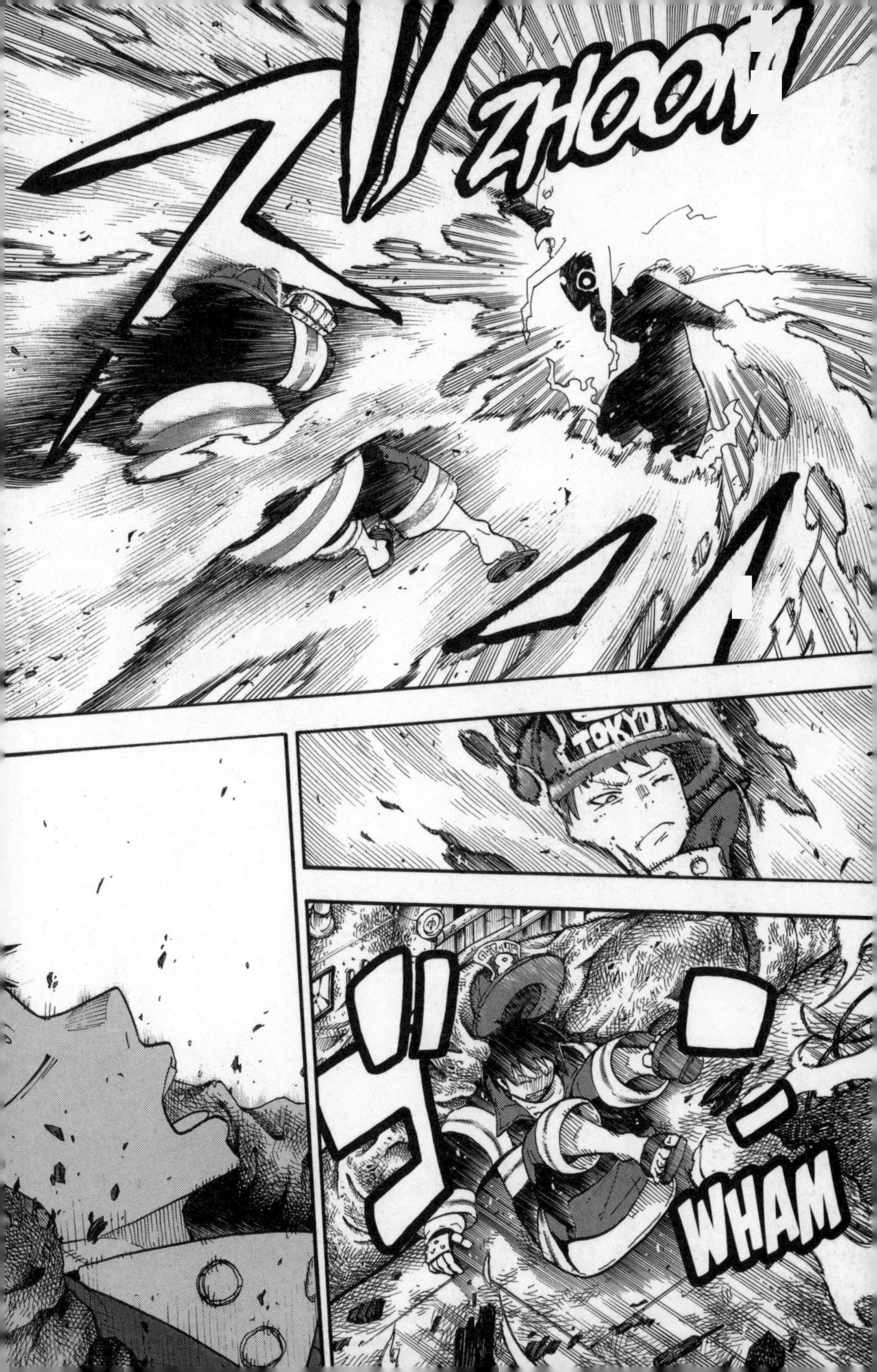
ZHOOM
TOKYO
WHAM

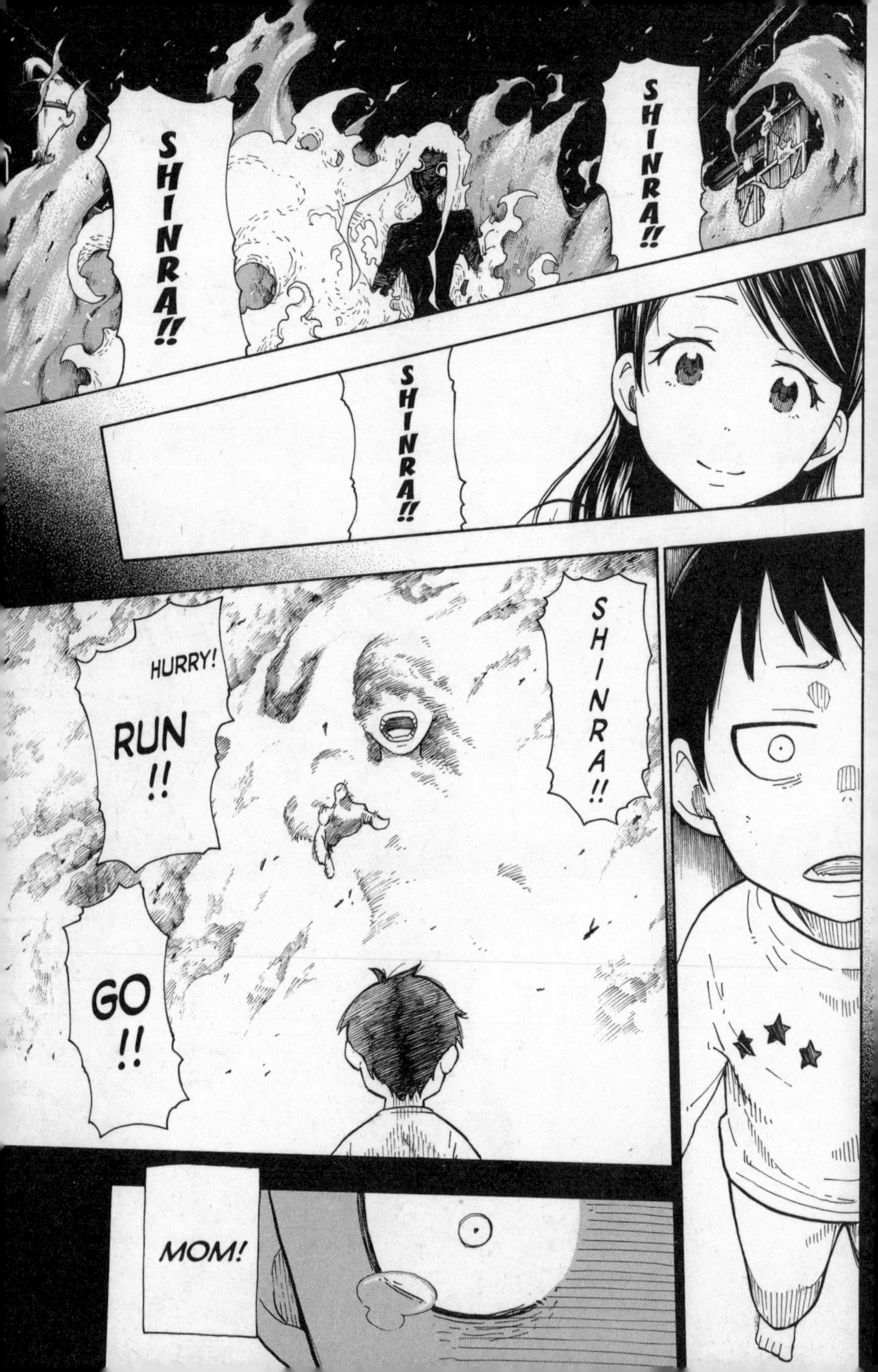
SHINRA!!
SHINRA!!
SHINRA!!
SHINRA!!
HURRY! RUN!!
GO!!
MOM!

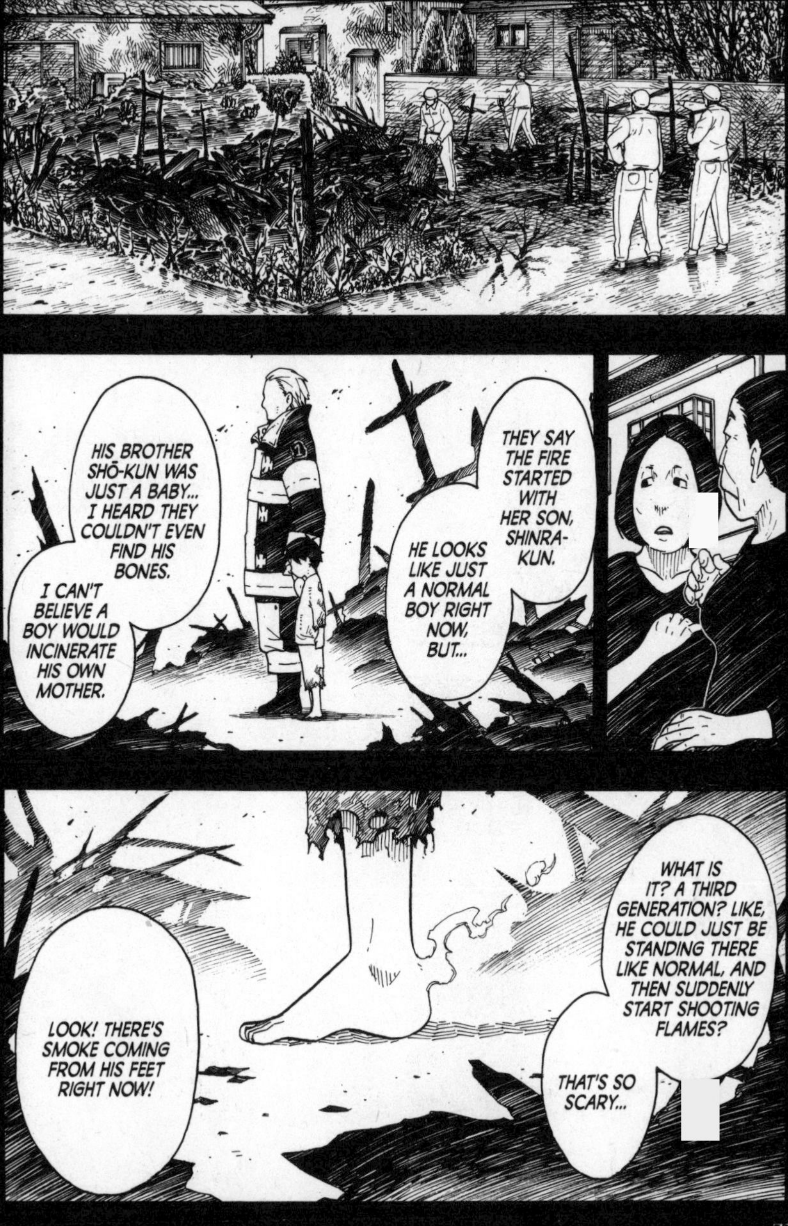
THEY SAY THE FIRE STARTED WITH HER SON, SHINRA-KUN.
HE LOOKS LIKE JUST A NORMAL BOY RIGHT NOW, BUT...
HIS BROTHER SHŌ-KUN WAS JUST A BABY... I HEARD THEY COULDN'T EVEN FIND HIS BONES.
I CAN'T BELIEVE A BOY WOULD INCINERATE HIS OWN MOTHER.
WHAT IS IT? A THIRD GENERATION? LIKE, HE COULD JUST BE STANDING THERE LIKE NORMAL, AND THEN SUDDENLY START SHOOTING FLAMES?
THAT'S SO SCARY...
LOOK! THERE'S SMOKE COMING FROM HIS FEET RIGHT NOW!

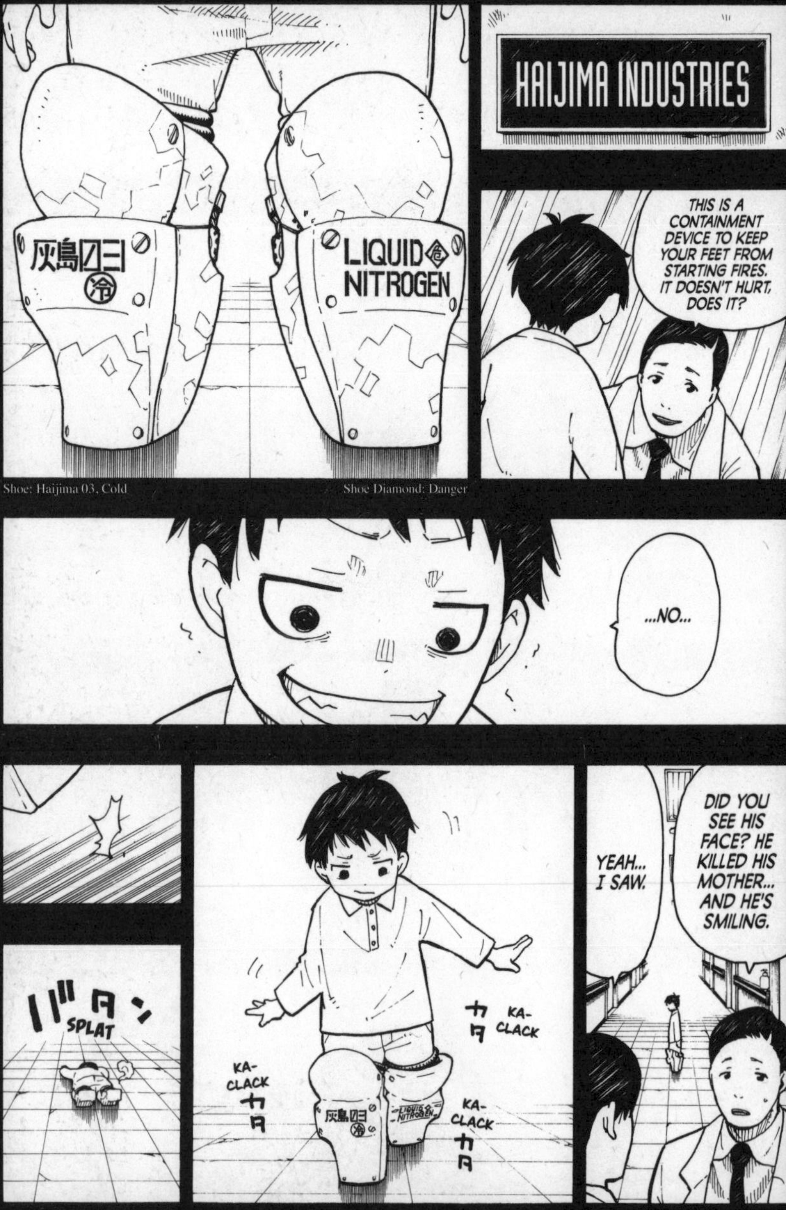
HAIJIMA INDUSTRIES
THIS IS A CONTAINMENT DEVICE TO KEEP YOUR FEET FROM STARTING FIRES. IT DOESN'T HURT, DOES IT?
灰島03 冷
LIQUID 危 NITROGEN
...NO...
DID YOU SEE HIS FACE? HE KILLED HIS MOTHER... AND HE'S SMILING.
YEAH... I SAW.
カタ KA-CLACK
KA-CLACK カタ
KA-CLACK カタ
灰島03 冷
LIQUID 危 NITROGEN
バタン SPLAT
Shoe: Haijima 03, Cold

Shoe Diamond: Danger

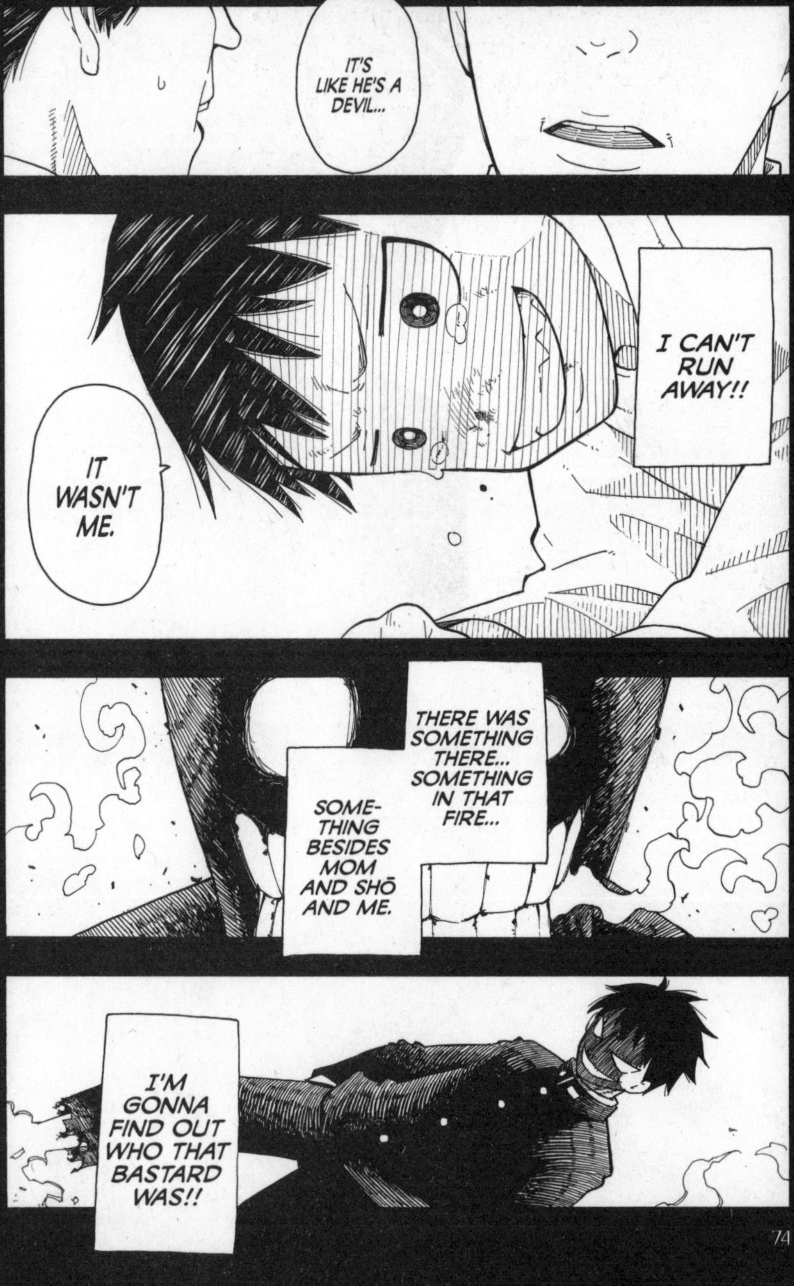
IT'S LIKE HE'S A DEVIL...
I CAN'T RUN AWAY!!
IT WASN'T ME.
THERE WAS SOMETHING THERE... SOMETHING IN THAT FIRE...
SOME-THING BESIDES MOM AND SHŌ AND ME.
I'M GONNA FIND OUT WHO THAT BASTARD WAS!!

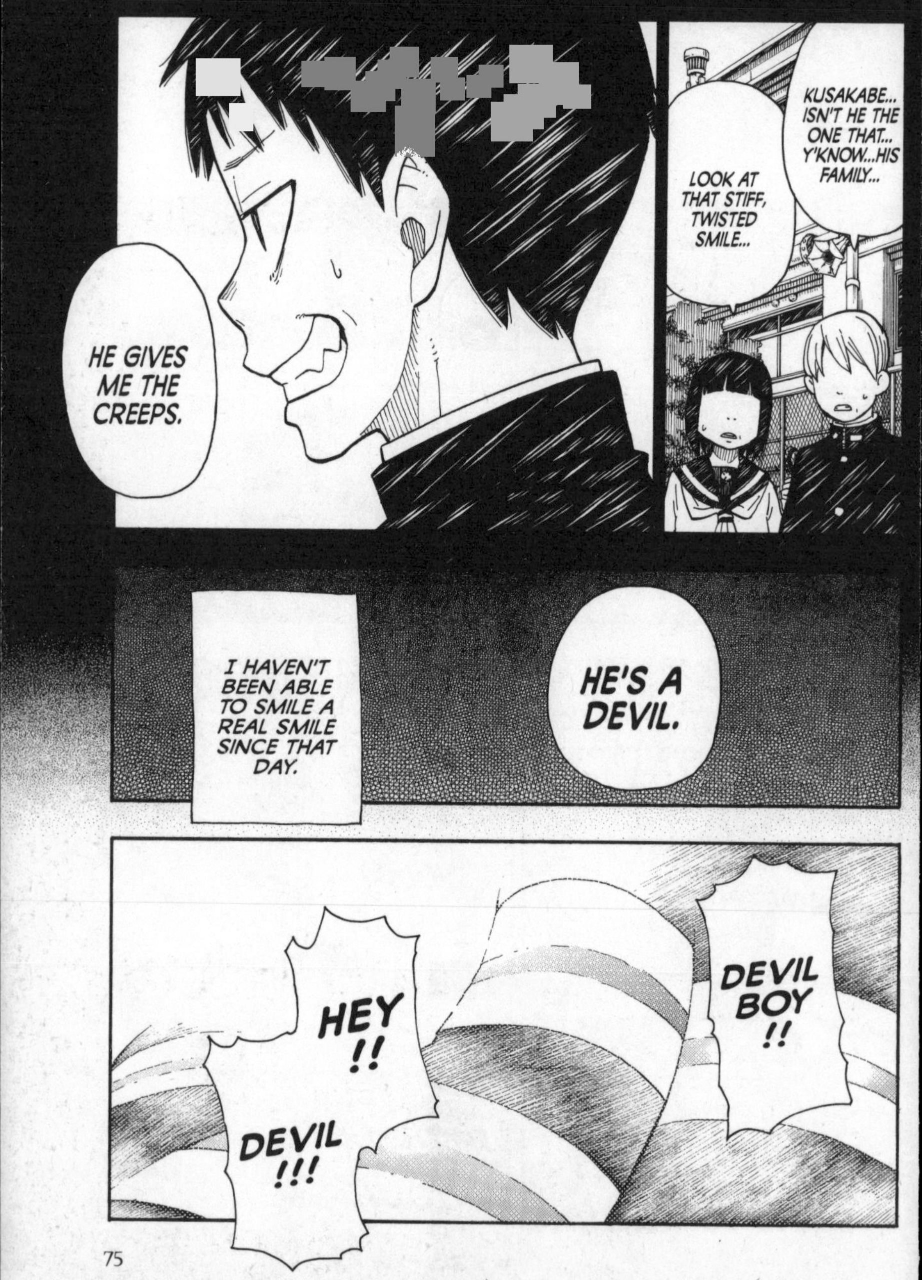
KUSAKABE... ISN'T HE THE ONE THAT... Y'KNOW...HIS FAMILY...
LOOK AT THAT STIFF, TWISTED SMILE...
HE GIVES ME THE CREEPS.
HE'S A DEVIL.
I HAVEN'T BEEN ABLE TO SMILE A REAL SMILE SINCE THAT DAY.
DEVIL BOY!!
HEY!!
DEVIL!!!

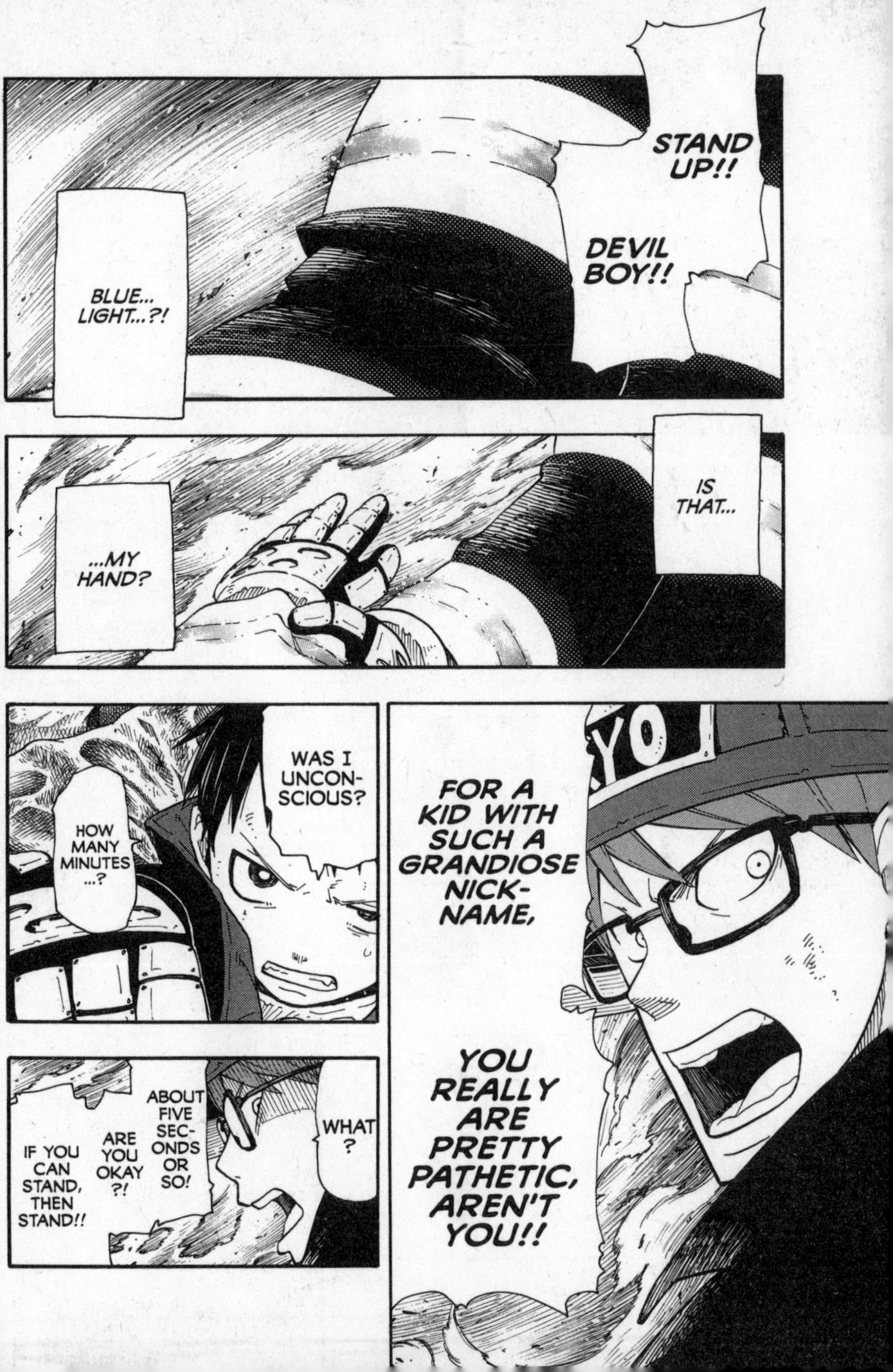
STAND UP!!
DEVIL BOY!!
BLUE... LIGHT...?!
IS THAT...
...MY HAND?
FOR A KID WITH SUCH A GRANDIOSE NICK-NAME,
YOU REALLY ARE PRETTY PATHETIC, AREN'T YOU!!
WAS I UNCON-SCIOUS?
HOW MANY MINUTES ...?
WHAT?
ABOUT FIVE SEC-ONDS OR SO!
ARE YOU OKAY ?!
IF YOU CAN STAND, THEN STAND!!

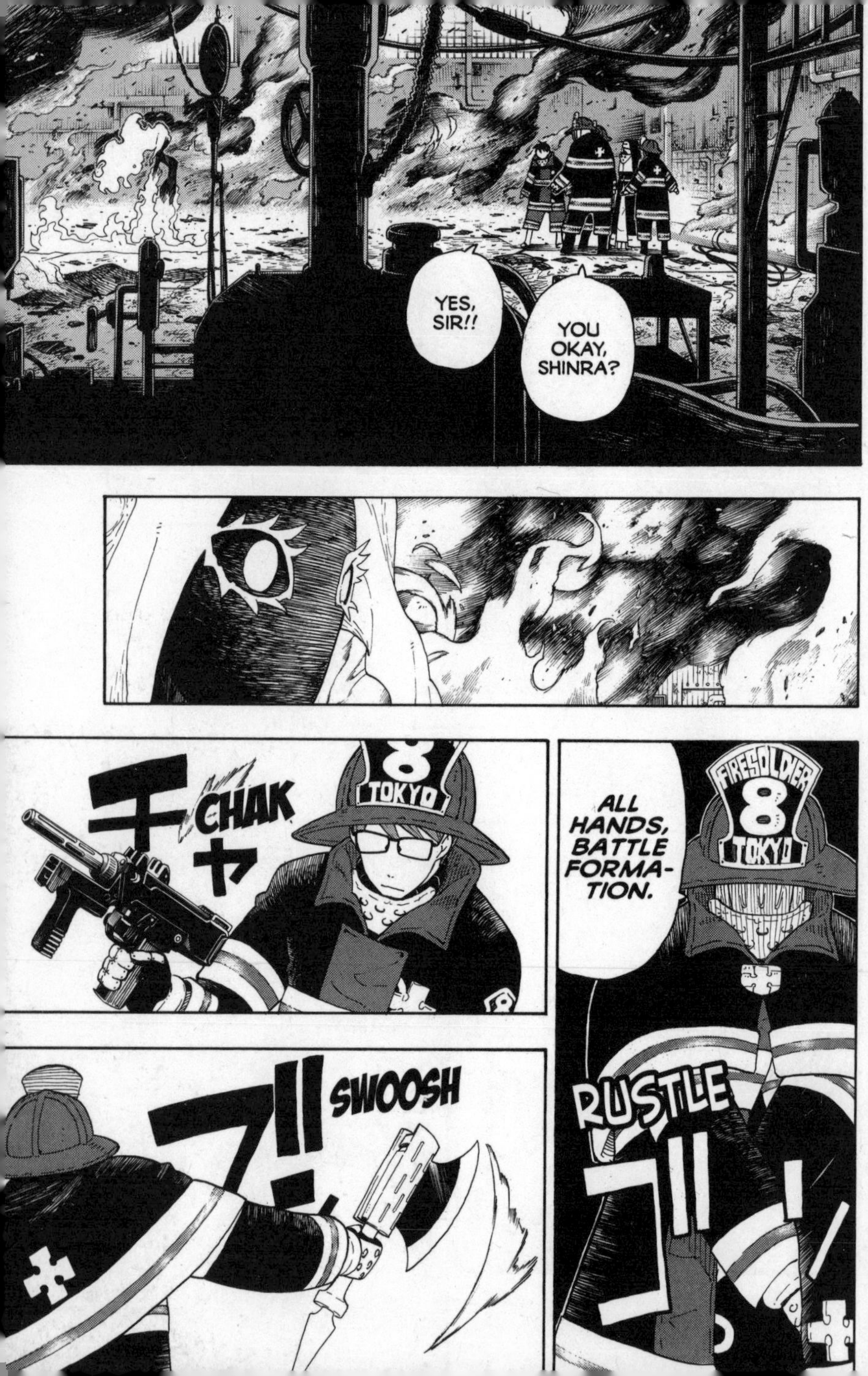
YOU OKAY, SHINRA?
YES, SIR!!
ALL HANDS, BATTLE FORMATION.
RUSTLE
CHAK
SWOOSH

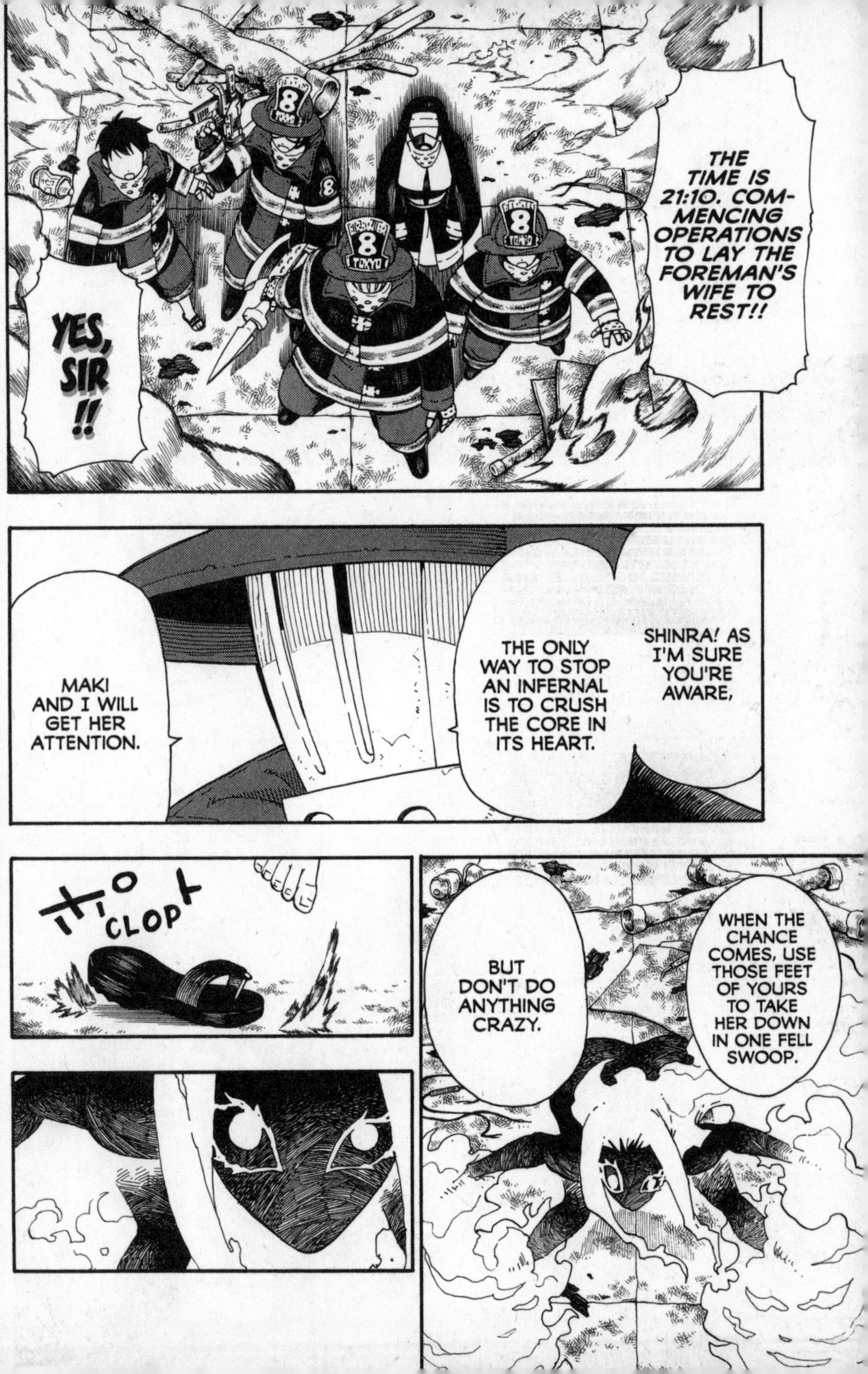
THE TIME IS 21:10. COMMENCING OPERATIONS TO LAY THE FOREMAN'S WIFE TO REST!!
YES, SIR!!
SHINRA! AS I'M SURE YOU'RE AWARE,
THE ONLY WAY TO STOP AN INFERNAL IS TO CRUSH THE CORE IN ITS HEART.
MAKI AND I WILL GET HER ATTENTION.
WHEN THE CHANCE COMES, USE THOSE FEET OF YOURS TO TAKE HER DOWN IN ONE FELL SWOOP.
BUT DON'T DO ANYTHING CRAZY.
CLOP

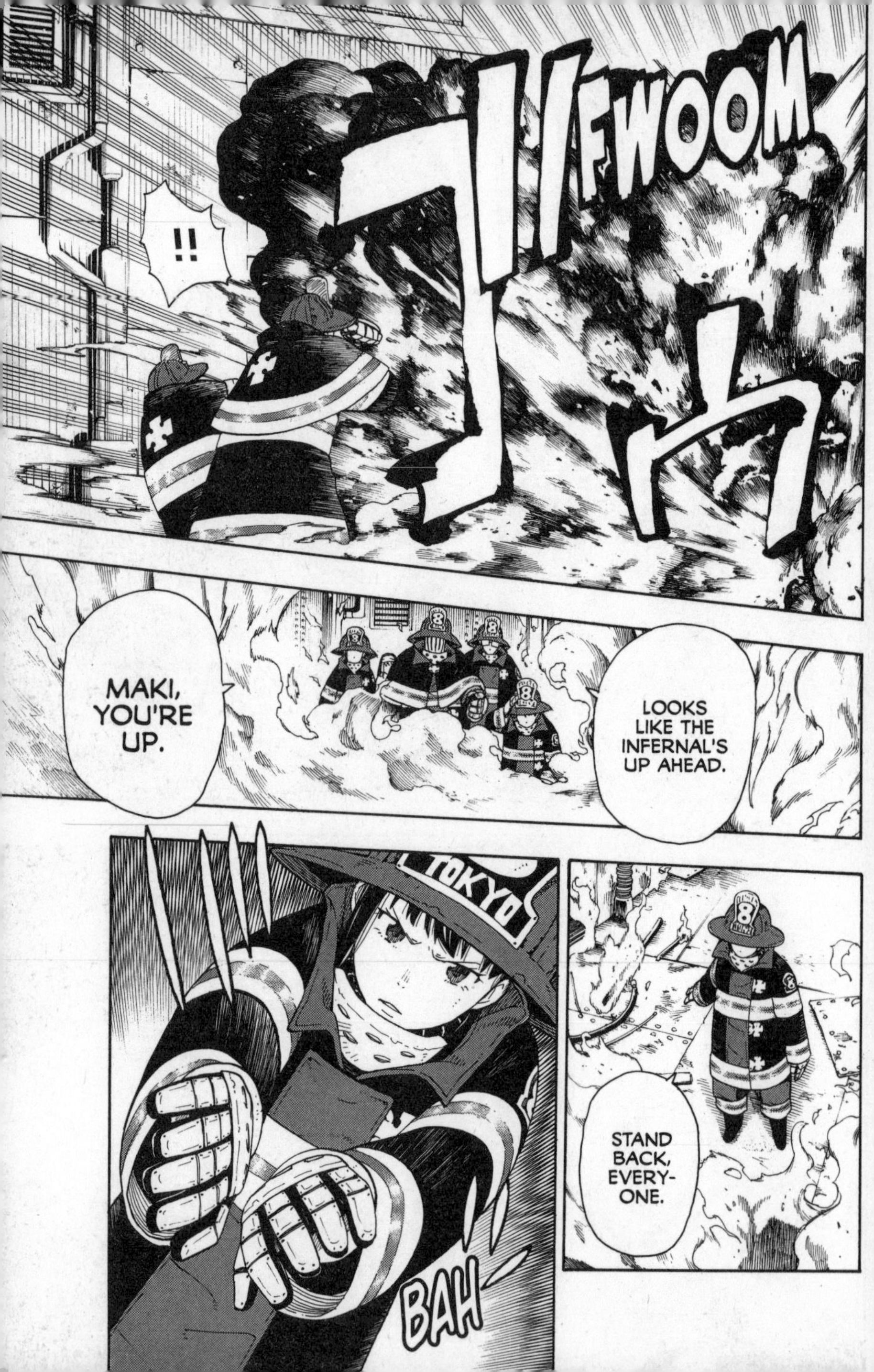
FWOOM
!!
LOOKS LIKE THE INFERNAL'S UP AHEAD.
MAKI, YOU'RE UP.
STAND BACK, EVERY-ONE.
TOKYO
BAH

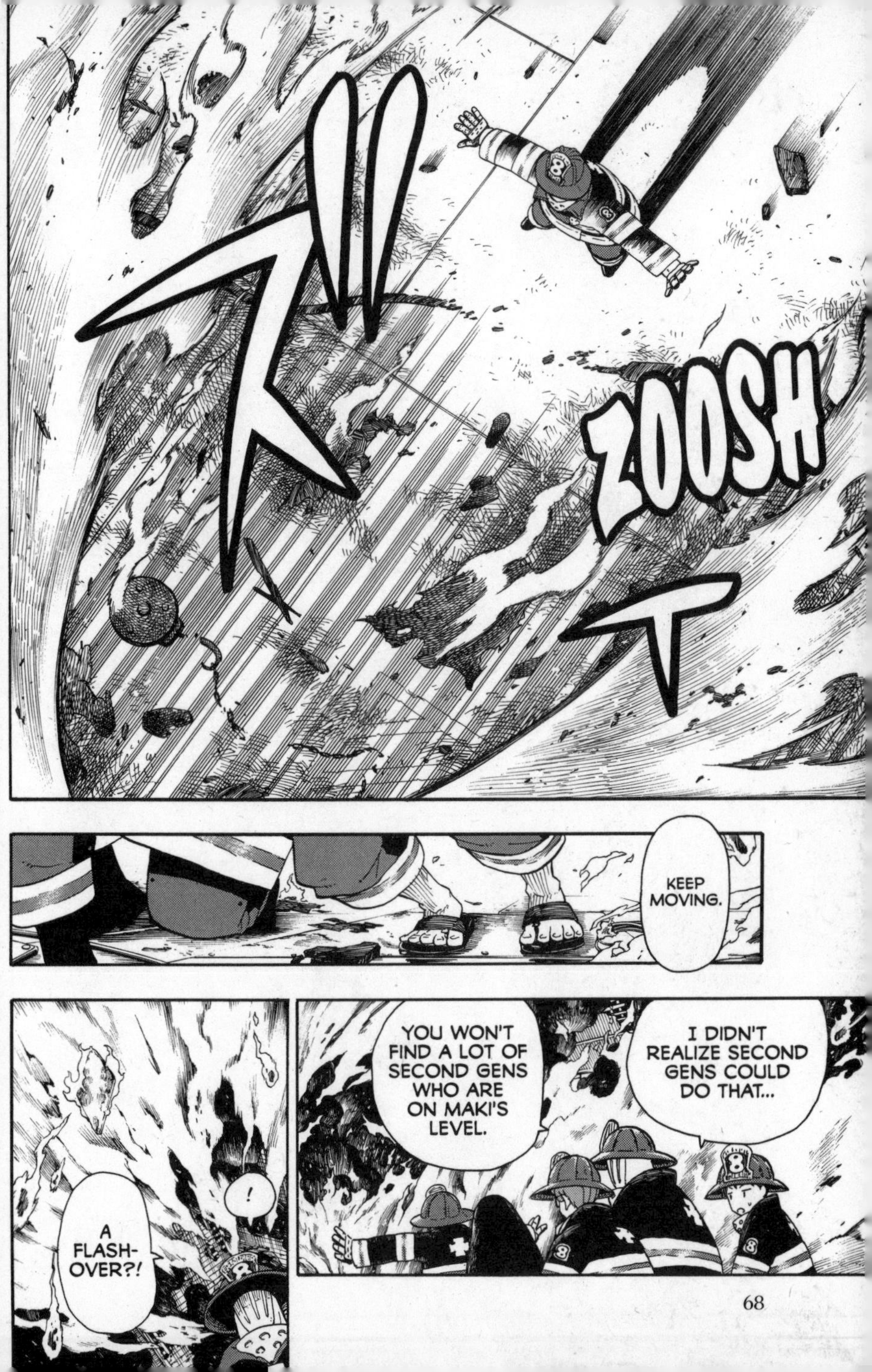
ZOOSH
KEEP MOVING.
I DIDN'T REALIZE SECOND GENS COULD DO THAT...
YOU WON'T FIND A LOT OF SECOND GENS WHO ARE ON MAKI'S LEVEL.
!
A FLASH-OVER?!

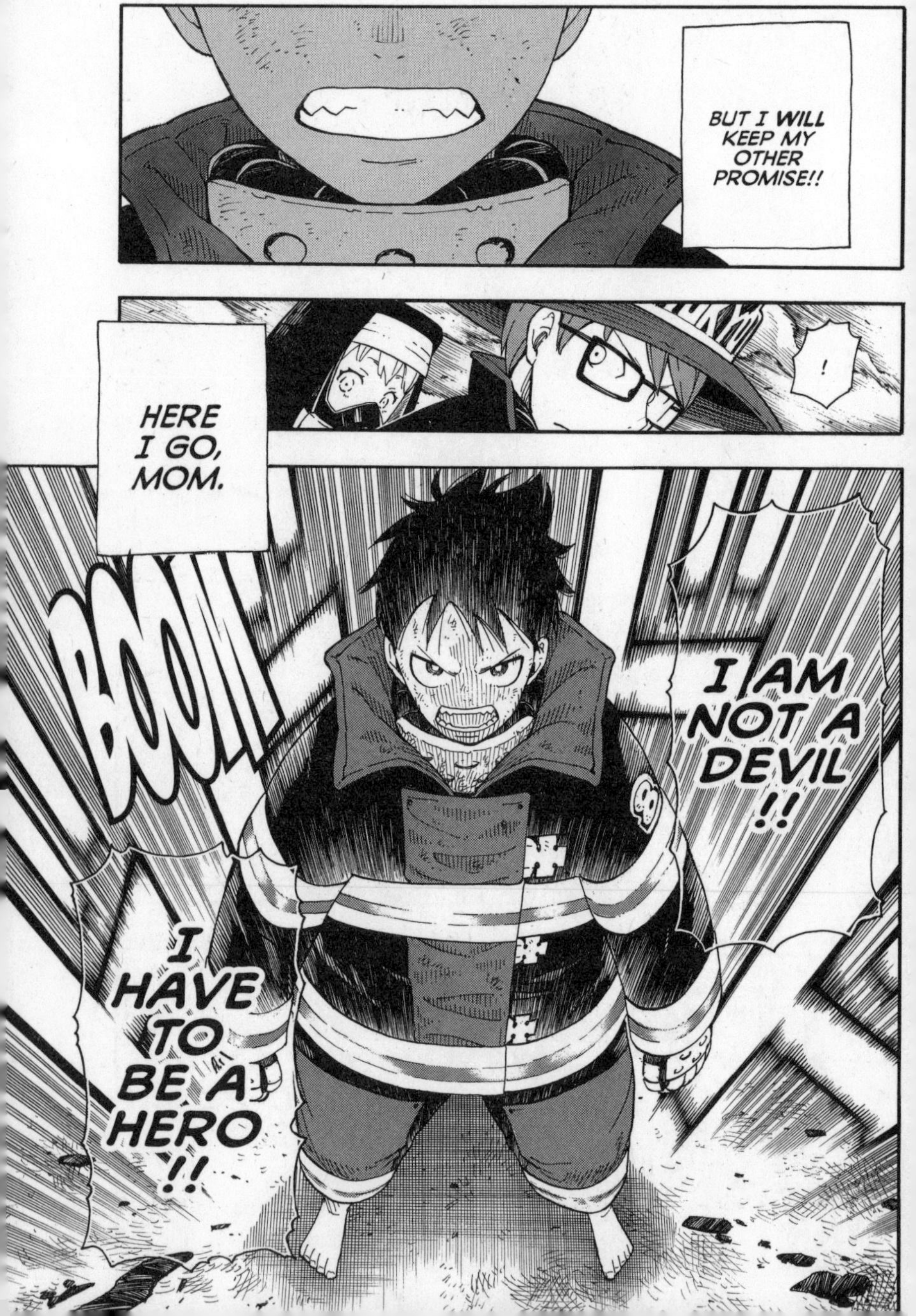
BUT I **WILL** KEEP MY OTHER PROMISE!!
!
HERE I GO, MOM.
I AM NOT A DEVIL!!
BOOM
I HAVE TO BE A HERO!!

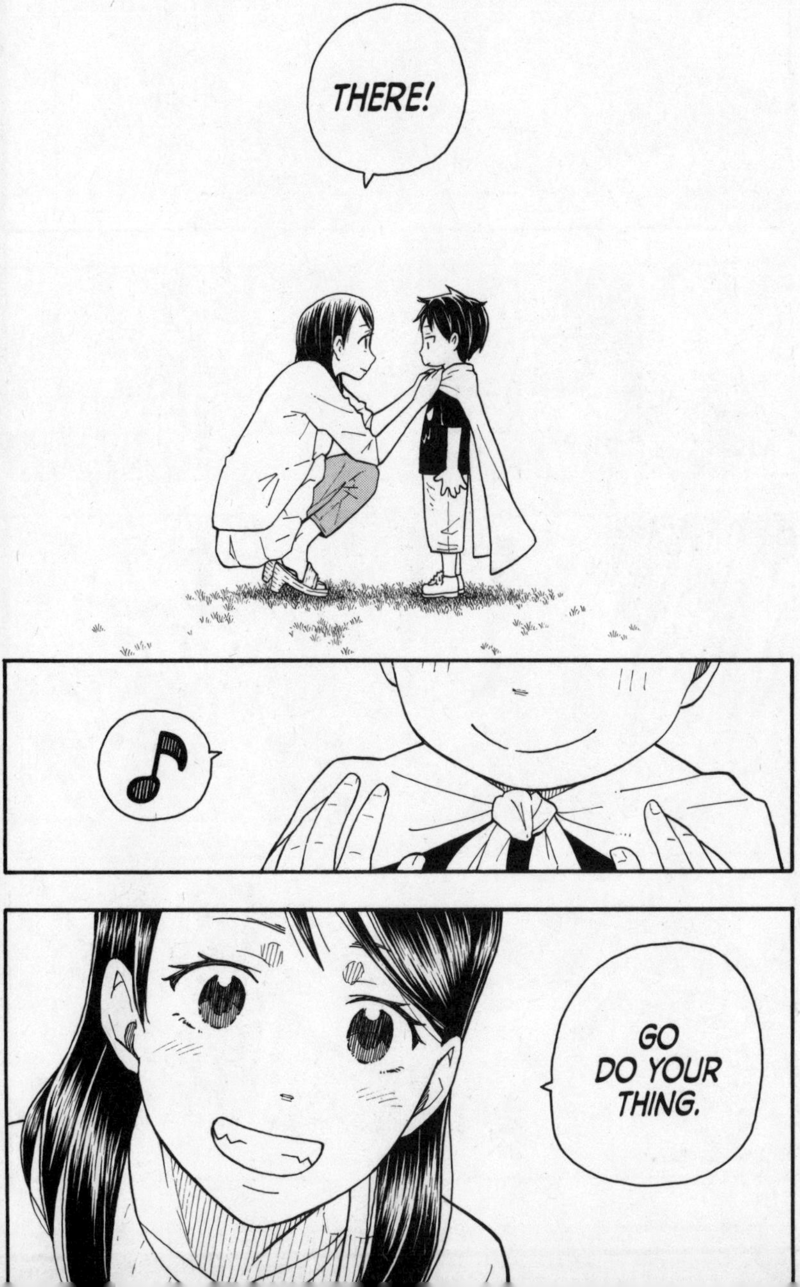
THERE!
GO DO YOUR THING.

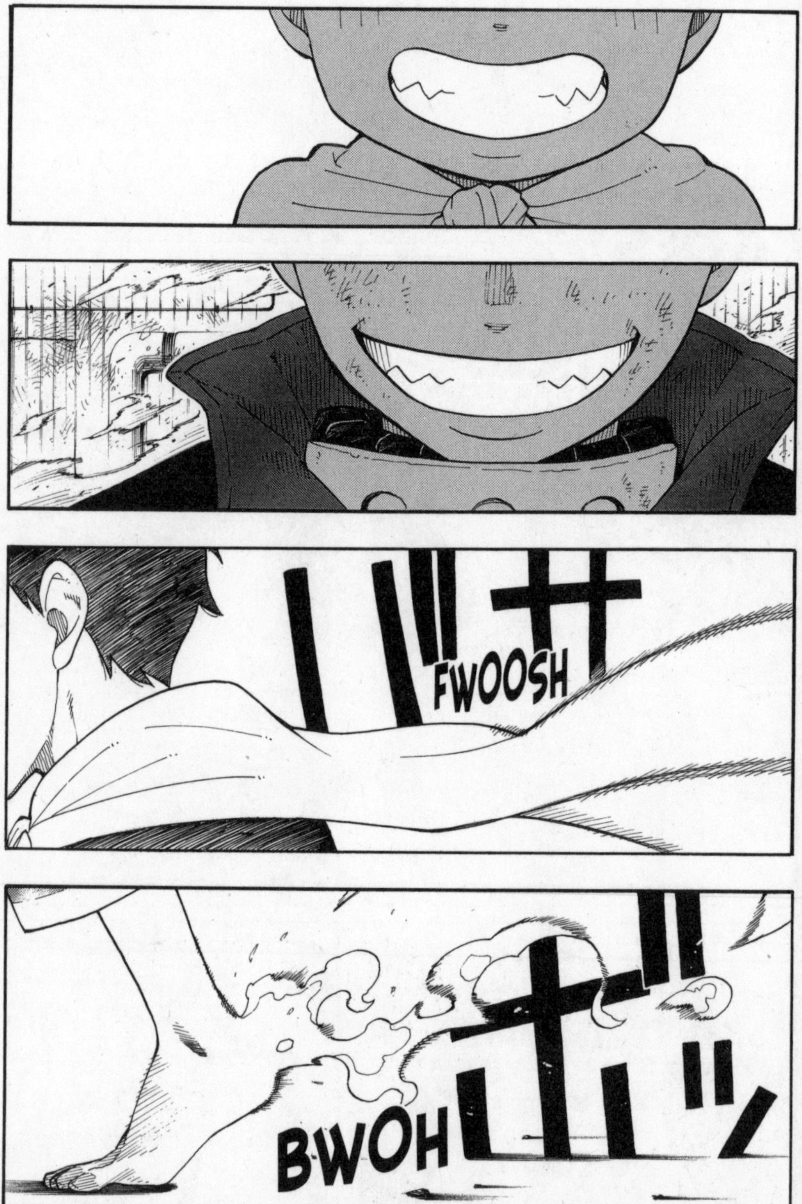
FWOOSH
BWOH

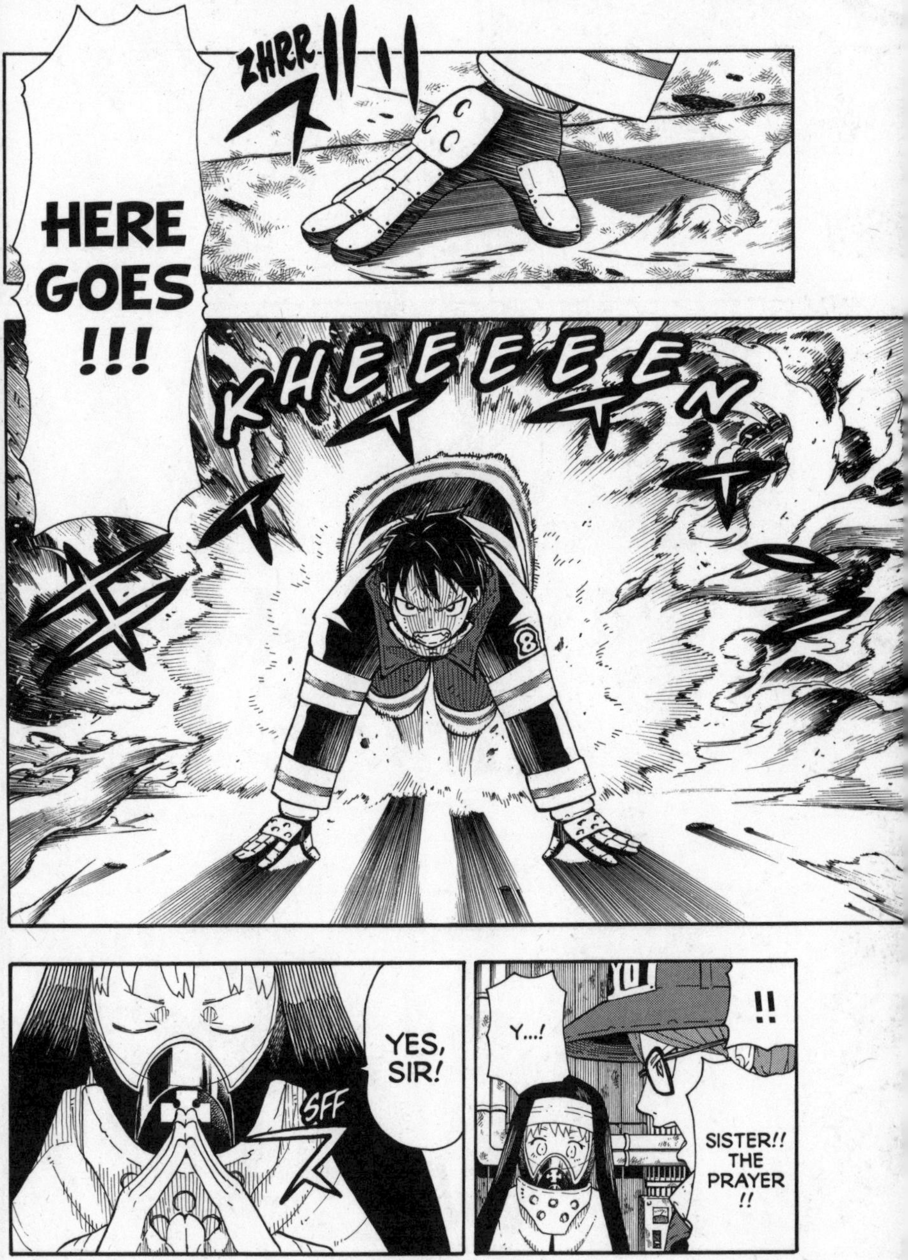
ZHRR
HERE GOES!!!
KHEEEEEN
!!
SISTER!! THE PRAYER!!
Y...!
YES, SIR!
SFF

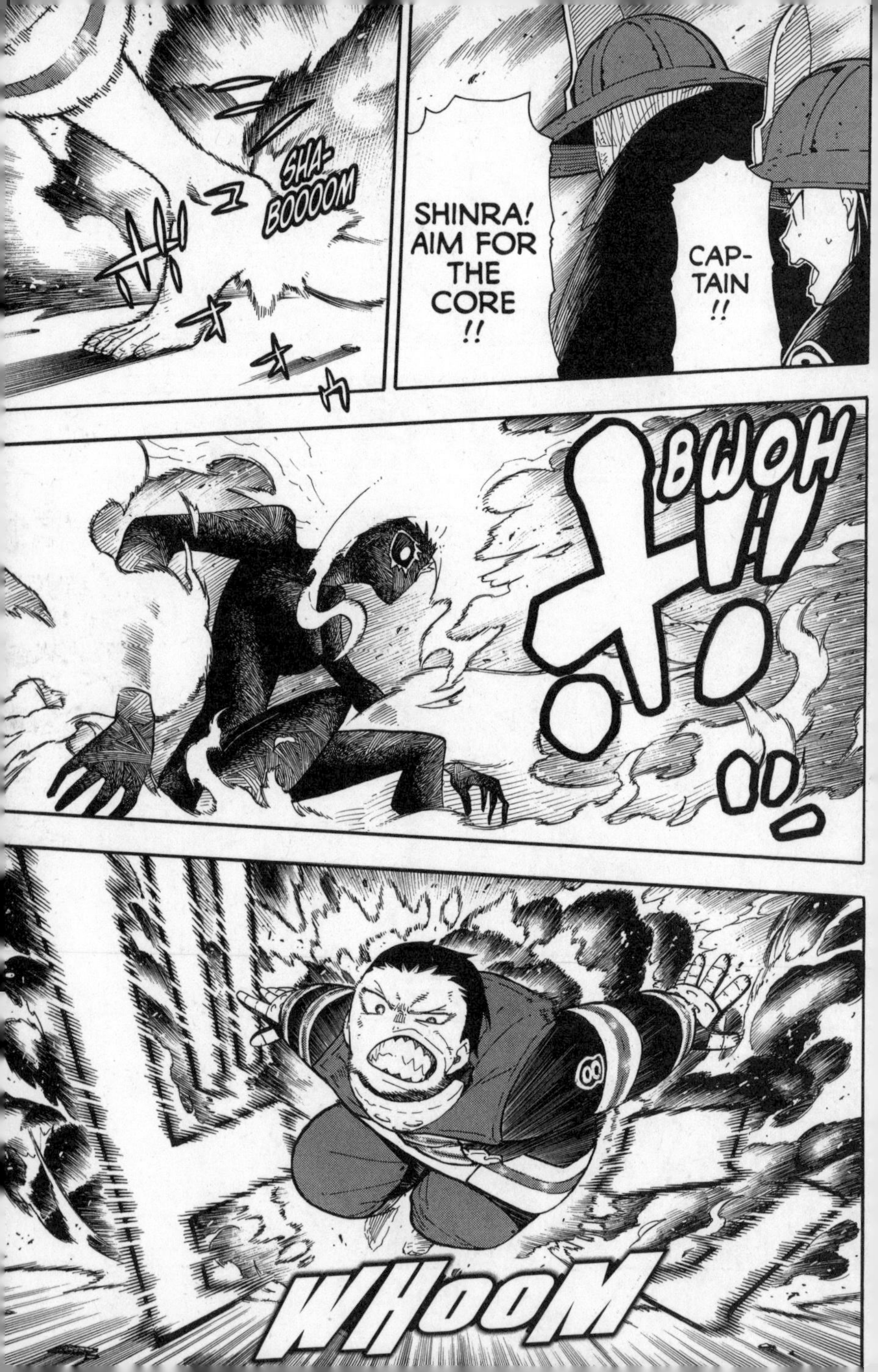
CAP-TAIN!!
SHINRA! AIM FOR THE CORE!!
SHA-BOOOOM
BWOH!!
WHOOM

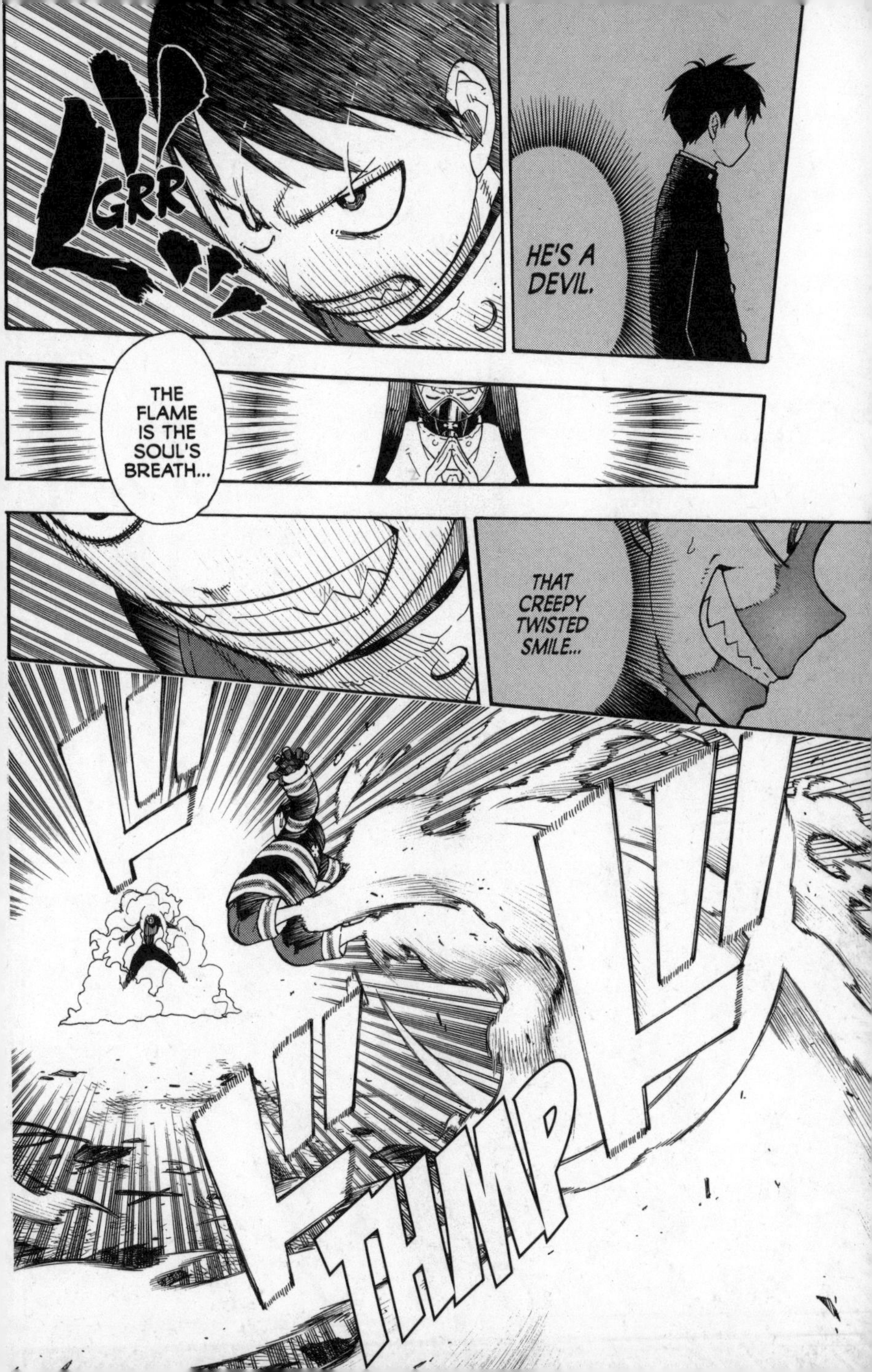
HE'S A DEVIL.
GRR
THE FLAME IS THE SOUL'S BREATH...
THAT CREEPY TWISTED SMILE...
THMP

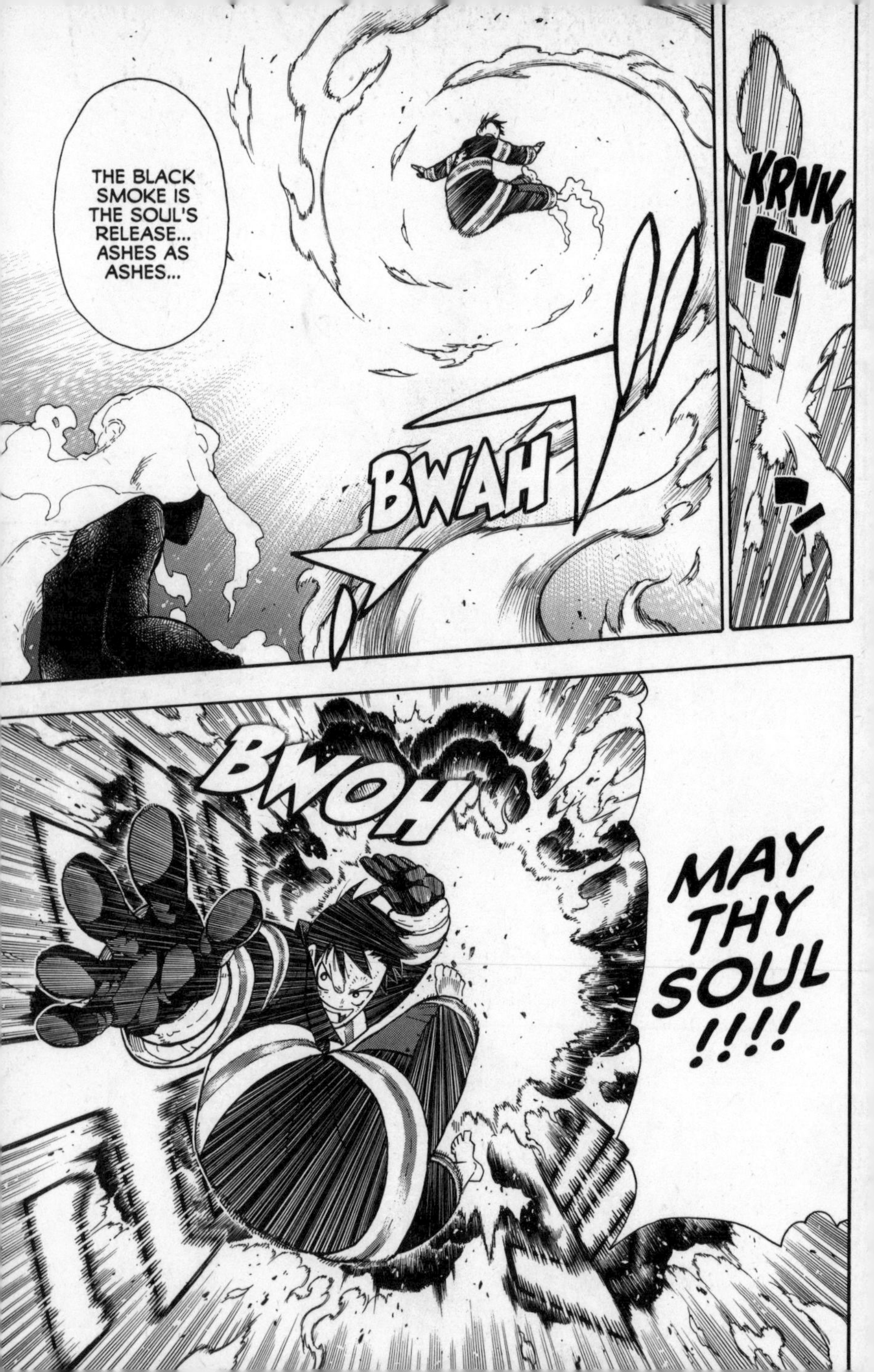
KRNK
THE BLACK SMOKE IS THE SOUL'S RELEASE... ASHES AS ASHES...
BWAH
MAY THY SOUL !!!!
BWOH

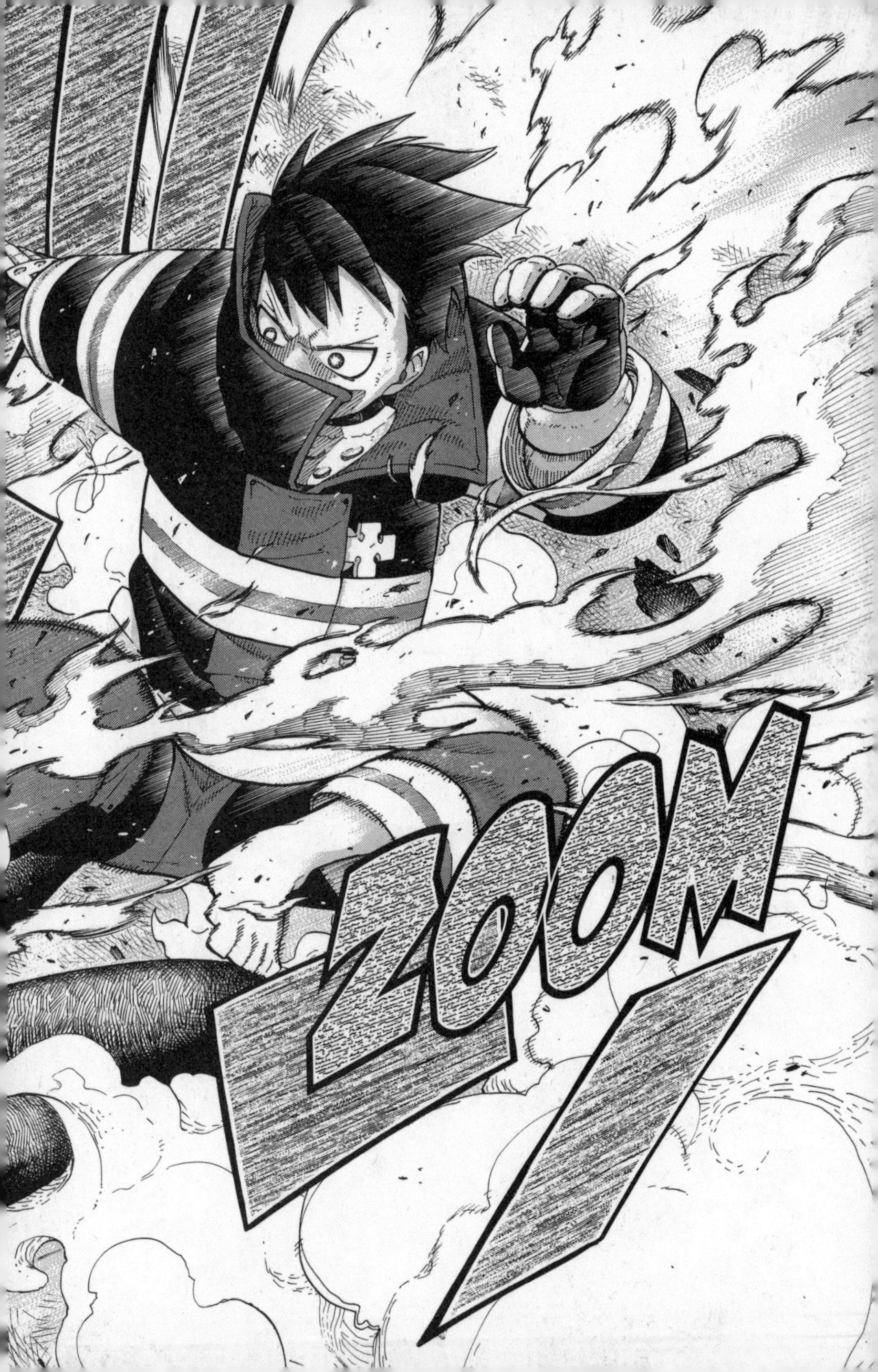
ZOOM

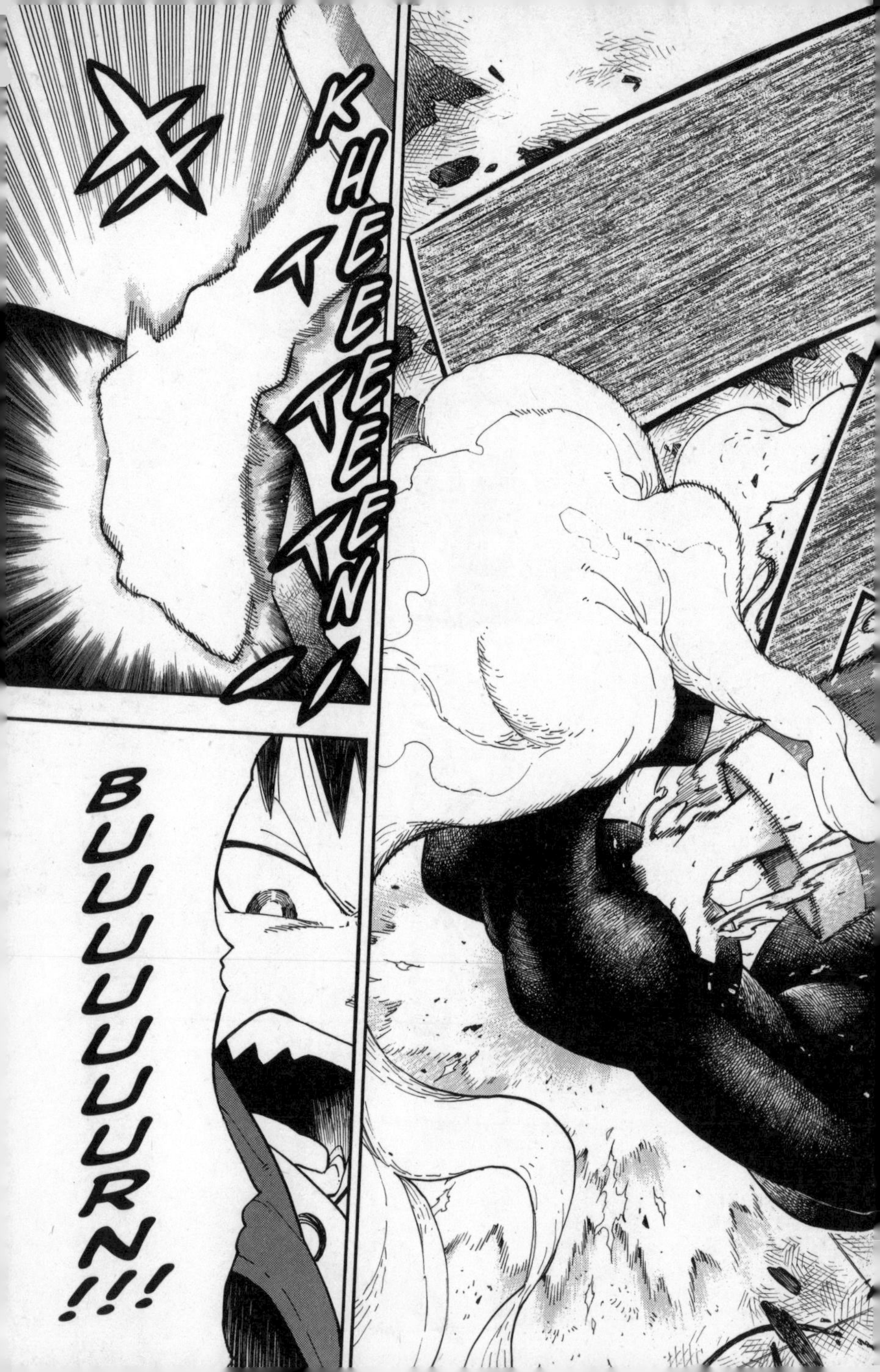
KHETEETEETEN!!
BUUUUUURN!!!

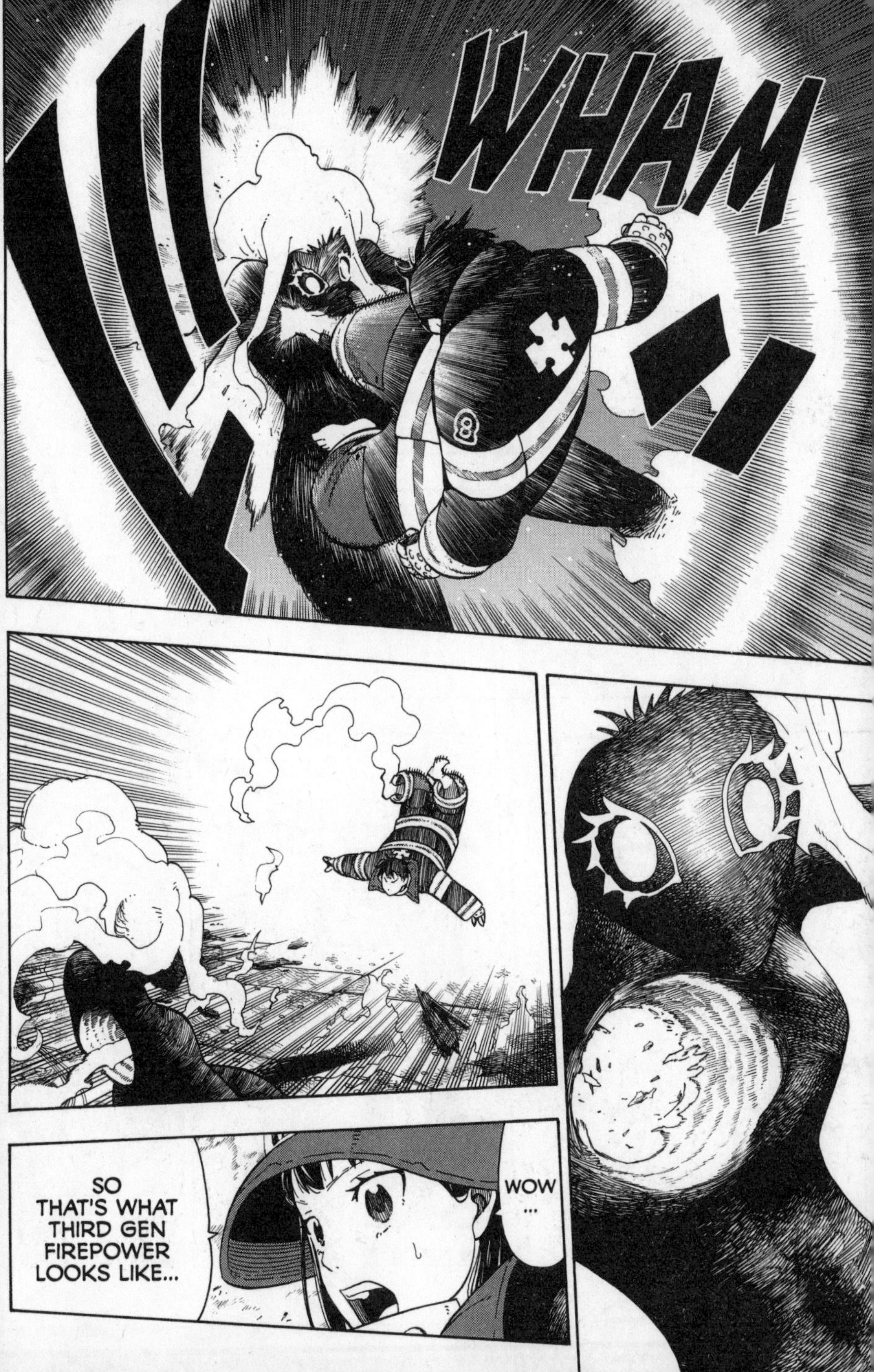
WHAM
WOW ...
SO THAT'S WHAT THIRD GEN FIREPOWER LOOKS LIKE...

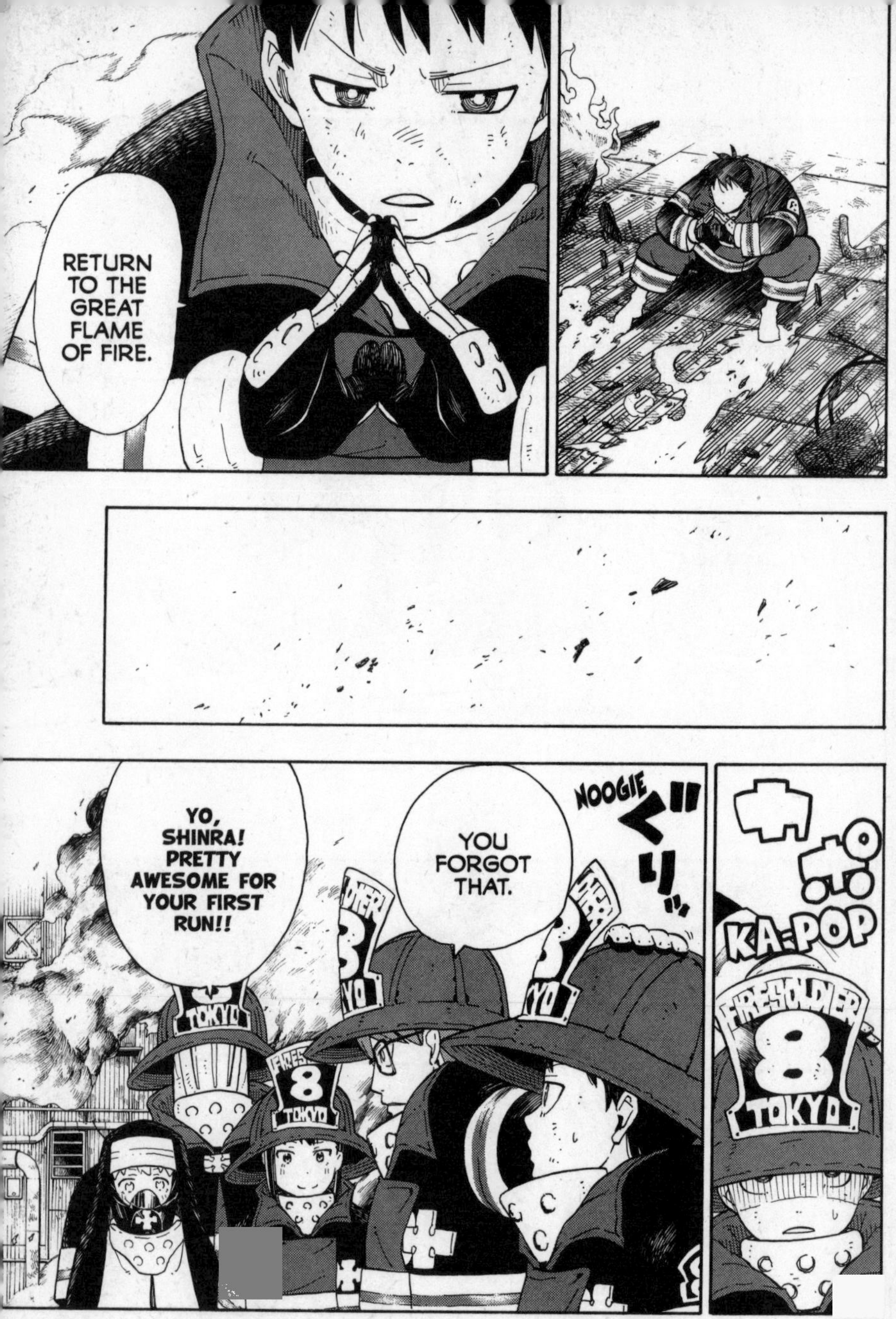
RETURN TO THE GREAT FLAME OF FIRE.
KA-POP
NOOGIE
YOU FORGOT THAT.
YO, SHINRA! PRETTY AWESOME FOR YOUR FIRST RUN!!

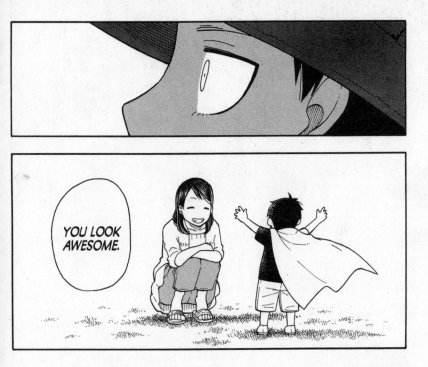

YOU LOOK
AWESOME.

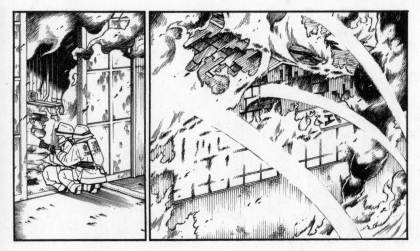

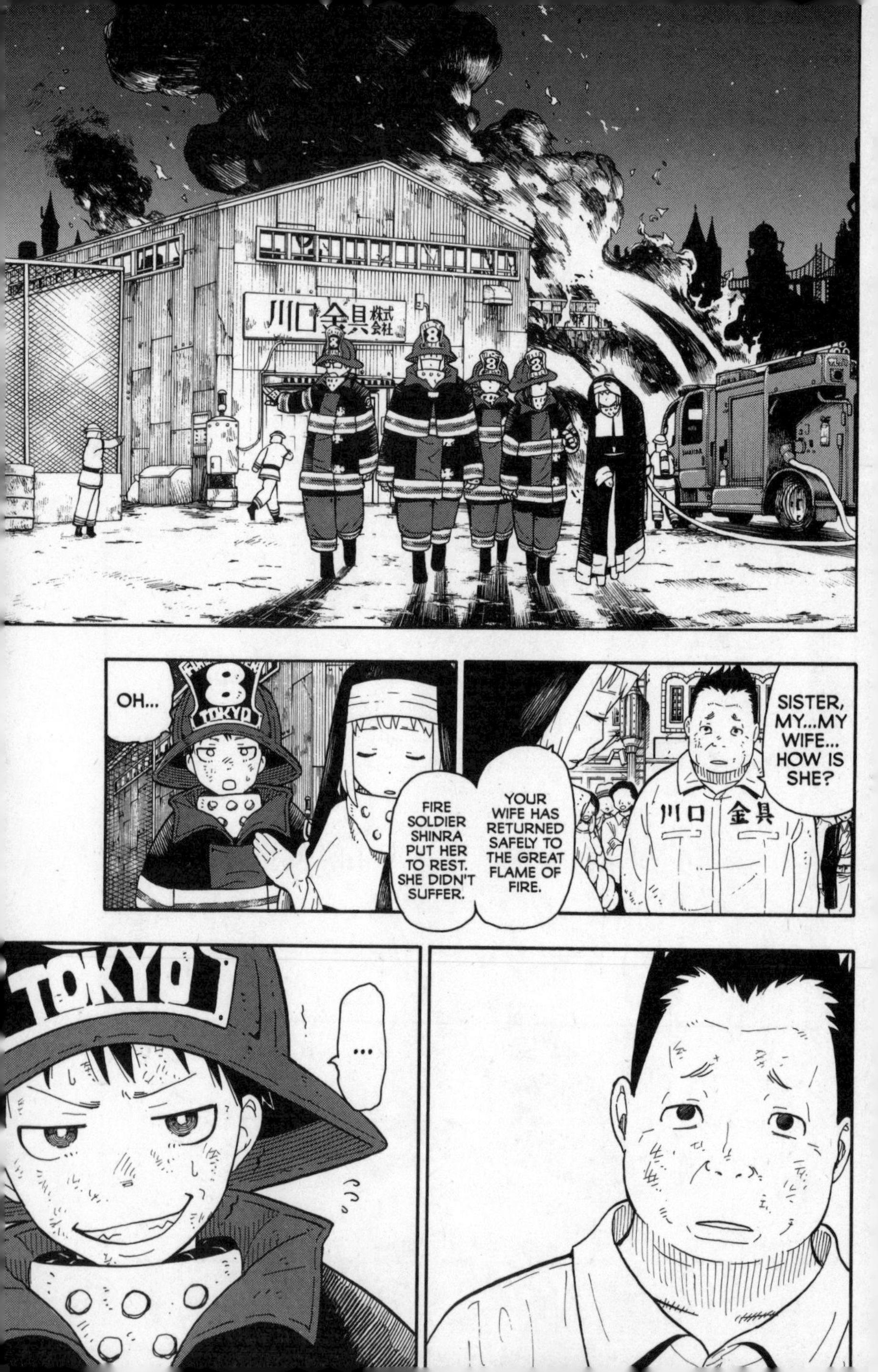

川口金具 株式会社
SISTER, MY...MY WIFE... HOW IS SHE?
川口 金具
YOUR WIFE HAS RETURNED SAFELY TO THE GREAT FLAME OF FIRE.
FIRE SOLDIER SHINRA PUT HER TO REST. SHE DIDN'T SUFFER.
OH...
8 TOKYO
...
TOKYO

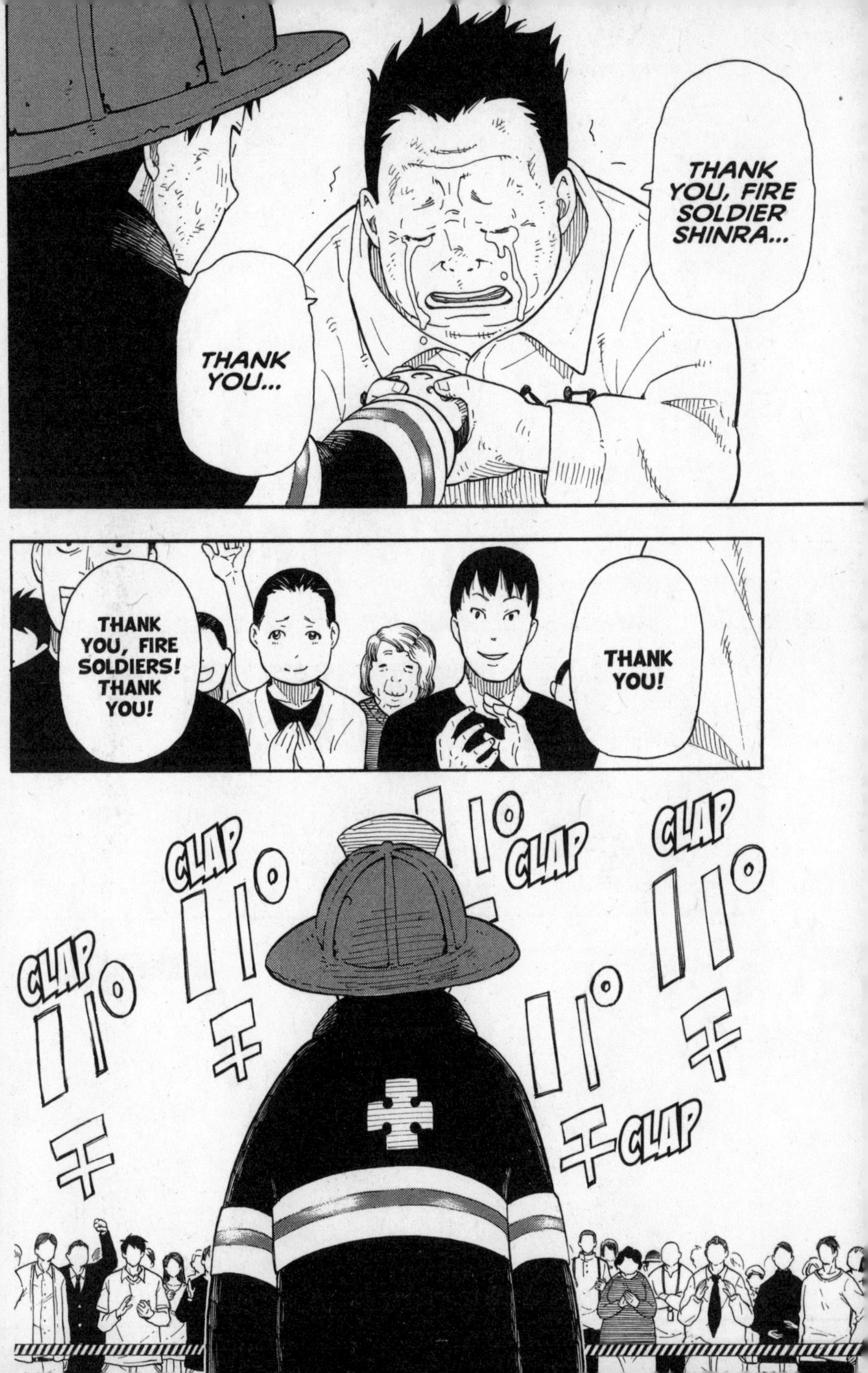
THANK YOU, FIRE SOLDIER SHINRA...
THANK YOU...
THANK YOU!
THANK YOU, FIRE SOLDIERS! THANK YOU!
CLAP
パチ
CLAP
パチ
CLAP
パチ
CLAP
パチ
CLAP
パチ

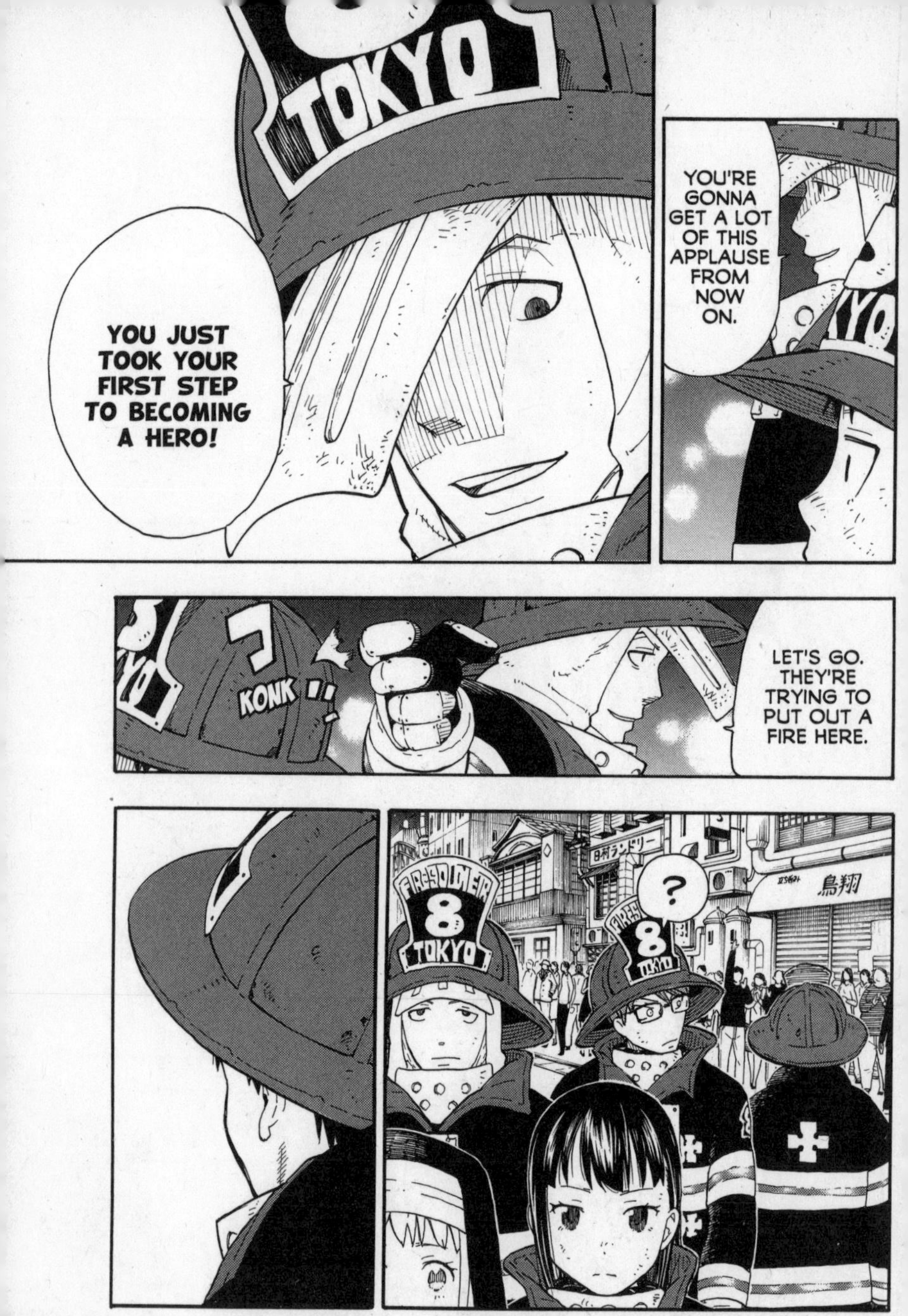
YOU'RE GONNA GET A LOT OF THIS APPLAUSE FROM NOW ON.
YOU JUST TOOK YOUR FIRST STEP TO BECOMING A HERO!
LET'S GO. THEY'RE TRYING TO PUT OUT A FIRE HERE.
KONK
?

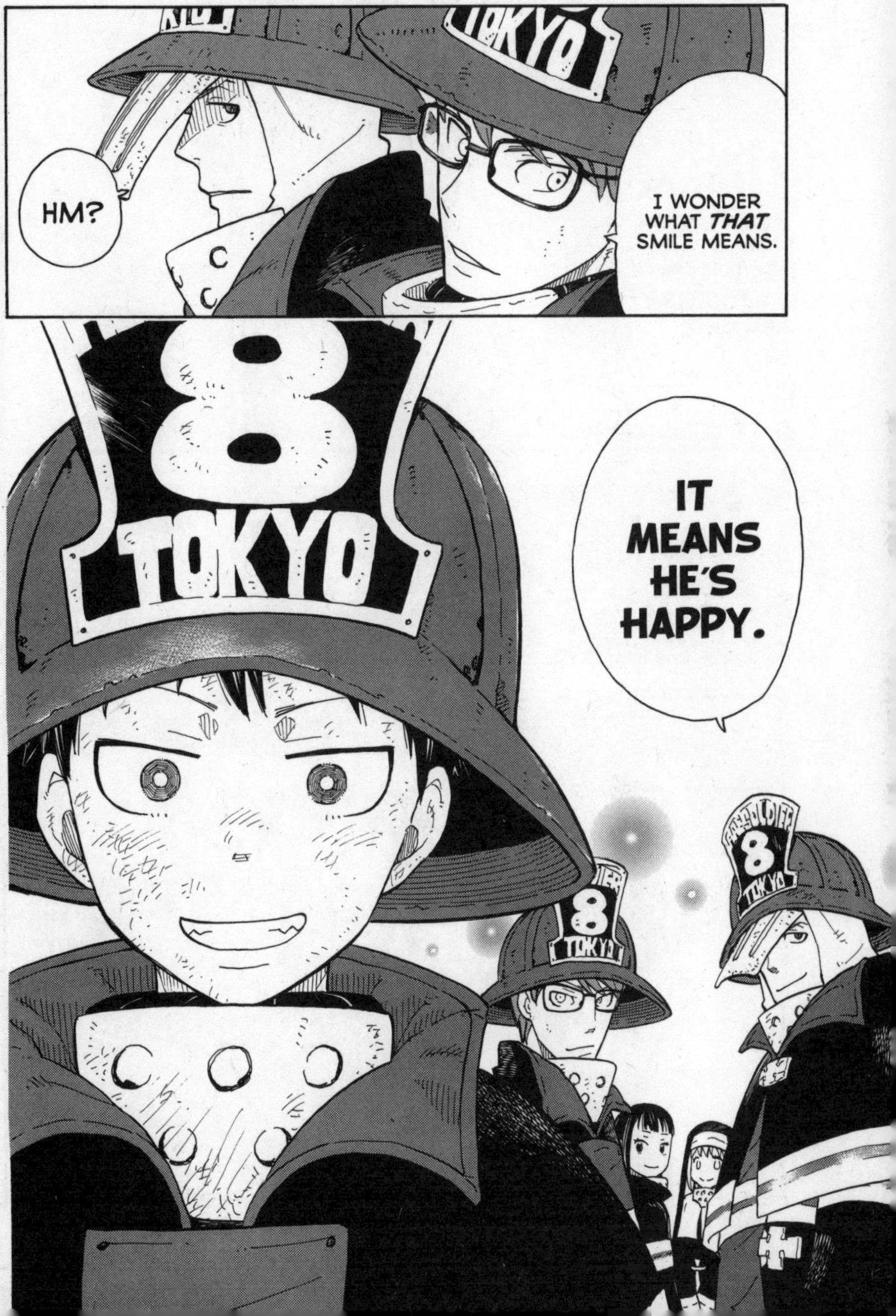
I WONDER WHAT *THAT* SMILE MEANS.
HM?
IT MEANS HE'S HAPPY.

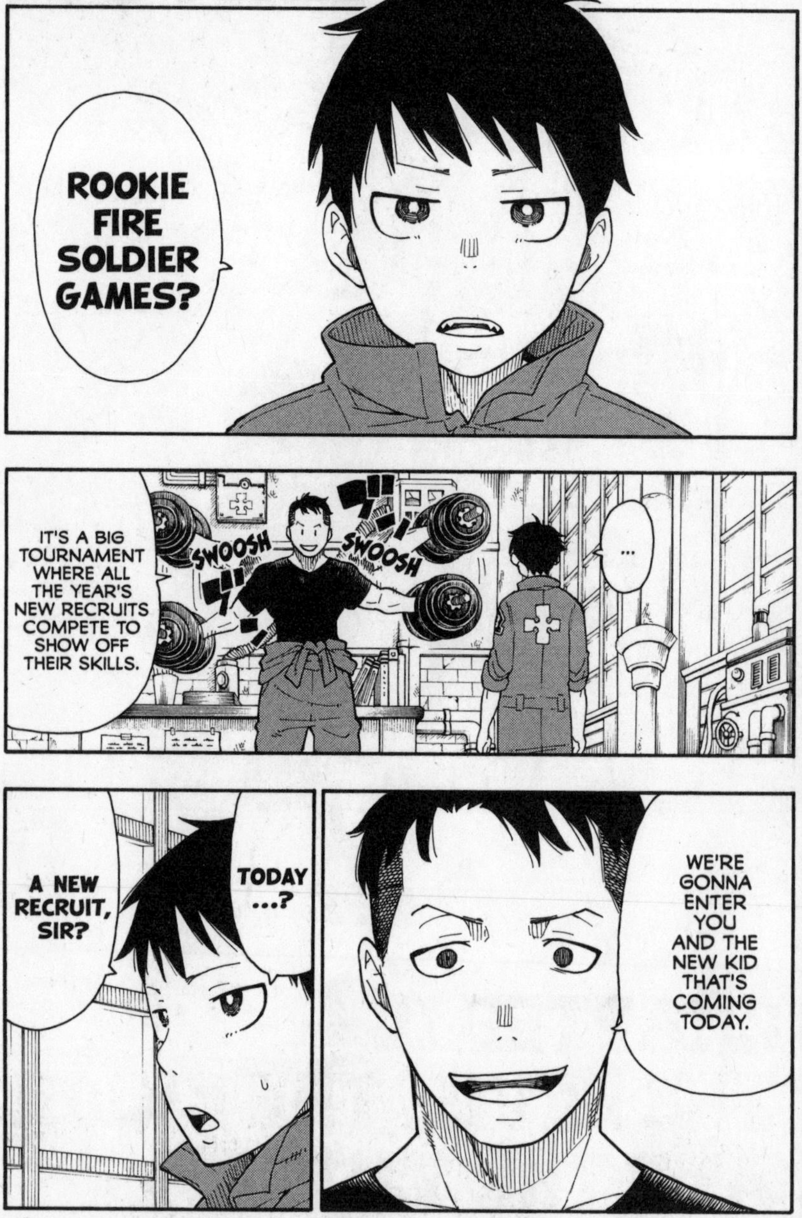
ROOKIE FIRE SOLDIER GAMES?
...
SWOOSH
SWOOSH
IT'S A BIG TOURNAMENT WHERE ALL THE YEAR'S NEW RECRUITS COMPETE TO SHOW OFF THEIR SKILLS.
WE'RE GONNA ENTER YOU AND THE NEW KID THAT'S COMING TODAY.
TODAY ...?
A NEW RECRUIT, SIR?

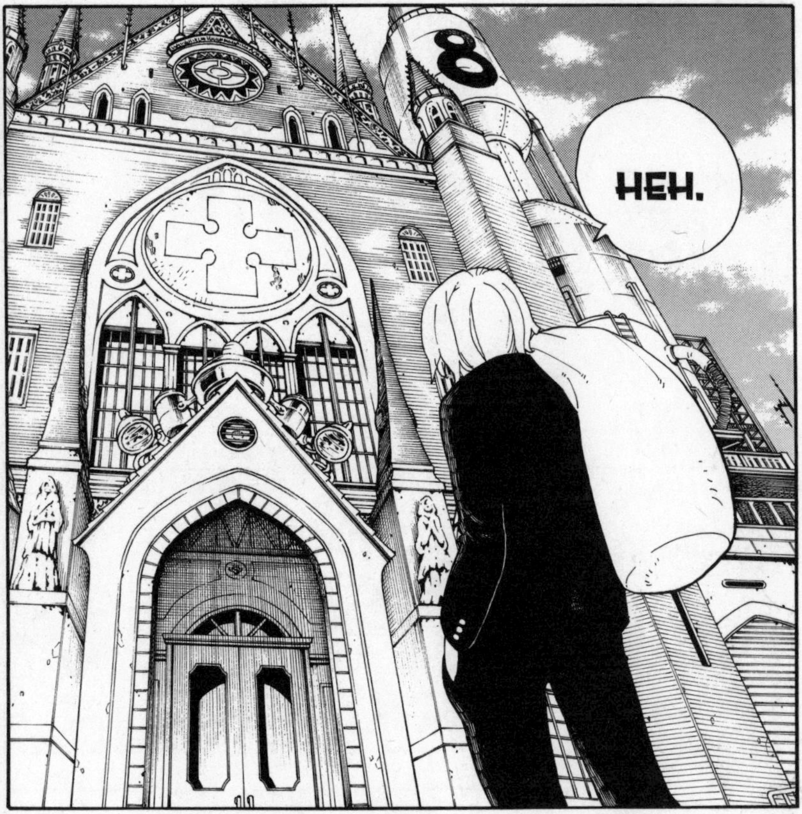
8
HEH.

CHAPTER II: THE DEVIL, THE KNIGHT, ND THE WITC

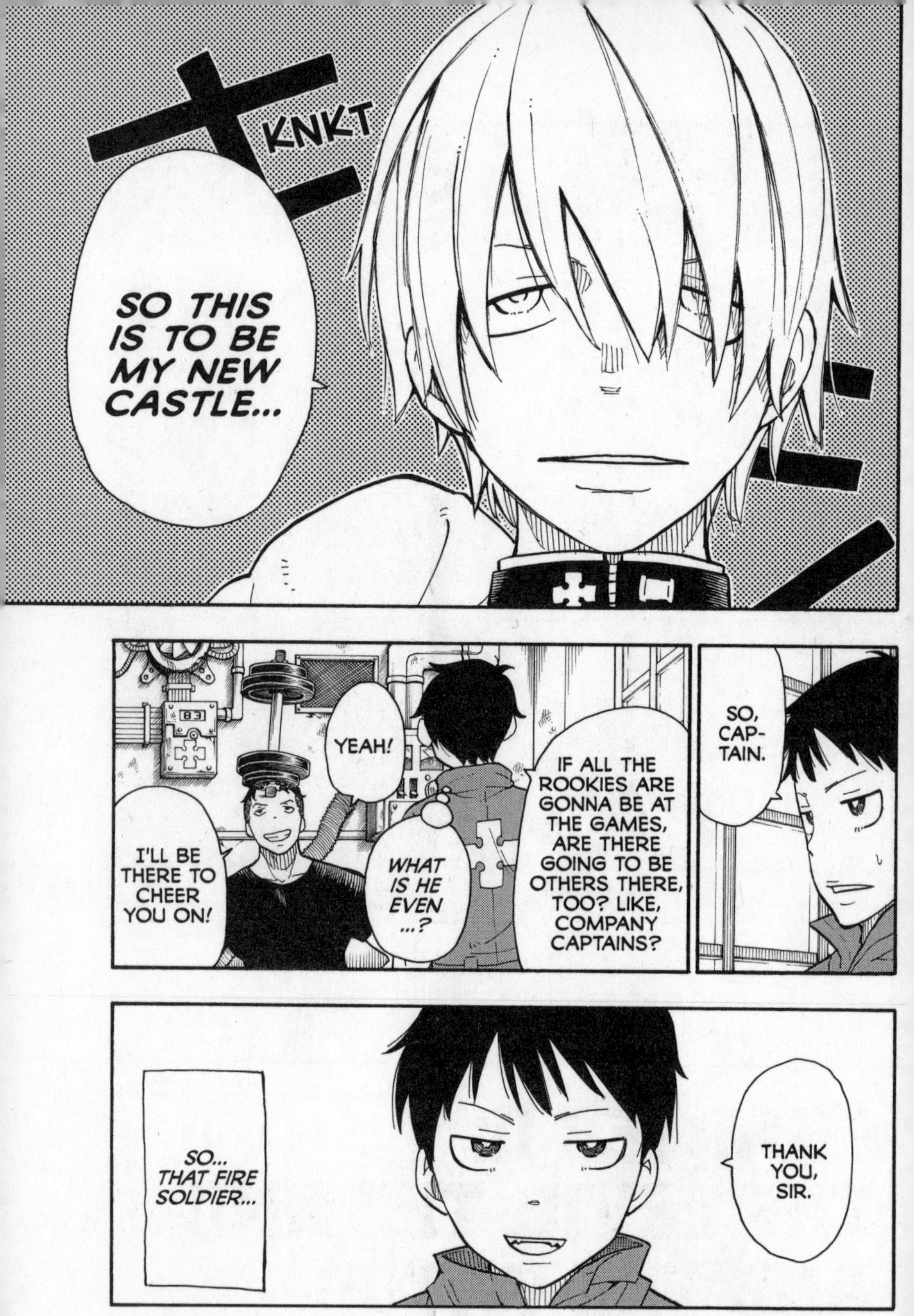
KNKT
SO THIS IS TO BE MY NEW CASTLE...
SO, CAP-TAIN.
IF ALL THE ROOKIES ARE GONNA BE AT THE GAMES, ARE THERE GOING TO BE OTHERS THERE, TOO? LIKE, COMPANY CAPTAINS?
YEAH!
WHAT IS HE EVEN ...?
I'LL BE THERE TO CHEER YOU ON!
THANK YOU, SIR.
SO... THAT FIRE SOLDIER...

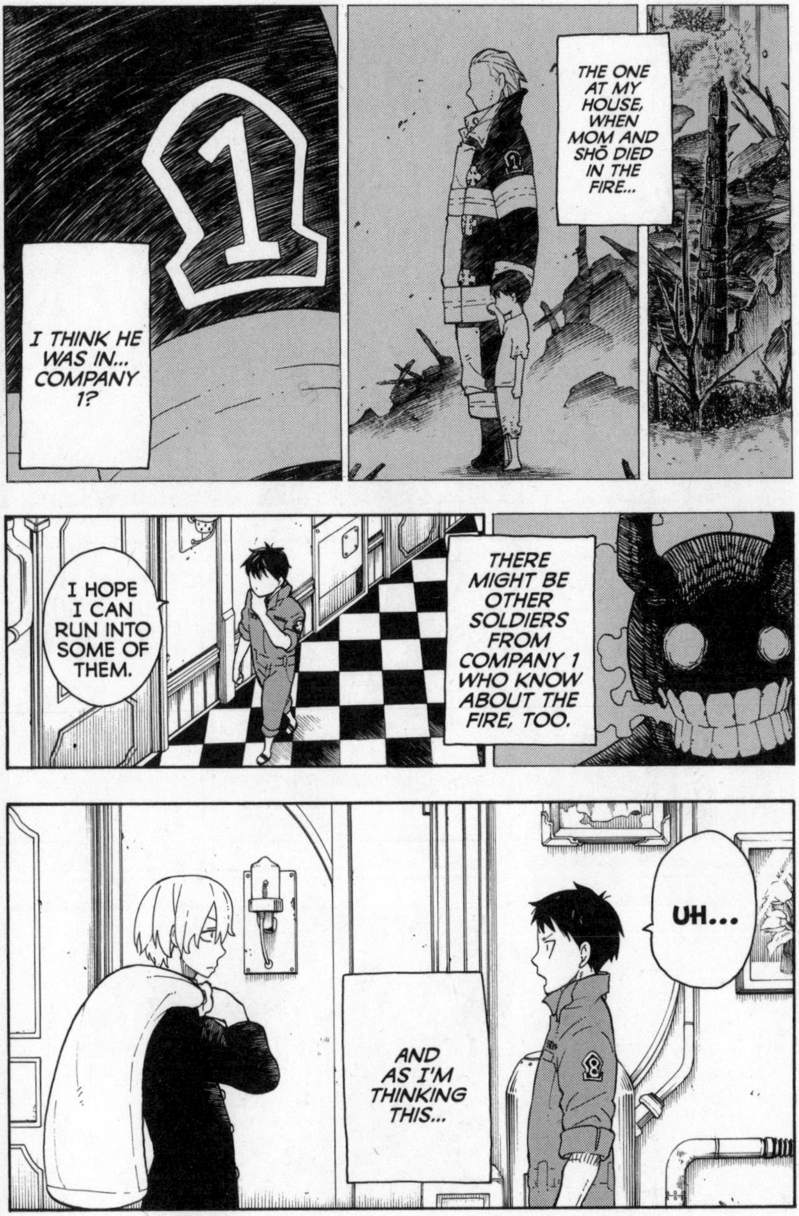
THE ONE AT MY HOUSE, WHEN MOM AND SHŌ DIED IN THE FIRE...
I THINK HE WAS IN... COMPANY 1?
THERE MIGHT BE OTHER SOLDIERS FROM COMPANY 1 WHO KNOW ABOUT THE FIRE, TOO.
I HOPE I CAN RUN INTO SOME OF THEM.
UH...
AND AS I'M THINKING THIS...

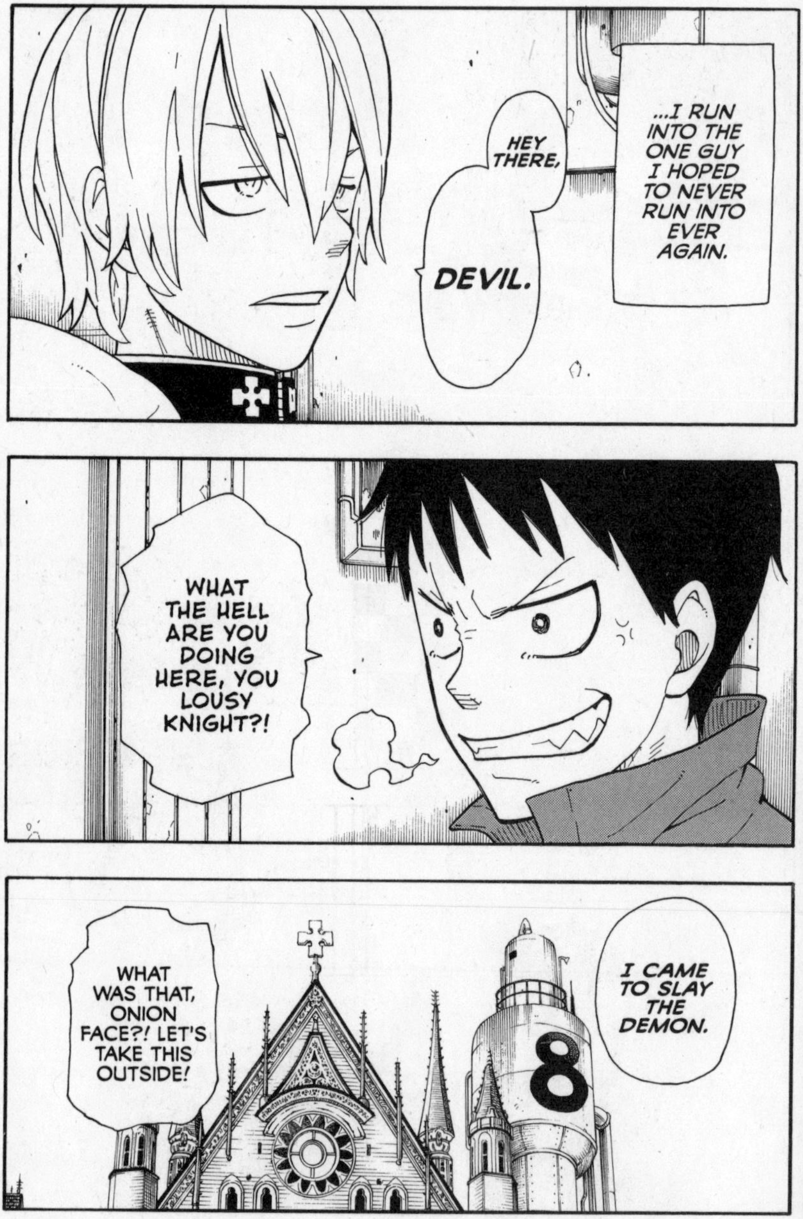
...I RUN INTO THE ONE GUY I HOPED TO NEVER RUN INTO EVER AGAIN.
HEY THERE,
DEVIL.
WHAT THE HELL ARE YOU DOING HERE, YOU LOUSY KNIGHT?!
I CAME TO SLAY THE DEMON.
WHAT WAS THAT, ONION FACE?! LET'S TAKE THIS OUTSIDE!

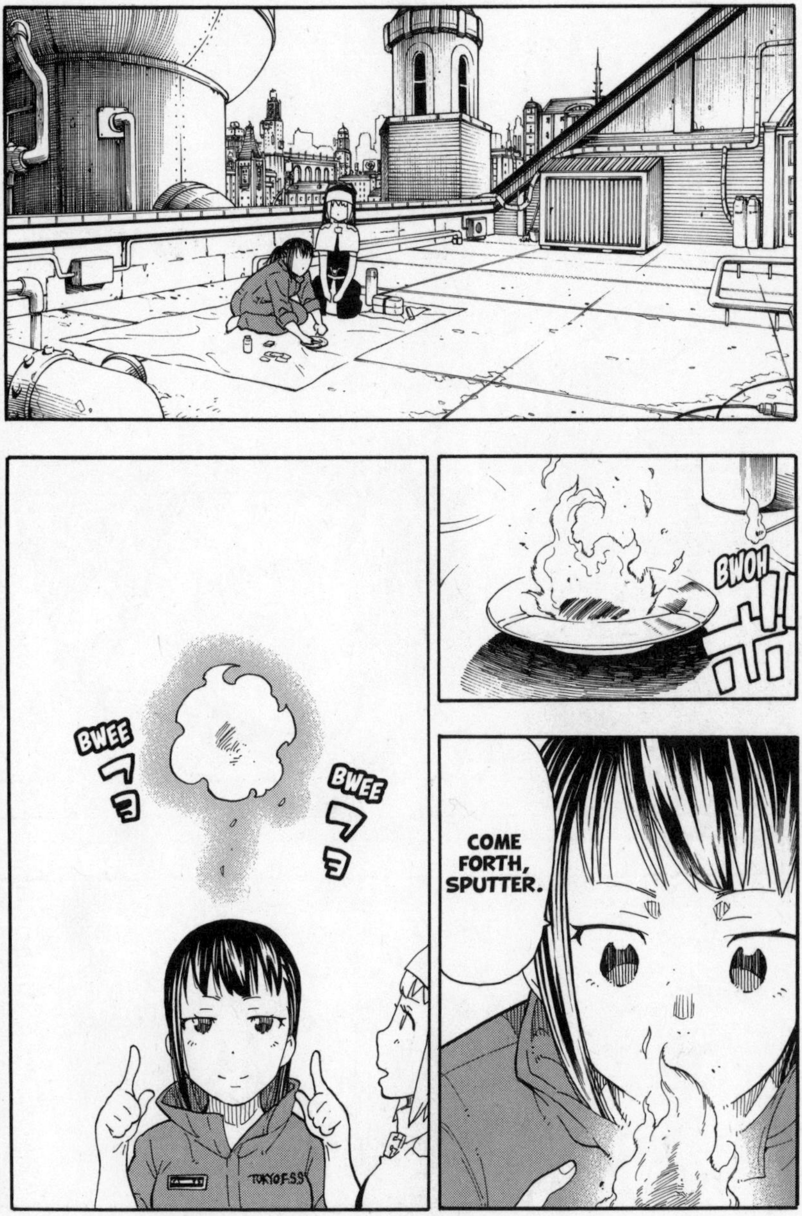
BWOH
COME FORTH, SPUTTER.
BWEE
BWEE

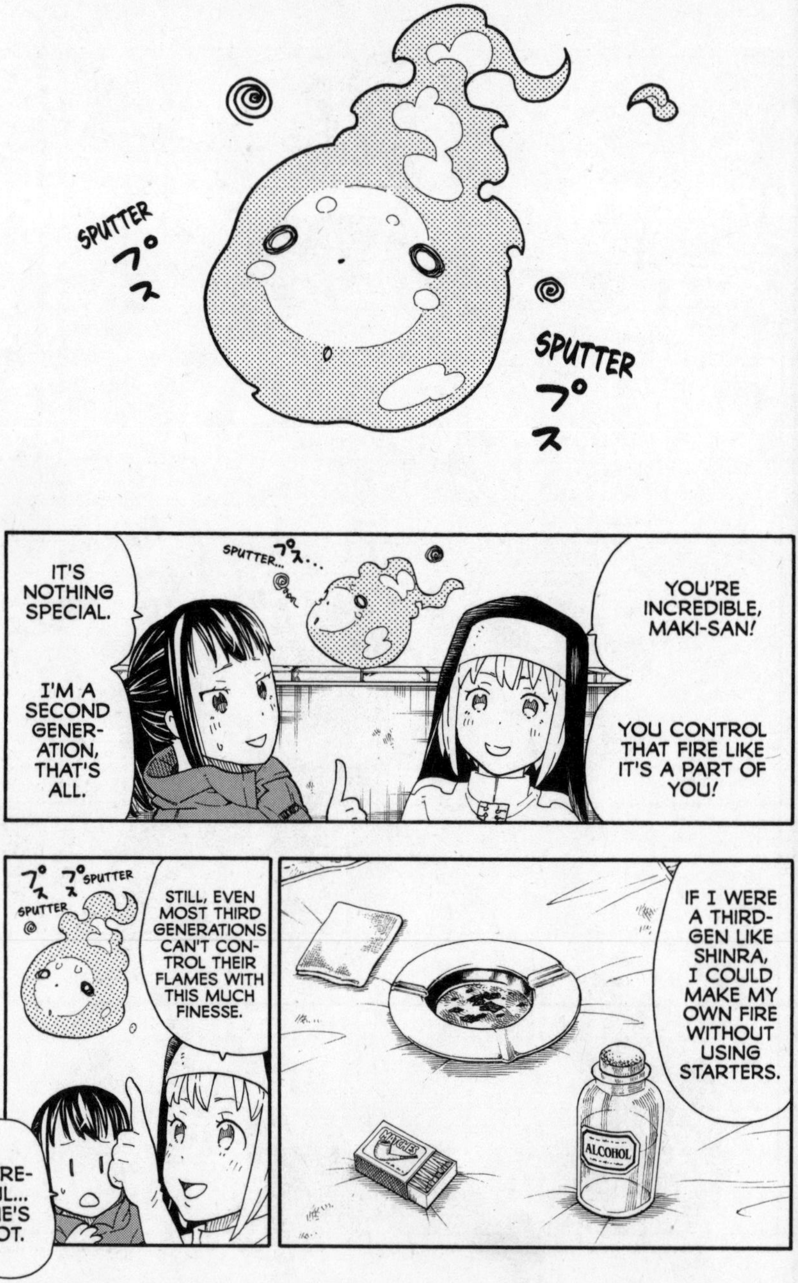
SPUTTER
プス
SPUTTER
プス
SPUTTER... プス...
YOU'RE INCREDIBLE, MAKI-SAN!
YOU CONTROL THAT FIRE LIKE IT'S A PART OF YOU!
IT'S NOTHING SPECIAL.
I'M A SECOND GENER-ATION, THAT'S ALL.
IF I WERE A THIRD-GEN LIKE SHINRA, I COULD MAKE MY OWN FIRE WITHOUT USING STARTERS.
MATCHES
ALCOHOL
プス SPUTTER
プス SPUTTER
STILL, EVEN MOST THIRD GENERATIONS CAN'T CON-TROL THEIR FLAMES WITH THIS MUCH FINESSE.
CARE-FUL... SHE'S HOT.

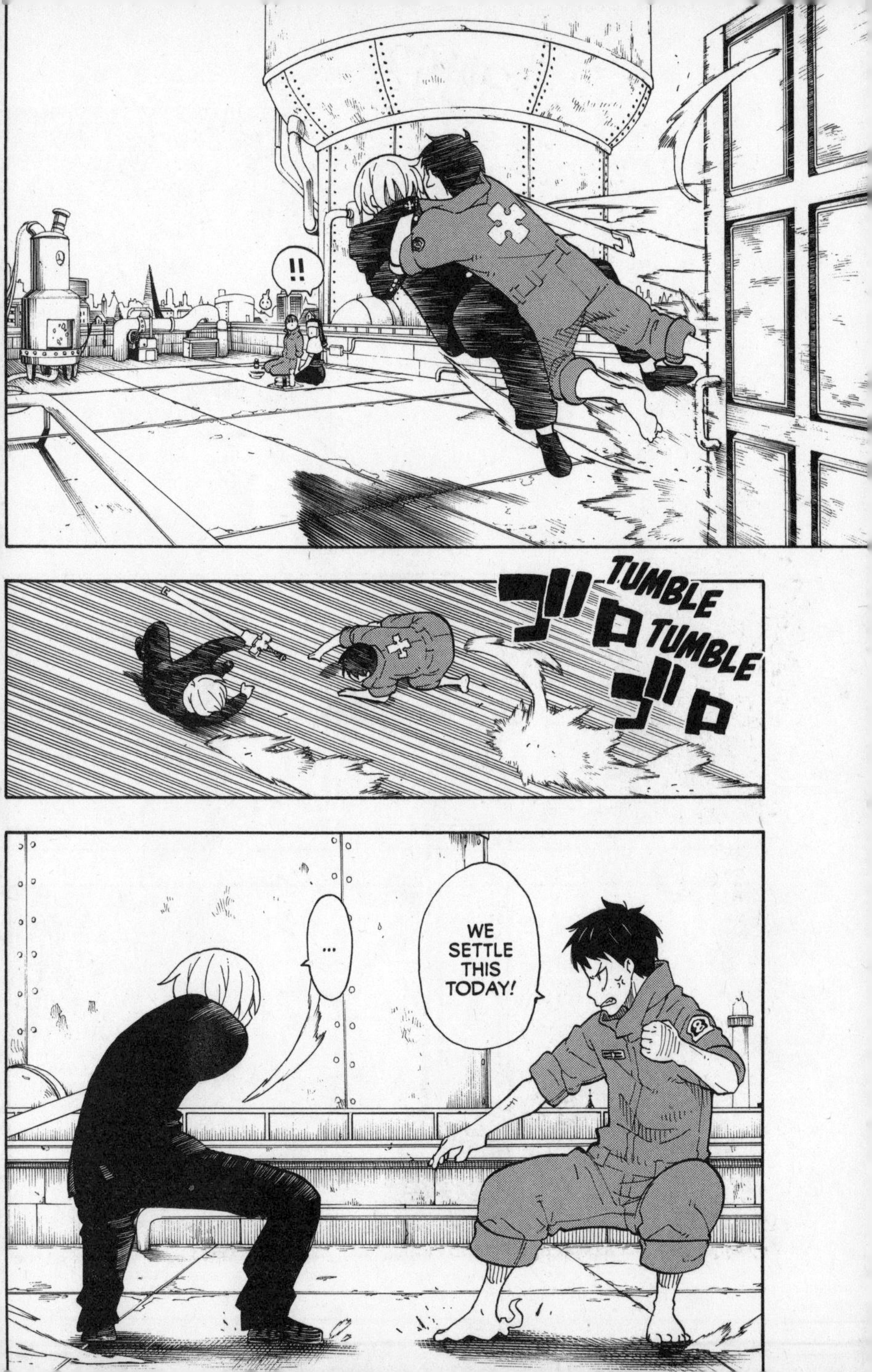
!!
ゴロ TUMBLE
ゴロ TUMBLE
WE SETTLE THIS TODAY!
...

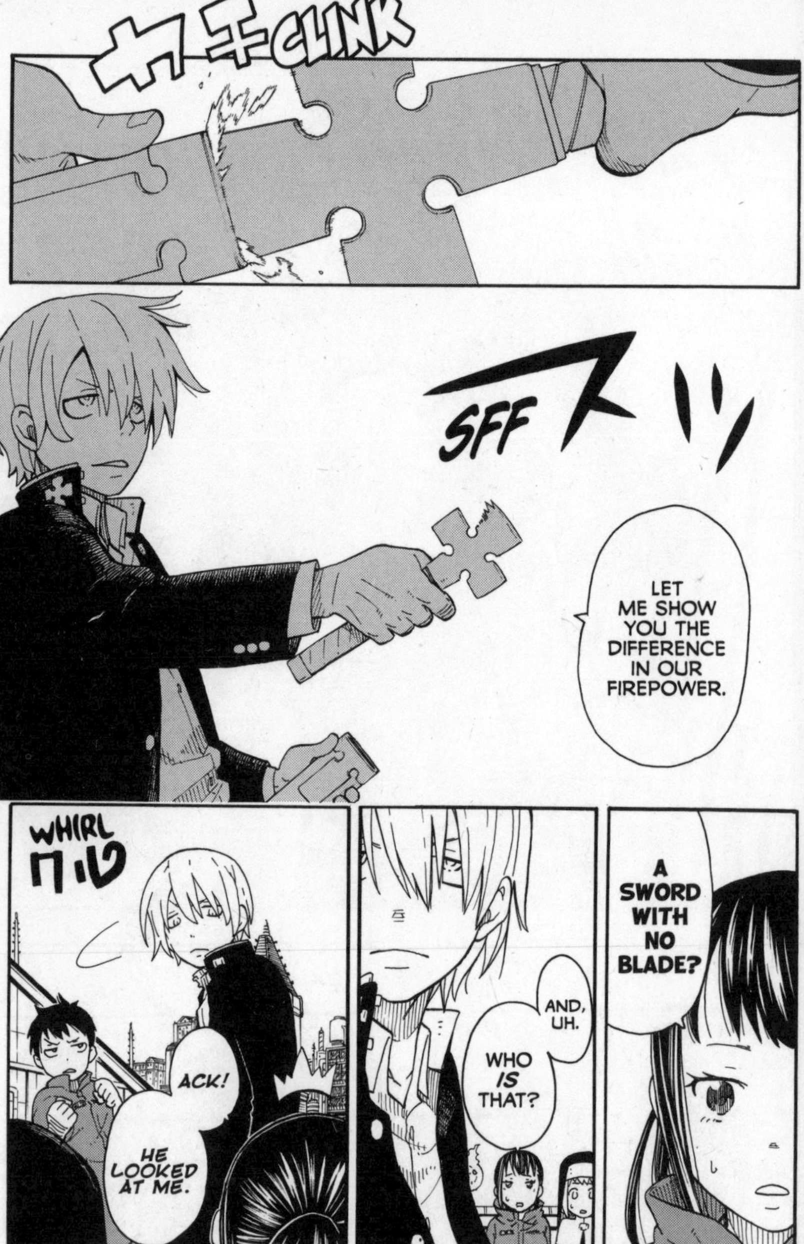
CLINK
SFF
LET ME SHOW YOU THE DIFFERENCE IN OUR FIREPOWER.
A SWORD WITH NO BLADE?
AND, UH.
WHO IS THAT?
WHIRL
ACK!
HE LOOKED AT ME.

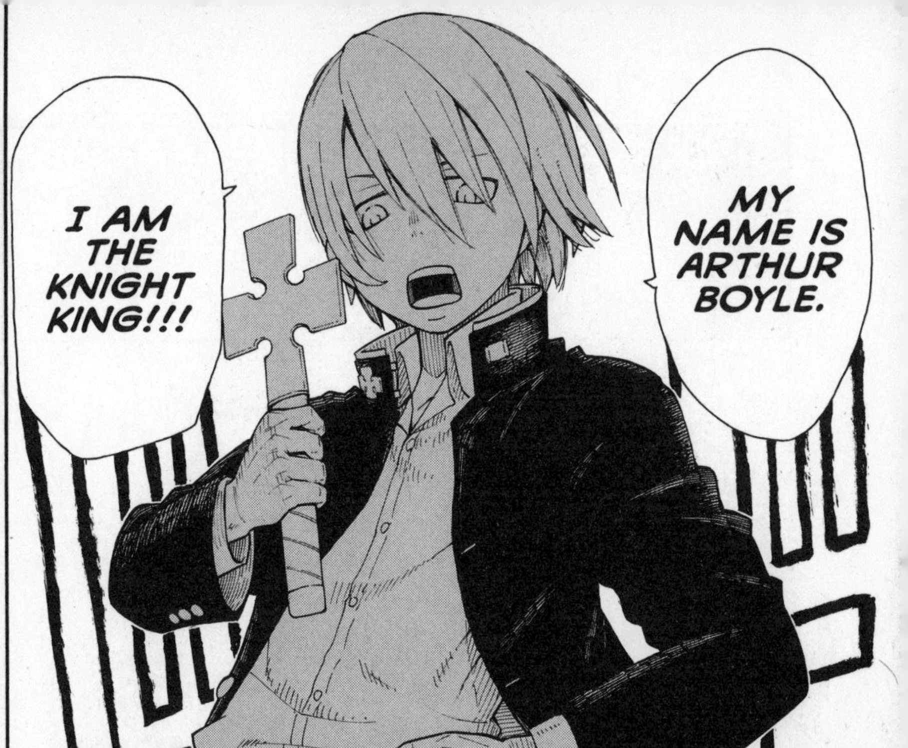
MY NAME IS ARTHUR BOYLE.
I AM THE KNIGHT KING!!!
DUN

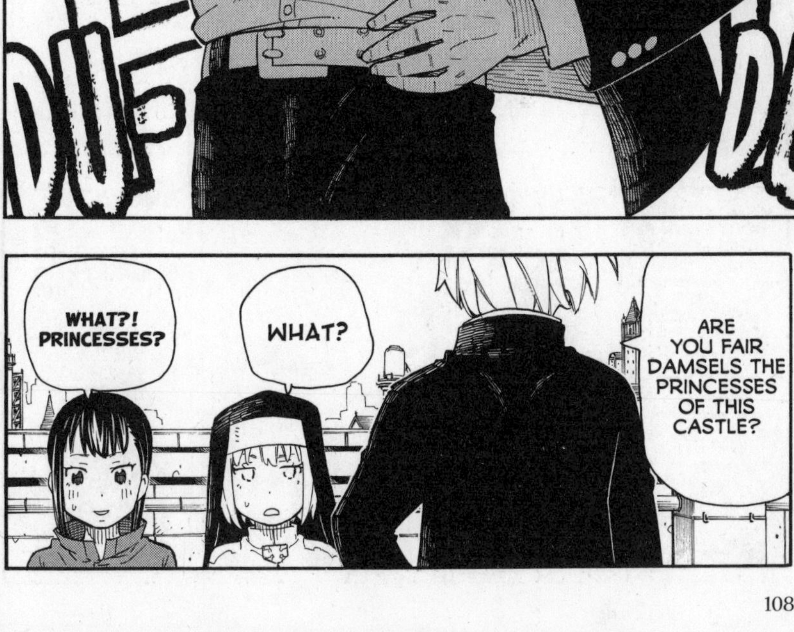
ARE YOU FAIR DAMSELS THE PRINCESSES OF THIS CASTLE?
WHAT?
WHAT?! PRINCESSES?

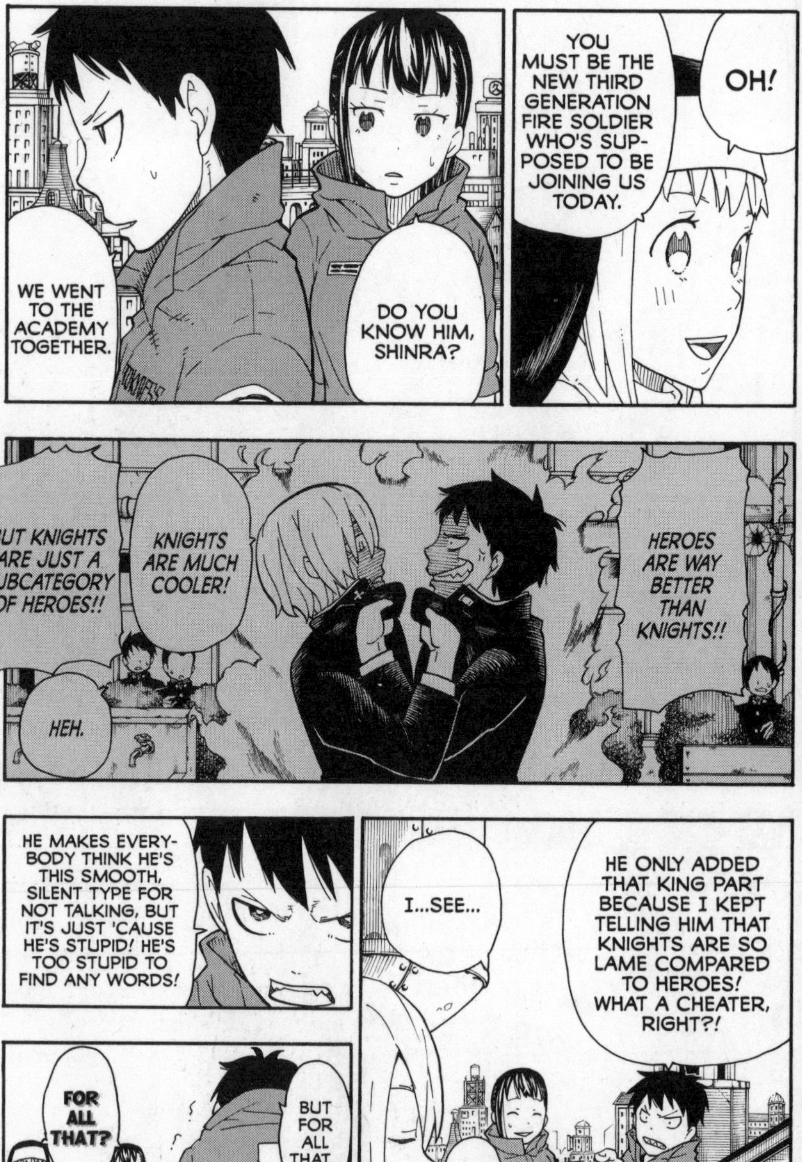
OH!
YOU MUST BE THE NEW THIRD GENERATION FIRE SOLDIER WHO'S SUP-POSED TO BE JOINING US TODAY.
DO YOU KNOW HIM, SHINRA?
WE WENT TO THE ACADEMY TOGETHER.
HEROES ARE WAY BETTER THAN KNIGHTS!!
KNIGHTS ARE MUCH COOLER!
BUT KNIGHTS ARE JUST A SUBCATEGORY OF HEROES!!
HEH.
HE ONLY ADDED THAT KING PART BECAUSE I KEPT TELLING HIM THAT KNIGHTS ARE SO LAME COMPARED TO HEROES! WHAT A CHEATER, RIGHT?!
I...SEE...
HEH.
HE MAKES EVERY-BODY THINK HE'S THIS SMOOTH, SILENT TYPE FOR NOT TALKING, BUT IT'S JUST 'CAUSE HE'S STUPID! HE'S TOO STUPID TO FIND ANY WORDS!
BUT FOR ALL THAT...
FOR ALL THAT?

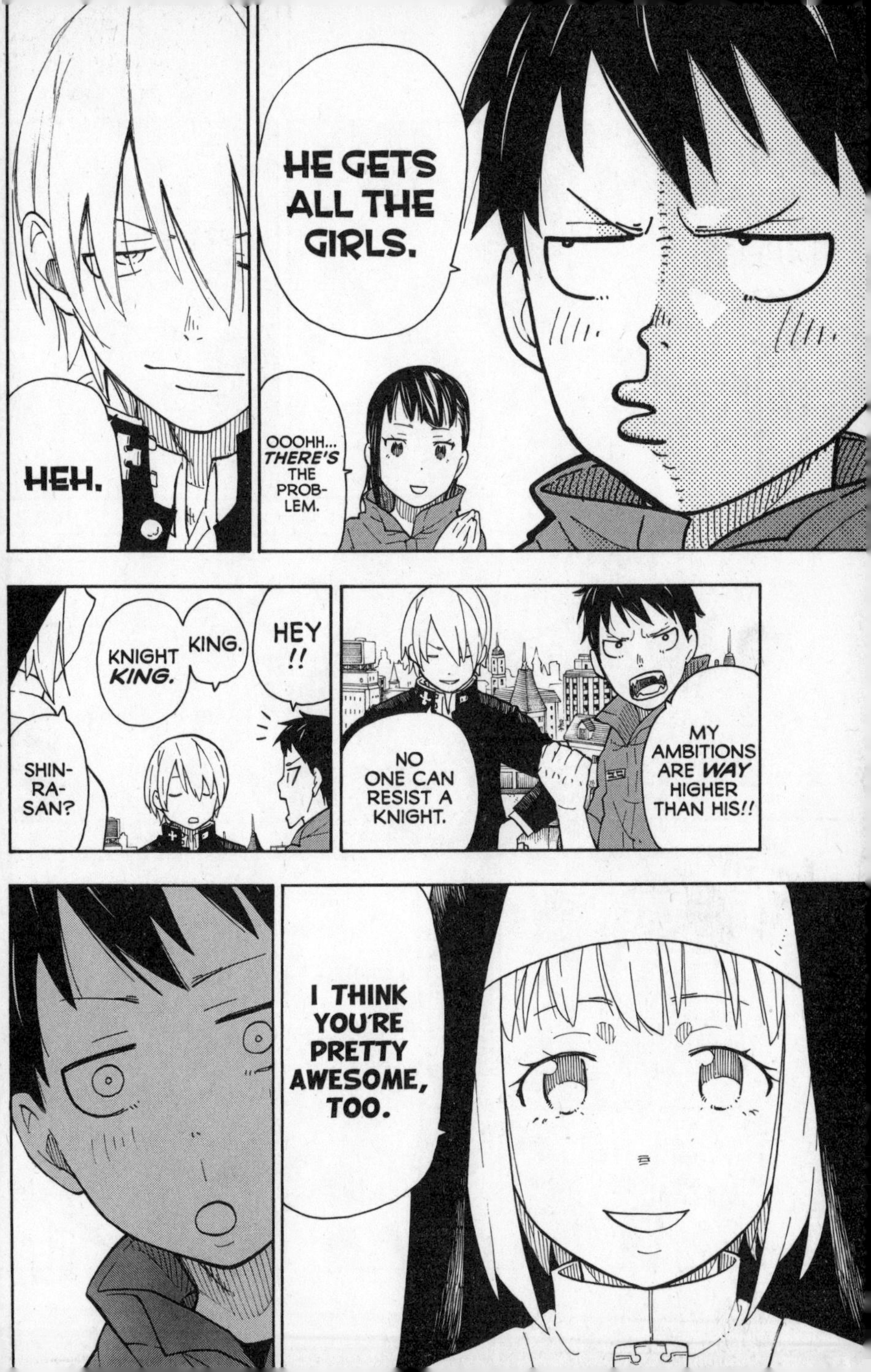
HE GETS ALL THE GIRLS.
OOOHH... *THERE'S* THE PROB-LEM.
HEH.
MY AMBITIONS ARE *WAY* HIGHER THAN HIS!!
NO ONE CAN RESIST A KNIGHT.
HEY!!
KING.
KNIGHT *KING.*
SHIN-RA-SAN?
I THINK YOU'RE PRETTY AWESOME, TOO.

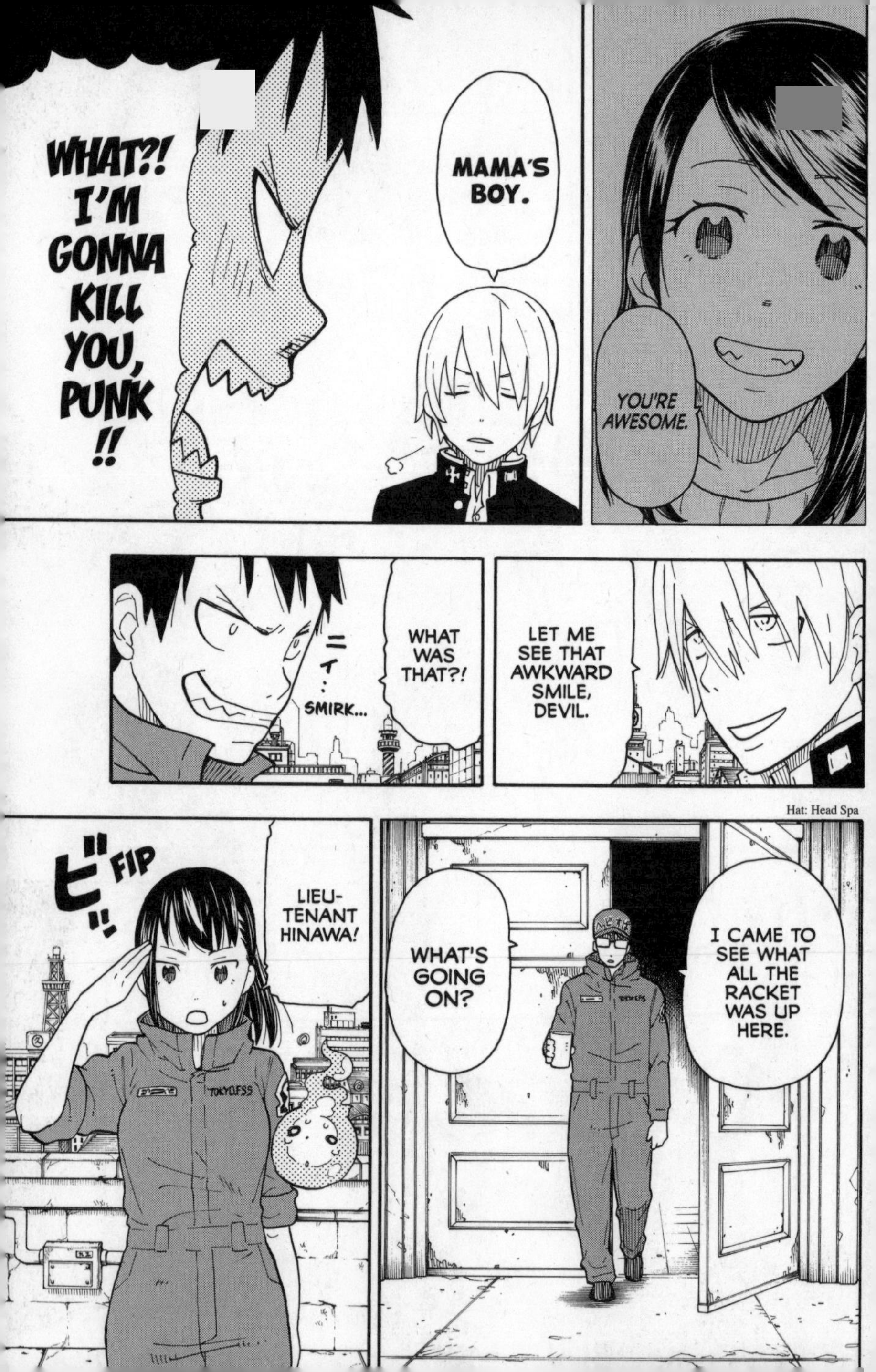
YOU'RE AWESOME.
MAMA'S BOY.
WHAT?! I'M GONNA KILL YOU, PUNK!!
LET ME SEE THAT AWKWARD SMILE, DEVIL.
WHAT WAS THAT?!
ニィ… SMIRK...
I CAME TO SEE WHAT ALL THE RACKET WAS UP HERE.
WHAT'S GOING ON?
LIEU-TENANT HINAWA!
ビ FIP
TOKYO.F.S.S
Hat: Head Spa

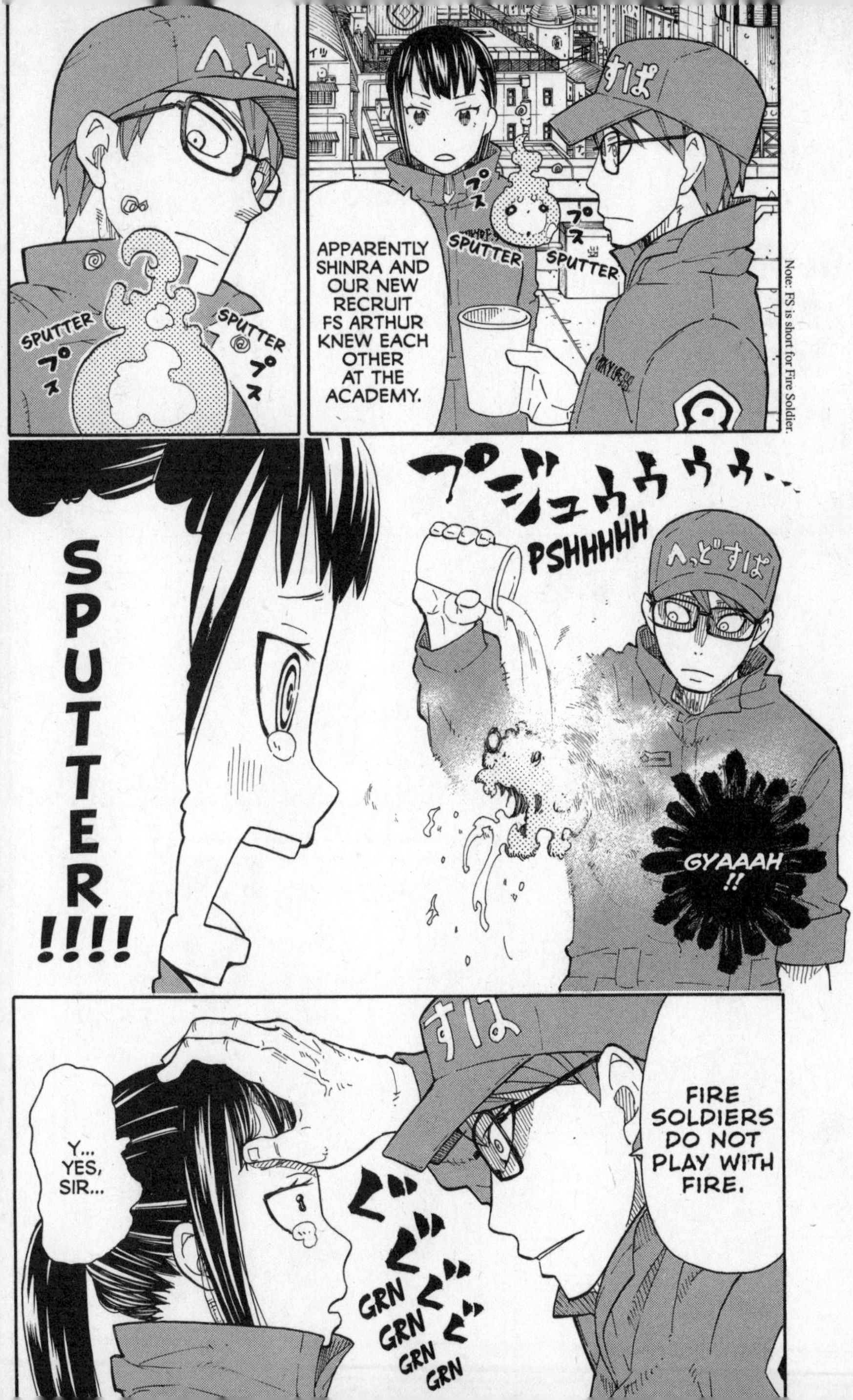
すぱ
APPARENTLY SHINRA AND OUR NEW RECRUIT FS ARTHUR KNEW EACH OTHER AT THE ACADEMY.
プス
SPUTTER
プス
SPUTTER
SPUTTER
プス
SPUTTER
プス
プシュううう…
PSHHHHH
へっどすぱ
GYAAAH!!
SPUTTER!!!!
FIRE SOLDIERS DO NOT PLAY WITH FIRE.
Y... YES, SIR...
GRN
GRN
GRN
GRN
GRN

Note: FS is short for Fire Soldier.

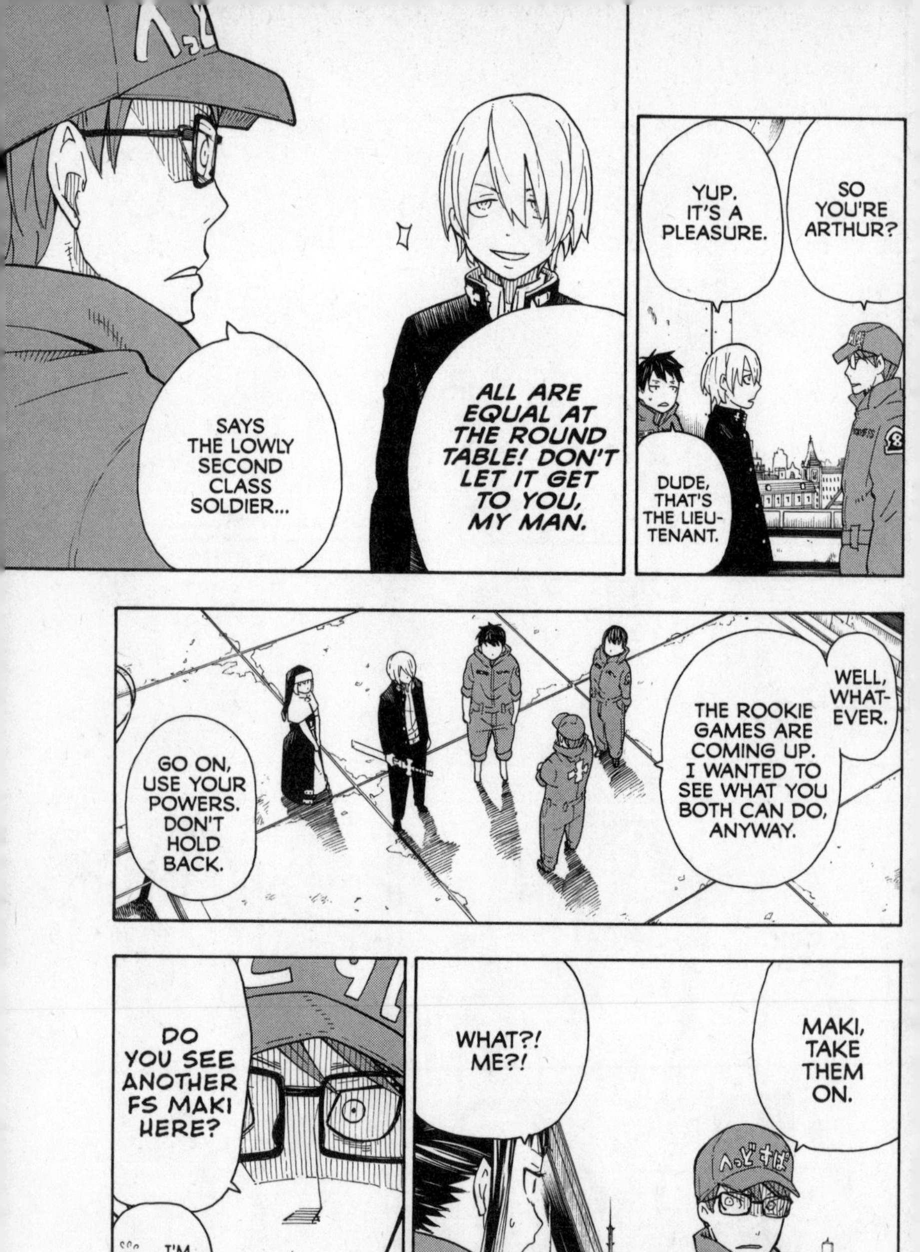
SO YOU'RE ARTHUR?
YUP. IT'S A PLEASURE.
DUDE, THAT'S THE LIEU-TENANT.
ALL ARE EQUAL AT THE ROUND TABLE! DON'T LET IT GET TO YOU, MY MAN.
SAYS THE LOWLY SECOND CLASS SOLDIER...
WELL, WHAT-EVER.
THE ROOKIE GAMES ARE COMING UP. I WANTED TO SEE WHAT YOU BOTH CAN DO, ANYWAY.
GO ON, USE YOUR POWERS. DON'T HOLD BACK.
MAKI, TAKE THEM ON.
WHAT?! ME?!
DO YOU SEE ANOTHER FS MAKI HERE?
I'M SORRY, SIR.

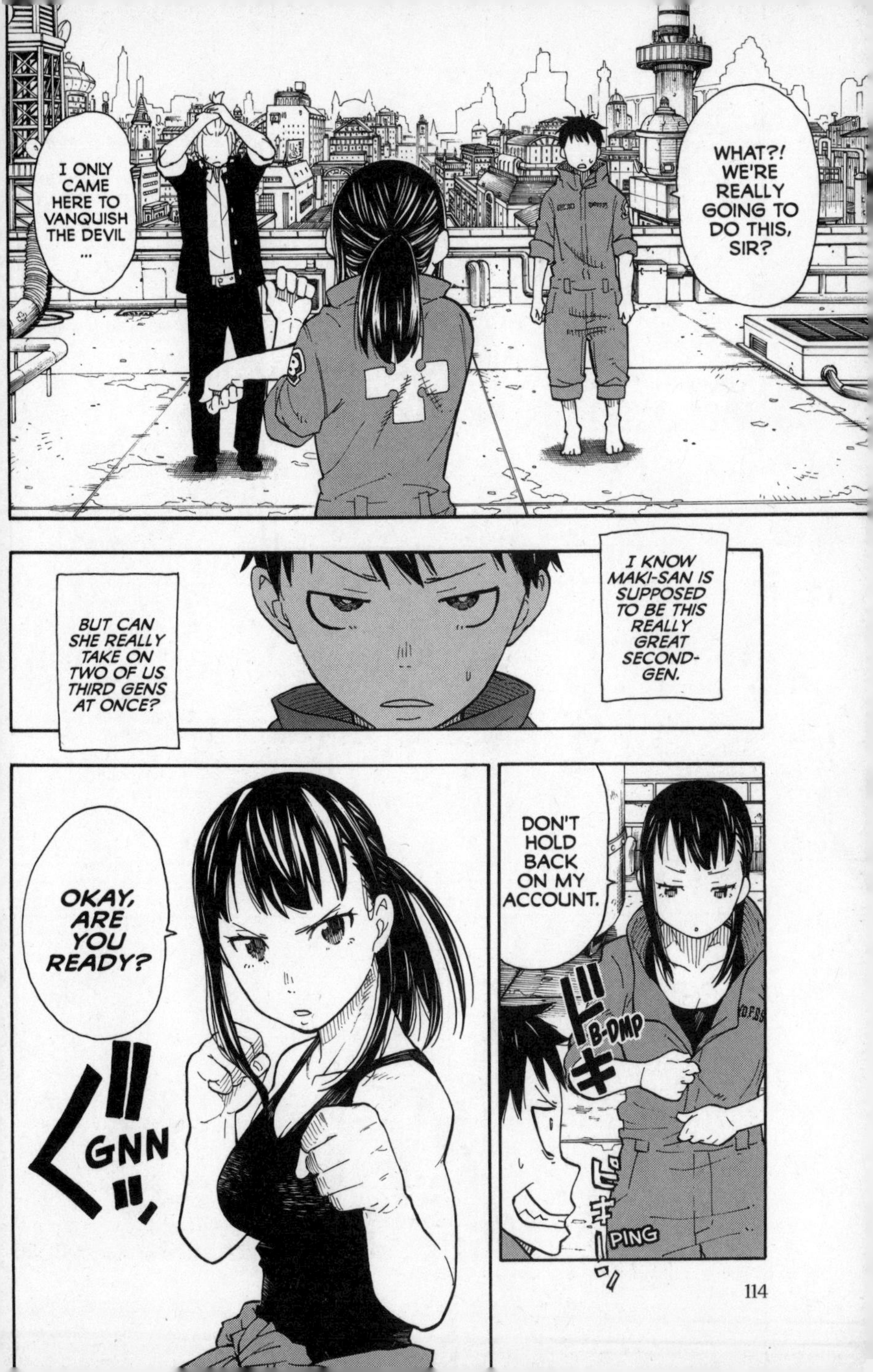
WHAT?! WE'RE REALLY GOING TO DO THIS, SIR?
I ONLY CAME HERE TO VANQUISH THE DEVIL ...
I KNOW MAKI-SAN IS SUPPOSED TO BE THIS REALLY GREAT SECOND-GEN.
BUT CAN SHE REALLY TAKE ON TWO OF US THIRD GENS AT ONCE?
DON'T HOLD BACK ON MY ACCOUNT.
B-DMP
PING
OKAY, ARE YOU READY?
GNN

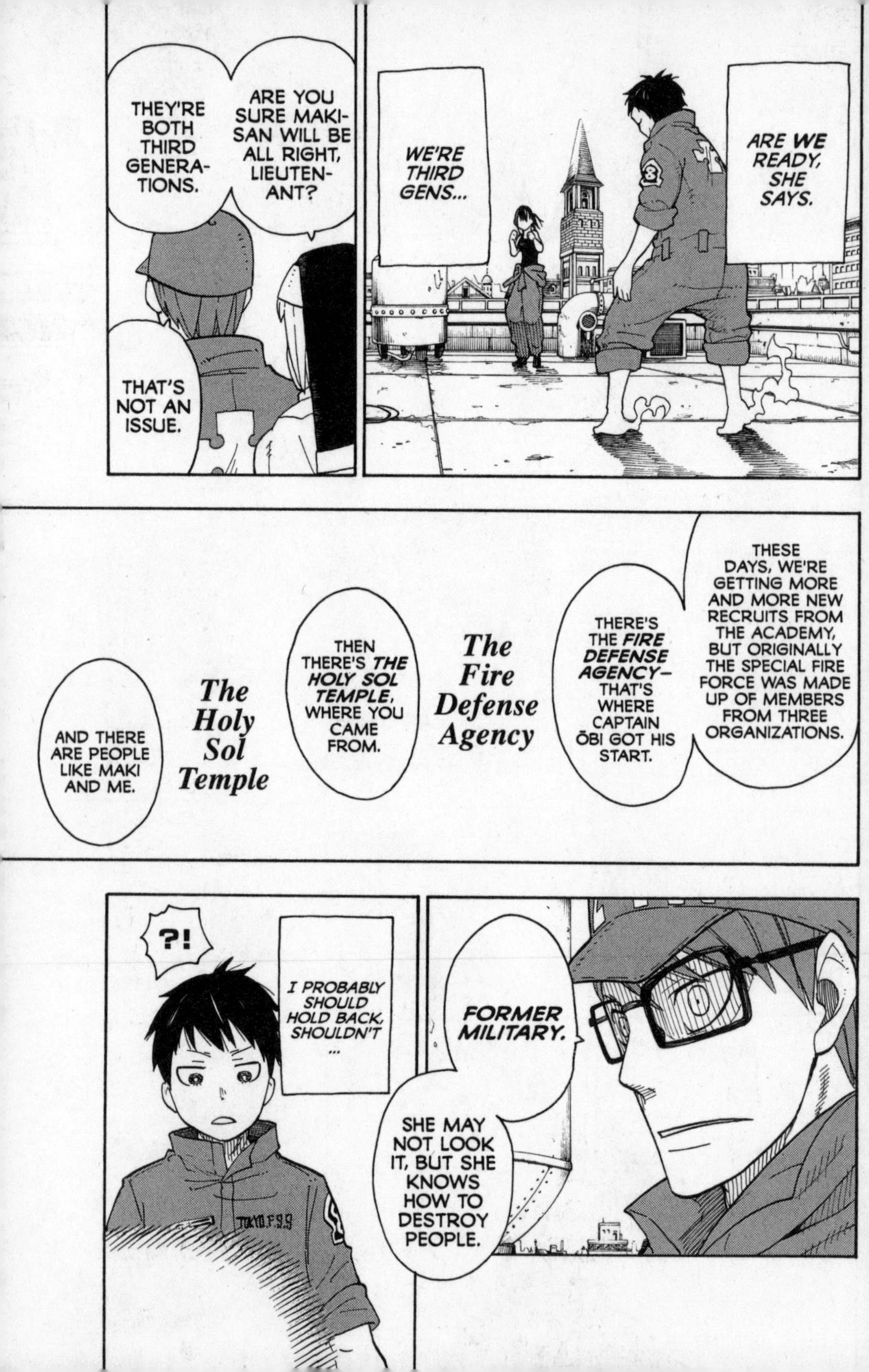
ARE WE READY, SHE SAYS.
WE'RE THIRD GENS...
ARE YOU SURE MAKI-SAN WILL BE ALL RIGHT, LIEUTENANT?
THEY'RE BOTH THIRD GENERATIONS.
THAT'S NOT AN ISSUE.
THESE DAYS, WE'RE GETTING MORE AND MORE NEW RECRUITS FROM THE ACADEMY, BUT ORIGINALLY THE SPECIAL FIRE FORCE WAS MADE UP OF MEMBERS FROM THREE ORGANIZATIONS.
THERE'S THE FIRE DEFENSE AGENCY— THAT'S WHERE CAPTAIN ŌBI GOT HIS START.
The Fire Defense Agency
THEN THERE'S THE HOLY SOL TEMPLE, WHERE YOU CAME FROM.
The Holy Sol Temple
AND THERE ARE PEOPLE LIKE MAKI AND ME.
FORMER MILITARY.
SHE MAY NOT LOOK IT, BUT SHE KNOWS HOW TO DESTROY PEOPLE.
I PROBABLY SHOULD HOLD BACK, SHOULDN'T ...
?!
TOKYO.F.S.8

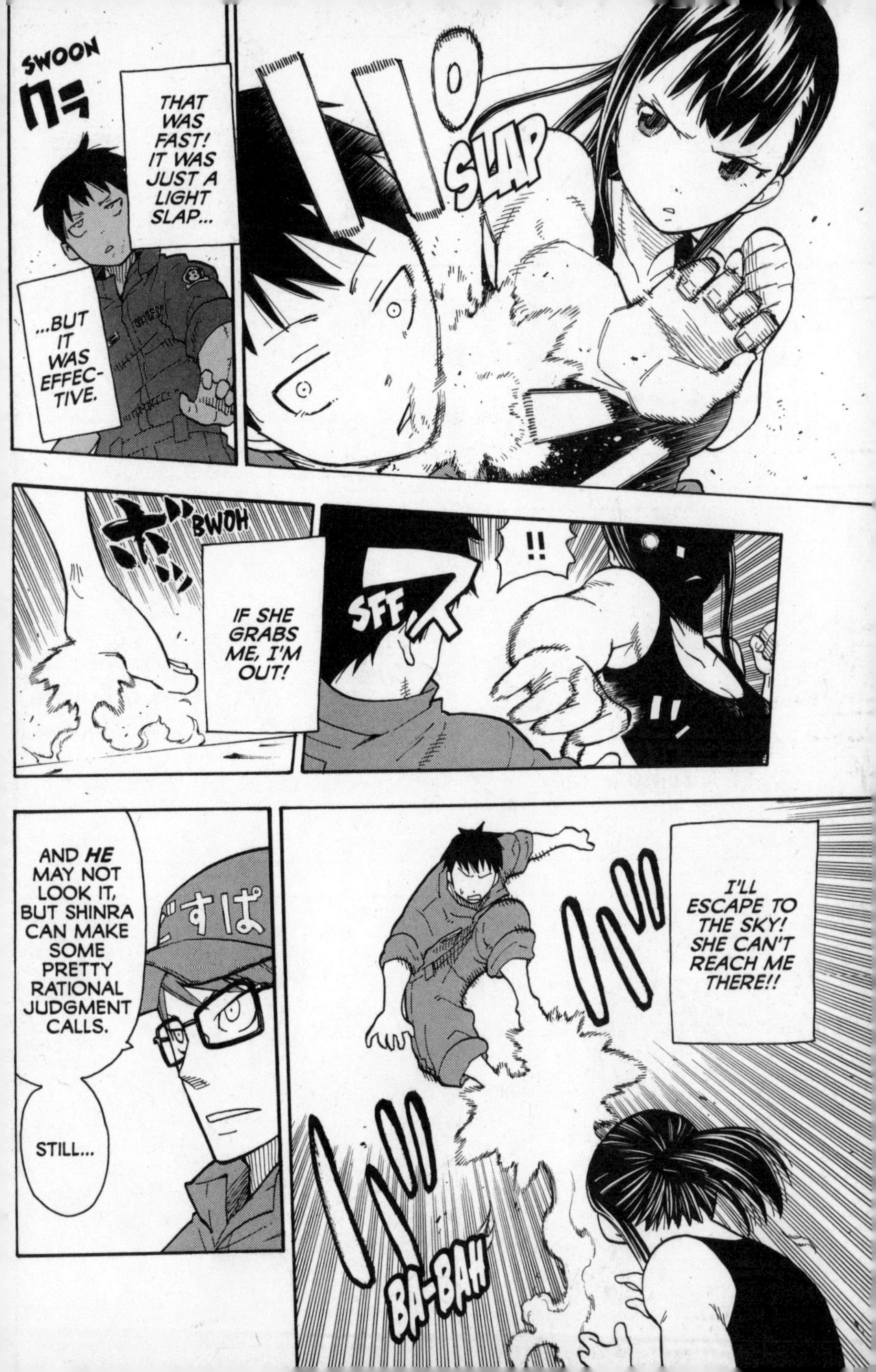
SLAP
SWOON
クラ
THAT WAS FAST! IT WAS JUST A LIGHT SLAP...
...BUT IT WAS EFFECTIVE.
!!
SFF
!!
BWOH
IF SHE GRABS ME, I'M OUT!
I'LL ESCAPE TO THE SKY! SHE CAN'T REACH ME THERE!!
BA-BAH
AND *HE* MAY NOT LOOK IT, BUT SHINRA CAN MAKE SOME PRETTY RATIONAL JUDGMENT CALLS.
STILL...

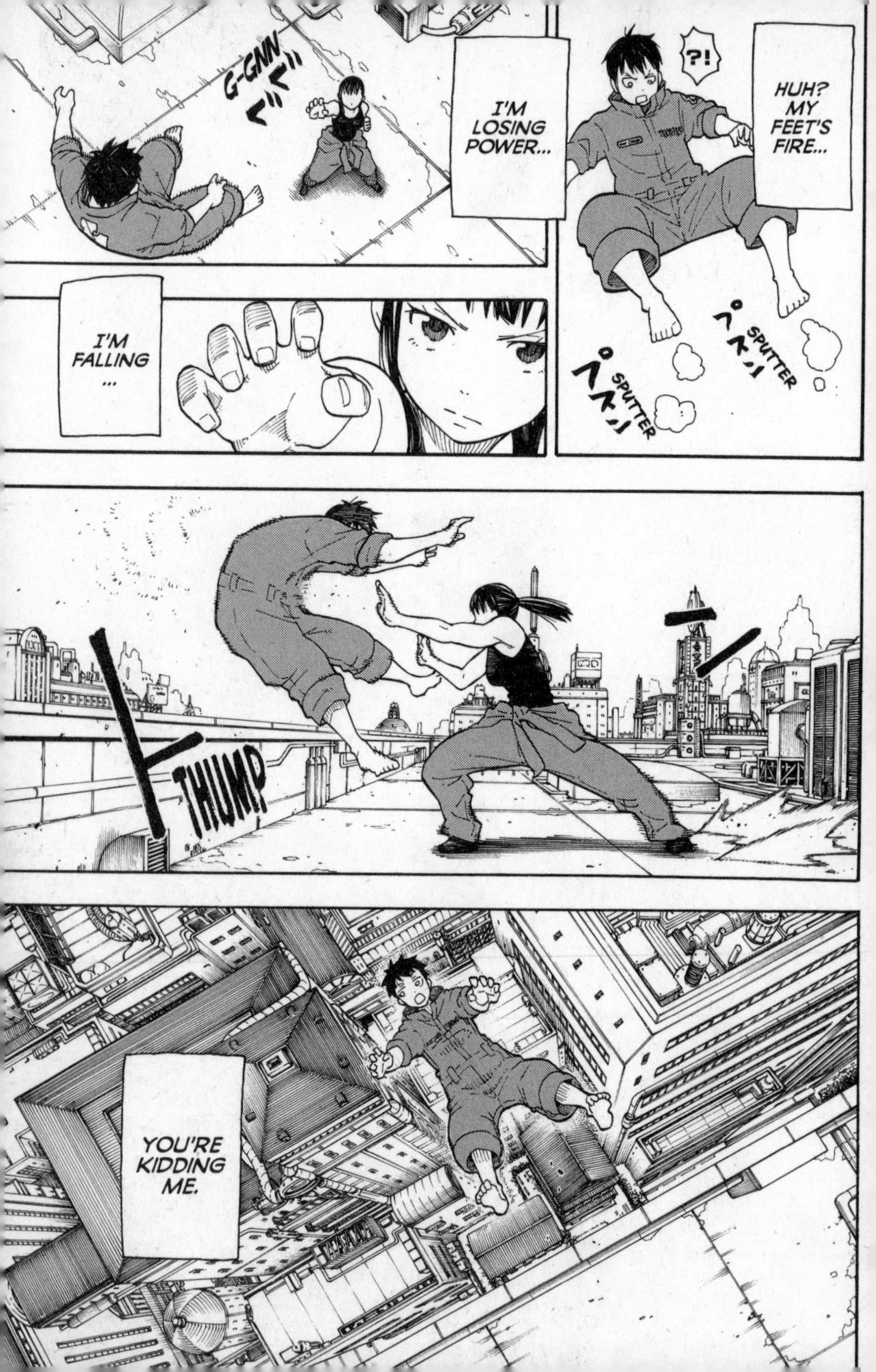
?!
HUH? MY FEET'S FIRE...
SPUTTER
SPUTTER
I'M LOSING POWER...
G-GNN
I'M FALLING ...
THUMP
YOU'RE KIDDING ME.

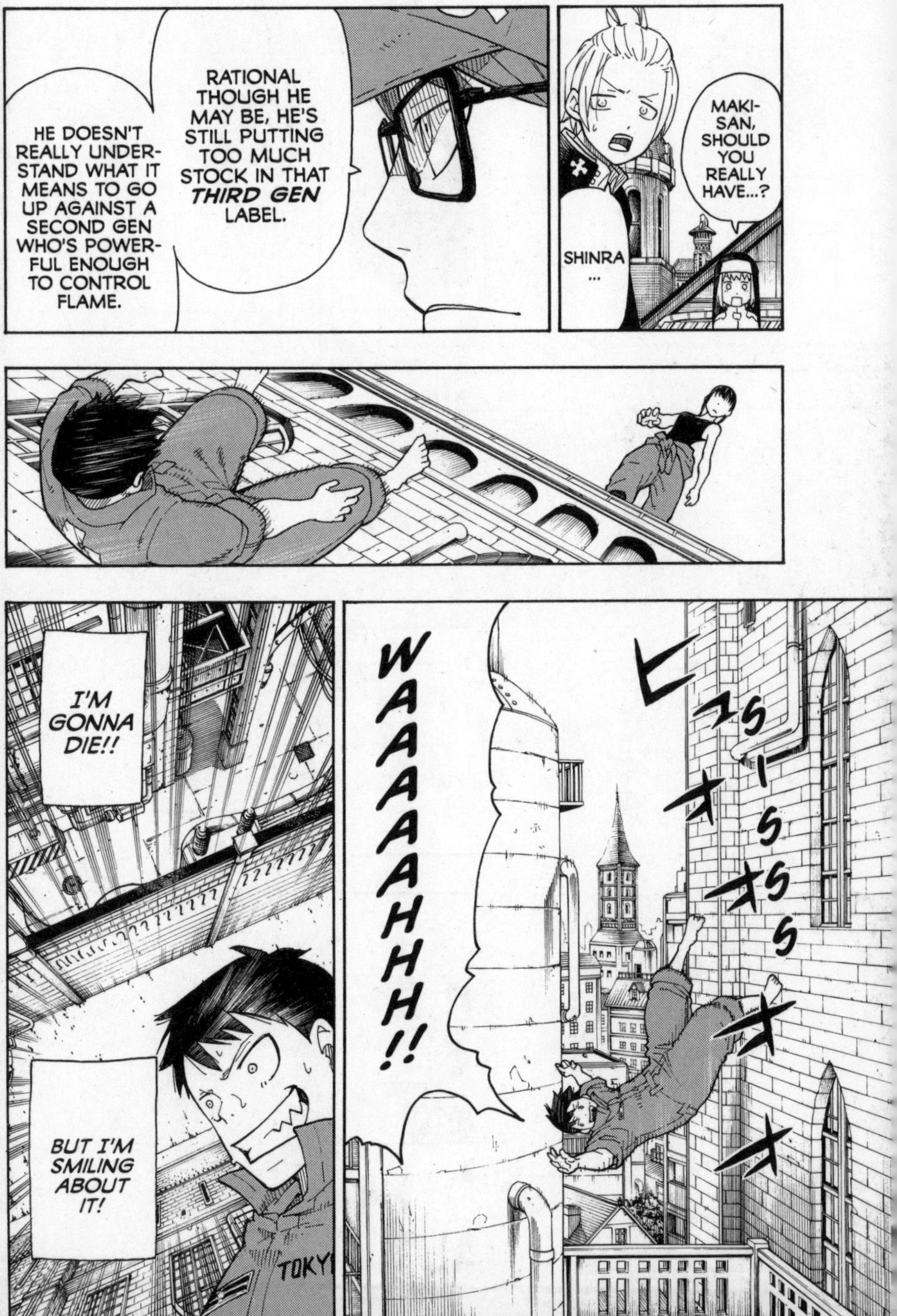
MAKI-SAN, SHOULD YOU REALLY HAVE...?
SHINRA...
RATIONAL THOUGH HE MAY BE, HE'S STILL PUTTING TOO MUCH STOCK IN THAT *THIRD GEN* LABEL.
HE DOESN'T REALLY UNDER-STAND WHAT IT MEANS TO GO UP AGAINST A SECOND GEN WHO'S POWER-FUL ENOUGH TO CONTROL FLAME.
ヒューオオオオ
S-SSSS
WAAAAAAHHH!!
I'M GONNA DIE!!
BUT I'M SMILING ABOUT IT!

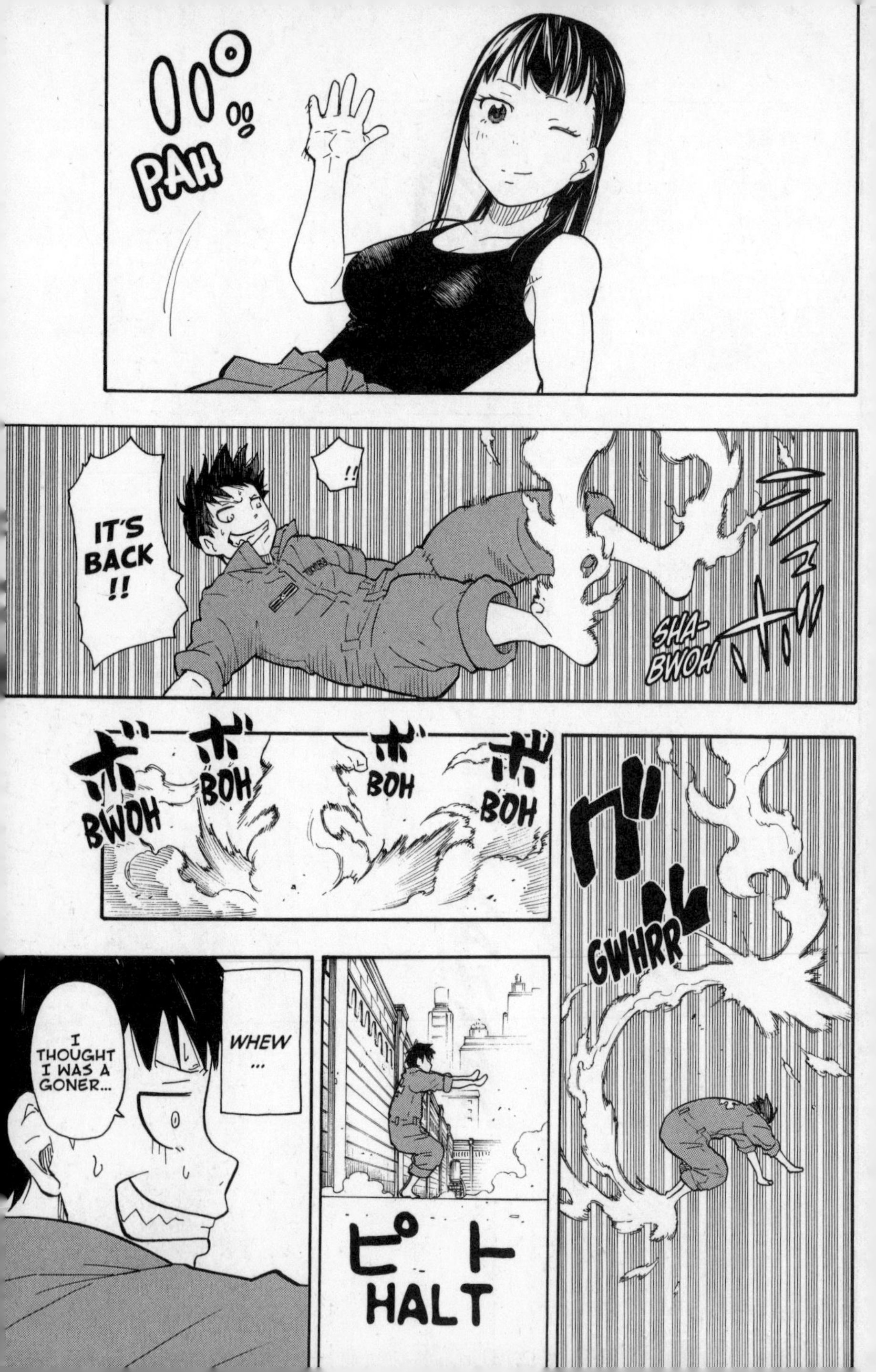
PAH
!!
IT'S BACK !!
SHA-BWOH
GWHRR
ボ BOH
ボ BOH
ボ BOH
ボ BWOH
ピト
HALT
WHEW ...
I THOUGHT I WAS A GONER...

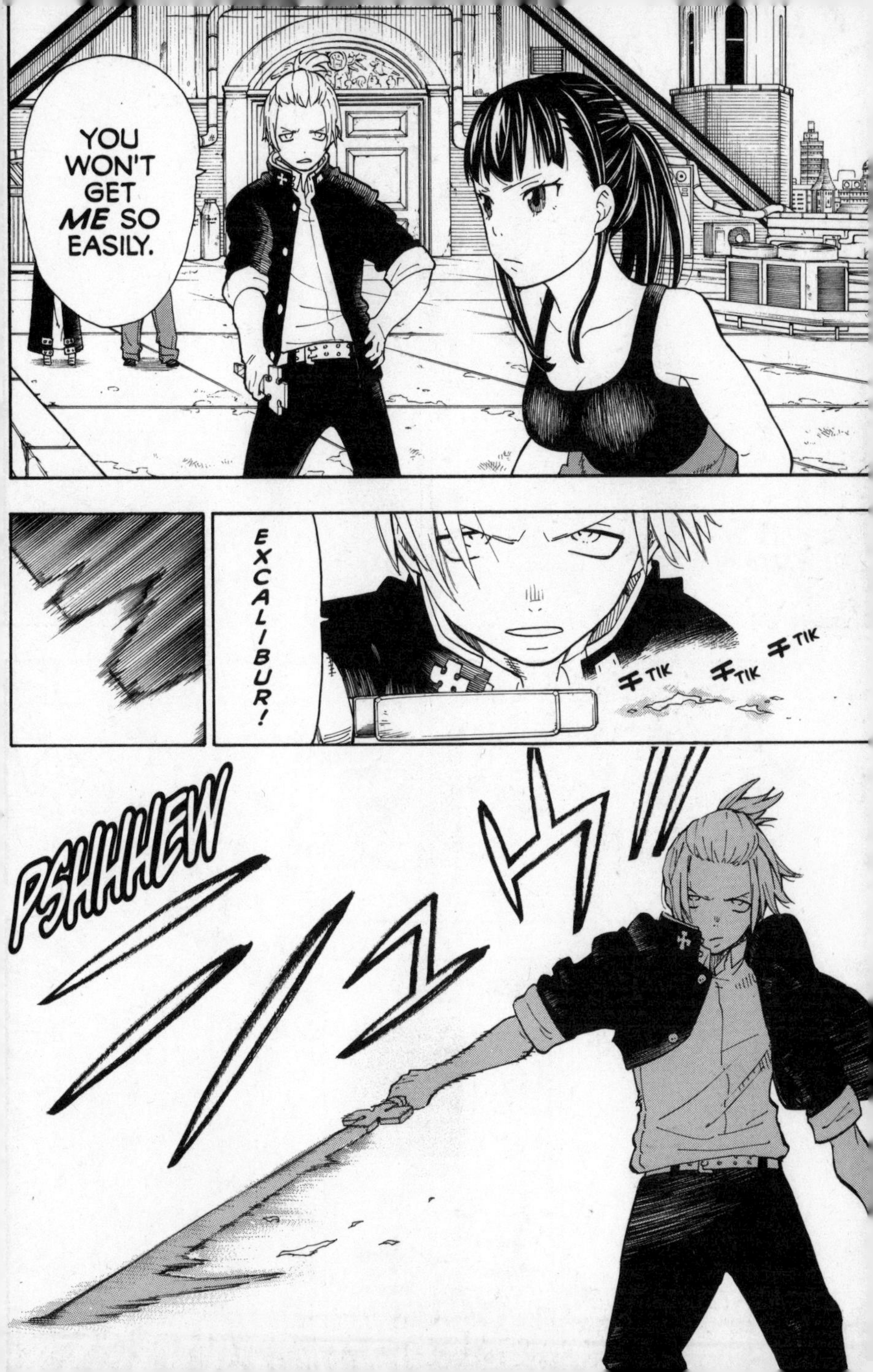
YOU WON'T GET *ME* SO EASILY.
EXCALIBUR!
TIK
TIK
TIK
PSHHEW

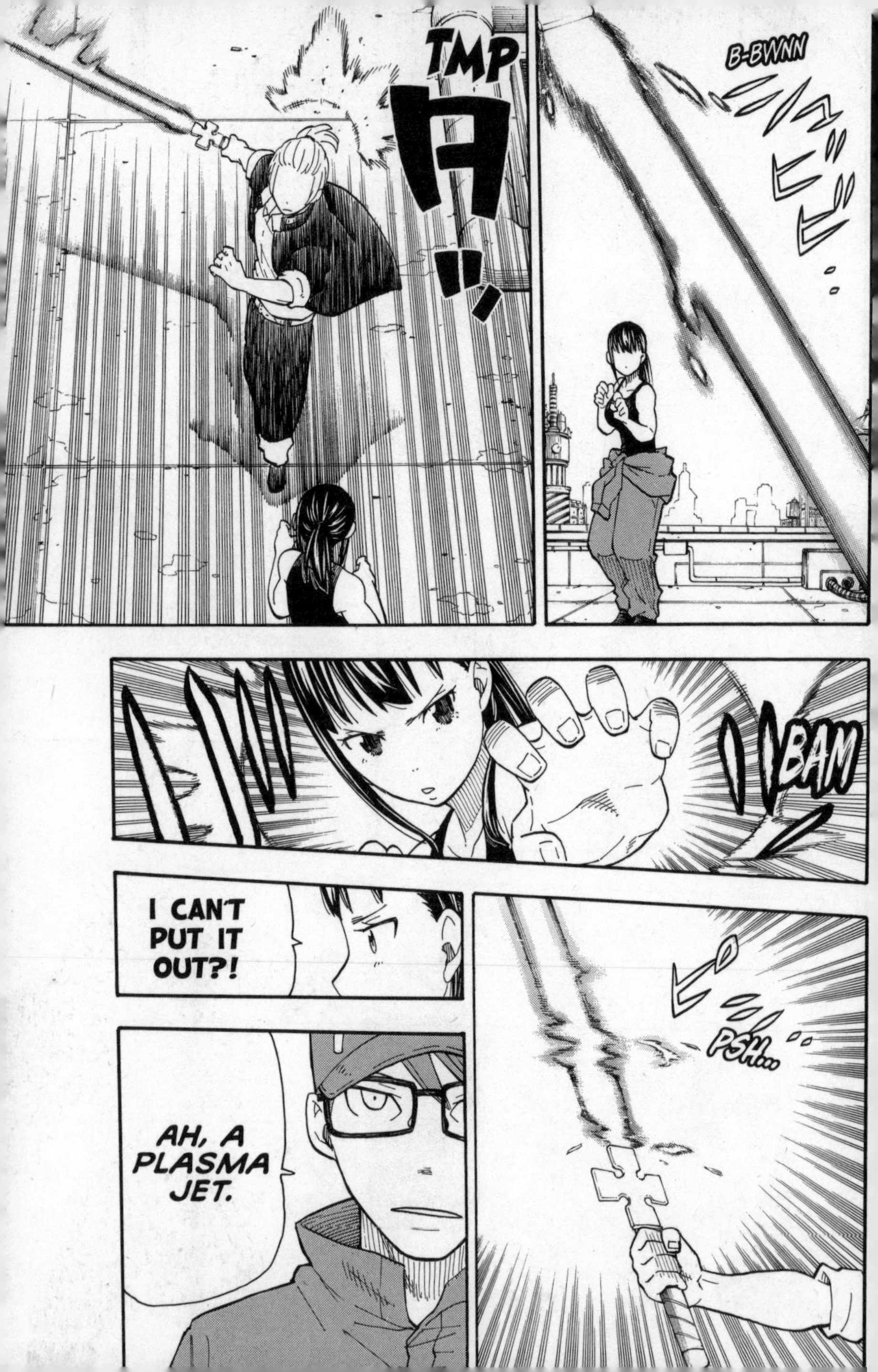
B-BWNN
TMP
BAM
PSH...
I CAN'T PUT IT OUT?!
AH, A PLASMA JET.

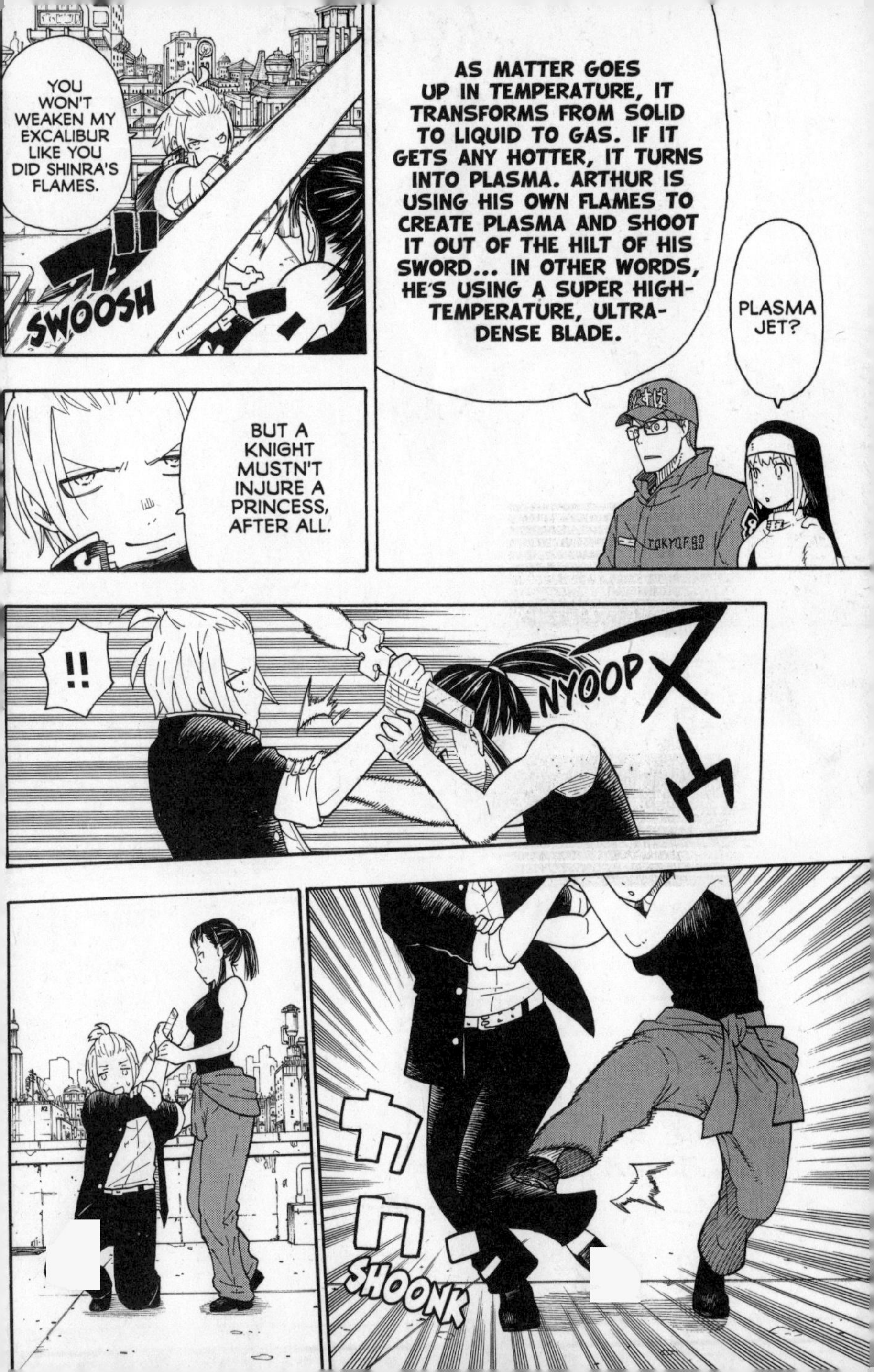
PLASMA JET?
AS MATTER GOES UP IN TEMPERATURE, IT TRANSFORMS FROM SOLID TO LIQUID TO GAS. IF IT GETS ANY HOTTER, IT TURNS INTO PLASMA. ARTHUR IS USING HIS OWN FLAMES TO CREATE PLASMA AND SHOOT IT OUT OF THE HILT OF HIS SWORD... IN OTHER WORDS, HE'S USING A SUPER HIGH-TEMPERATURE, ULTRA-DENSE BLADE.
YOU WON'T WEAKEN MY EXCALIBUR LIKE YOU DID SHINRA'S FLAMES.
SWOOSH
BUT A KNIGHT MUSTN'T INJURE A PRINCESS, AFTER ALL.
NYOOP
!!
SHOONK

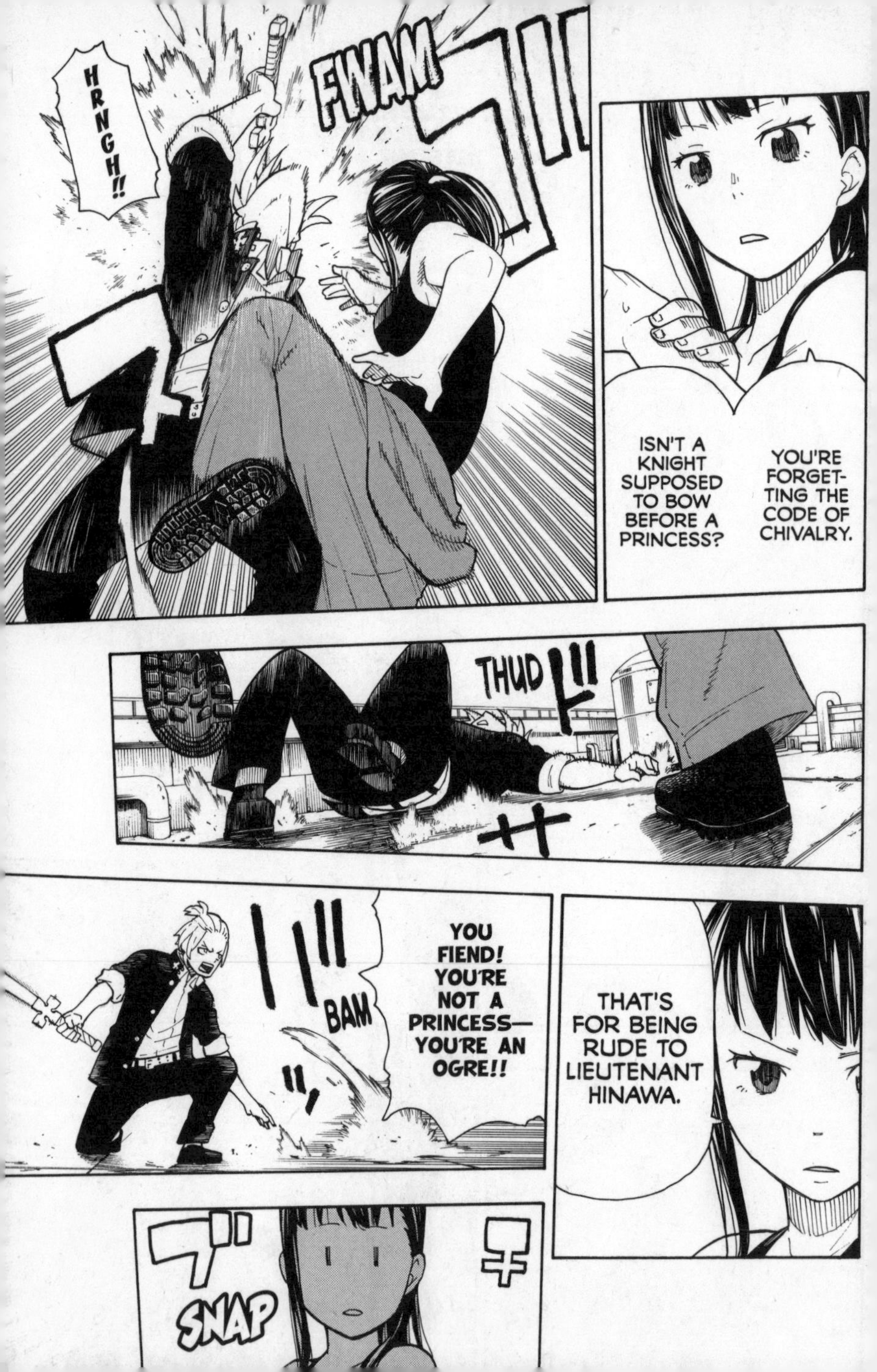
YOU'RE FORGETTING THE CODE OF CHIVALRY.
ISN'T A KNIGHT SUPPOSED TO BOW BEFORE A PRINCESS?
FWAM
HRNGH!!
THUD
THAT'S FOR BEING RUDE TO LIEUTENANT HINAWA.
YOU FIEND! YOU'RE NOT A PRINCESS—YOU'RE AN OGRE!!
BAM
SNAP

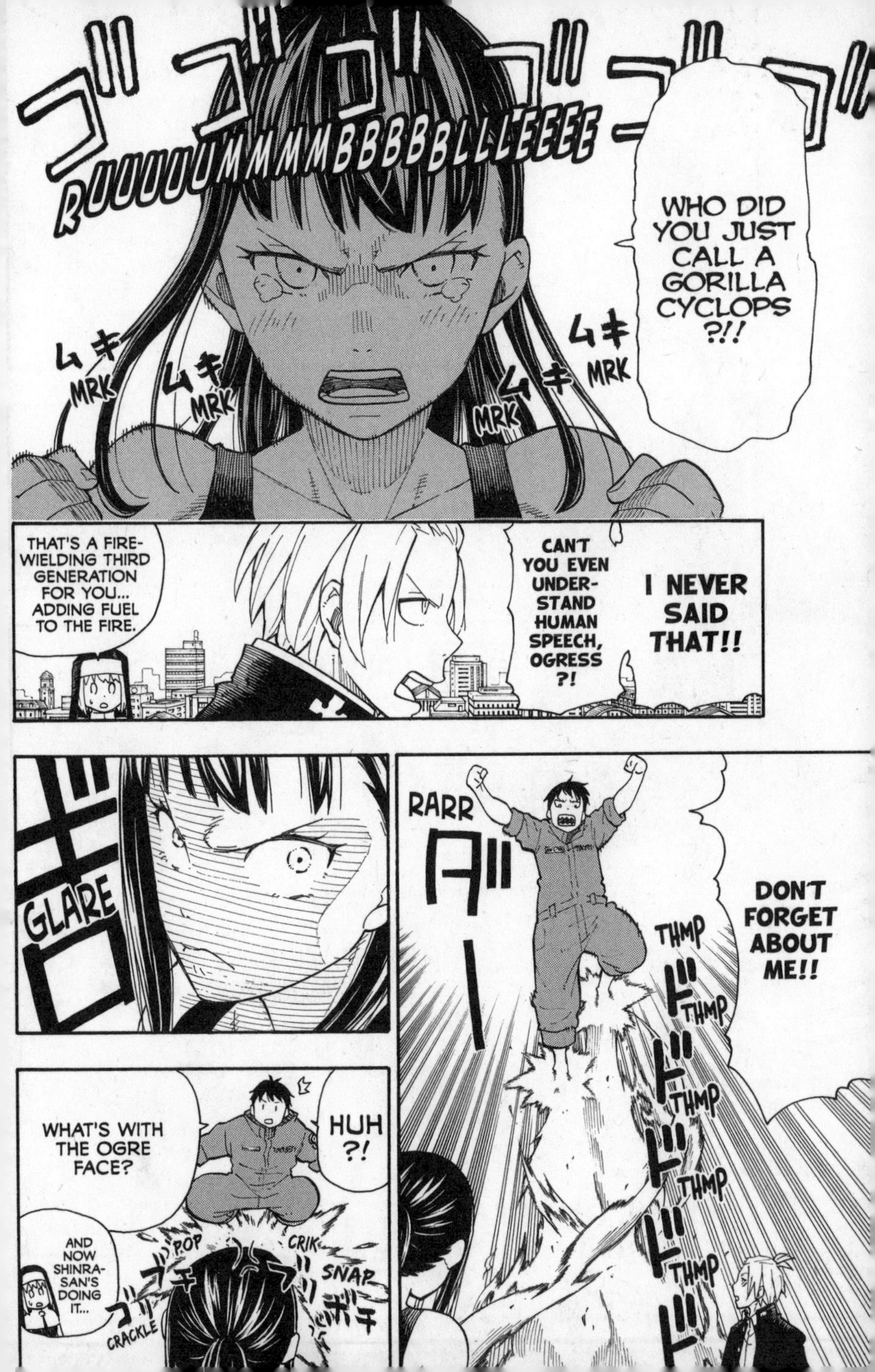
RUUUUUMMMMMBBBBBLLLEEEE
WHO DID YOU JUST CALL A GORILLA CYCLOPS ?!!
ムキ MRK
ムキ MRK
ムキ MRK
ムキ MRK
I NEVER SAID THAT!!
CAN'T YOU EVEN UNDER-STAND HUMAN SPEECH, OGRESS ?!
THAT'S A FIRE-WIELDING THIRD GENERATION FOR YOU... ADDING FUEL TO THE FIRE.
DON'T FORGET ABOUT ME!!
RARR
ダー
THMP
THMP
THMP
THMP
THMP
ギロ
GLARE
HUH ?!
WHAT'S WITH THE OGRE FACE?
AND NOW SHINRA-SAN'S DOING IT...
POP
CRIK
SNAP
CRACKLE

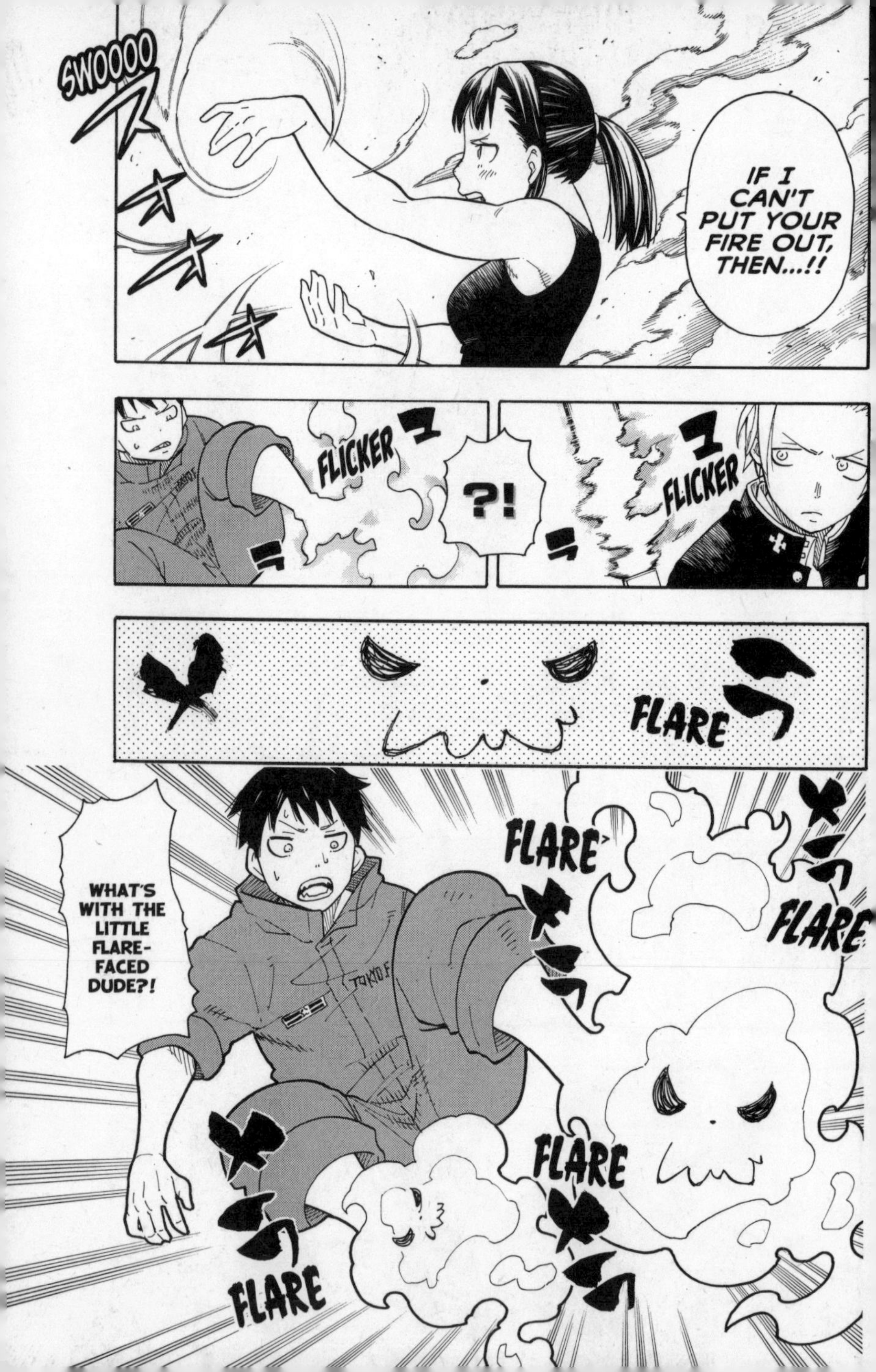
IF I CAN'T PUT YOUR FIRE OUT, THEN...!!
SWOOOO
FLICKER
?!
FLICKER
FLARE
FLARE
FLARE
WHAT'S WITH THE LITTLE FLARE-FACED DUDE?!
FLARE
FLARE

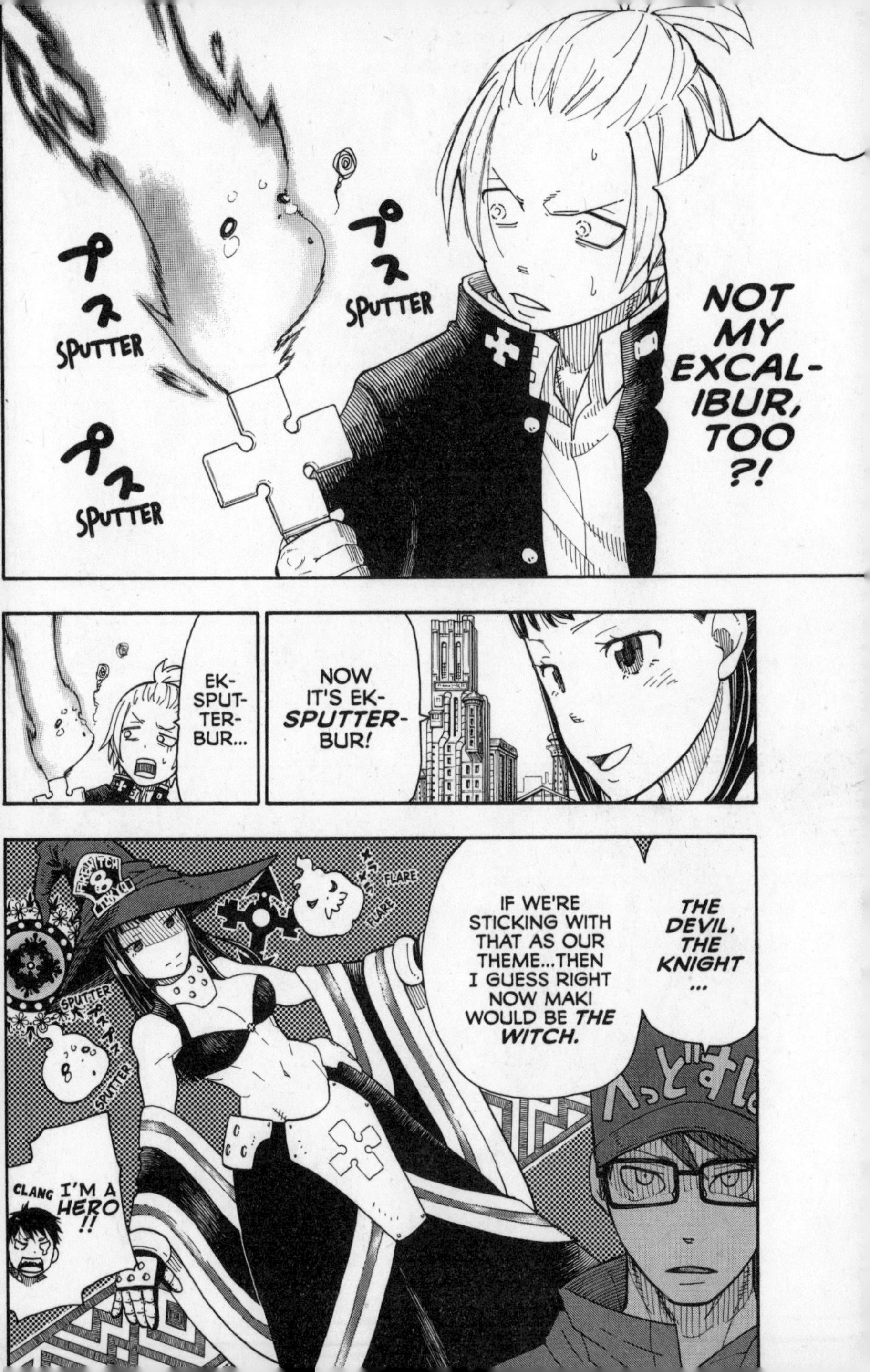

NOT MY EXCAL-IBUR, TOO?!
SPUTTER
SPUTTER
SPUTTER
NOW IT'S EK-SPUTTER-BUR!
EK-SPUT-TER-BUR...
THE DEVIL, THE KNIGHT...
IF WE'RE STICKING WITH THAT AS OUR THEME...THEN I GUESS RIGHT NOW MAKI WOULD BE THE WITCH.
FLARE
FLARE
SPUTTER
SPUTTER
CLANG
I'M A HERO!!

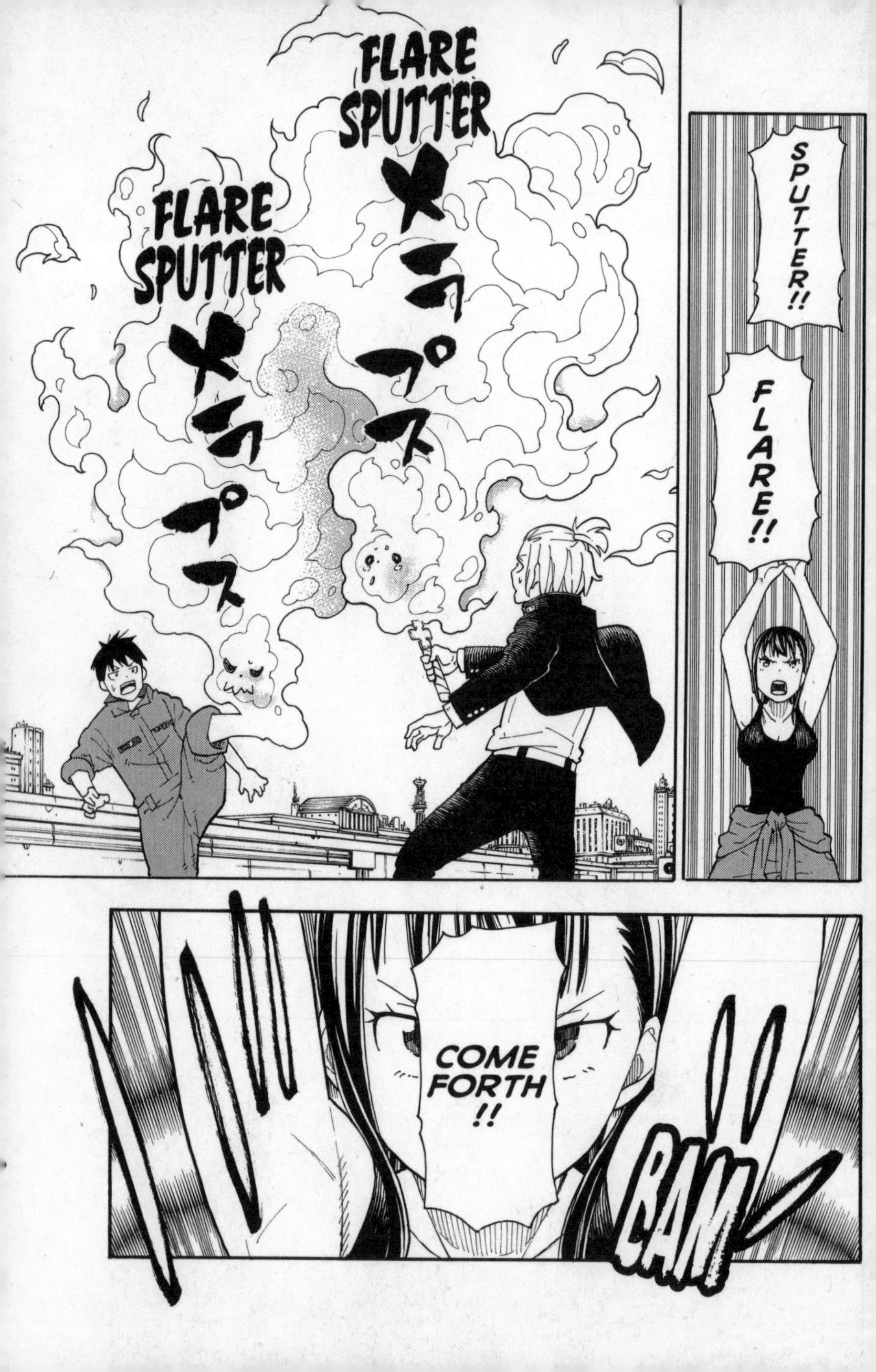
SPUTTER!!
FLARE!!
FLARE SPUTTER
メラプス
FLARE SPUTTER
メラプス
COME FORTH!!
BAM

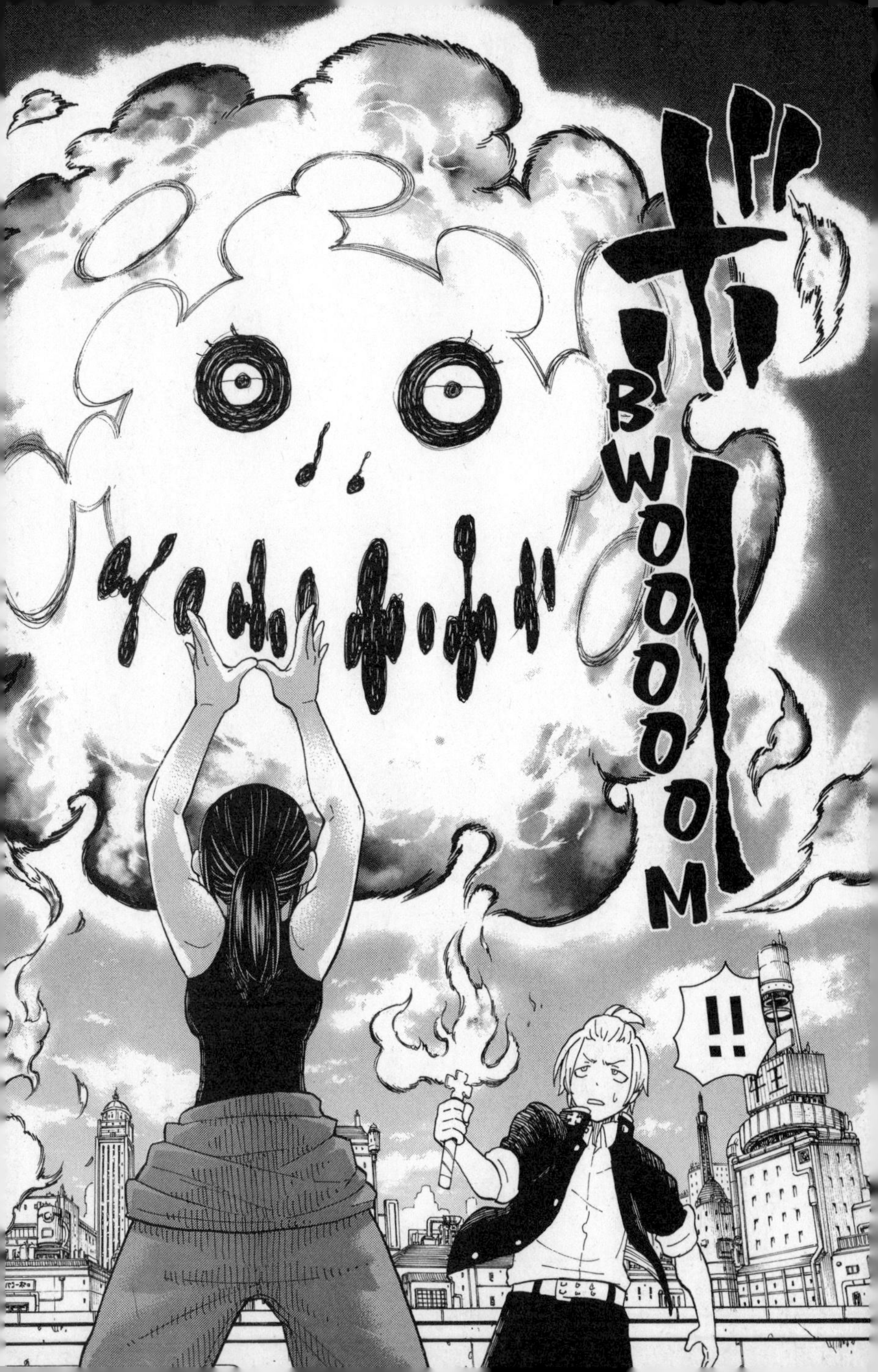

BWOOOOOOM
!!

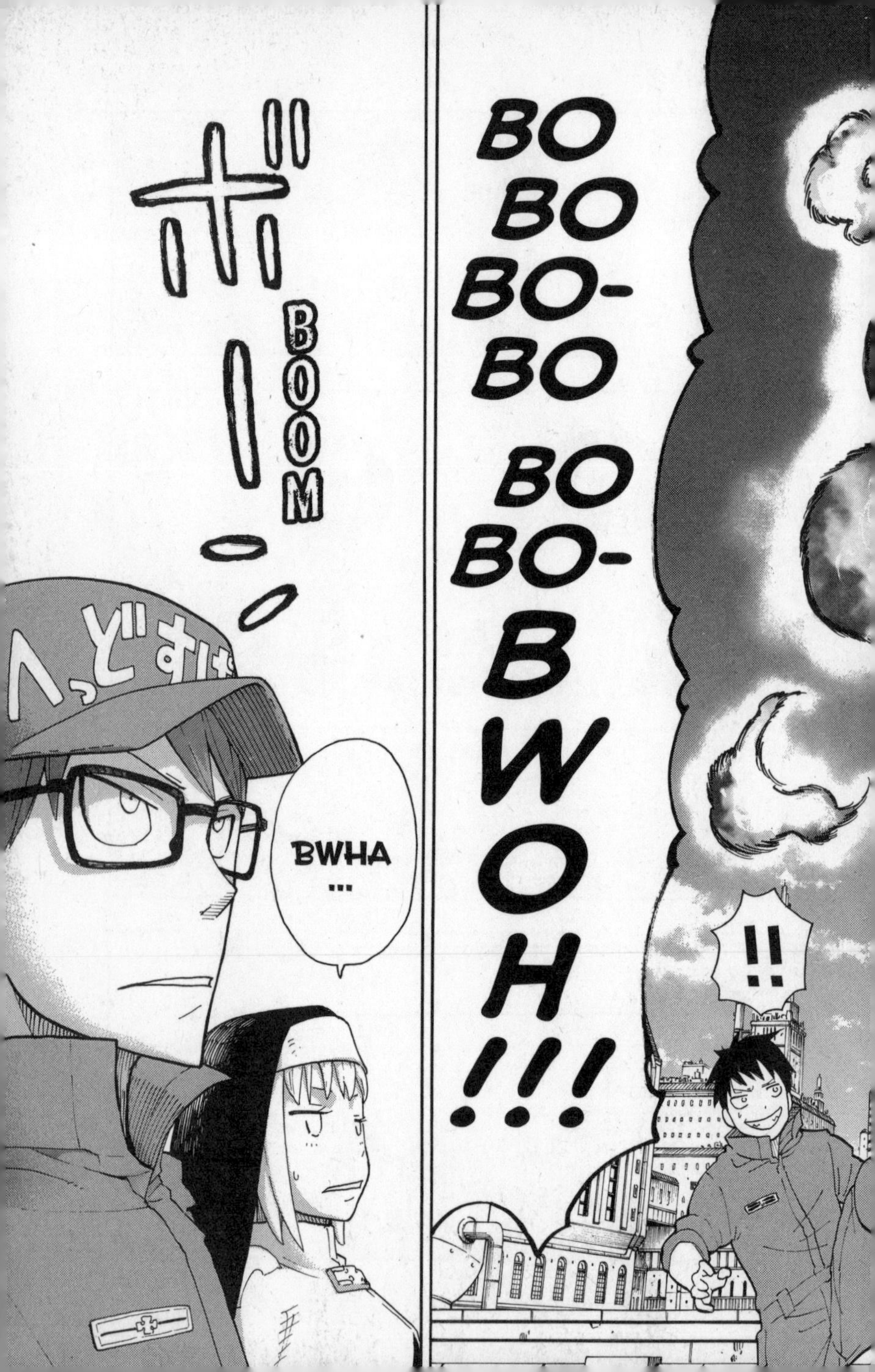
BO BO BO-BO BO BO-BWOOH!!!
!!
BOOM
BWHA ...

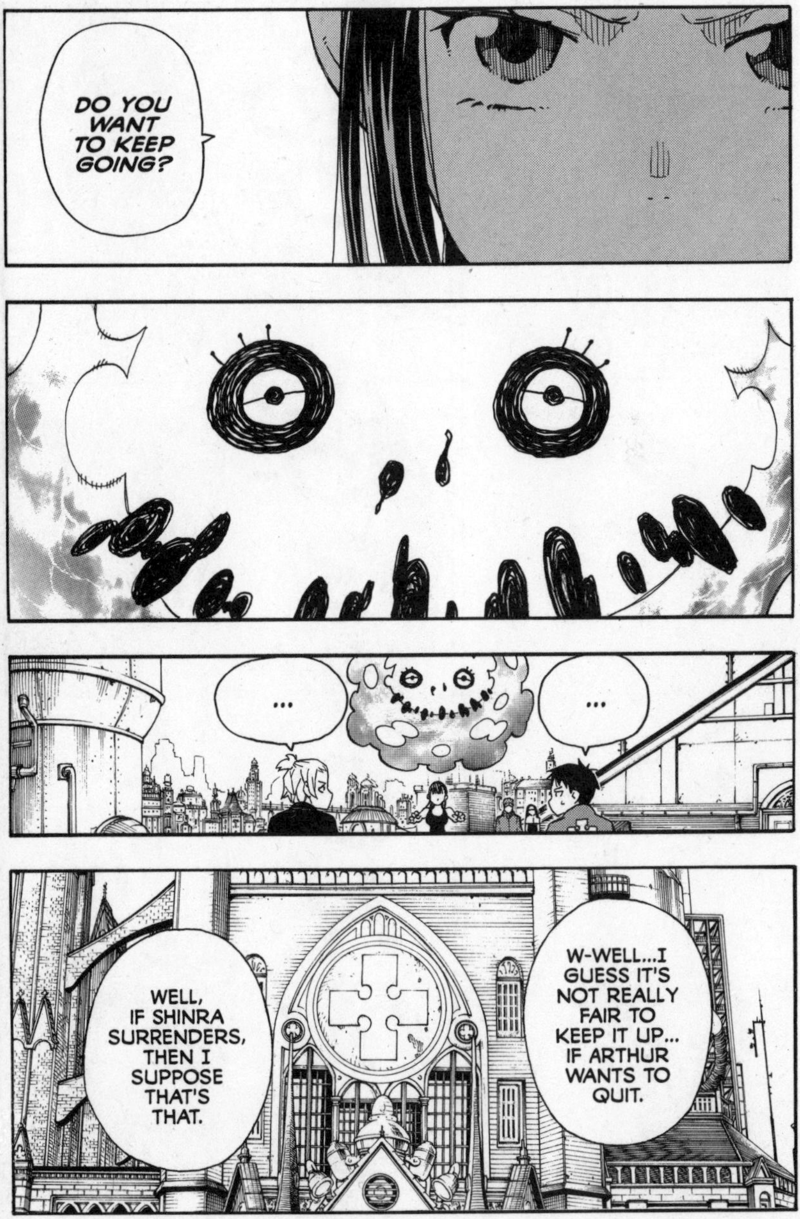
DO YOU WANT TO KEEP GOING?
...
...
W-WELL...I GUESS IT'S NOT REALLY FAIR TO KEEP IT UP... IF ARTHUR WANTS TO QUIT.
WELL, IF SHINRA SURRENDERS, THEN I SUPPOSE THAT'S THAT.

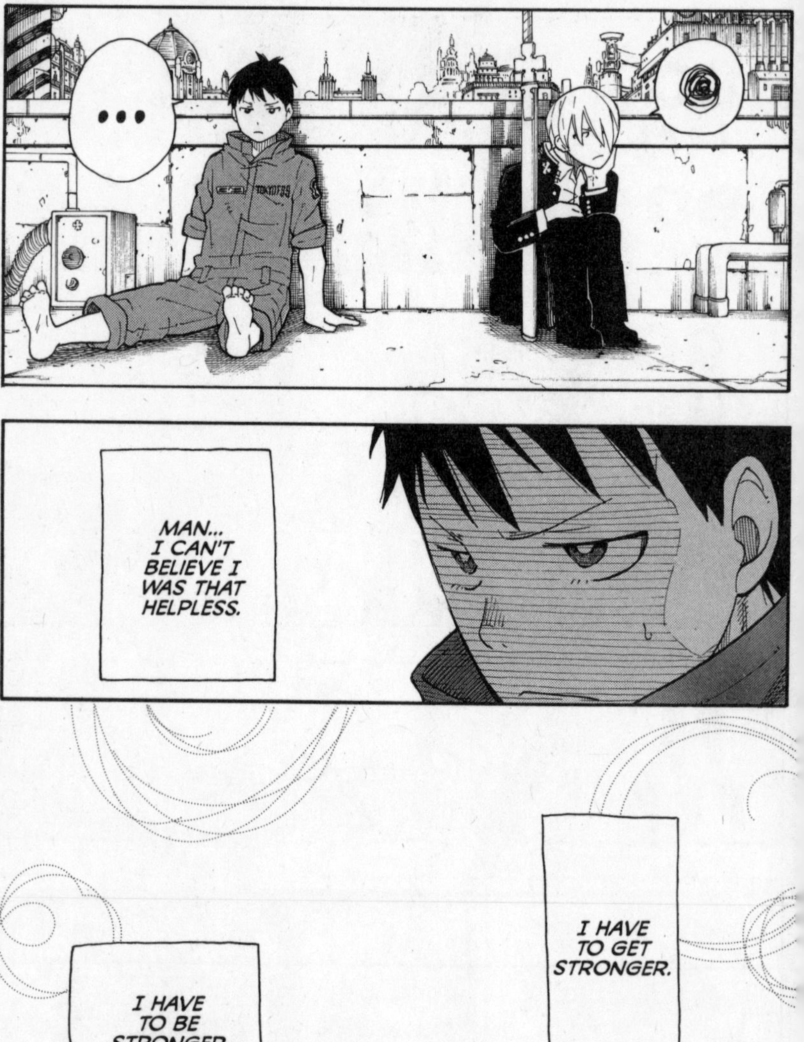
...
MAN... I CAN'T BELIEVE I WAS THAT HELPLESS.
I HAVE TO GET STRONGER.
I HAVE TO BE STRONGER THAN ANY-ONE, IF I WANT TO BE A HERO THAT CAN PROTECT EVERYONE!!

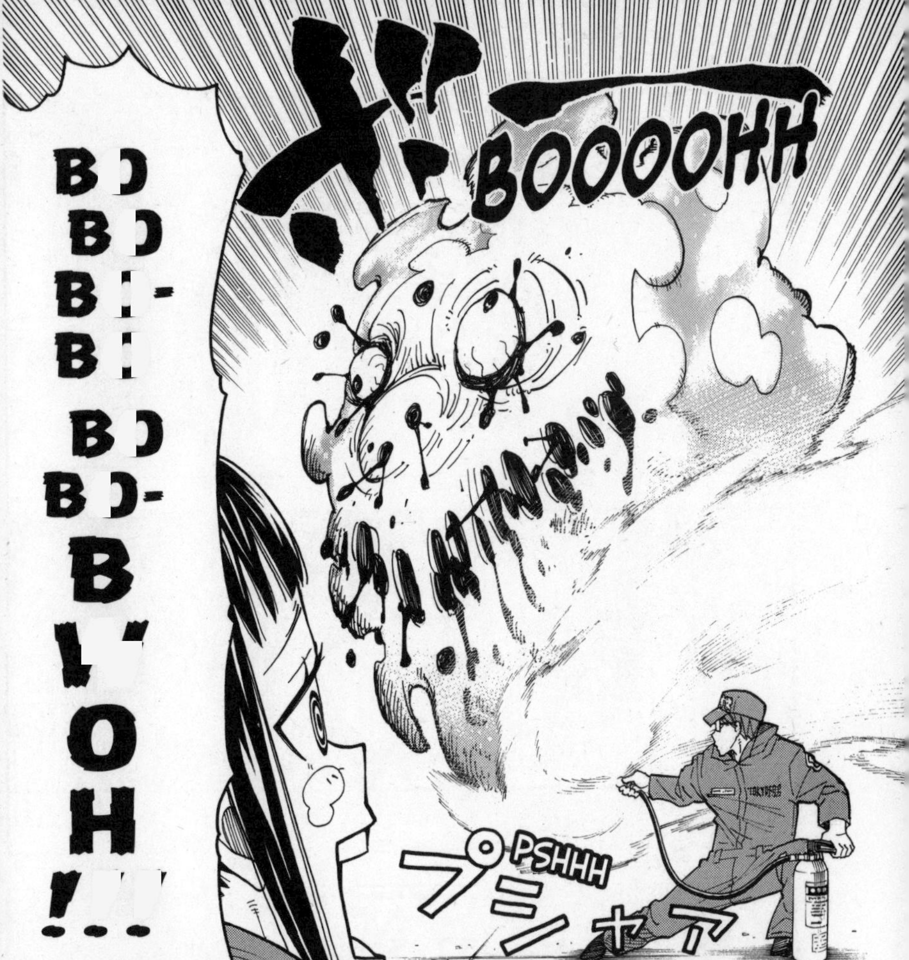
BOOOOHH
PSHHH
プシャア
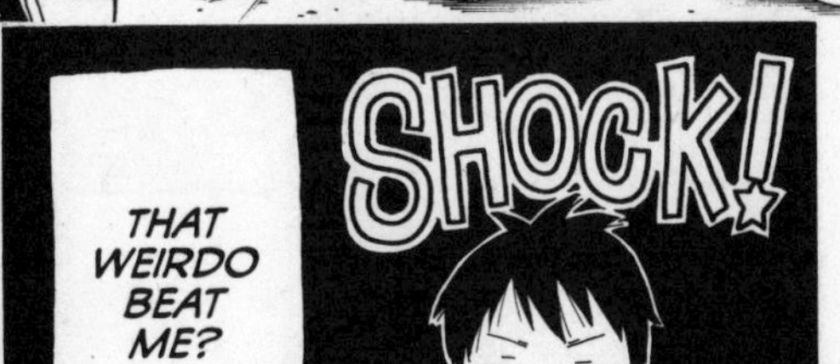
SHOCK!
THAT WEIRDO BEAT ME?
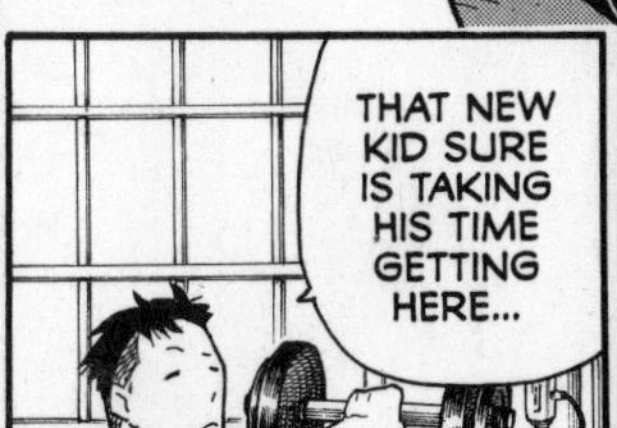
THAT NEW KID SURE IS TAKING HIS TIME GETTING HERE...

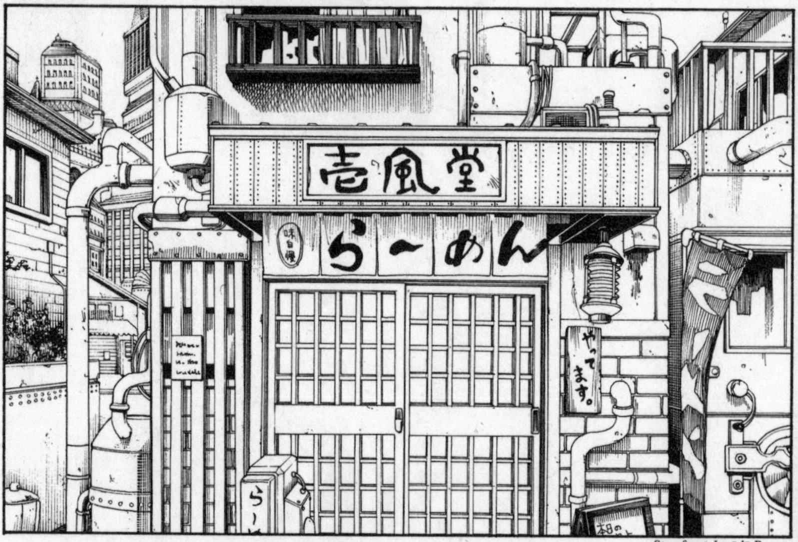
壱風堂
らーめん
やってます。

Storefront: Ippūdō Ramen

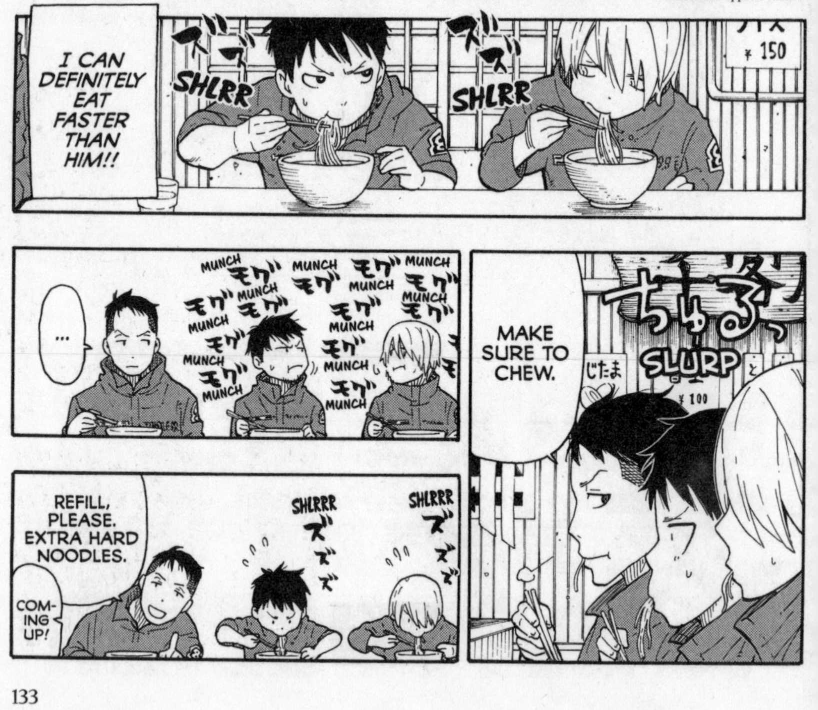
¥150
SHLRR
SHLRR
I CAN DEFINITELY EAT FASTER THAN HIM!!
SLURP
MAKE SURE TO CHEW.
¥100
MUNCH
MUNCH
MUNCH
MUNCH
MUNCH
MUNCH
MUNCH
MUNCH
MUNCH
MUNCH
MUNCH
...
SHLRRR
SHLRRR
REFILL, PLEASE. EXTRA HARD NOODLES.
COMING UP!

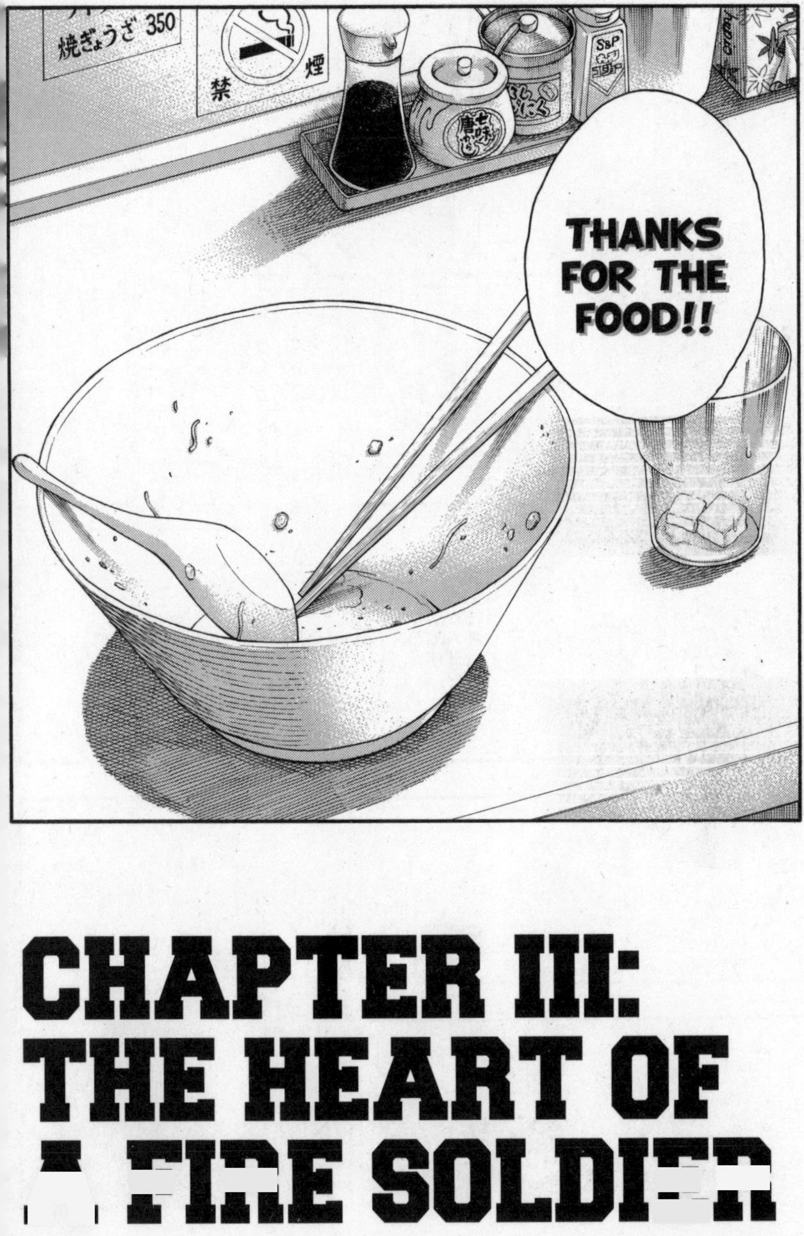
焼ぎょうざ 350
禁 煙
S&P
THANKS FOR THE FOOD!!

CHAPTER III: THE HEART OF A FIRE SOLDIER

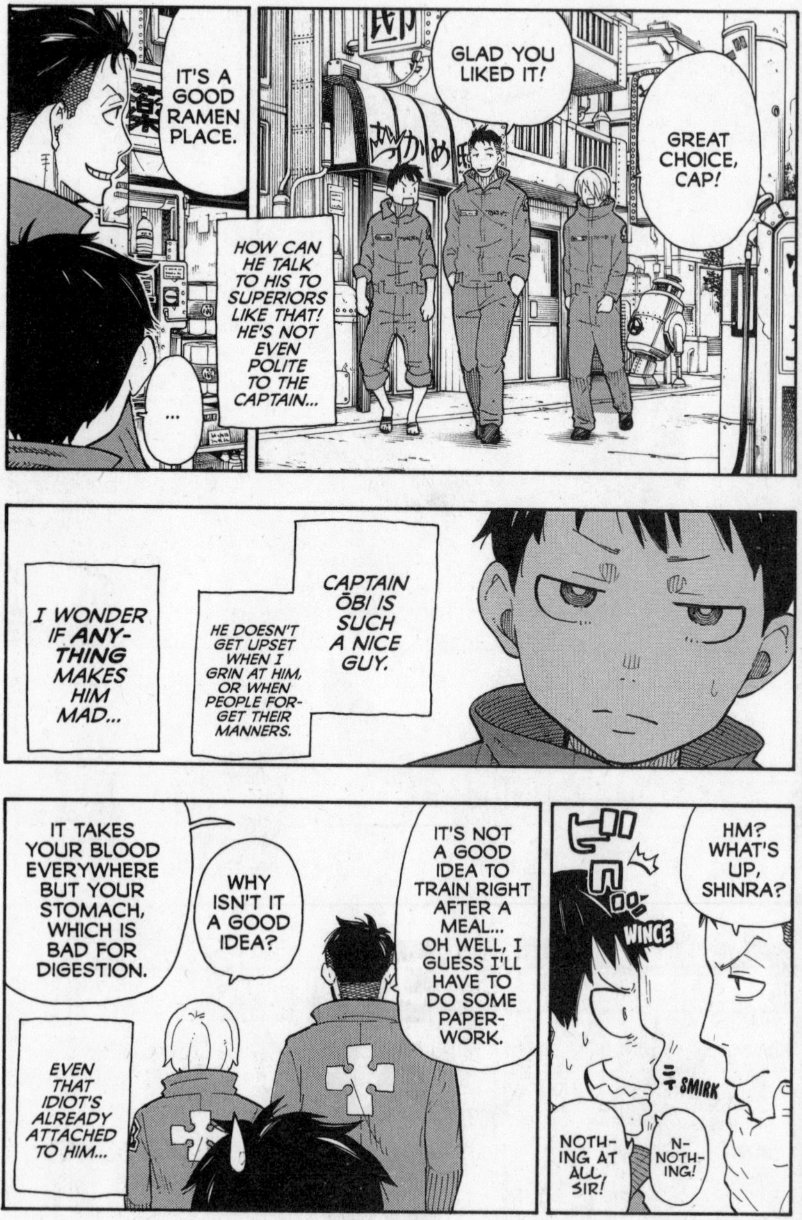
GREAT CHOICE, CAP!
GLAD YOU LIKED IT!
HOW CAN HE TALK TO HIS TO SUPERIORS LIKE THAT! HE'S NOT EVEN POLITE TO THE CAPTAIN...
IT'S A GOOD RAMEN PLACE.
...
CAPTAIN ŌBI IS SUCH A NICE GUY.
HE DOESN'T GET UPSET WHEN I GRIN AT HIM, OR WHEN PEOPLE FORGET THEIR MANNERS.
I WONDER IF ANYTHING MAKES HIM MAD...
HM? WHAT'S UP, SHINRA?
WINCE
SMIRK
N-NOTHING!
NOTHING AT ALL, SIR!
IT'S NOT A GOOD IDEA TO TRAIN RIGHT AFTER A MEAL... OH WELL, I GUESS I'LL HAVE TO DO SOME PAPERWORK.
WHY ISN'T IT A GOOD IDEA?
IT TAKES YOUR BLOOD EVERYWHERE BUT YOUR STOMACH, WHICH IS BAD FOR DIGESTION.
EVEN THAT IDIOT'S ALREADY ATTACHED TO HIM...

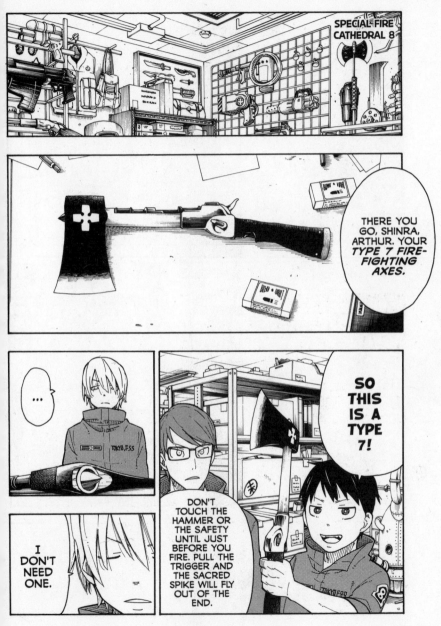

SPECIAL FIRE CATHEDRAL 8
THERE YOU GO, SHINRA, ARTHUR. YOUR *TYPE 7 FIRE-FIGHTING AXES.*
SO THIS IS A TYPE 7!
DON'T TOUCH THE HAMMER OR THE SAFETY UNTIL JUST BEFORE YOU FIRE. PULL THE TRIGGER AND THE SACRED SPIKE WILL FLY OUT OF THE END.
...
I DON'T NEED ONE.

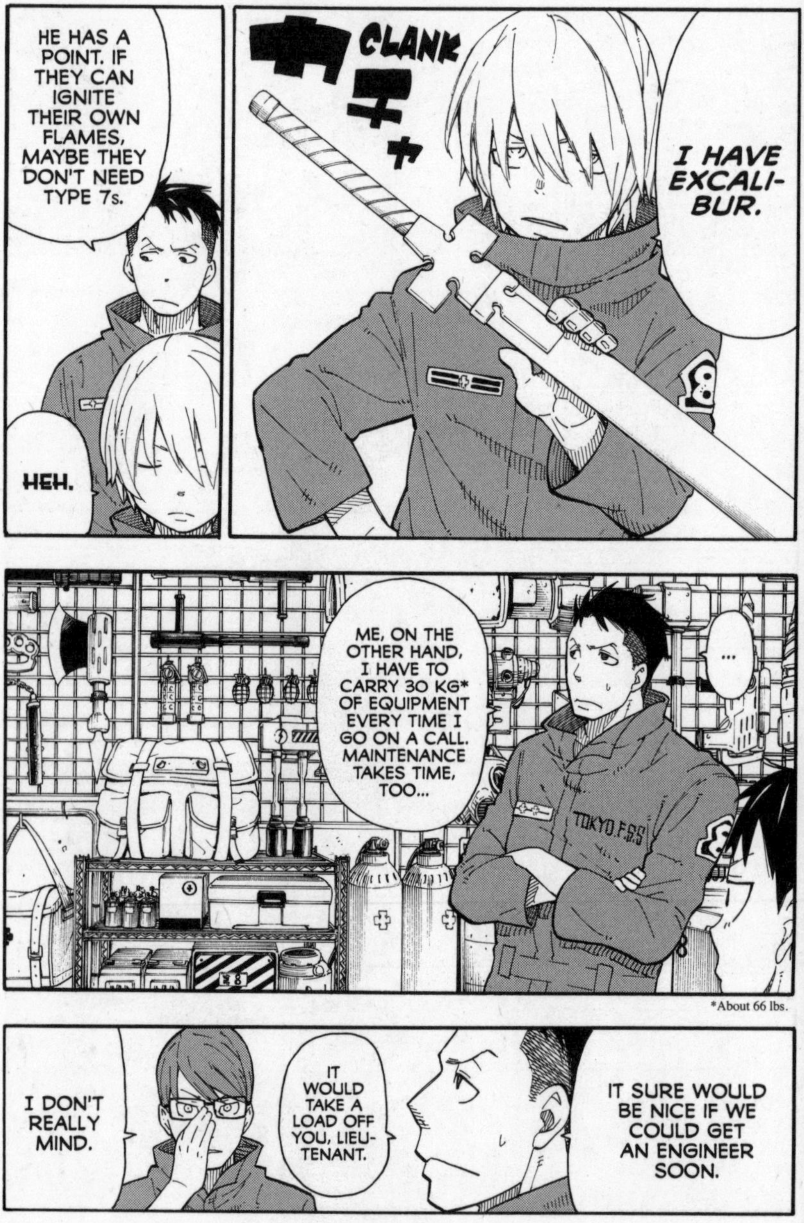
CLANK
I HAVE EXCALIBUR.
HE HAS A POINT. IF THEY CAN IGNITE THEIR OWN FLAMES, MAYBE THEY DON'T NEED TYPE 7s.
HEH.
ME, ON THE OTHER HAND, I HAVE TO CARRY 30 KG* OF EQUIPMENT EVERY TIME I GO ON A CALL. MAINTENANCE TAKES TIME, TOO...
...
IT SURE WOULD BE NICE IF WE COULD GET AN ENGINEER SOON.
IT WOULD TAKE A LOAD OFF YOU, LIEUTENANT.
I DON'T REALLY MIND.

*About 66 lbs.

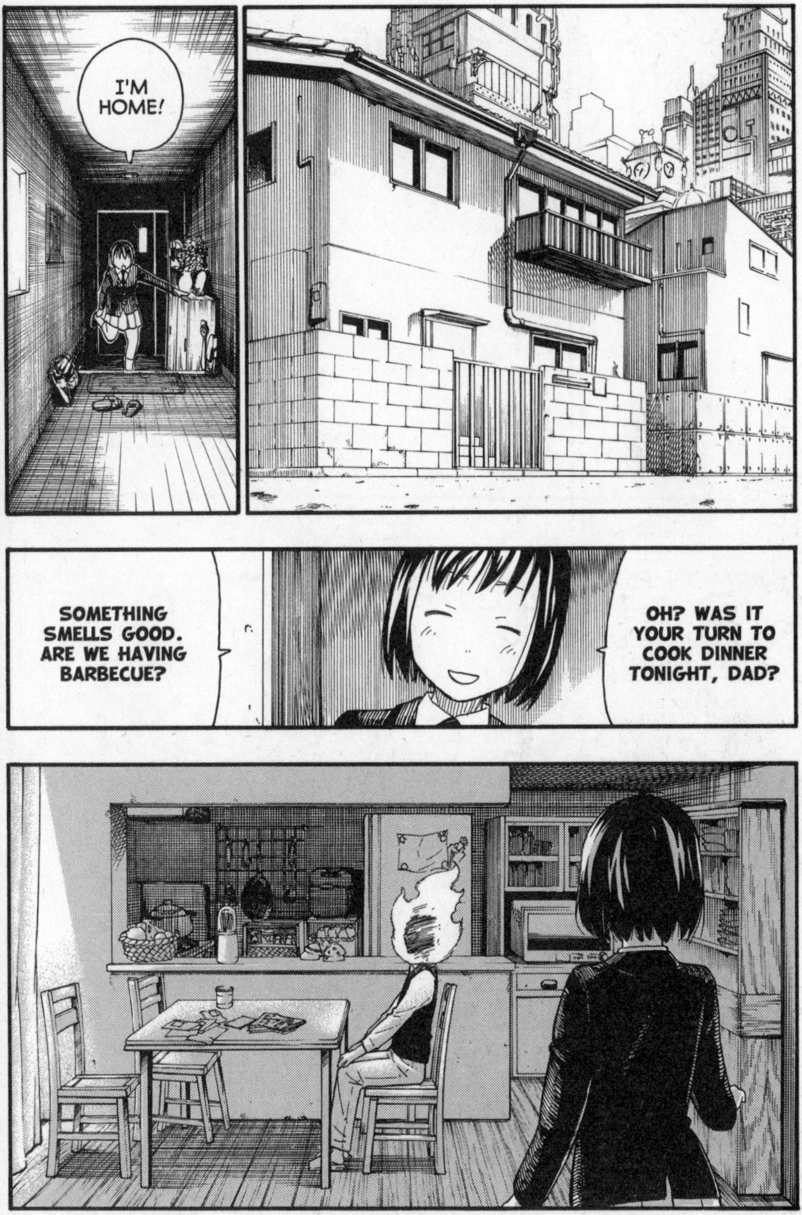
I'M HOME!
OH? WAS IT YOUR TURN TO COOK DINNER TONIGHT, DAD?
SOMETHING SMELLS GOOD. ARE WE HAVING BARBECUE?

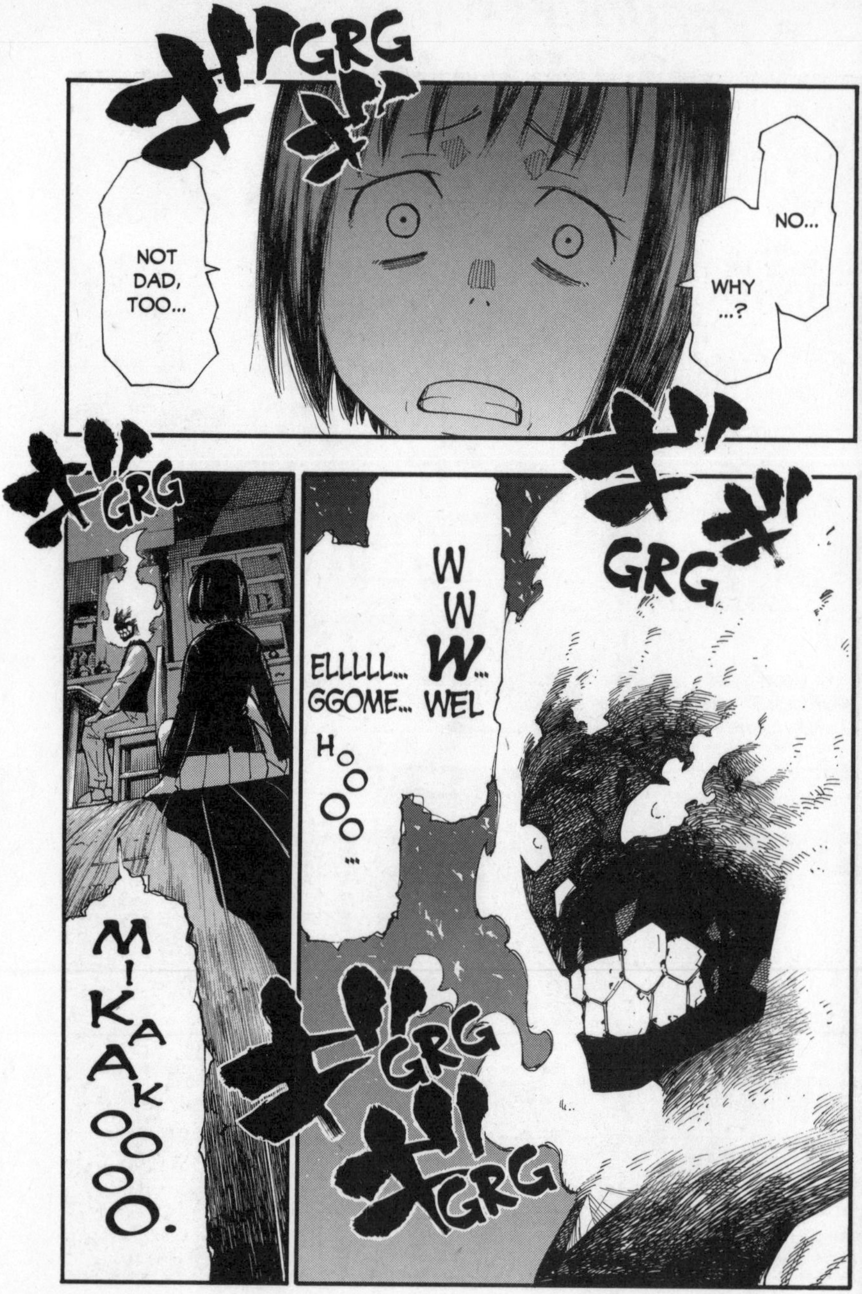
GRG
NO... WHY ...?
NOT DAD, TOO...
GRG
WWW...
WEL
ELLLLL...
GGOME...
HOOOO...
GRG
GRG
GRG
MIKAKOOOO.

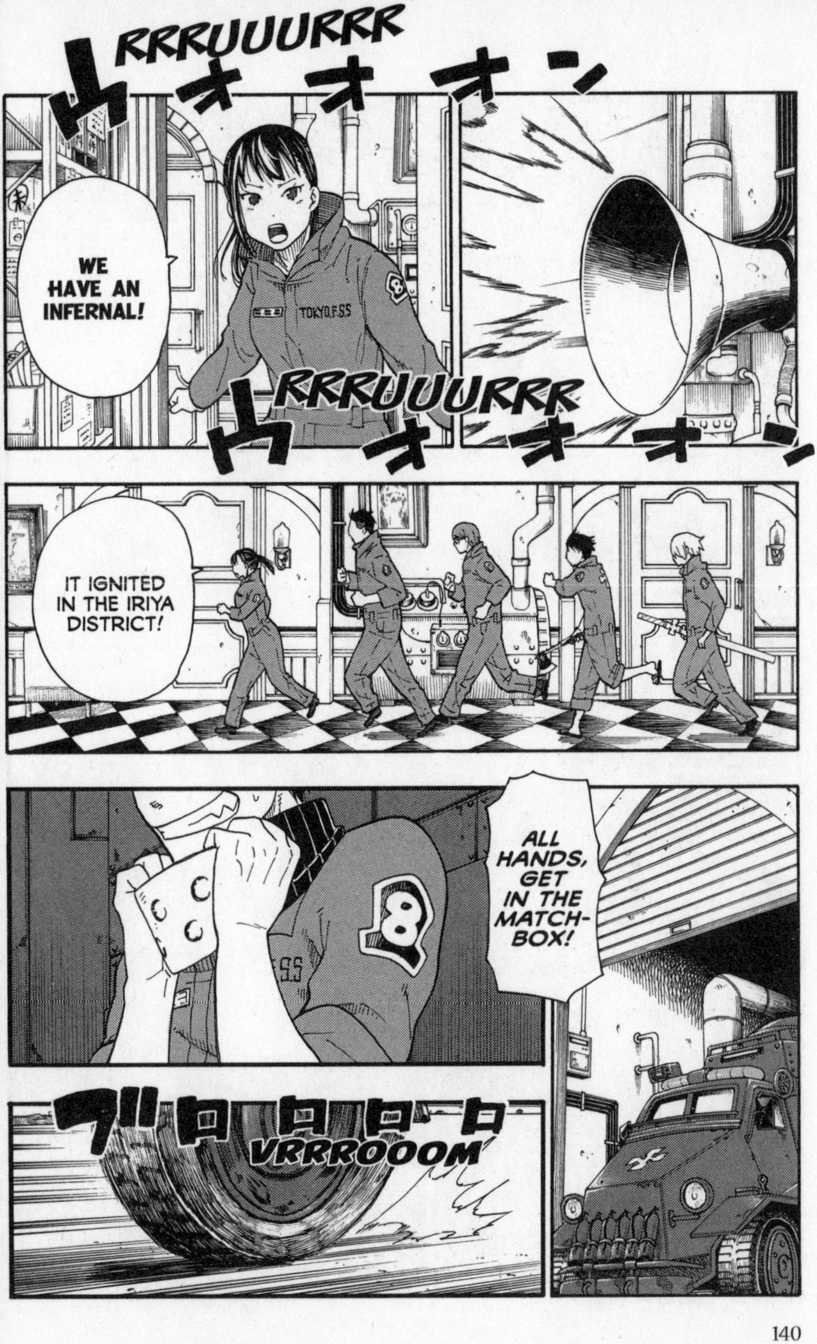
RRRUUURRR
RRRUUURRR
WE HAVE AN INFERNAL!
IT IGNITED IN THE IRIYA DISTRICT!
ALL HANDS, GET IN THE MATCH-BOX!
VRRROOOM

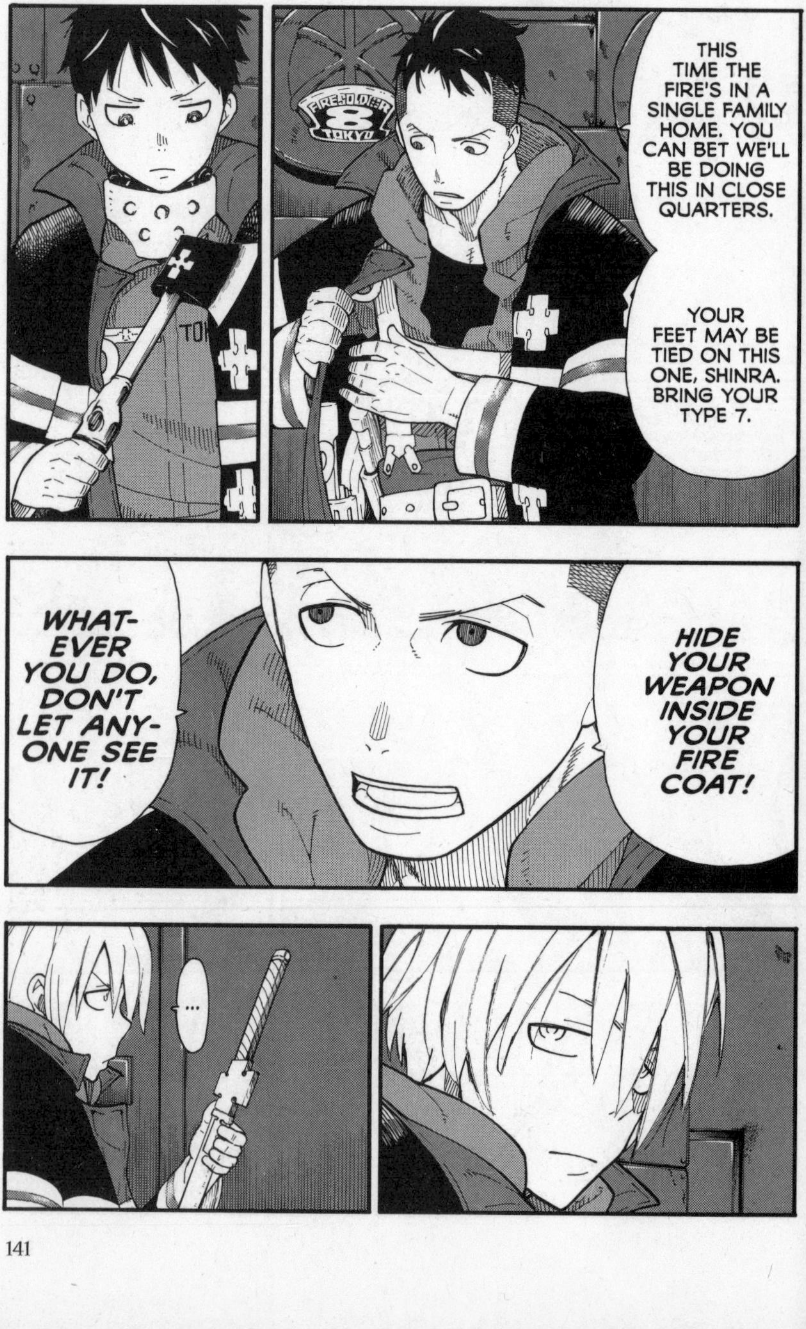
THIS TIME THE FIRE'S IN A SINGLE FAMILY HOME. YOU CAN BET WE'LL BE DOING THIS IN CLOSE QUARTERS.
YOUR FEET MAY BE TIED ON THIS ONE, SHINRA. BRING YOUR TYPE 7.
HIDE YOUR WEAPON INSIDE YOUR FIRE COAT!
WHAT-EVER YOU DO, DON'T LET ANY-ONE SEE IT!
—....

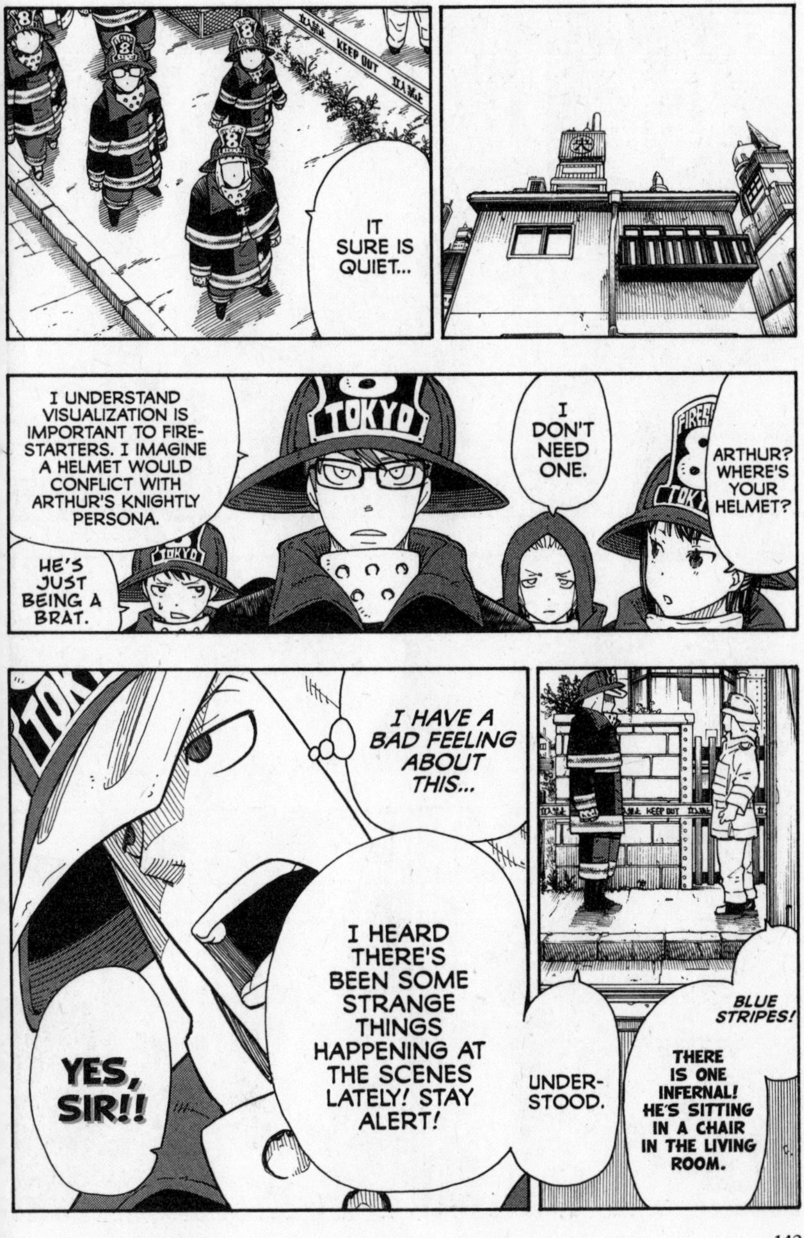
IT SURE IS QUIET...
ARTHUR? WHERE'S YOUR HELMET?
I DON'T NEED ONE.
I UNDERSTAND VISUALIZATION IS IMPORTANT TO FIRE-STARTERS. I IMAGINE A HELMET WOULD CONFLICT WITH ARTHUR'S KNIGHTLY PERSONA.
HE'S JUST BEING A BRAT.
BLUE STRIPES!
THERE IS ONE INFERNAL! HE'S SITTING IN A CHAIR IN THE LIVING ROOM.
UNDER-STOOD.
I HAVE A BAD FEELING ABOUT THIS...
I HEARD THERE'S BEEN SOME STRANGE THINGS HAPPENING AT THE SCENES LATELY! STAY ALERT!
YES, SIR!!

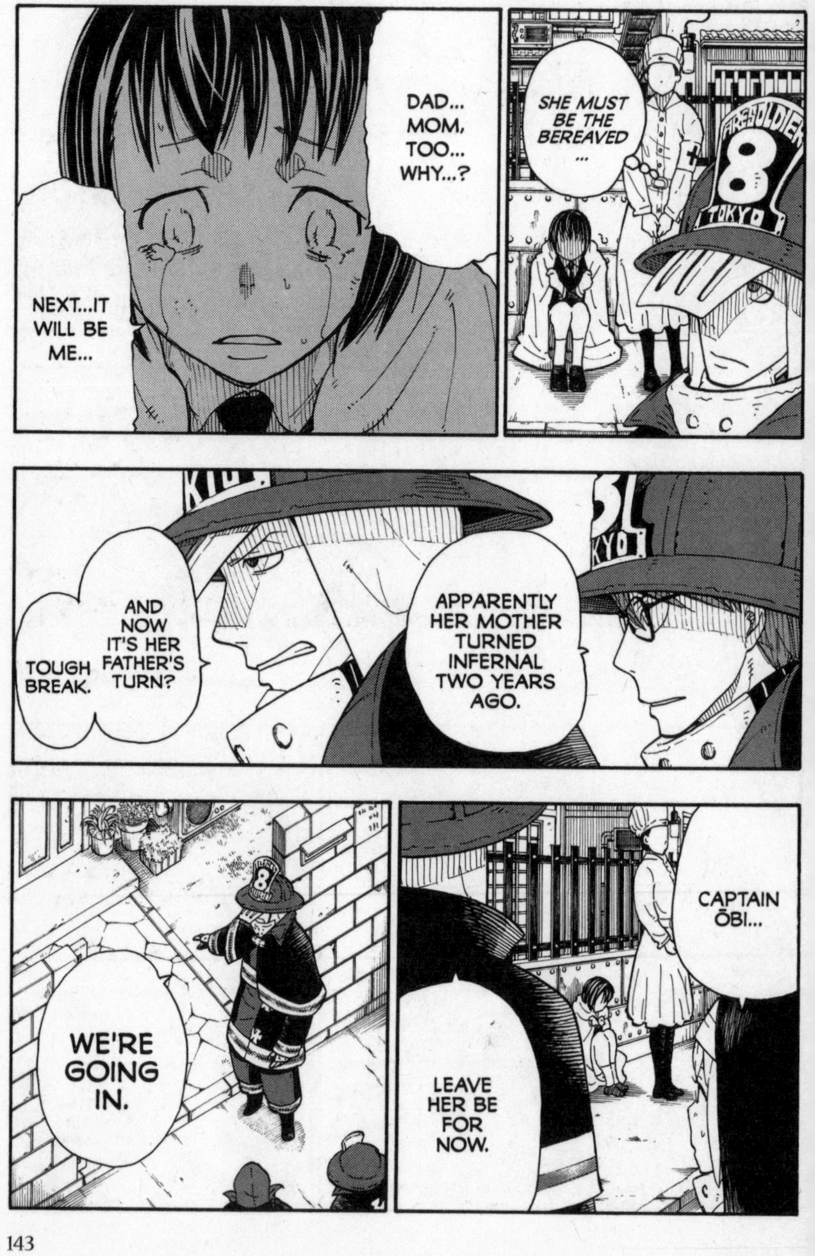
SHE MUST BE THE BEREAVED ...
DAD... MOM, TOO... WHY...?
NEXT...IT WILL BE ME...
APPARENTLY HER MOTHER TURNED INFERNAL TWO YEARS AGO.
AND NOW IT'S HER FATHER'S TURN?
TOUGH BREAK.
CAPTAIN ŌBI...
LEAVE HER BE FOR NOW.
WE'RE GOING IN.

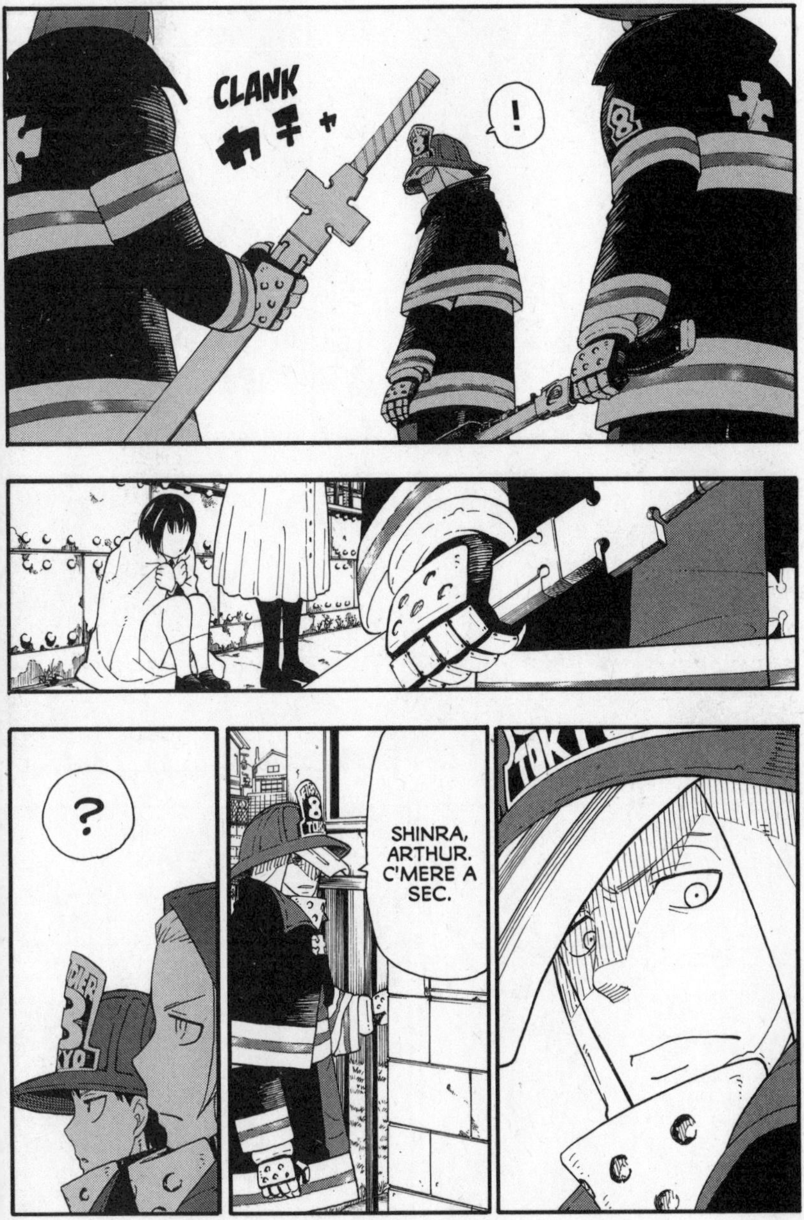
CLANK
カチャ
!
SHINRA, ARTHUR. C'MERE A SEC.
?

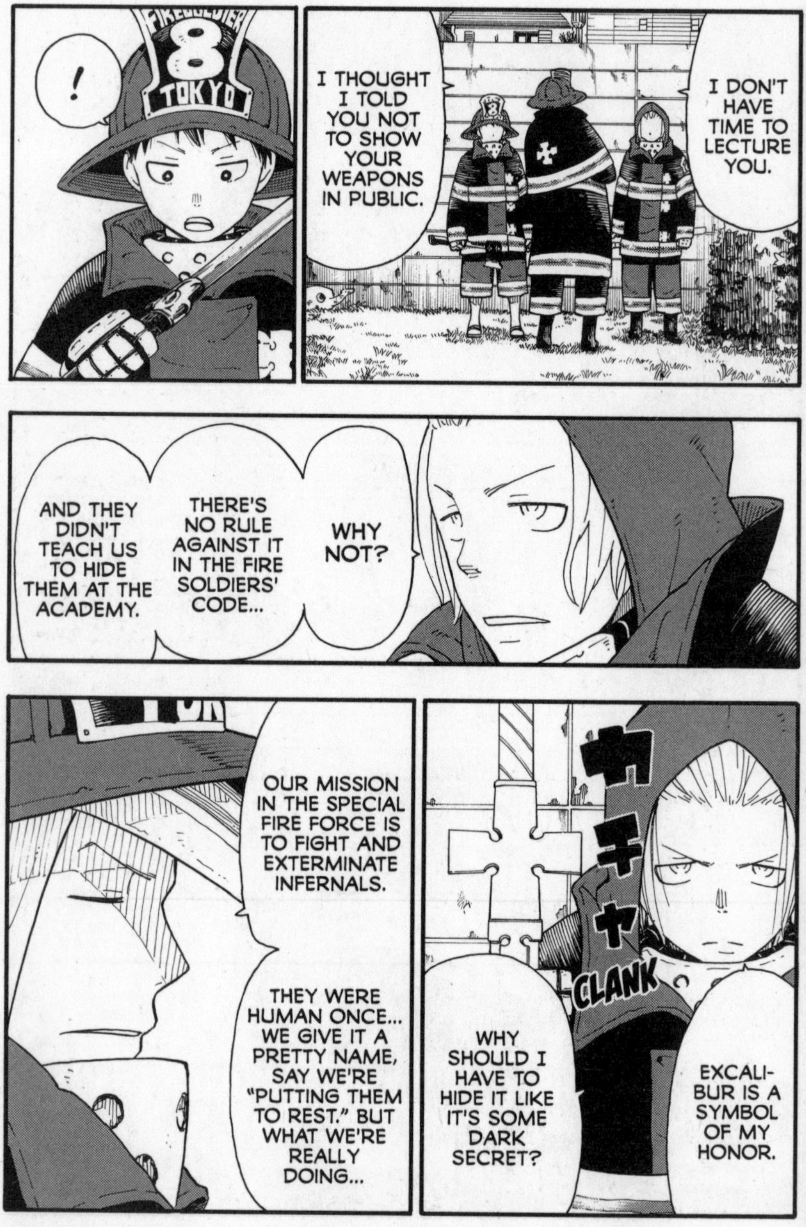
I DON'T HAVE TIME TO LECTURE YOU.
I THOUGHT I TOLD YOU NOT TO SHOW YOUR WEAPONS IN PUBLIC.
FIRE SOLDIER 8 TOKYO
!
WHY NOT?
THERE'S NO RULE AGAINST IT IN THE FIRE SOLDIERS' CODE...
AND THEY DIDN'T TEACH US TO HIDE THEM AT THE ACADEMY.
カチャ
CLANK
EXCALIBUR IS A SYMBOL OF MY HONOR.
WHY SHOULD I HAVE TO HIDE IT LIKE IT'S SOME DARK SECRET?
OUR MISSION IN THE SPECIAL FIRE FORCE IS TO FIGHT AND EXTERMINATE INFERNALS.
THEY WERE HUMAN ONCE... WE GIVE IT A PRETTY NAME, SAY WE'RE "PUTTING THEM TO REST." BUT WHAT WE'RE REALLY DOING...

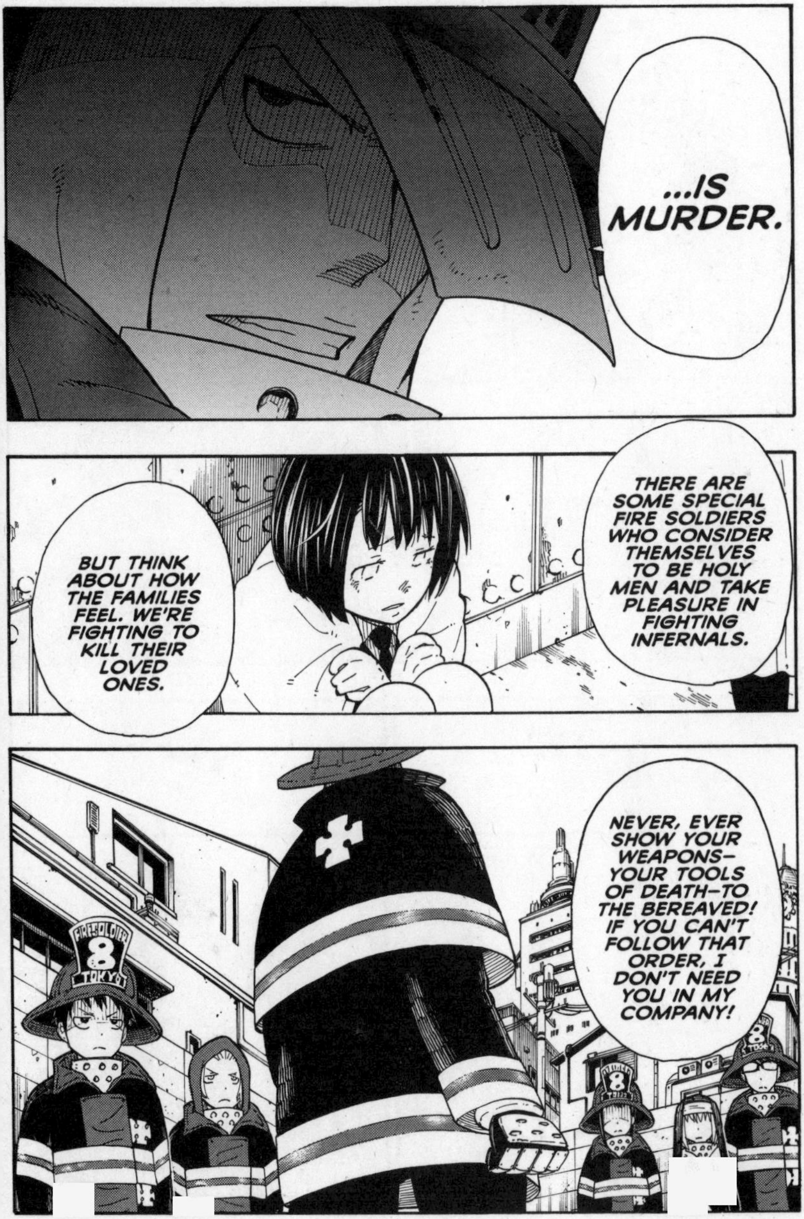
...IS MURDER.
THERE ARE SOME SPECIAL FIRE SOLDIERS WHO CONSIDER THEMSELVES TO BE HOLY MEN AND TAKE PLEASURE IN FIGHTING INFERNALS.
BUT THINK ABOUT HOW THE FAMILIES FEEL. WE'RE FIGHTING TO KILL THEIR LOVED ONES.
NEVER, EVER SHOW YOUR WEAPONS—YOUR TOOLS OF DEATH—TO THE BEREAVED! IF YOU CAN'T FOLLOW THAT ORDER, I DON'T NEED YOU IN MY COMPANY!

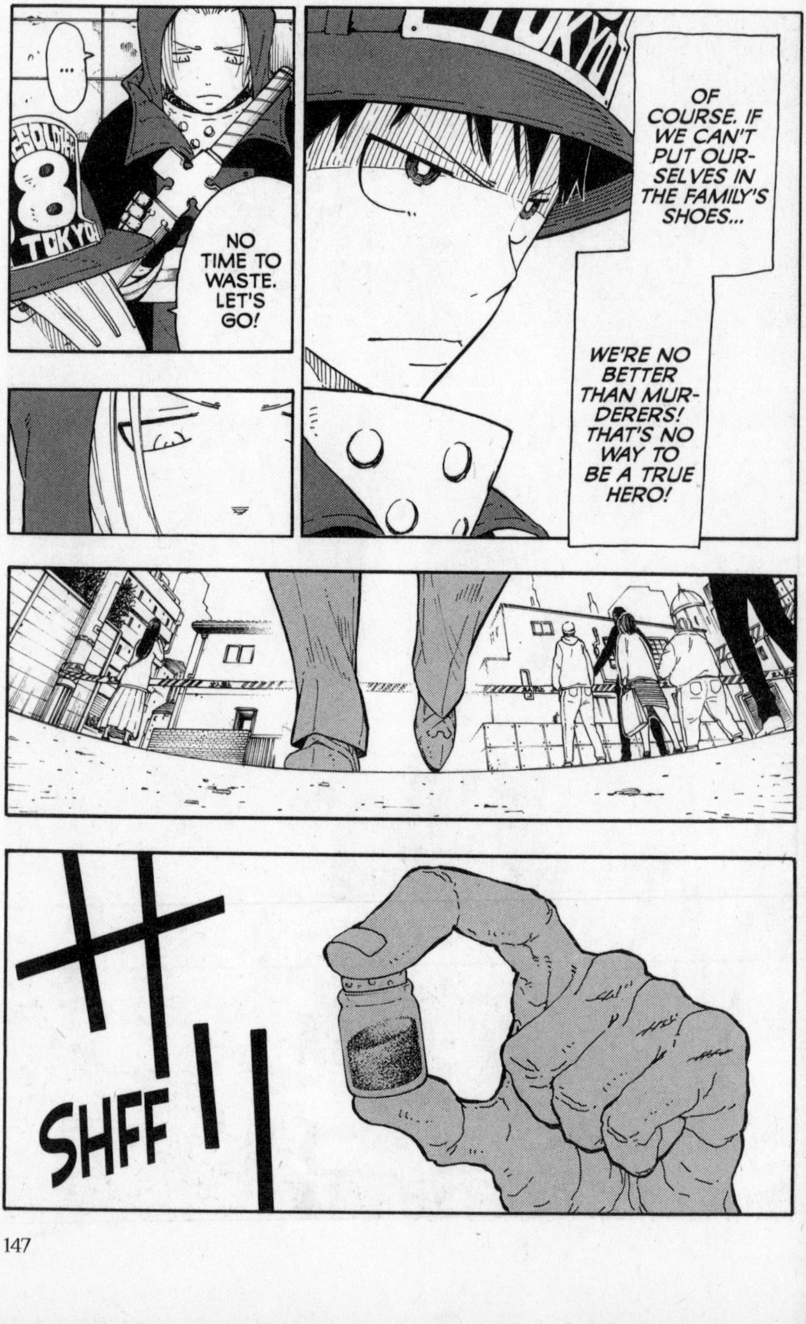
OF COURSE. IF WE CAN'T PUT OURSELVES IN THE FAMILY'S SHOES...
WE'RE NO BETTER THAN MURDERERS! THAT'S NO WAY TO BE A TRUE HERO!
...
NO TIME TO WASTE. LET'S GO!
SHFF

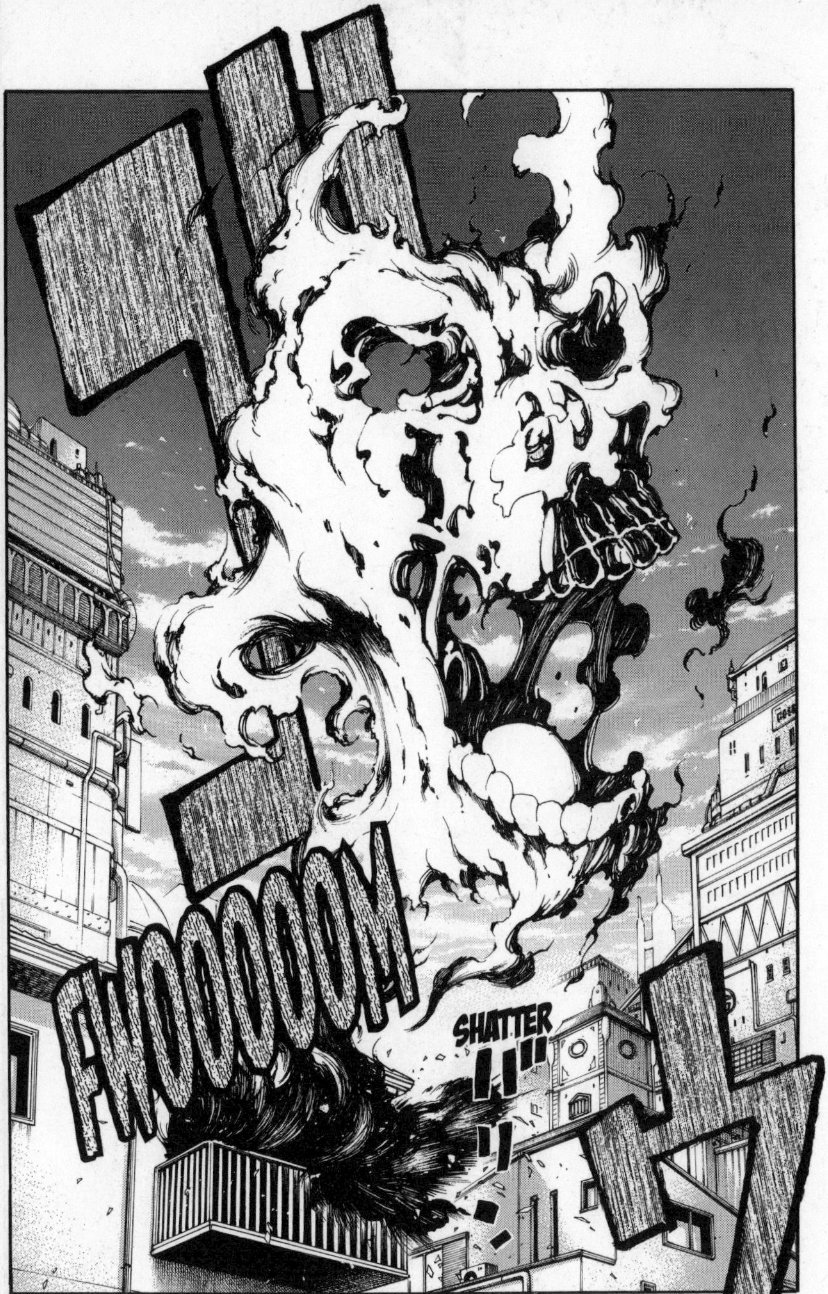
FWOOOOOM
SHATTER!!

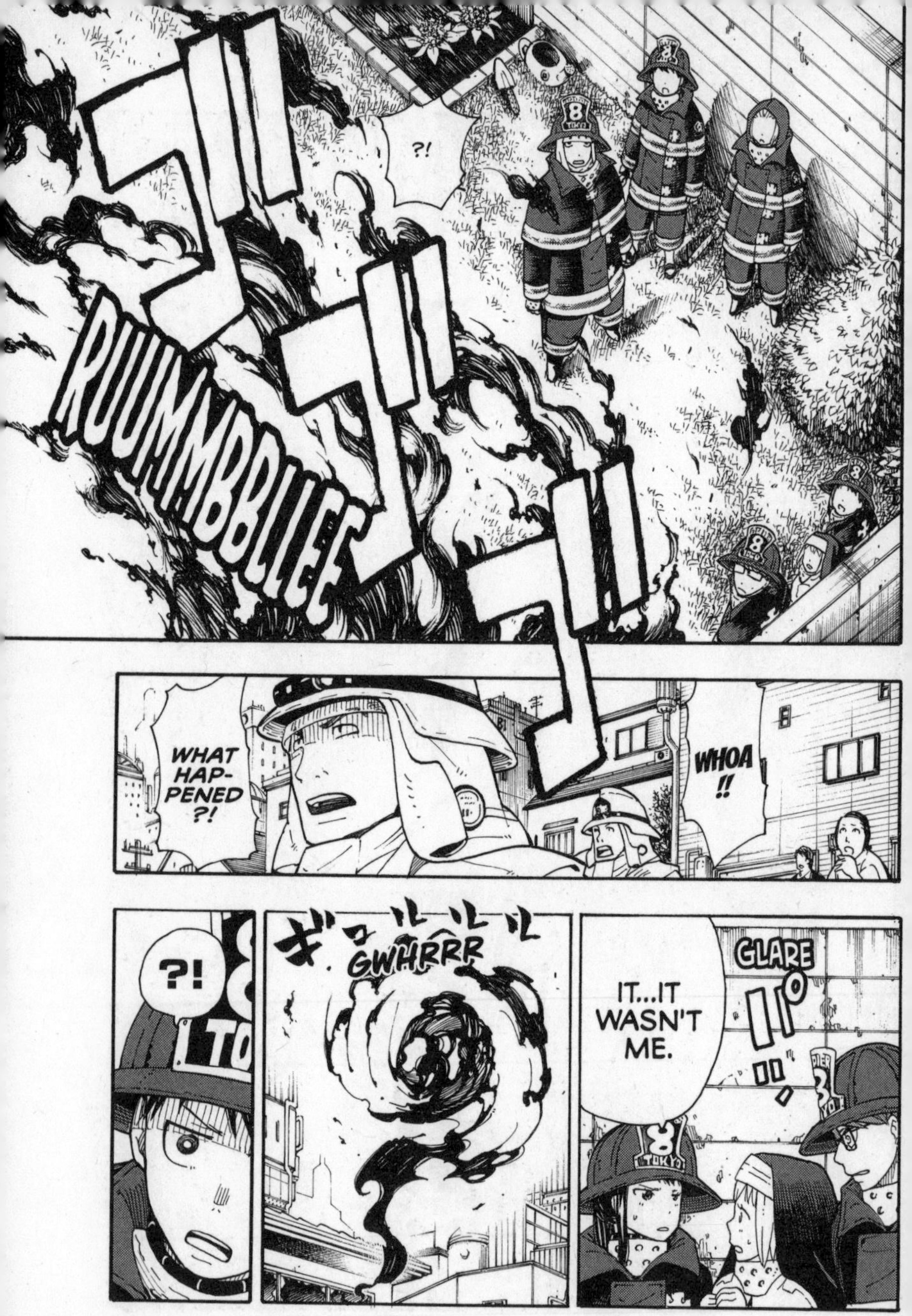
?!
RUUMMBBLLEE
WHOA!!
WHAT HAPPENED?!
GLARE
IT...IT WASN'T ME.
GWHRRR
?!

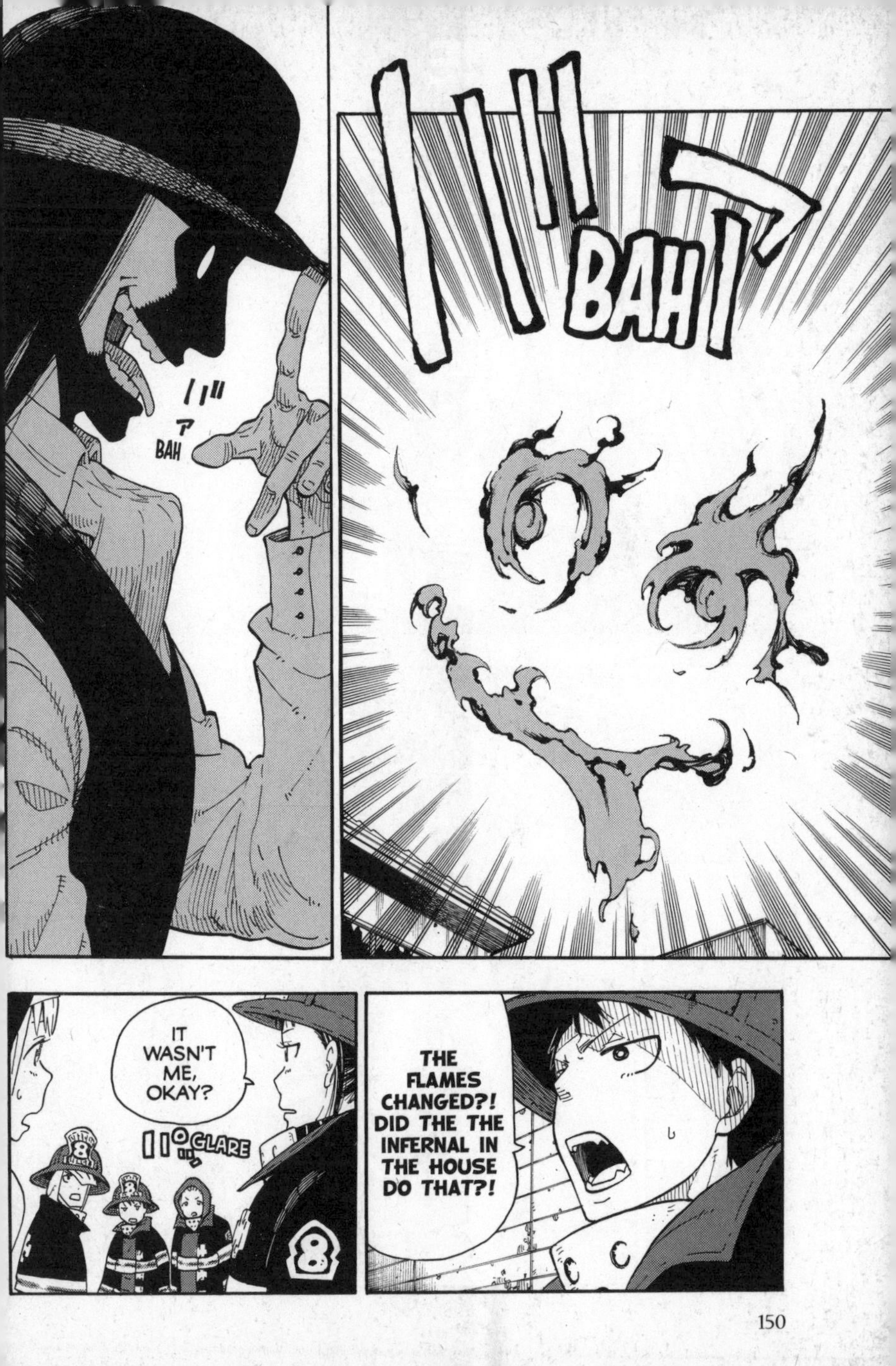
BAH
BAH
THE FLAMES CHANGED?! DID THE THE INFERNAL IN THE HOUSE DO THAT?!
IT WASN'T ME, OKAY?
GLARE

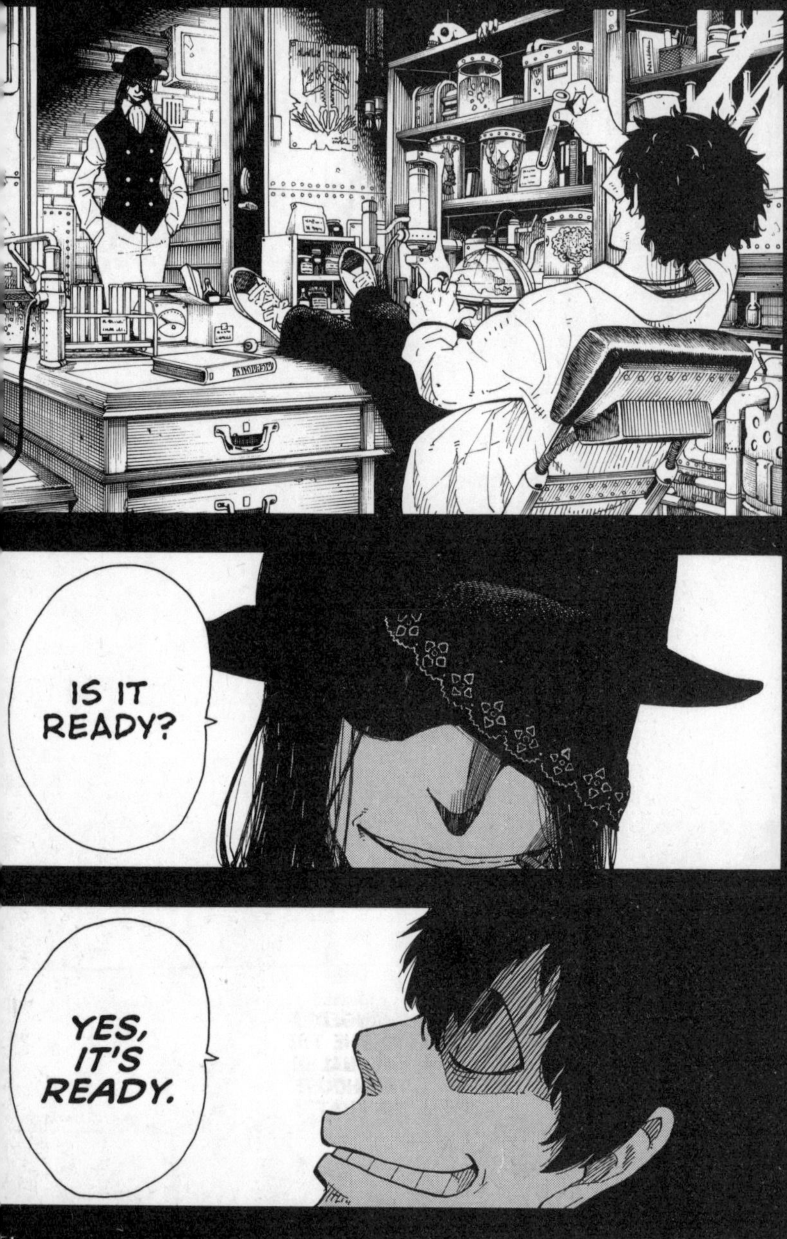
IS IT READY?
YES, IT'S READY.

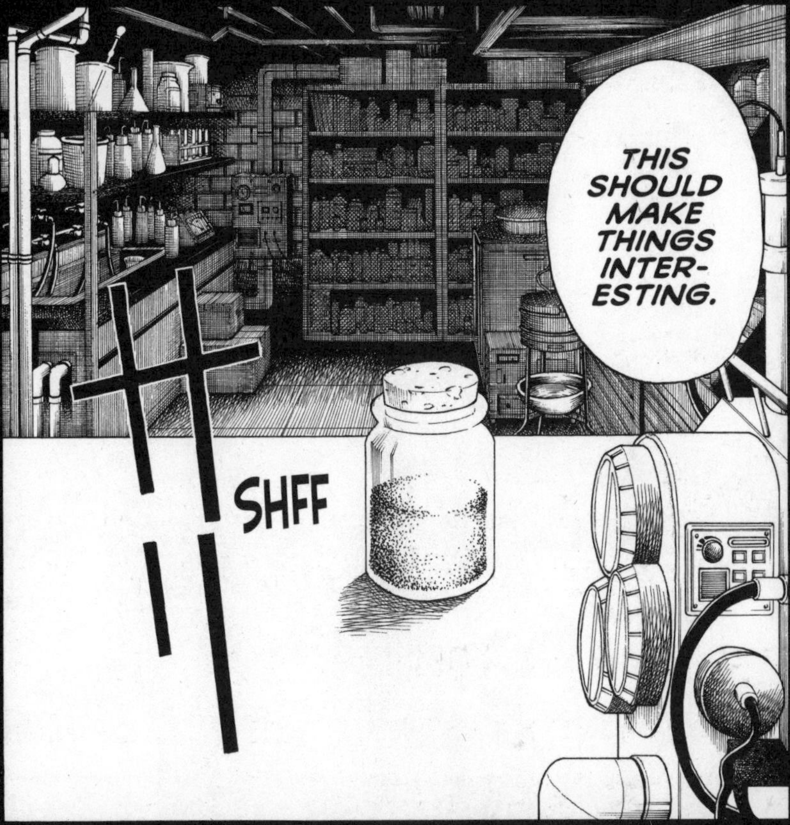
THIS SHOULD MAKE THINGS INTER-ESTING.
SHFF

CHAPTER IV: THE SINISTER BLASPHEMER

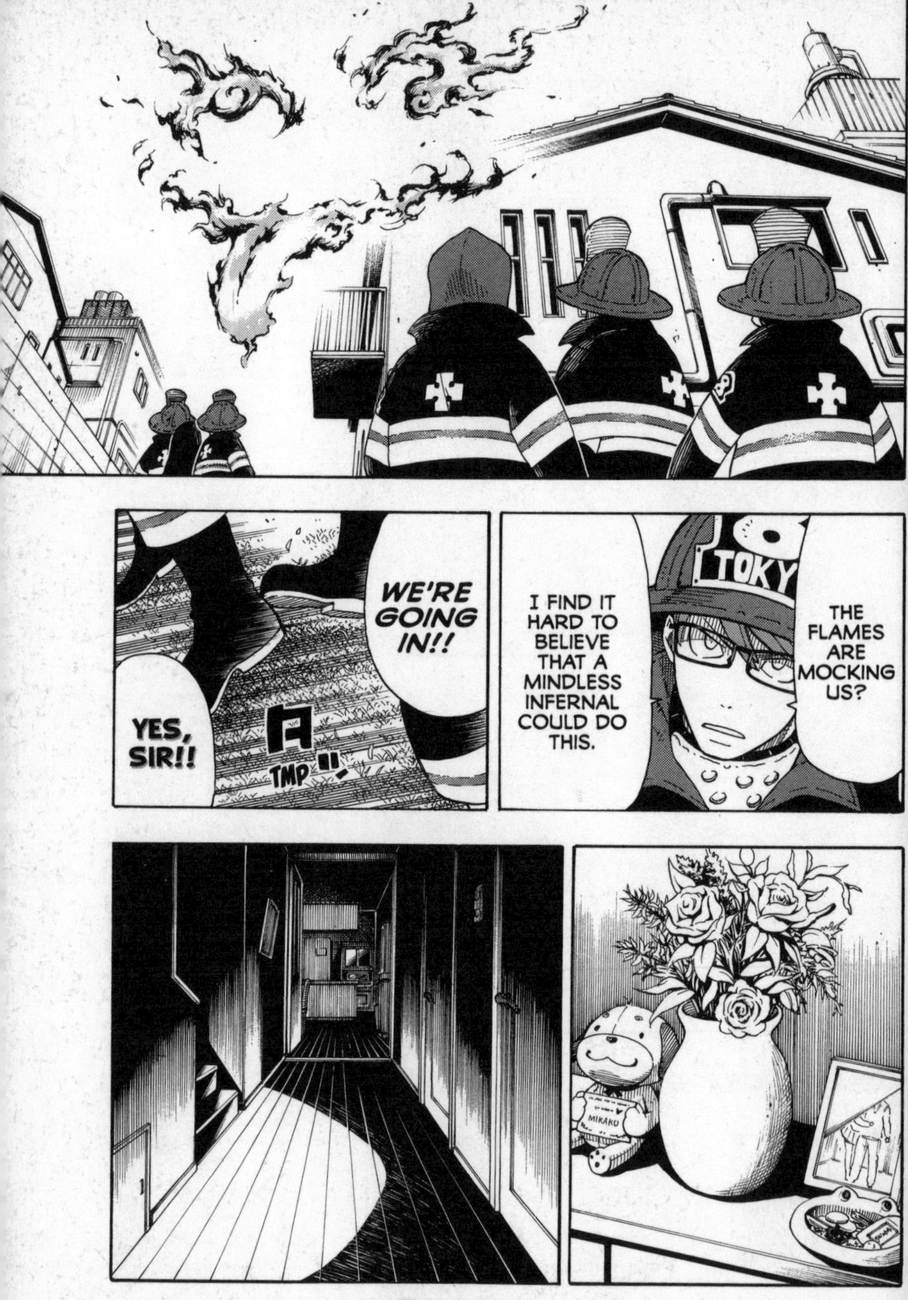
THE FLAMES ARE MOCKING US?
TOKY
I FIND IT HARD TO BELIEVE THAT A MINDLESS INFERNAL COULD DO THIS.
WE'RE GOING IN!!
YES, SIR!!
TMP
MIKAKO

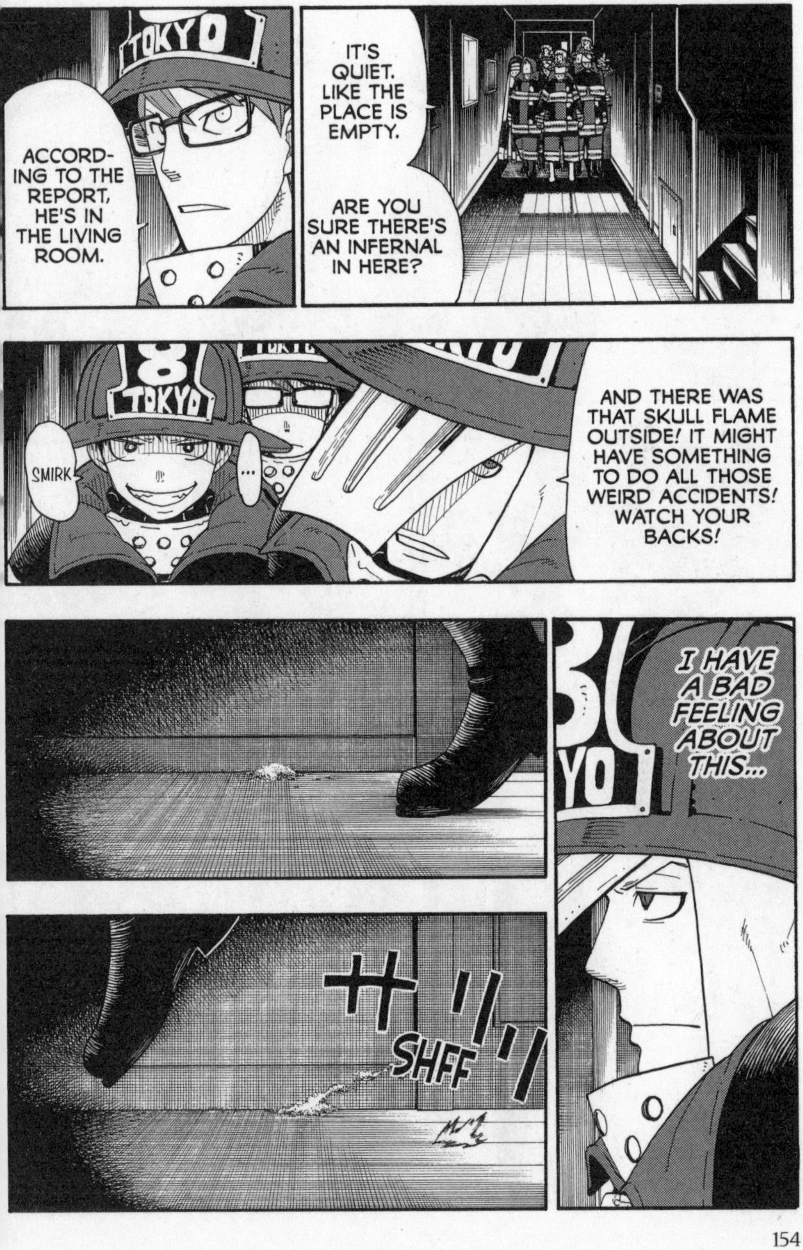
IT'S QUIET. LIKE THE PLACE IS EMPTY.
ARE YOU SURE THERE'S AN INFERNAL IN HERE?
ACCORD-ING TO THE REPORT, HE'S IN THE LIVING ROOM.
AND THERE WAS THAT SKULL FLAME OUTSIDE! IT MIGHT HAVE SOMETHING TO DO ALL THOSE WEIRD ACCIDENTS! WATCH YOUR BACKS!
...
SMIRK
I HAVE A BAD FEELING ABOUT THIS...
SHFF

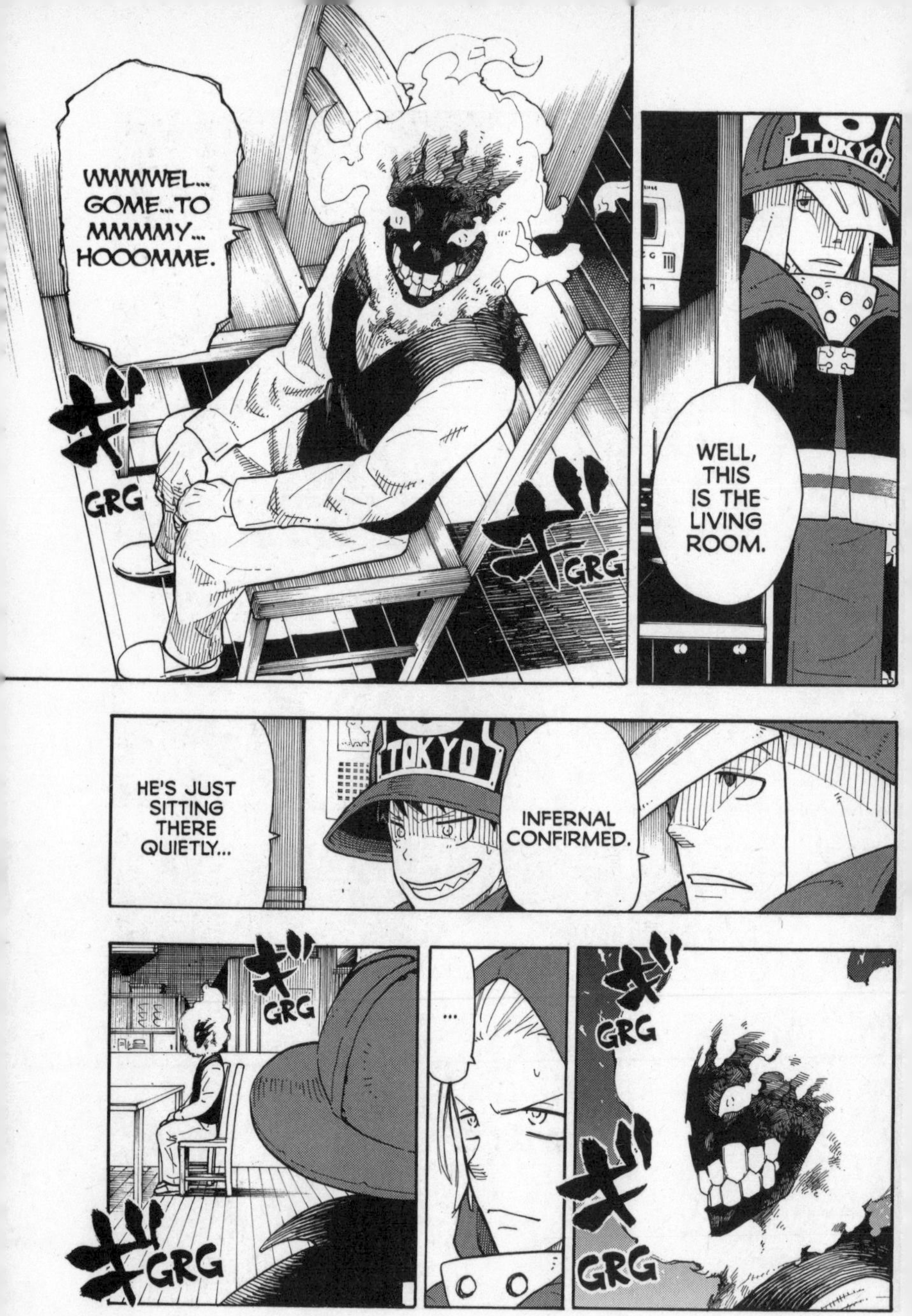
WELL, THIS IS THE LIVING ROOM.
WWWWEL... GOME...TO MMMMY... HOOOMME.
GRG
GRG
INFERNAL CONFIRMED.
HE'S JUST SITTING THERE QUIETLY...
GRG
GRG
GRG
...
GRG
GRG

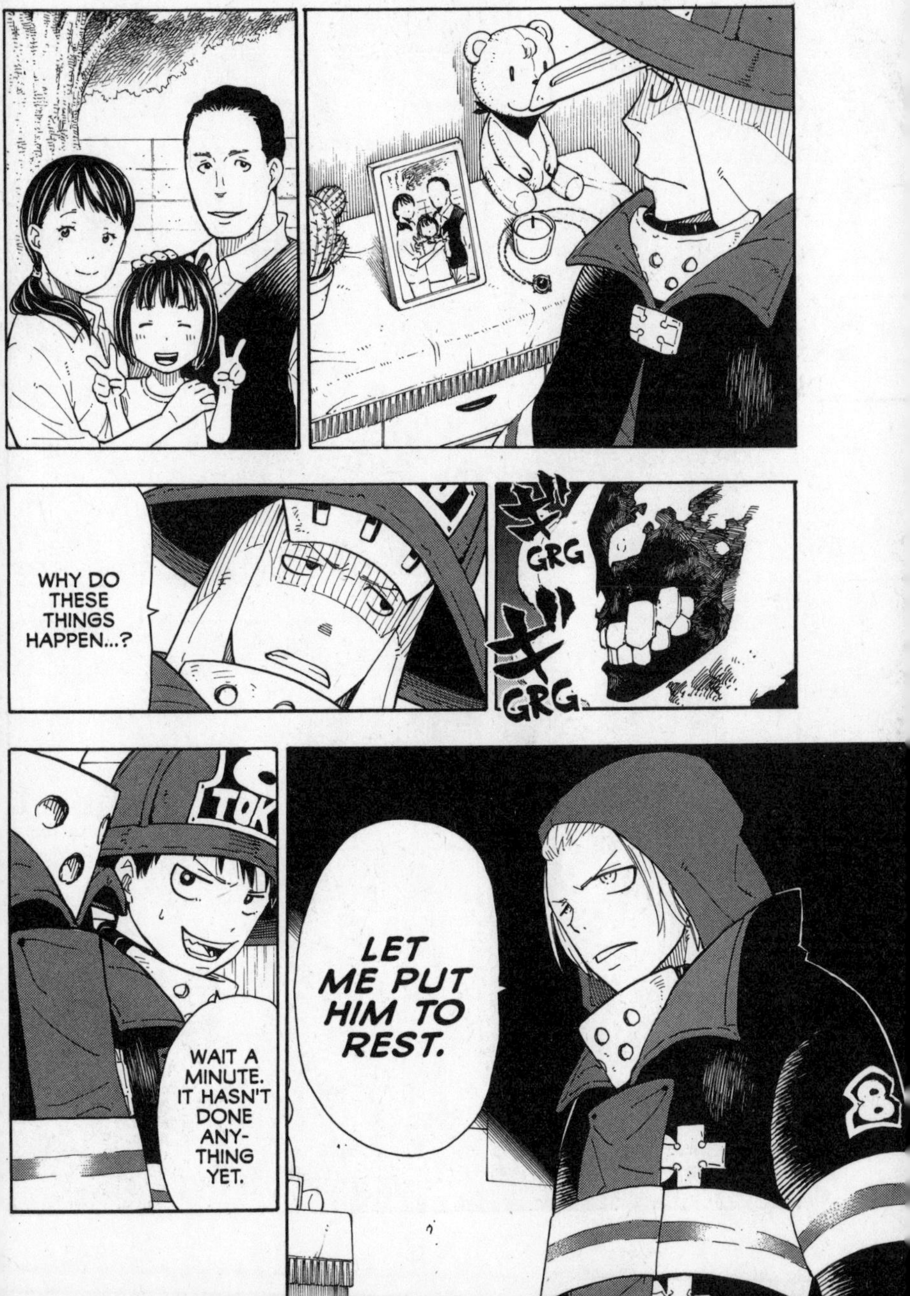
GRG
GRG
WHY DO THESE THINGS HAPPEN...?
LET ME PUT HIM TO REST.
WAIT A MINUTE. IT HASN'T DONE ANY-THING YET.

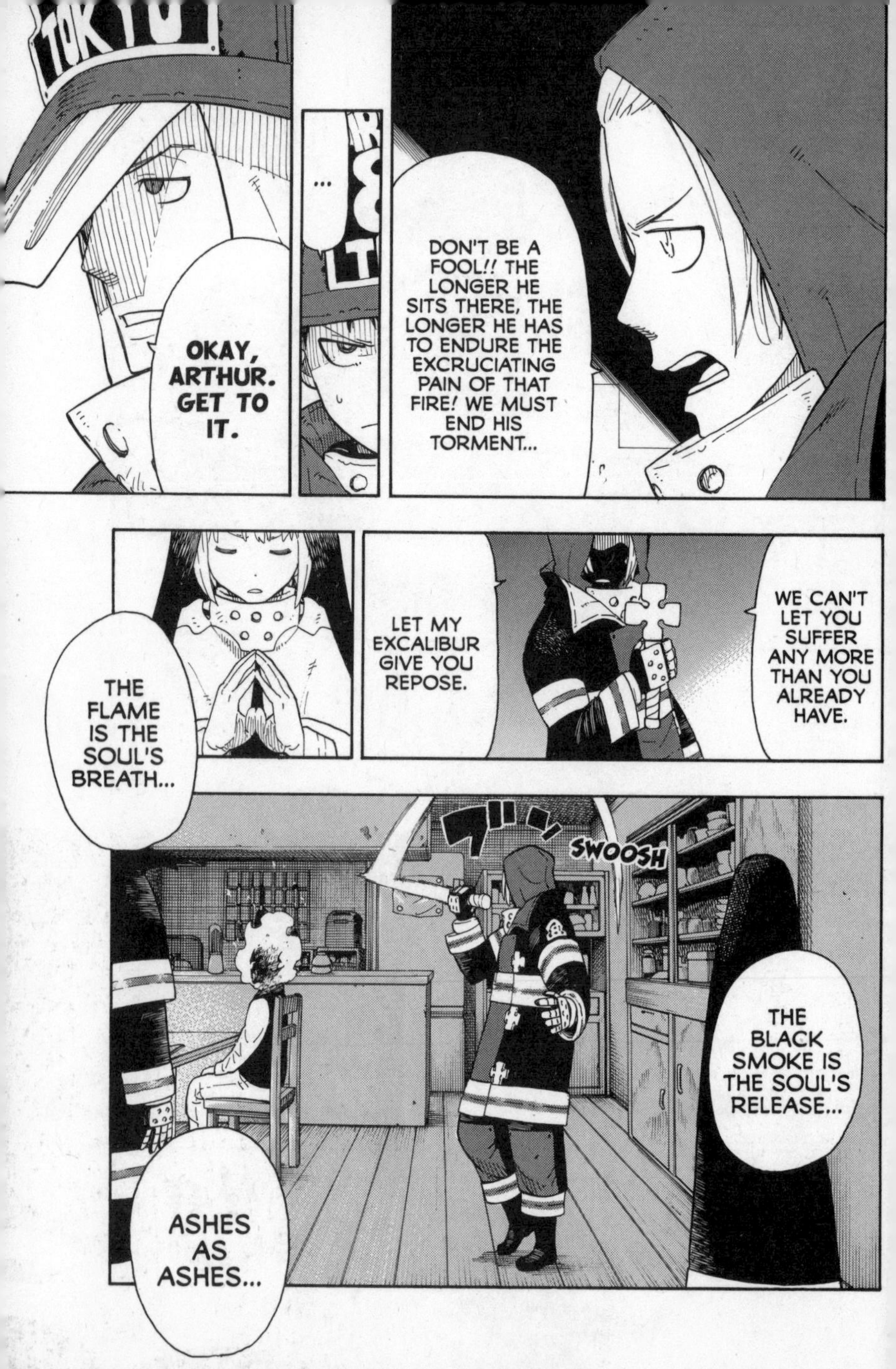
DON'T BE A FOOL!! THE LONGER HE SITS THERE, THE LONGER HE HAS TO ENDURE THE EXCRUCIATING PAIN OF THAT FIRE! WE MUST END HIS TORMENT...
...
OKAY, ARTHUR. GET TO IT.
WE CAN'T LET YOU SUFFER ANY MORE THAN YOU ALREADY HAVE.
LET MY EXCALIBUR GIVE YOU REPOSE.
THE FLAME IS THE SOUL'S BREATH...
SWOOSH
THE BLACK SMOKE IS THE SOUL'S RELEASE...
ASHES AS ASHES...

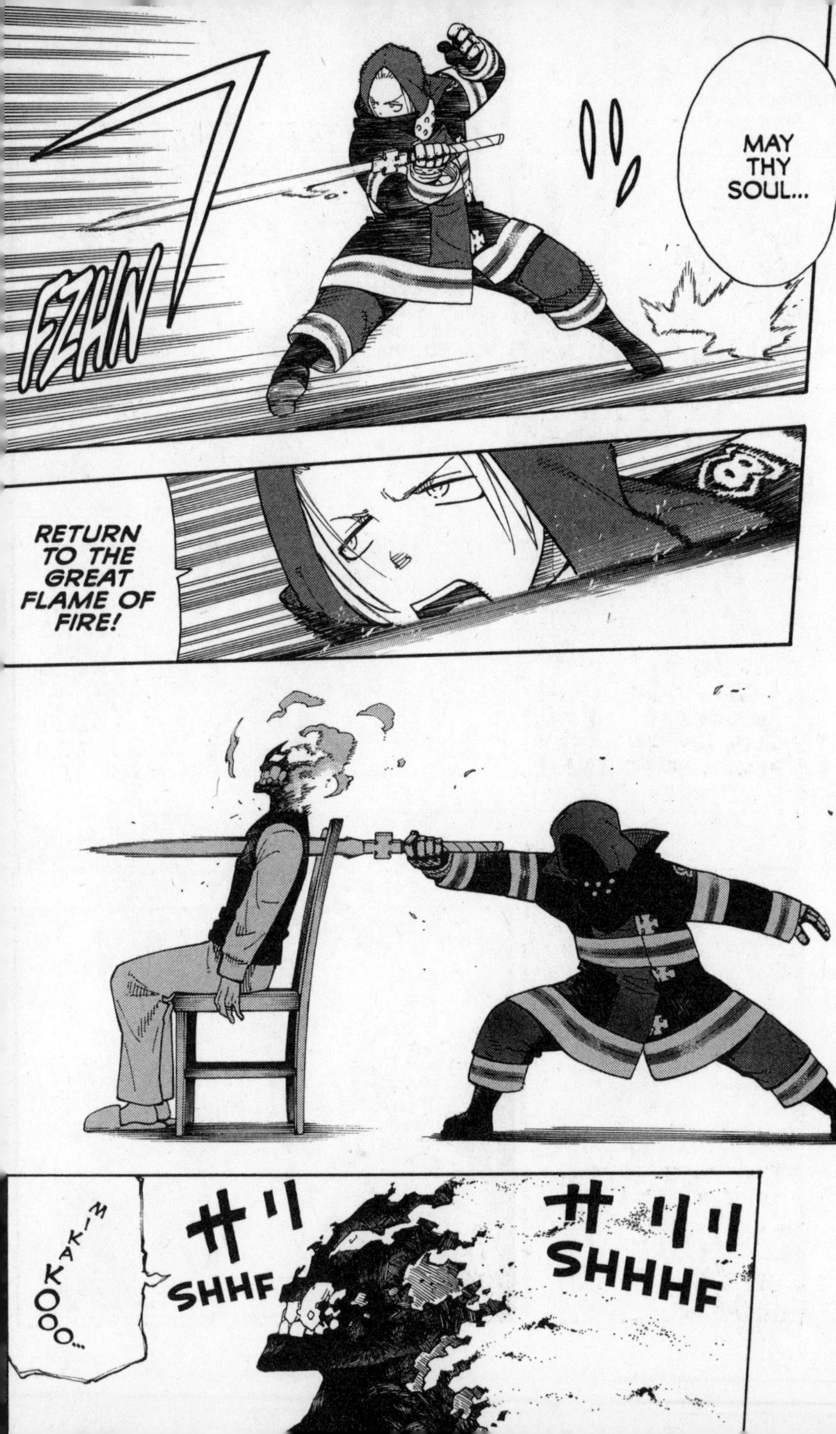
MAY THY SOUL...
FZHN
RETURN TO THE GREAT FLAME OF FIRE!
サリリ
SHHHF
サリ
SHHF
MIKAKOOO...

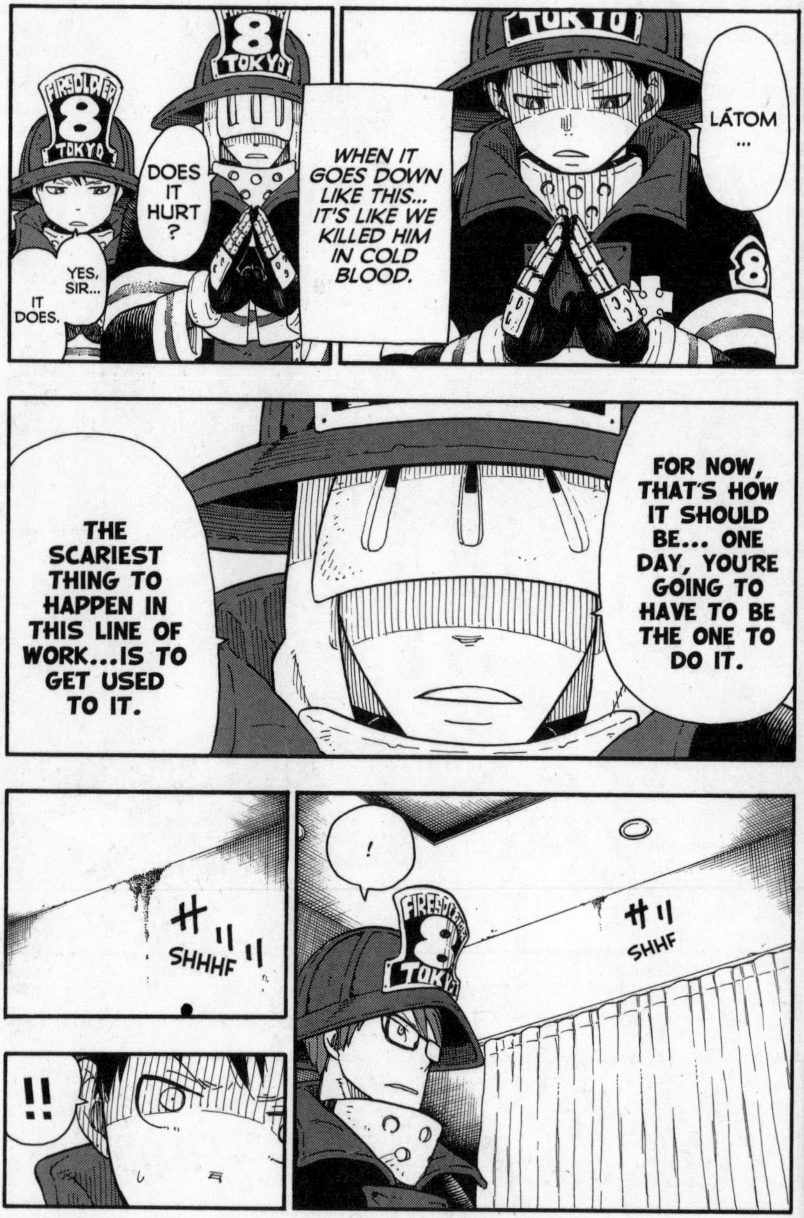
LÁTOM ...
WHEN IT GOES DOWN LIKE THIS... IT'S LIKE WE KILLED HIM IN COLD BLOOD.
DOES IT HURT?
YES, SIR... IT DOES.
FOR NOW, THAT'S HOW IT SHOULD BE... ONE DAY, YOU'RE GOING TO HAVE TO BE THE ONE TO DO IT.
THE SCARIEST THING TO HAPPEN IN THIS LINE OF WORK...IS TO GET USED TO IT.
!
サリ SHHF
サリリ SHHHF
!!

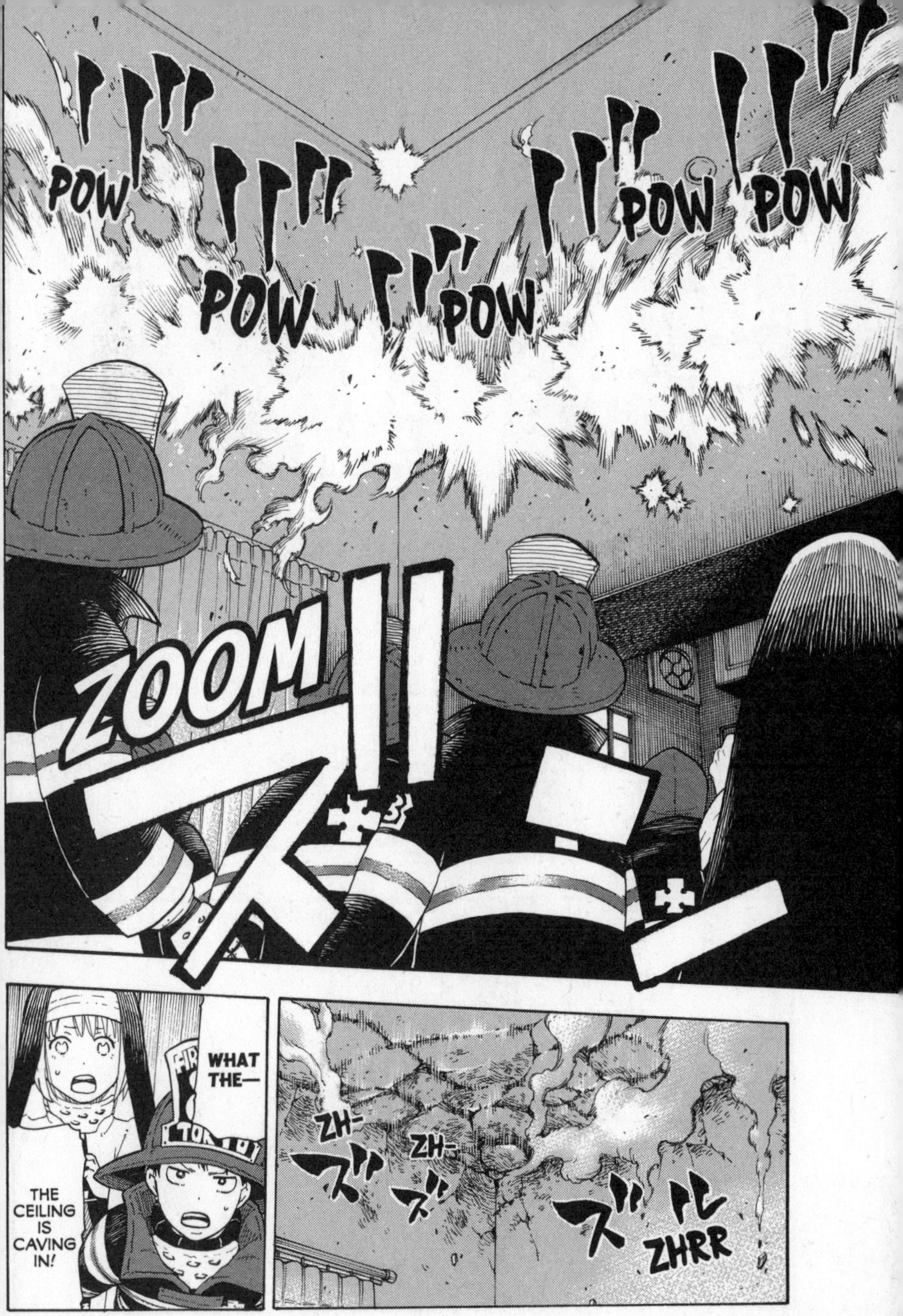
POW
POW
POW
POW
POW
ZOOM
ZH-
ZH-
ZHRR
WHAT THE—
THE CEILING IS CAVING IN!

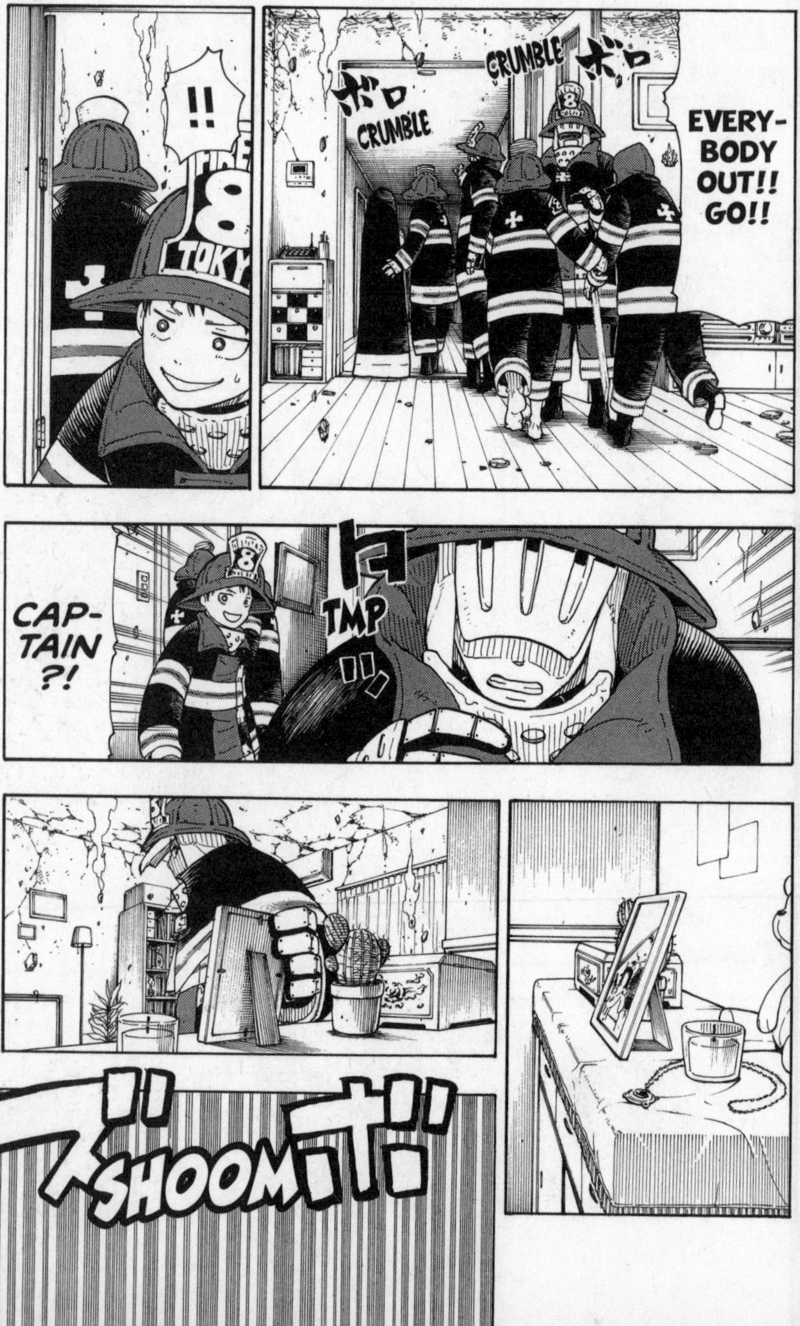
EVERY-BODY OUT!! GO!!
CRUMBLE ボロ
ボロ CRUMBLE
!!
トッ TMP
CAP-TAIN ?!
フッ!! SHOOM!!

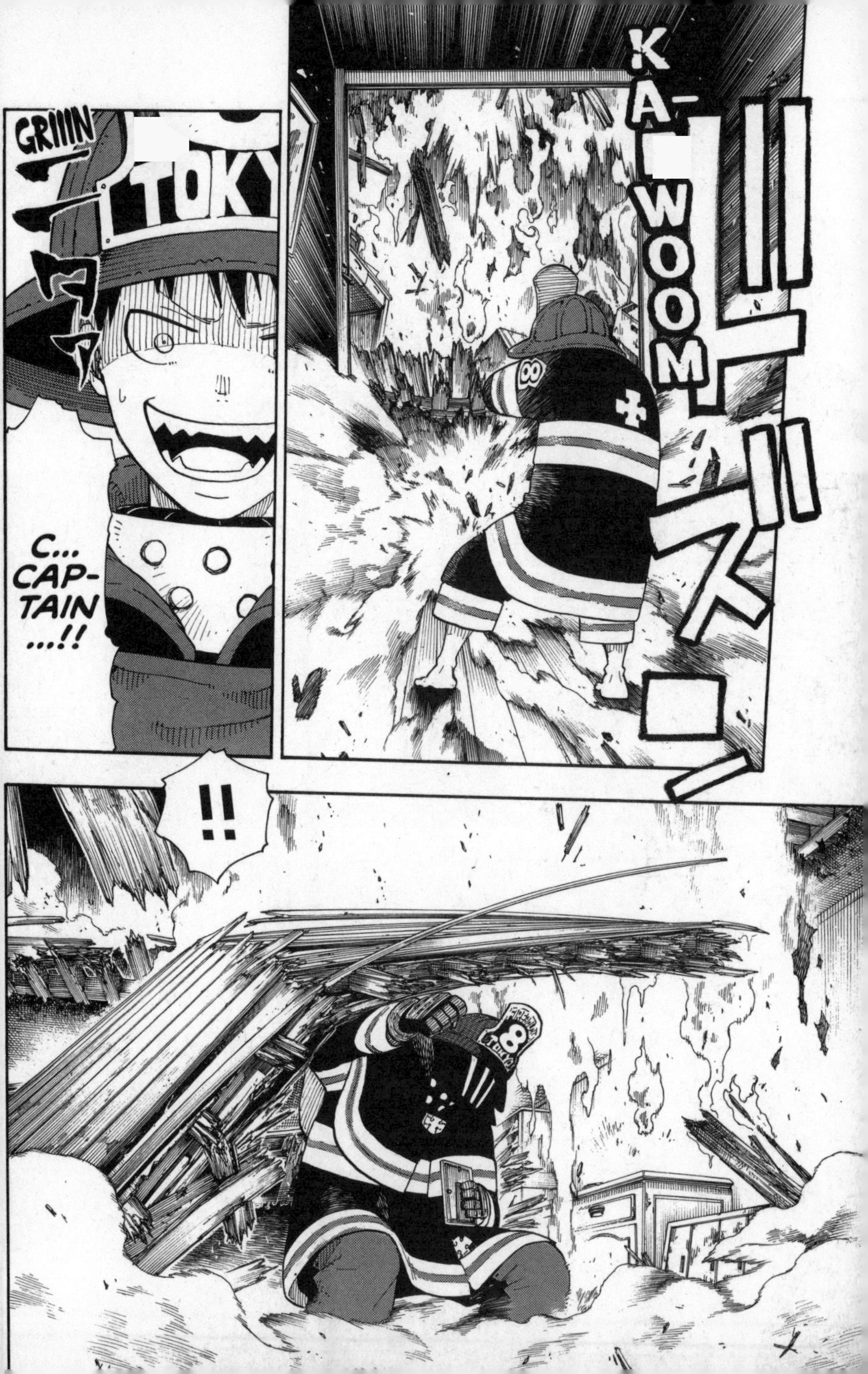
KA-WOOM
GRIIIN
C... CAP-TAIN ...!!
!!

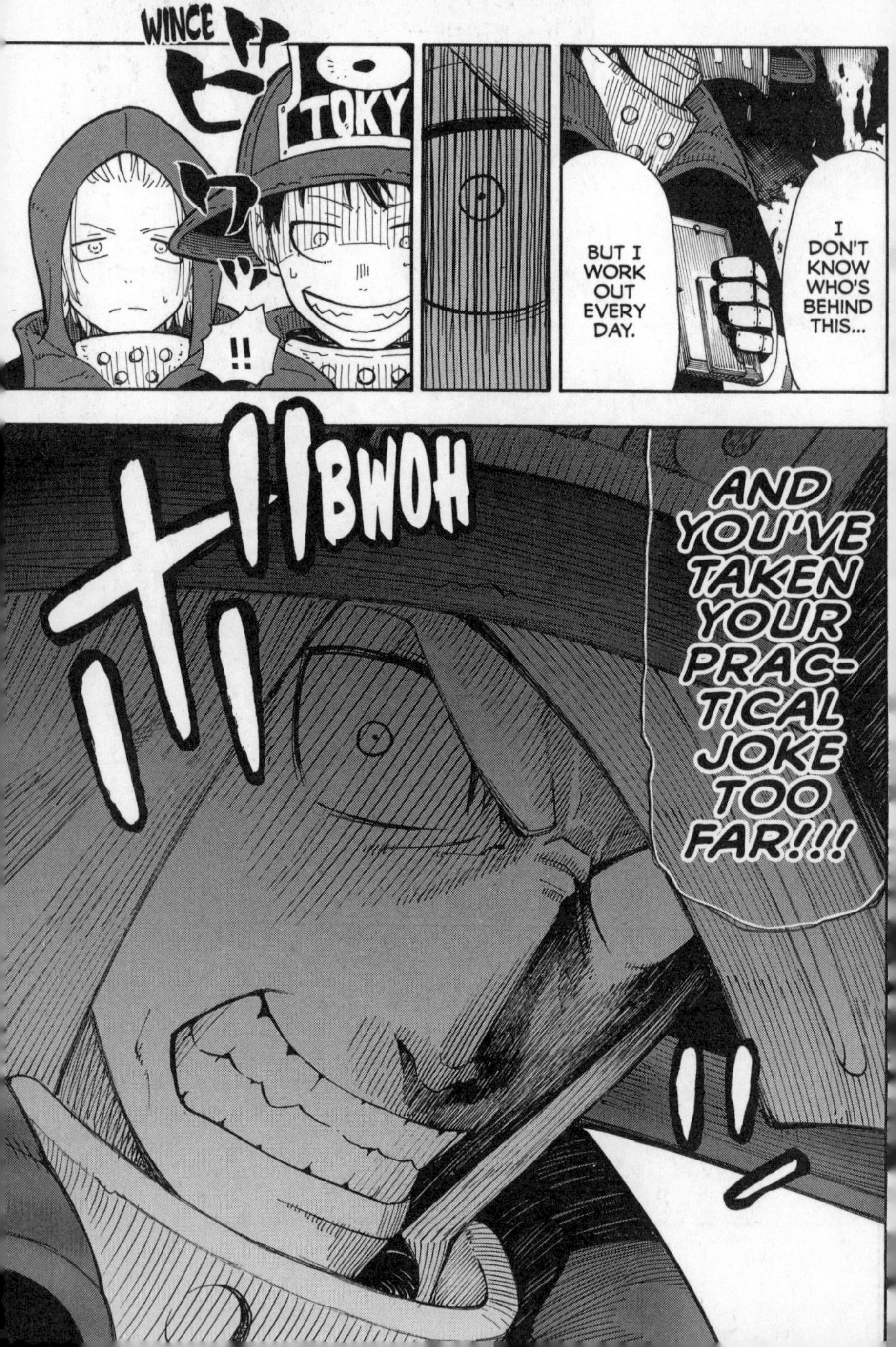
I DON'T KNOW WHO'S BEHIND THIS...
BUT I WORK OUT EVERY DAY.
WINCE
!!
AND YOU'VE TAKEN YOUR PRAC-TICAL JOKE TOO FAR!!!
BWOH

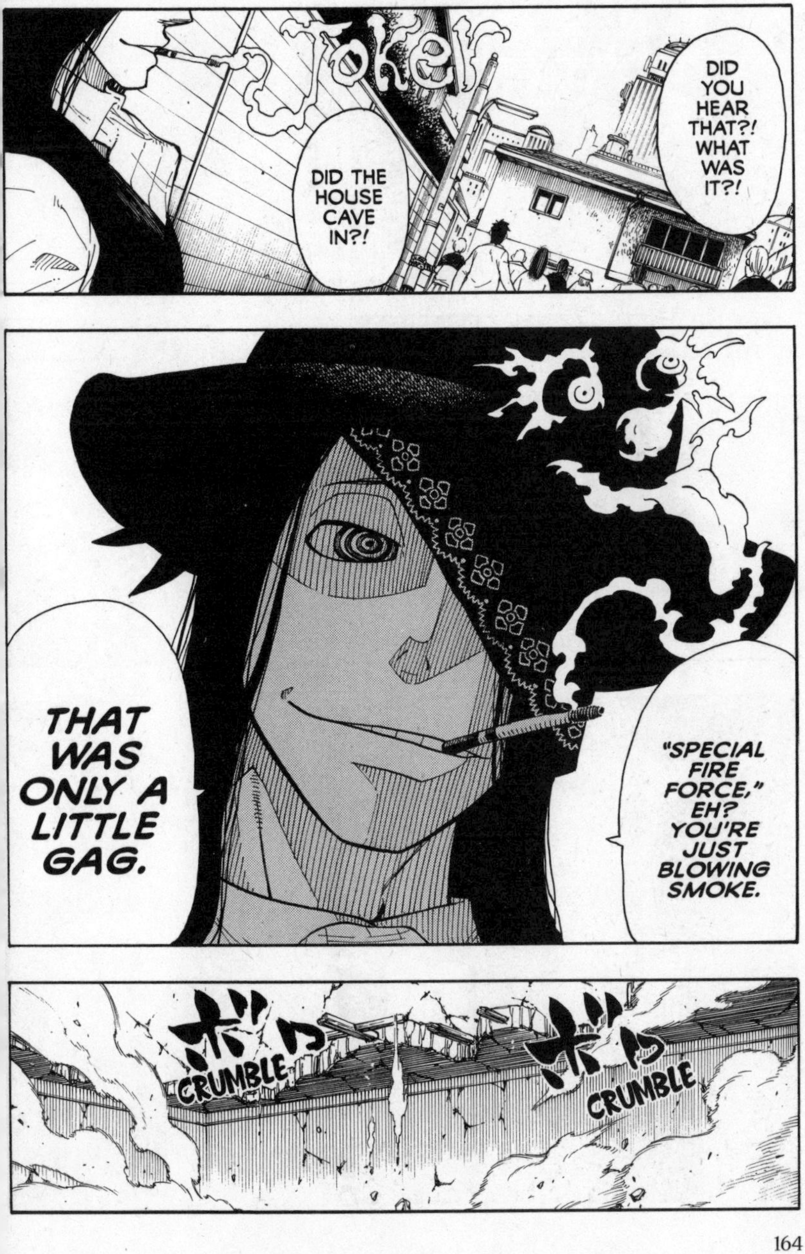
DID YOU HEAR THAT?! WHAT WAS IT?!
DID THE HOUSE CAVE IN?!
Joker
"SPECIAL FIRE FORCE," EH? YOU'RE JUST BLOWING SMOKE.
THAT WAS ONLY A LITTLE GAG.
ボロッ
CRUMBLE
ボロッ
CRUMBLE

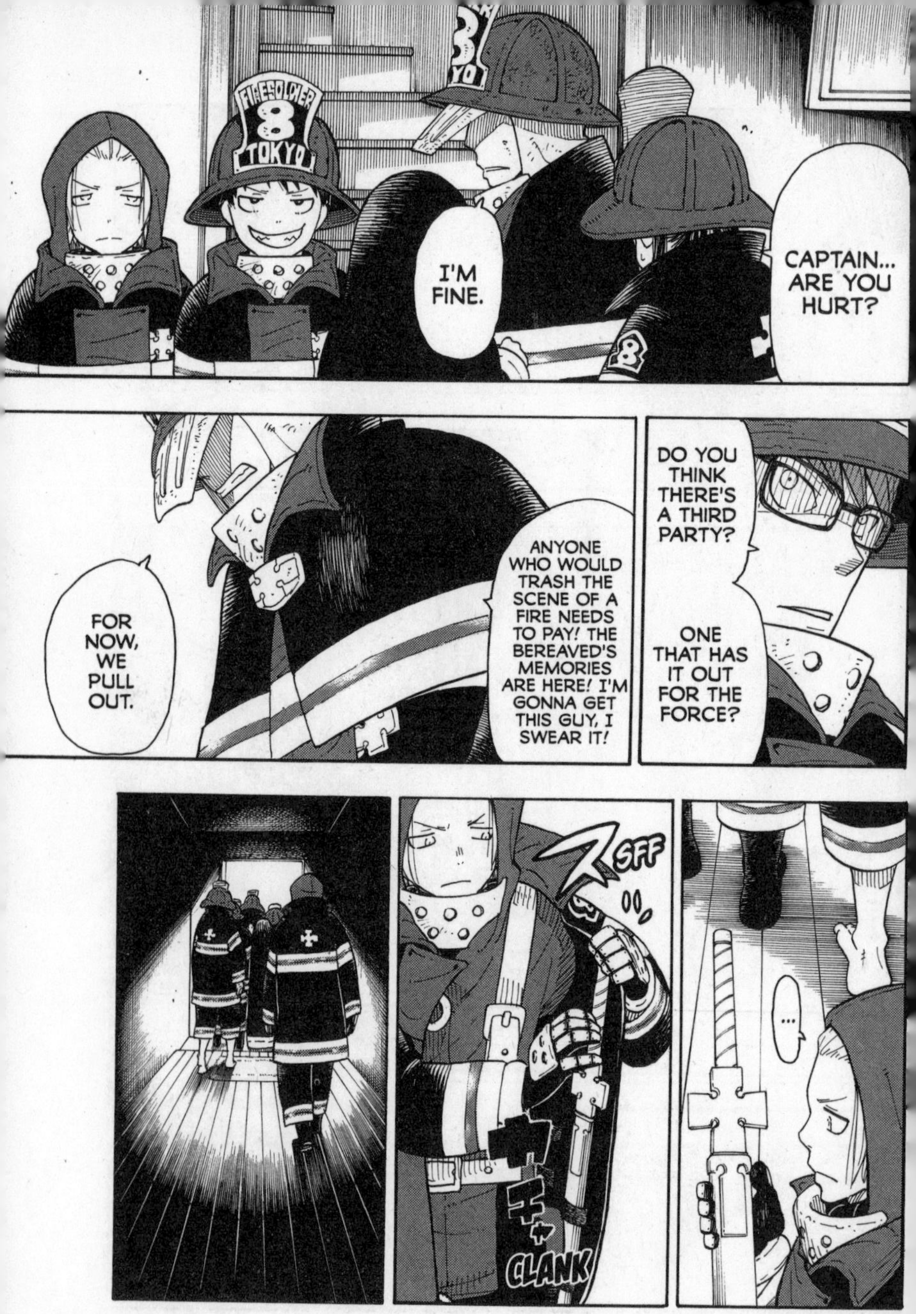
CAPTAIN... ARE YOU HURT?
I'M FINE.
DO YOU THINK THERE'S A THIRD PARTY?
ONE THAT HAS IT OUT FOR THE FORCE?
ANYONE WHO WOULD TRASH THE SCENE OF A FIRE NEEDS TO PAY! THE BEREAVED'S MEMORIES ARE HERE! I'M GONNA GET THIS GUY, I SWEAR IT!
FOR NOW, WE PULL OUT.
...
SFF
CLANK

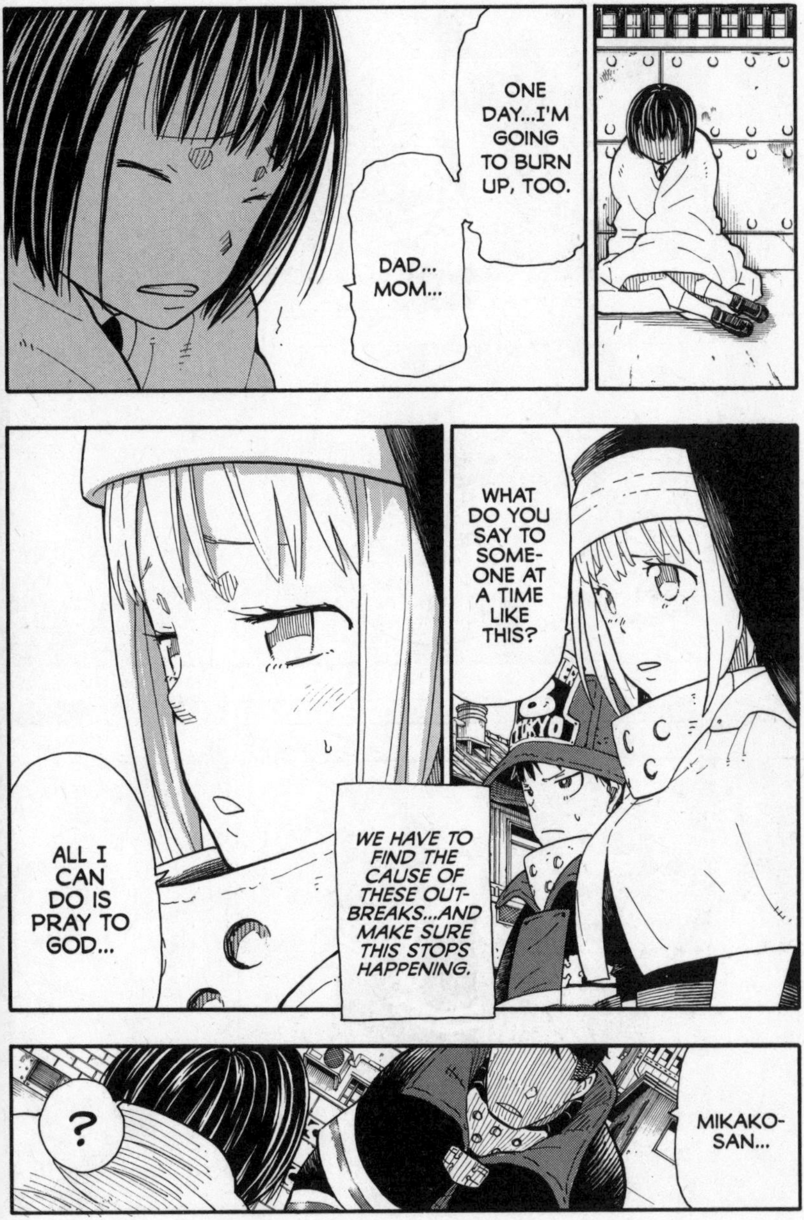
ONE DAY...I'M GOING TO BURN UP, TOO.
DAD... MOM...
WHAT DO YOU SAY TO SOME-ONE AT A TIME LIKE THIS?
WE HAVE TO FIND THE CAUSE OF THESE OUT-BREAKS...AND MAKE SURE THIS STOPS HAPPENING.
ALL I CAN DO IS PRAY TO GOD...
MIKAKO-SAN...
?

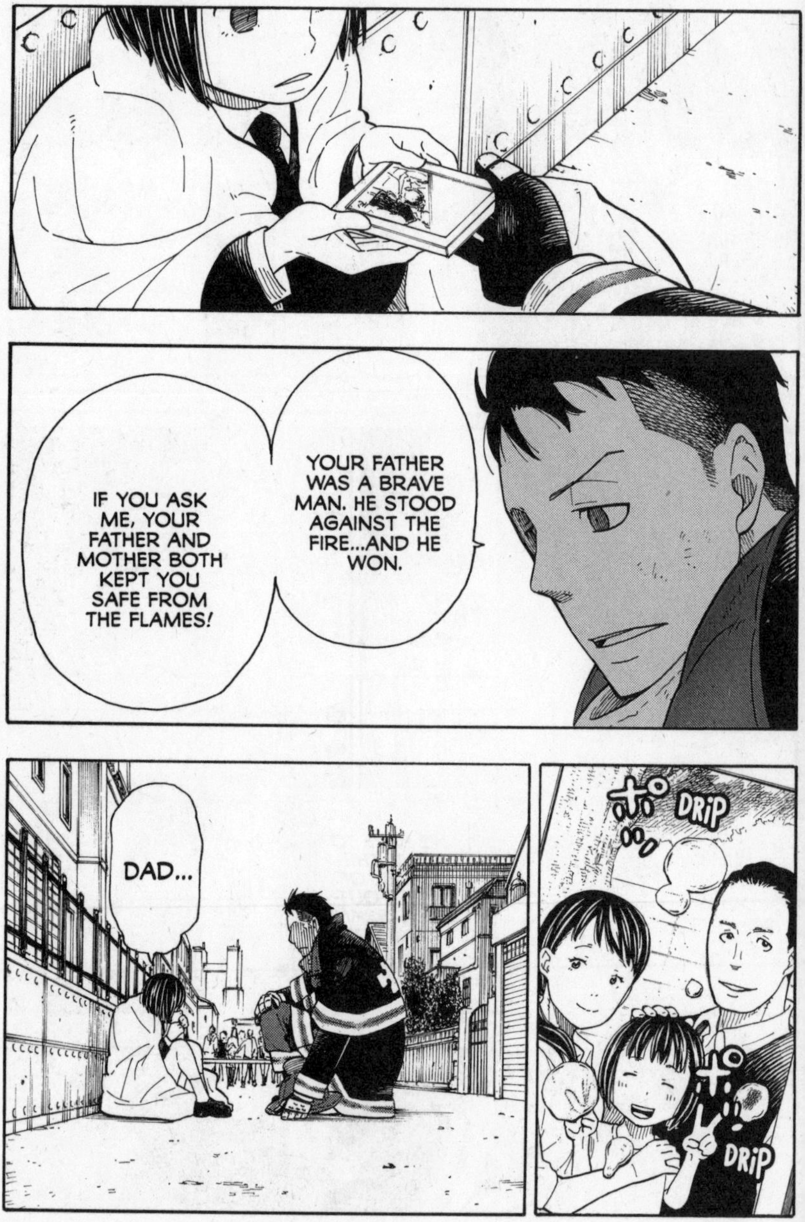
YOUR FATHER WAS A BRAVE MAN. HE STOOD AGAINST THE FIRE...AND HE WON.
IF YOU ASK ME, YOUR FATHER AND MOTHER BOTH KEPT YOU SAFE FROM THE FLAMES!
ポ
DRIP
ポ
DRIP
DAD...

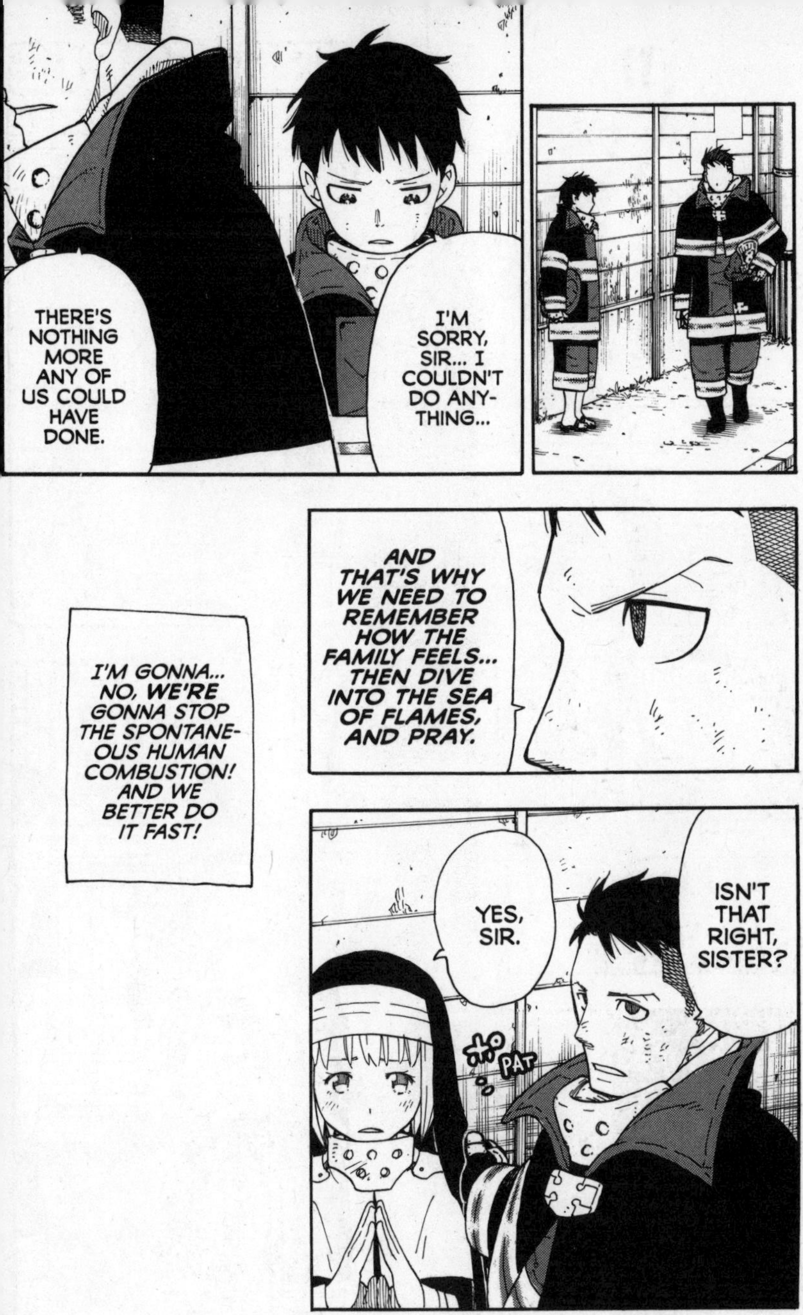
I'M SORRY, SIR... I COULDN'T DO ANY-THING...
THERE'S NOTHING MORE ANY OF US COULD HAVE DONE.
AND THAT'S WHY WE NEED TO REMEMBER HOW THE FAMILY FEELS... THEN DIVE INTO THE SEA OF FLAMES, AND PRAY.
ISN'T THAT RIGHT, SISTER?
YES, SIR.
PAT
I'M GONNA... NO, WE'RE GONNA STOP THE SPONTANE-OUS HUMAN COMBUSTION! AND WE BETTER DO IT FAST!

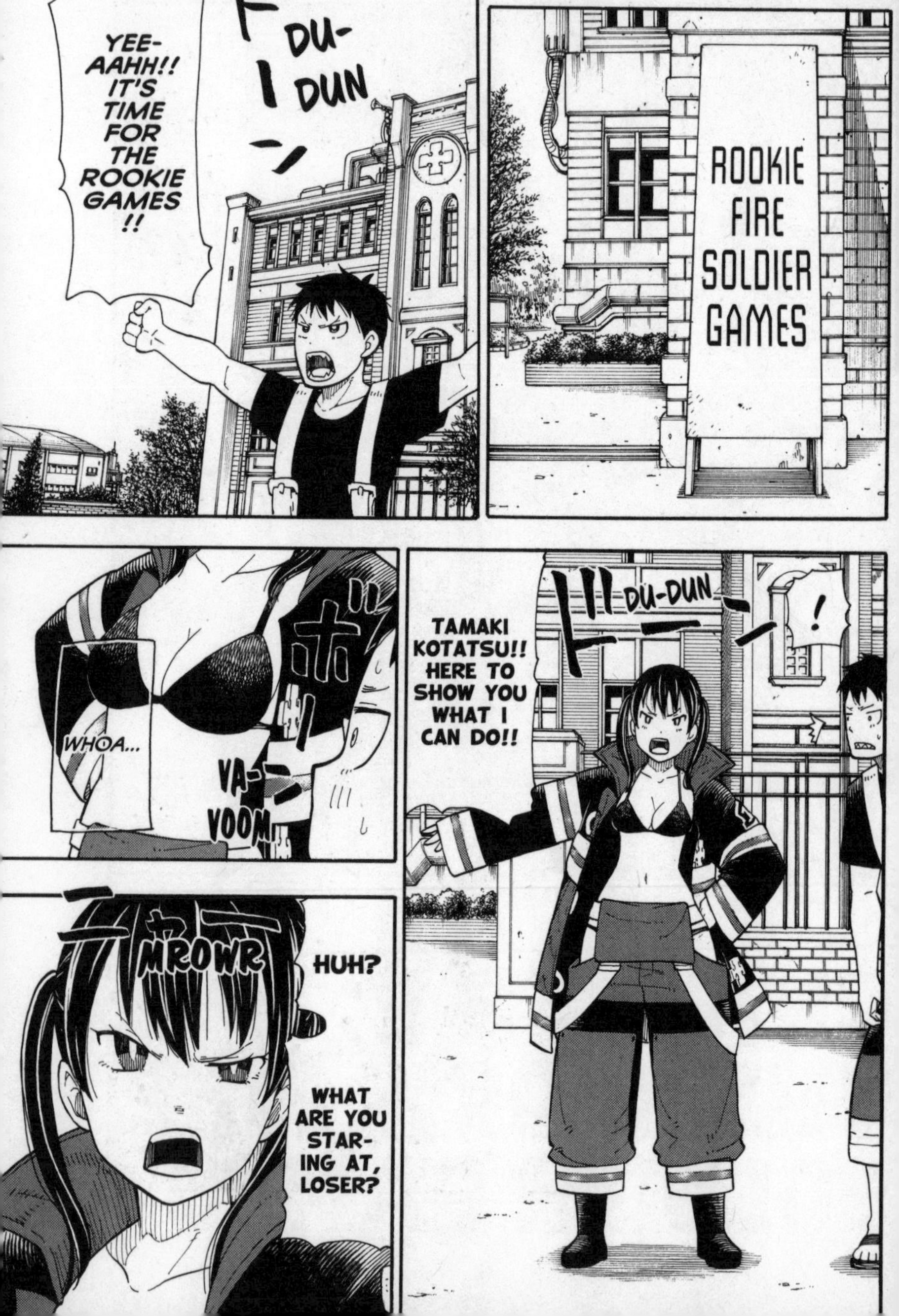
ROOKIE FIRE SOLDIER GAMES
YEE-AAHH!! IT'S TIME FOR THE ROOKIE GAMES!!
DU-DUN
DU-DUN
!
TAMAKI KOTATSU!! HERE TO SHOW YOU WHAT I CAN DO!!
VA-VOOM
WHOA...
MROWR
HUH?
WHAT ARE YOU STAR-ING AT, LOSER?

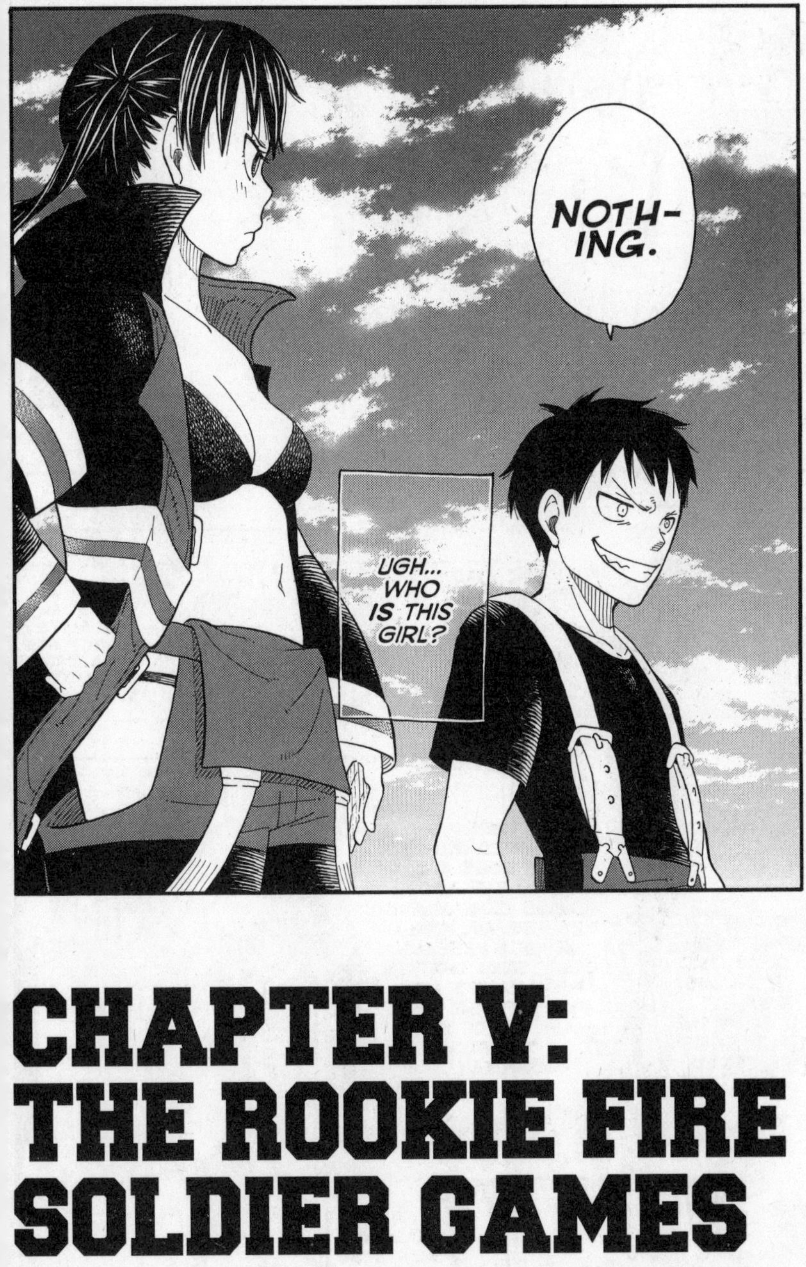
NOTH-ING.
UGH... WHO IS THIS GIRL?

CHAPTER V: THE ROOKIE FIRE SOLDIER GAMES

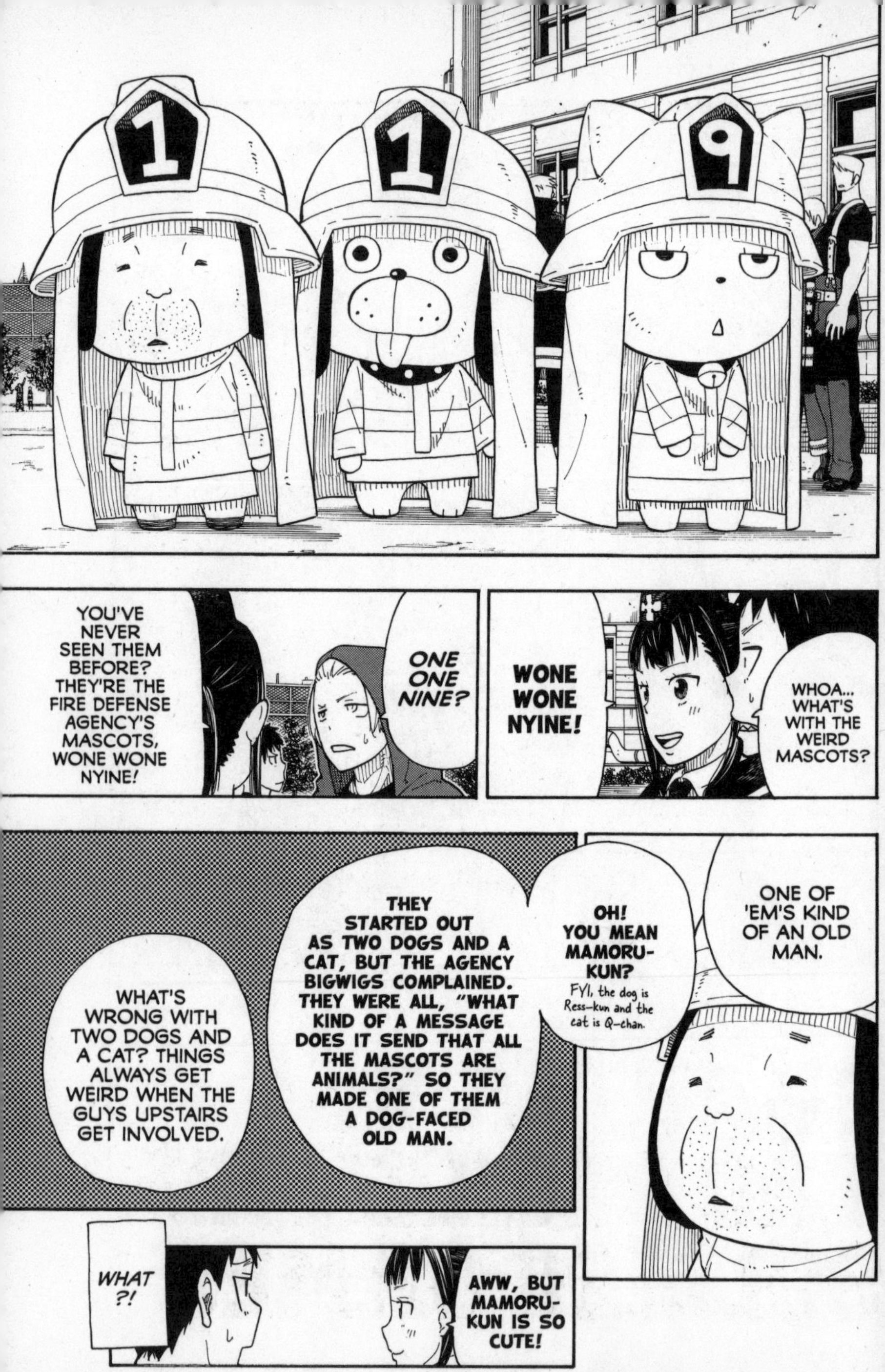
WHOA... WHAT'S WITH THE WEIRD MASCOTS?
WONE WONE NYINE!
ONE ONE NINE?
YOU'VE NEVER SEEN THEM BEFORE? THEY'RE THE FIRE DEFENSE AGENCY'S MASCOTS, WONE WONE NYINE!
ONE OF 'EM'S KIND OF AN OLD MAN.
OH! YOU MEAN MAMORU-KUN?
FYI, the dog is Ress-kun and the cat is Q-chan.
THEY STARTED OUT AS TWO DOGS AND A CAT, BUT THE AGENCY BIGWIGS COMPLAINED. THEY WERE ALL, "WHAT KIND OF A MESSAGE DOES IT SEND THAT ALL THE MASCOTS ARE ANIMALS?" SO THEY MADE ONE OF THEM A DOG-FACED OLD MAN.
WHAT'S WRONG WITH TWO DOGS AND A CAT? THINGS ALWAYS GET WEIRD WHEN THE GUYS UPSTAIRS GET INVOLVED.
AWW, BUT MAMORU-KUN IS SO CUTE!
WHAT ?!

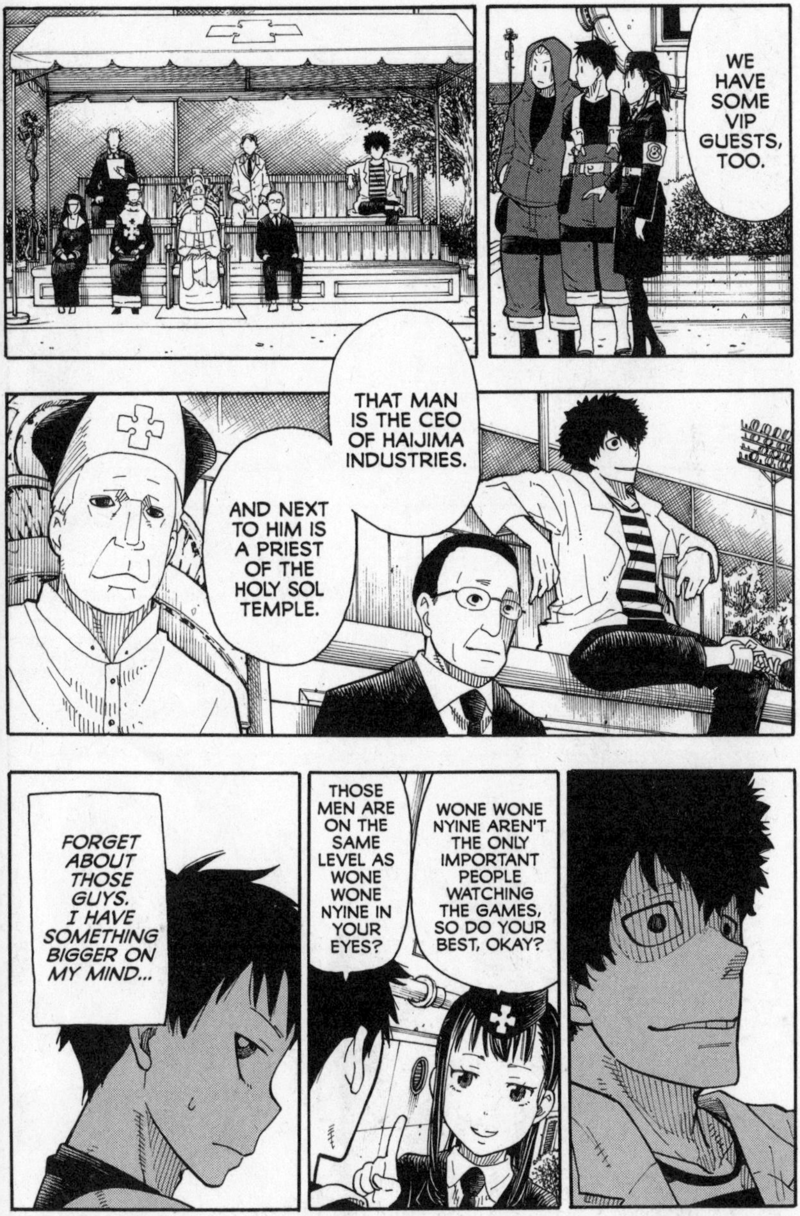
WE HAVE SOME VIP GUESTS, TOO.
THAT MAN IS THE CEO OF HAIJIMA INDUSTRIES.
AND NEXT TO HIM IS A PRIEST OF THE HOLY SOL TEMPLE.
WONE WONE NYINE AREN'T THE ONLY IMPORTANT PEOPLE WATCHING THE GAMES, SO DO YOUR BEST, OKAY?
THOSE MEN ARE ON THE SAME LEVEL AS WONE WONE NYINE IN YOUR EYES?
FORGET ABOUT THOSE GUYS. I HAVE SOMETHING BIGGER ON MY MIND...

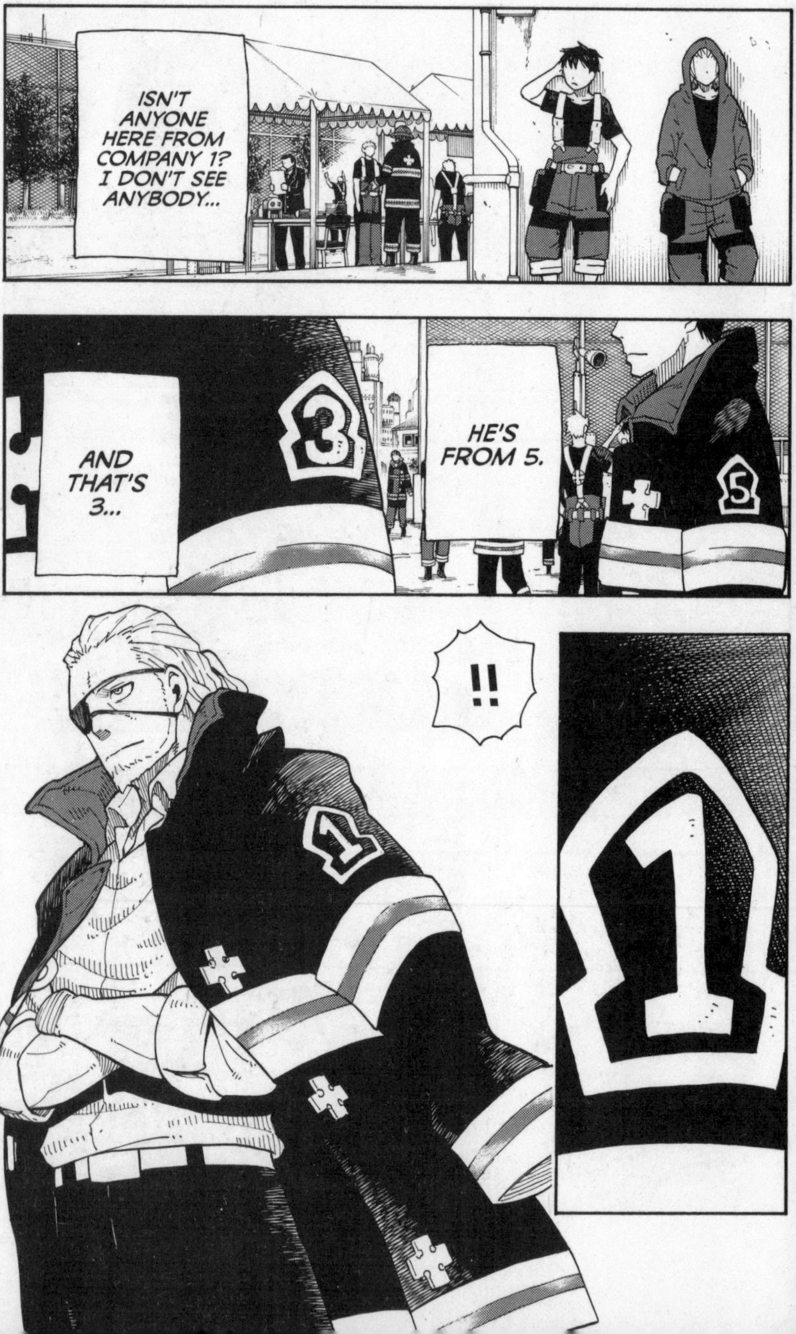
ISN'T ANYONE HERE FROM COMPANY 1? I DON'T SEE ANYBODY...
HE'S FROM 5.
AND THAT'S 3...
!!

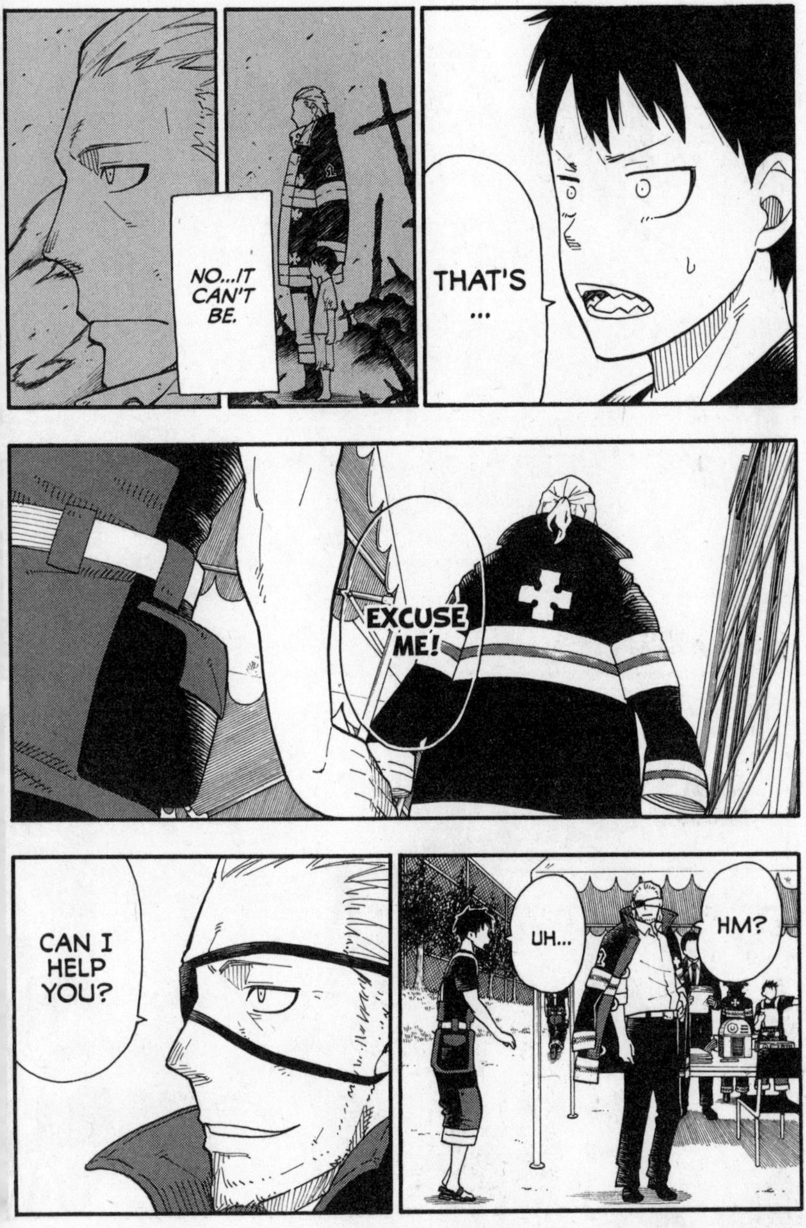
THAT'S ...
NO...IT CAN'T BE.
EXCUSE ME!
HM?
UH...
CAN I HELP YOU?

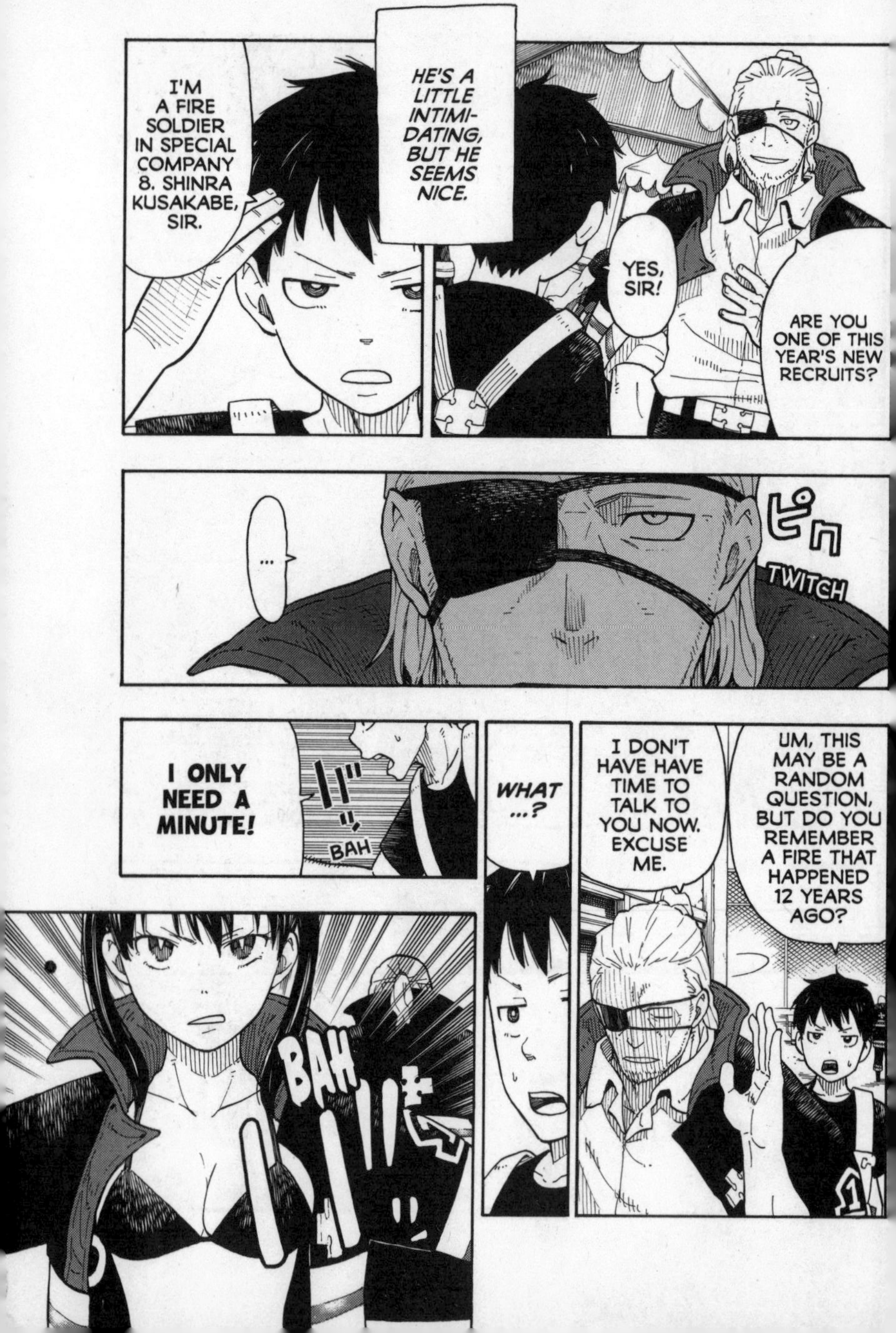
ARE YOU ONE OF THIS YEAR'S NEW RECRUITS?
YES, SIR!
I'M A FIRE SOLDIER IN SPECIAL COMPANY 8. SHINRA KUSAKABE, SIR.
HE'S A LITTLE INTIMI-DATING, BUT HE SEEMS NICE.
ピn
TWITCH
...
UM, THIS MAY BE A RANDOM QUESTION, BUT DO YOU REMEMBER A FIRE THAT HAPPENED 12 YEARS AGO?
I DON'T HAVE HAVE TIME TO TALK TO YOU NOW. EXCUSE ME.
WHAT ...?
I ONLY NEED A MINUTE!
BAH
BAH

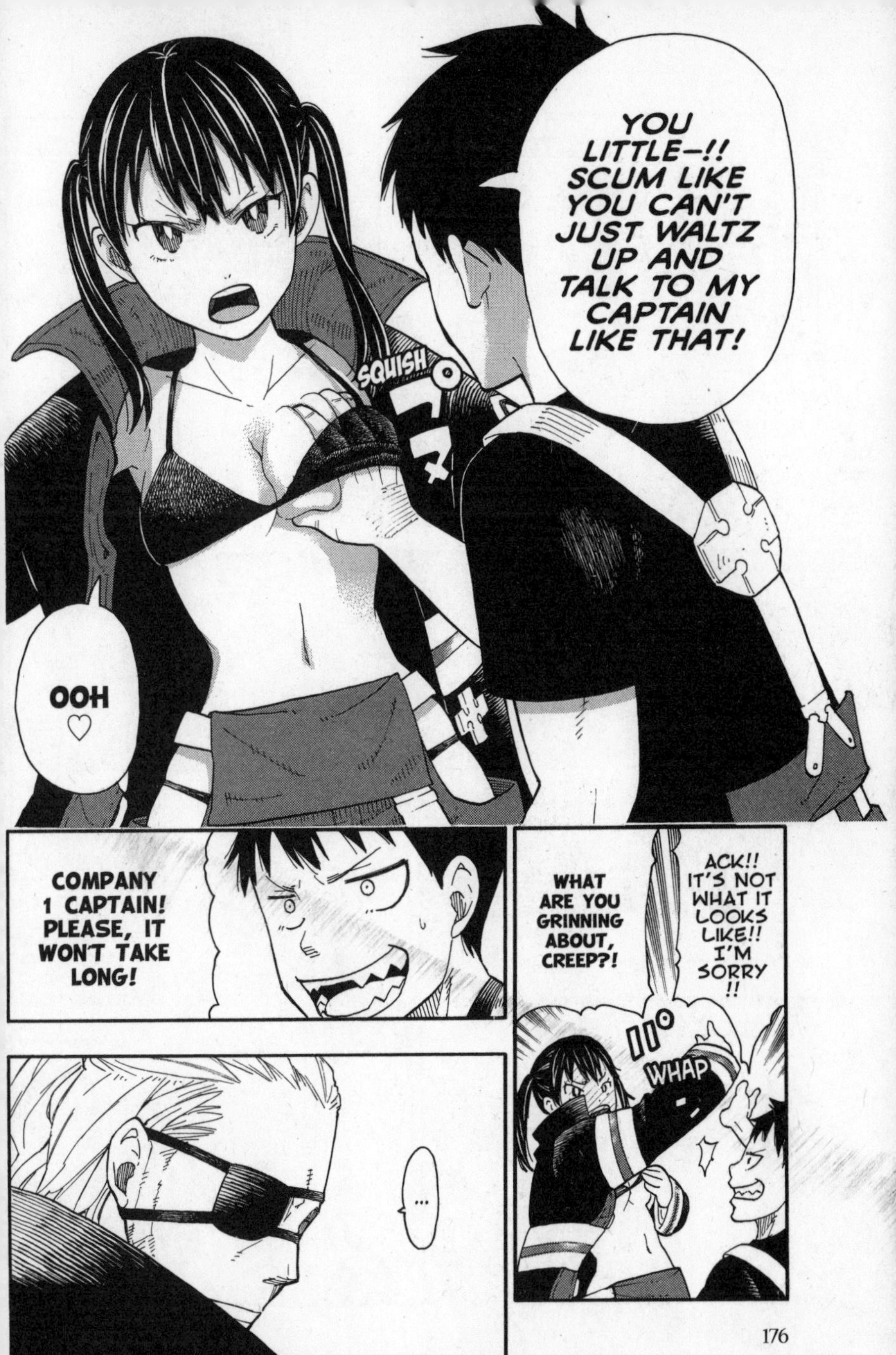
YOU LITTLE—!! SCUM LIKE YOU CAN'T JUST WALTZ UP AND TALK TO MY CAPTAIN LIKE THAT!
SQUISH
OOH ♡
ACK!! IT'S NOT WHAT IT LOOKS LIKE!! I'M SORRY !!
WHAT ARE YOU GRINNING ABOUT, CREEP?!
WHAP
COMPANY 1 CAPTAIN! PLEASE, IT WON'T TAKE LONG!
...

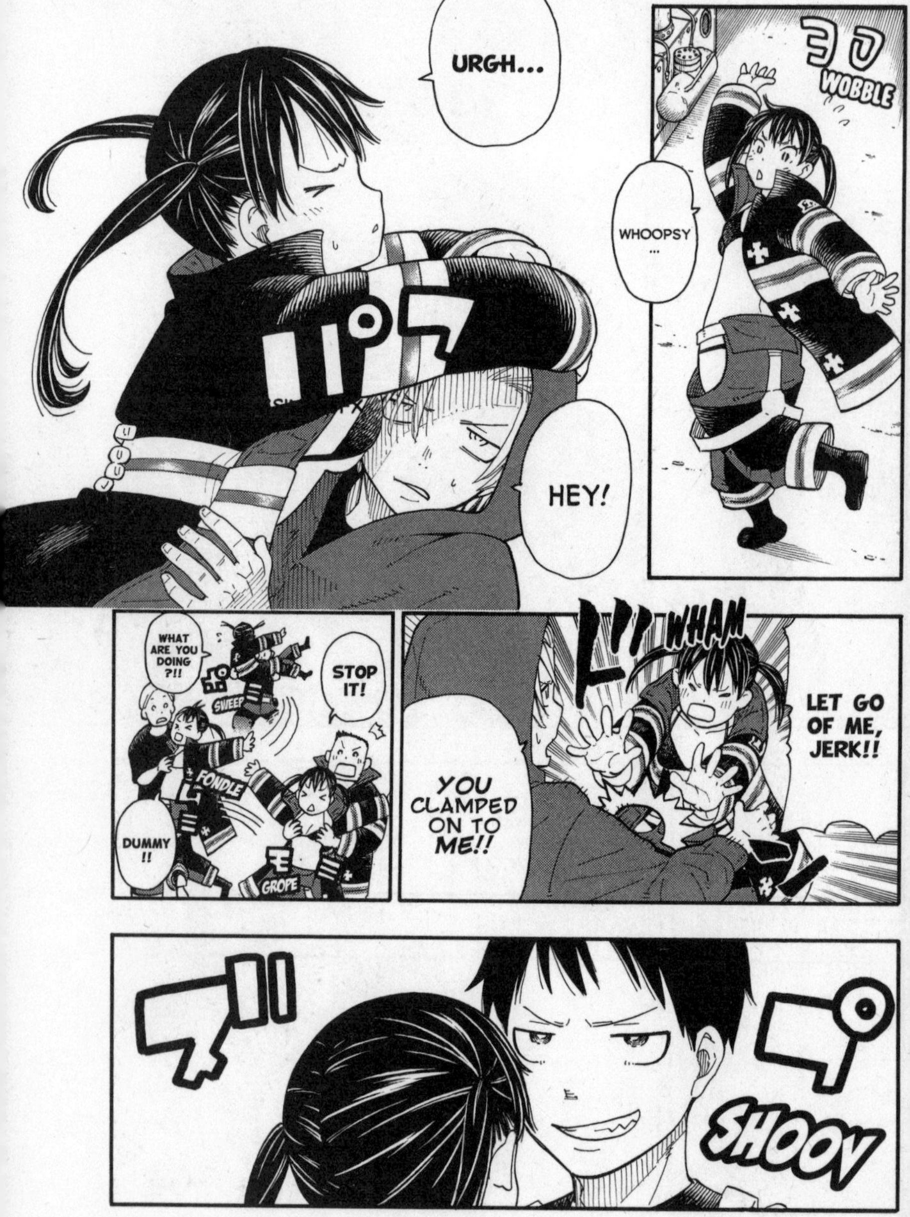
WOBBLE
WHOOPSY ...
URGH...
HEY!
WHAM
LET GO OF ME, JERK!!
YOU CLAMPED ON TO ME!!
STOP IT!
WHAT ARE YOU DOING ?!!
SWEEP
FONDLE
DUMMY !!
GROPE
SHOOV

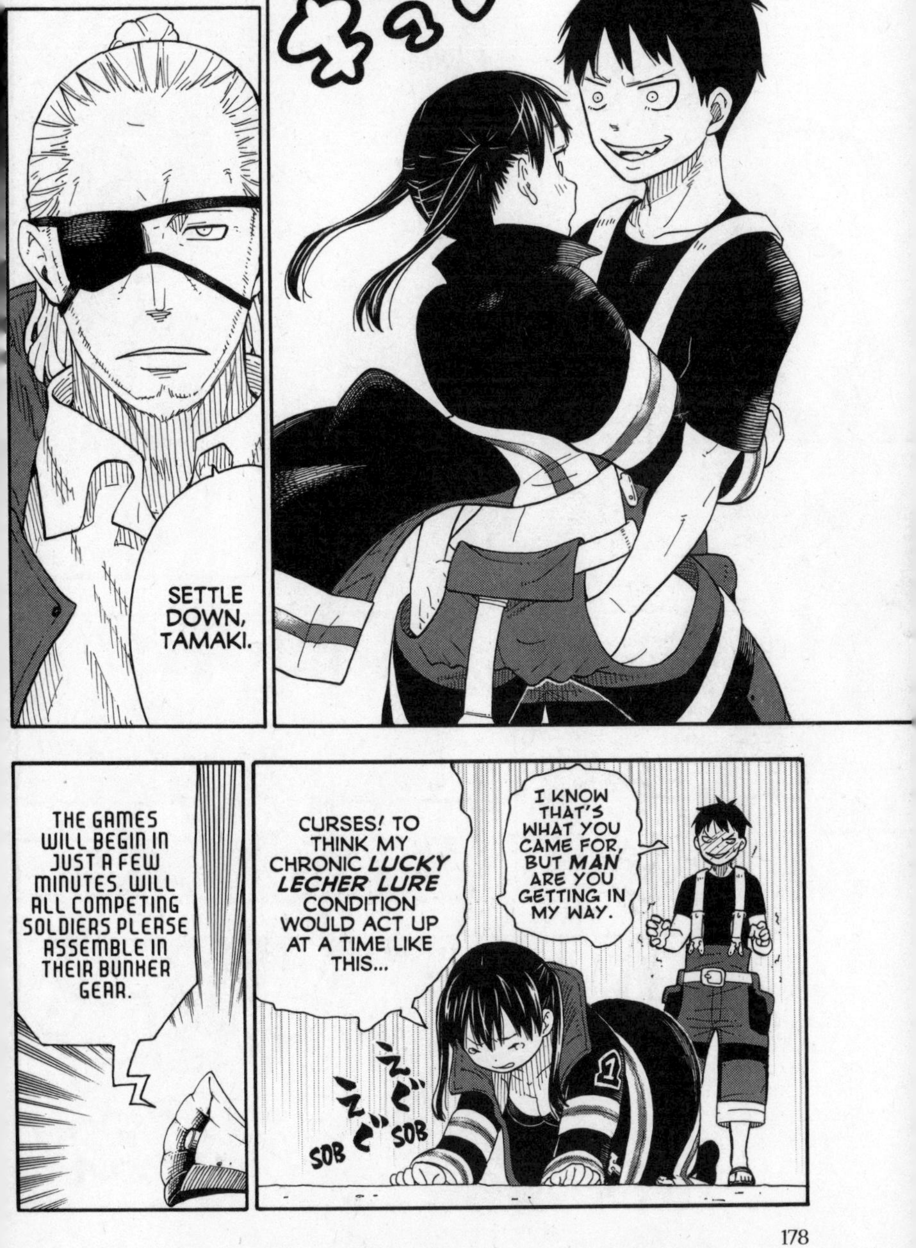
SQUEEZE
SETTLE DOWN, TAMAKI.
I KNOW THAT'S WHAT YOU CAME FOR, BUT MAN ARE YOU GETTING IN MY WAY.
CURSES! TO THINK MY CHRONIC LUCKY LECHER LURE CONDITION WOULD ACT UP AT A TIME LIKE THIS...
SOB SOB
THE GAMES WILL BEGIN IN JUST A FEW MINUTES. WILL ALL COMPETING SOLDIERS PLEASE ASSEMBLE IN THEIR BUNKER GEAR.

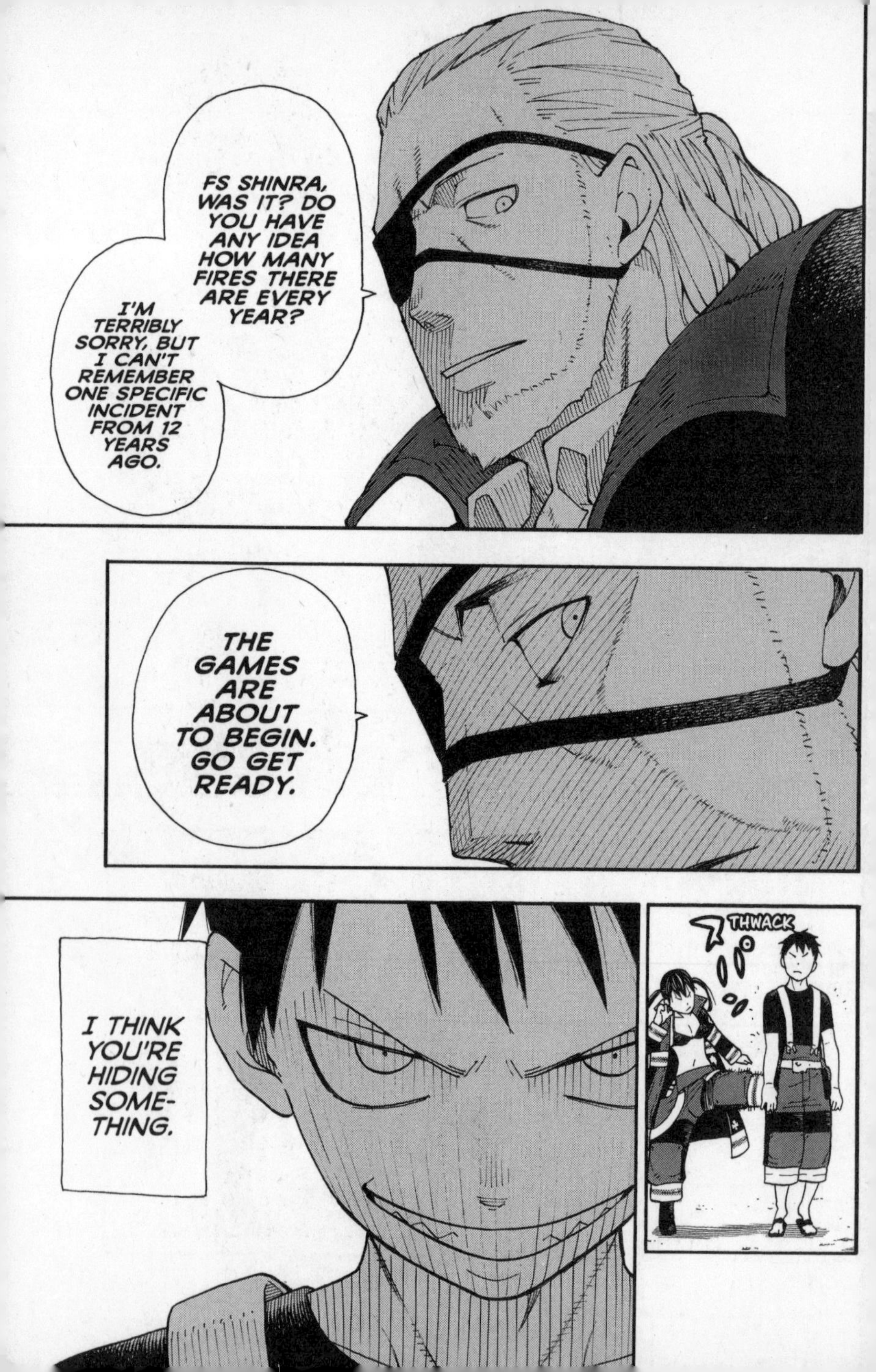
FS SHINRA, WAS IT? DO YOU HAVE ANY IDEA HOW MANY FIRES THERE ARE EVERY YEAR?
I'M TERRIBLY SORRY, BUT I CAN'T REMEMBER ONE SPECIFIC INCIDENT FROM 12 YEARS AGO.
THE GAMES ARE ABOUT TO BEGIN. GO GET READY.
THWACK
I THINK YOU'RE HIDING SOME-THING.

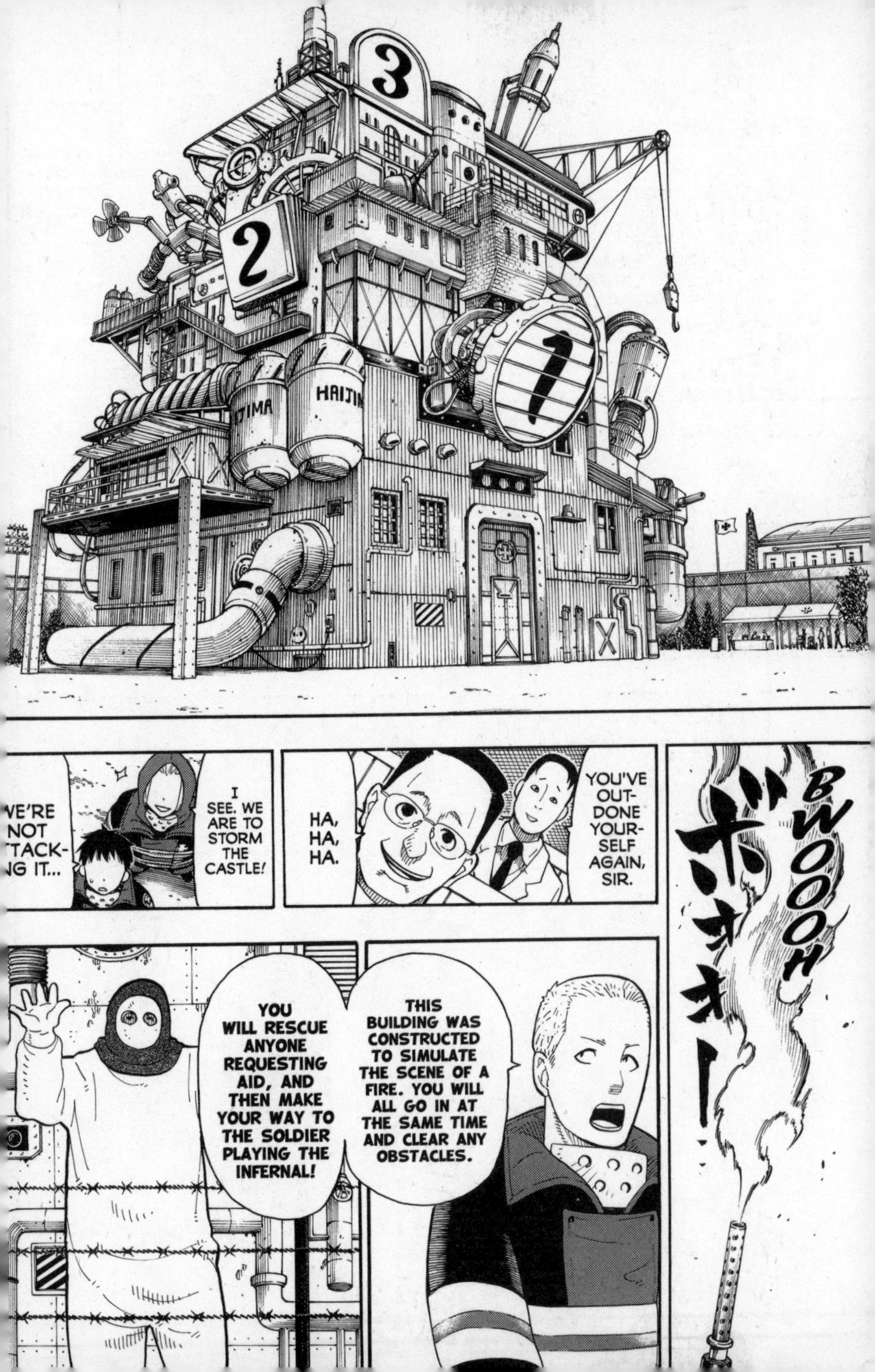
3
2
1
IJIMA
HAIJIN
BWOOOOH
YOU'VE OUT-DONE YOUR-SELF AGAIN, SIR.
HA, HA, HA.
I SEE. WE ARE TO STORM THE CASTLE!
VE'RE NOT TTACK- NG IT...
THIS BUILDING WAS CONSTRUCTED TO SIMULATE THE SCENE OF A FIRE. YOU WILL ALL GO IN AT THE SAME TIME AND CLEAR ANY OBSTACLES.
YOU WILL RESCUE ANYONE REQUESTING AID, AND THEN MAKE YOUR WAY TO THE SOLDIER PLAYING THE INFERNAL!

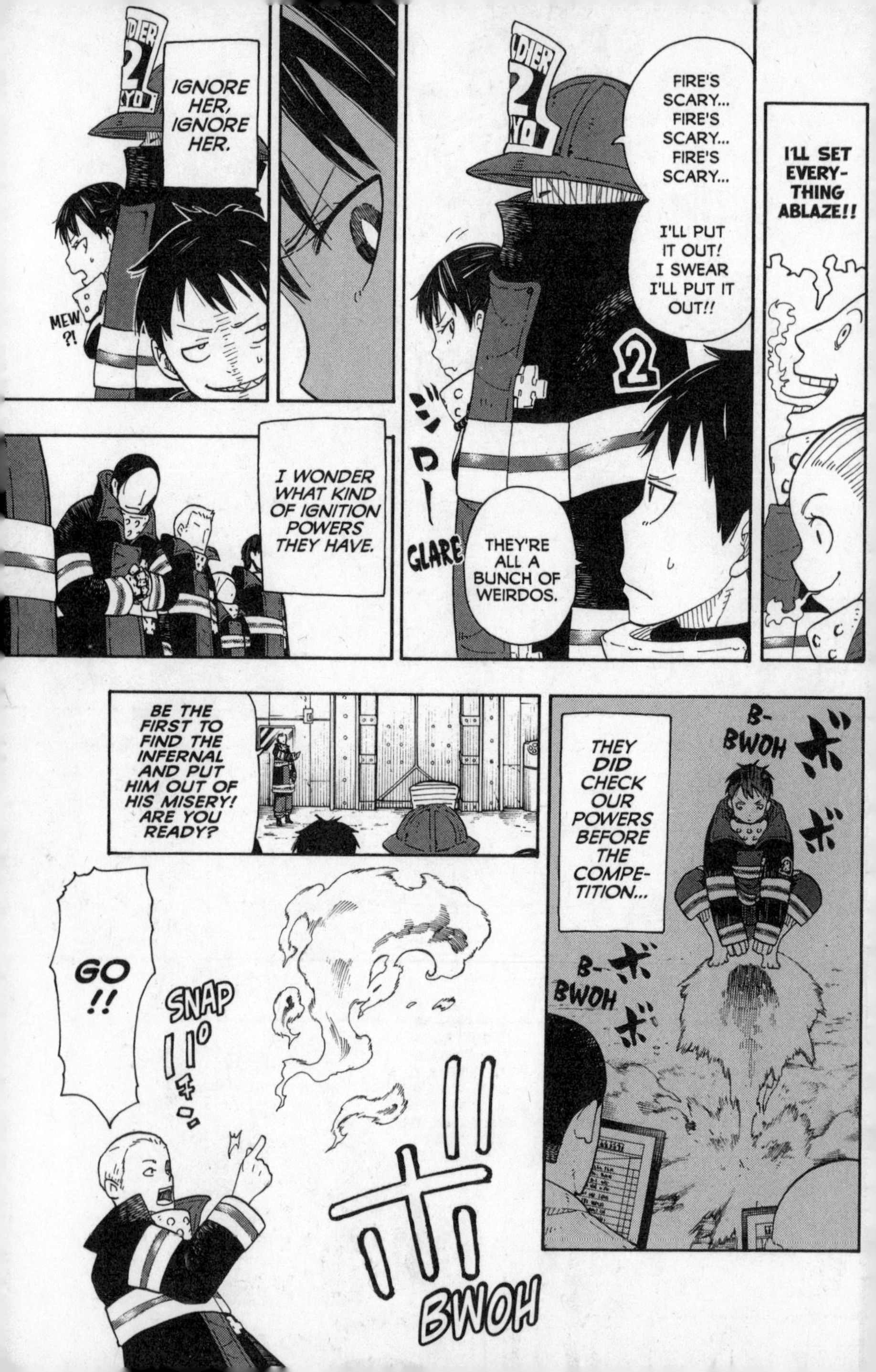
I'LL SET EVERYTHING ABLAZE!!
FIRE'S SCARY... FIRE'S SCARY... FIRE'S SCARY...
I'LL PUT IT OUT! I SWEAR I'LL PUT IT OUT!!
GLARE
THEY'RE ALL A BUNCH OF WEIRDOS.
IGNORE HER, IGNORE HER.
MEW ?!
I WONDER WHAT KIND OF IGNITION POWERS THEY HAVE.
B-BWOH
THEY DID CHECK OUR POWERS BEFORE THE COMPETITION...
B-BWOH
BE THE FIRST TO FIND THE INFERNAL AND PUT HIM OUT OF HIS MISERY! ARE YOU READY?
GO!!
SNAP
BWOH

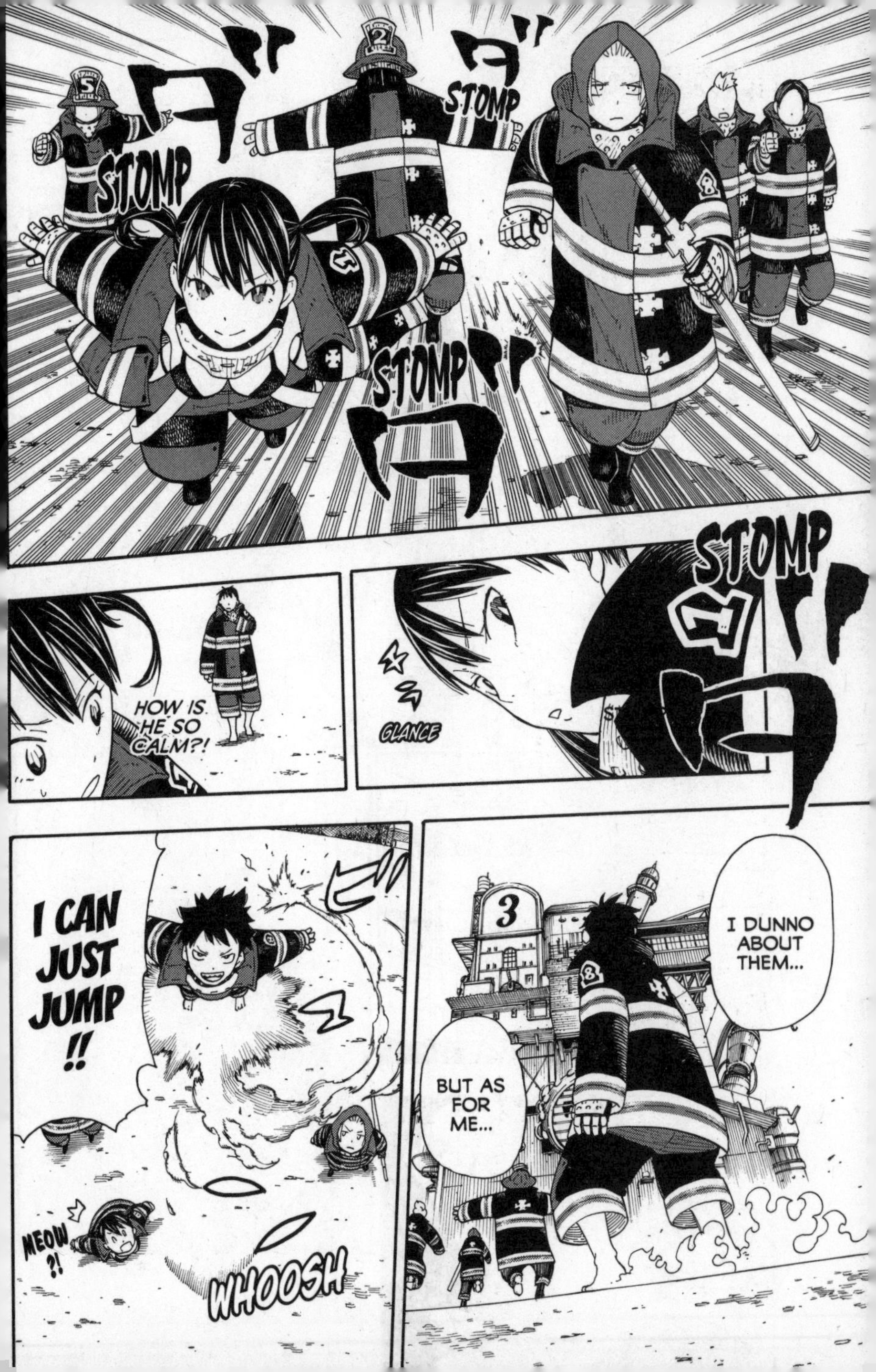
STOMP
STOMP
STOMP
STOMP
GLANCE
HOW IS HE SO CALM?!
I DUNNO ABOUT THEM...
BUT AS FOR ME...
I CAN JUST JUMP!!
MEOW?!
WHOOSH

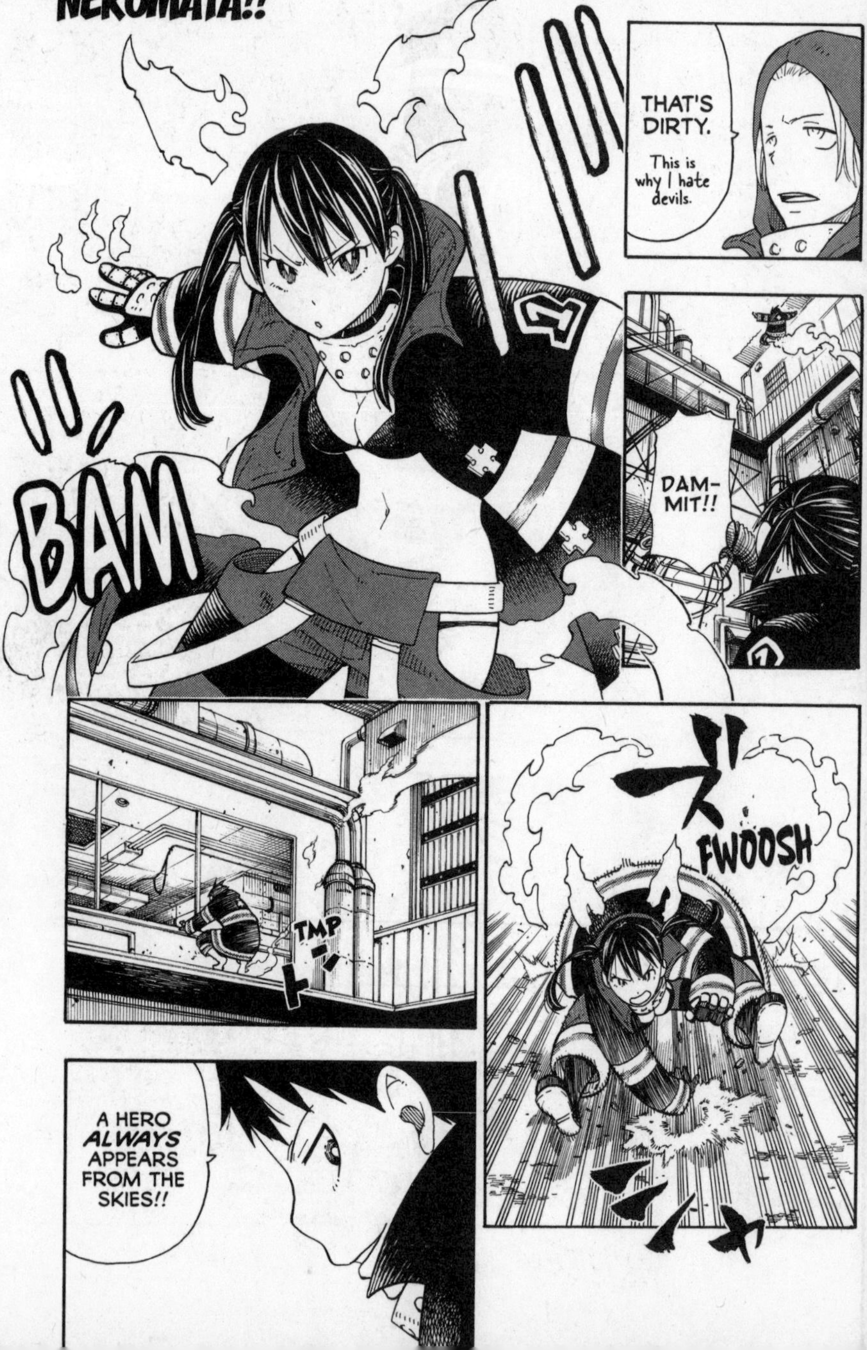
THAT'S DIRTY.
This is why I hate devils.
DAM-MIT!!
NEKOMATA!!
BAM
FWOOSH
TMP
A HERO ALWAYS APPEARS FROM THE SKIES!!

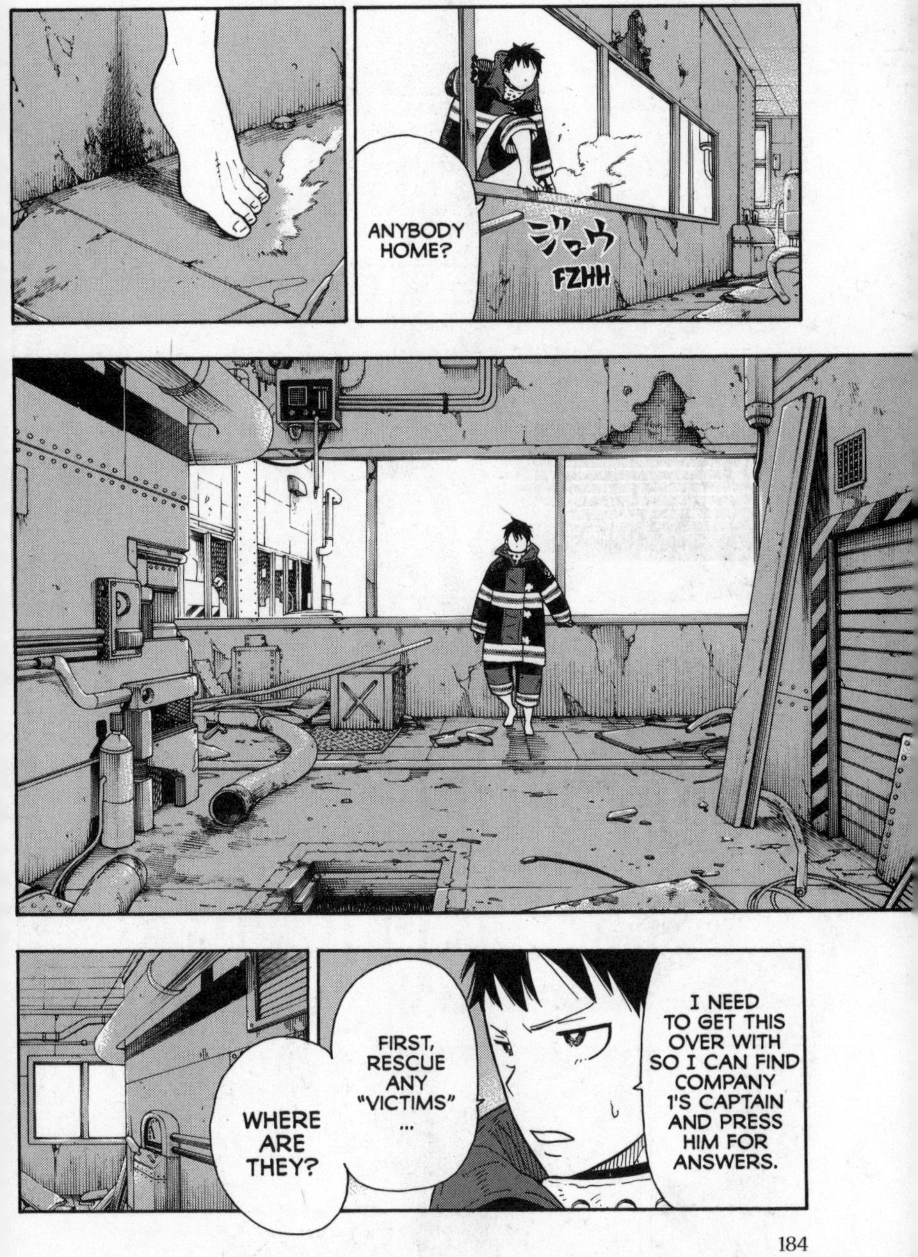
ANYBODY HOME?
ジュウ
FZHH
I NEED TO GET THIS OVER WITH SO I CAN FIND COMPANY 1'S CAPTAIN AND PRESS HIM FOR ANSWERS.
FIRST, RESCUE ANY "VICTIMS" ...
WHERE ARE THEY?

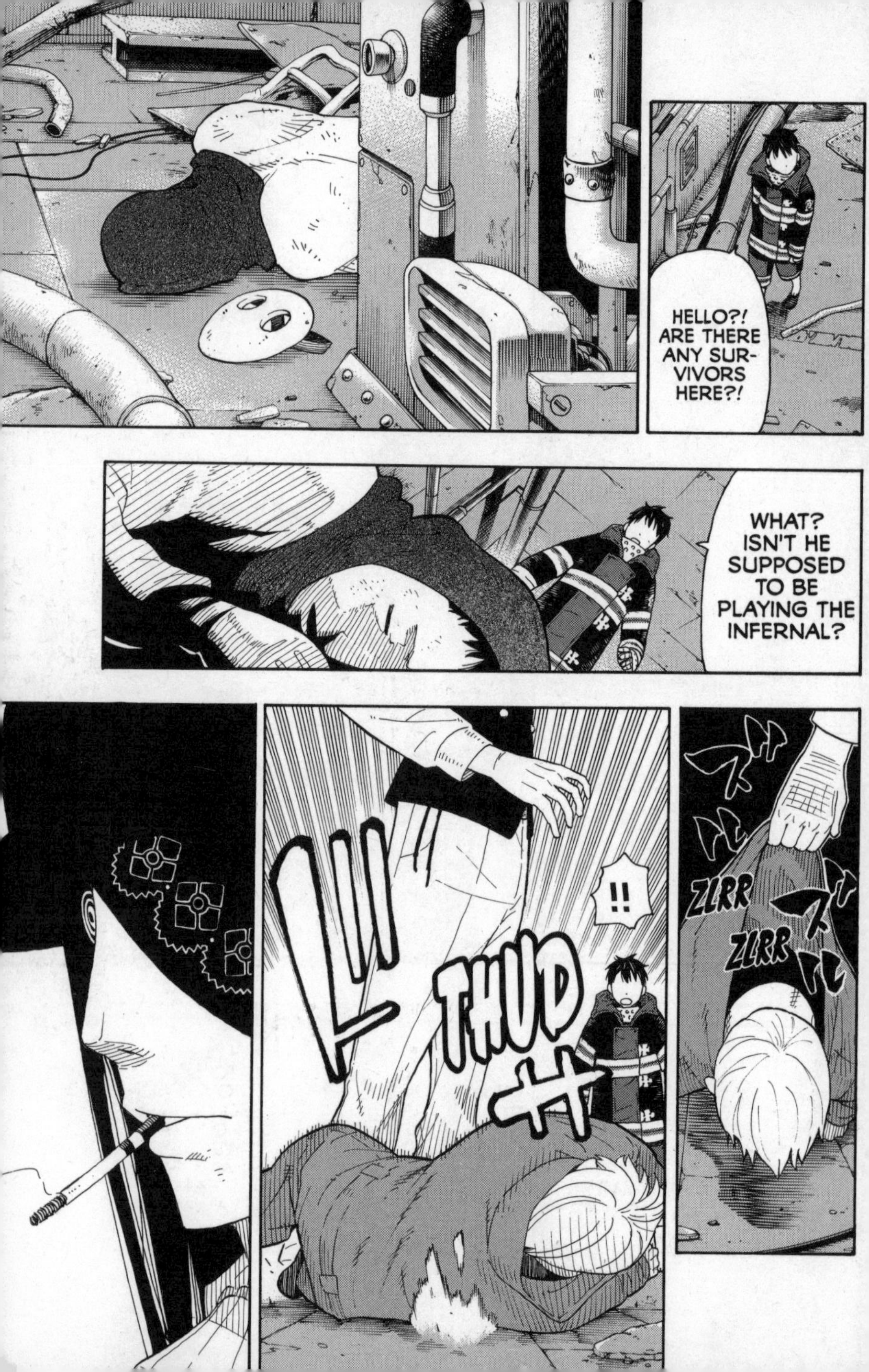
HELLO?! ARE THERE ANY SUR- VIVORS HERE?!
WHAT? ISN'T HE SUPPOSED TO BE PLAYING THE INFERNAL?
ZLRR
ZLRR
!!
THUD

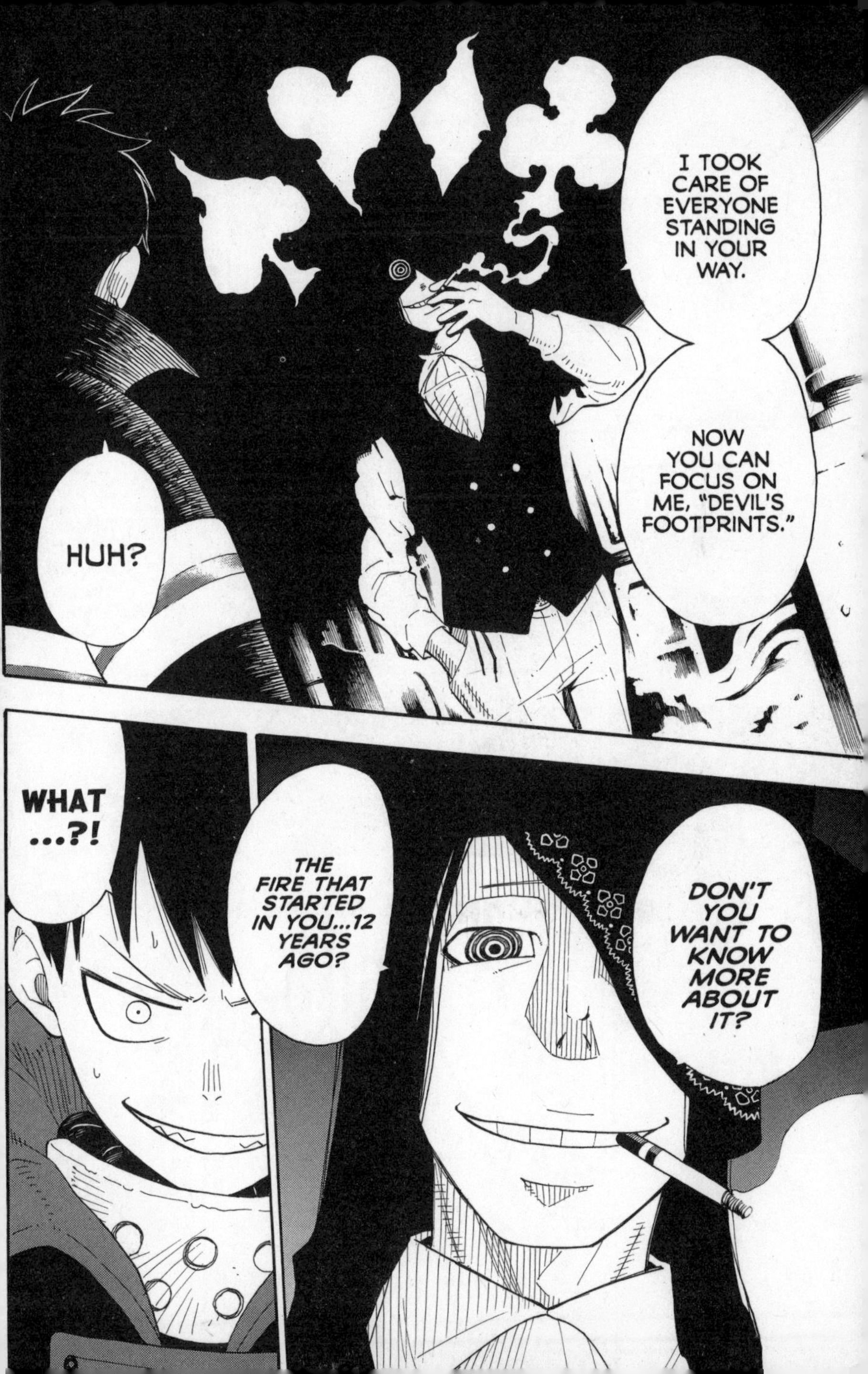
I TOOK CARE OF EVERYONE STANDING IN YOUR WAY.
NOW YOU CAN FOCUS ON ME, "DEVIL'S FOOTPRINTS."
HUH?
DON'T YOU WANT TO KNOW MORE ABOUT IT?
THE FIRE THAT STARTED IN YOU...12 YEARS AGO?
WHAT ...?!

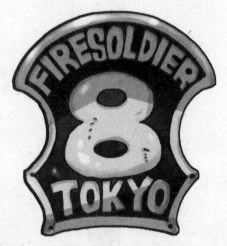

TO BE CONTINUED IN VOLUME 2!!

AFTERWORD MANGA: ATSUSHIYA

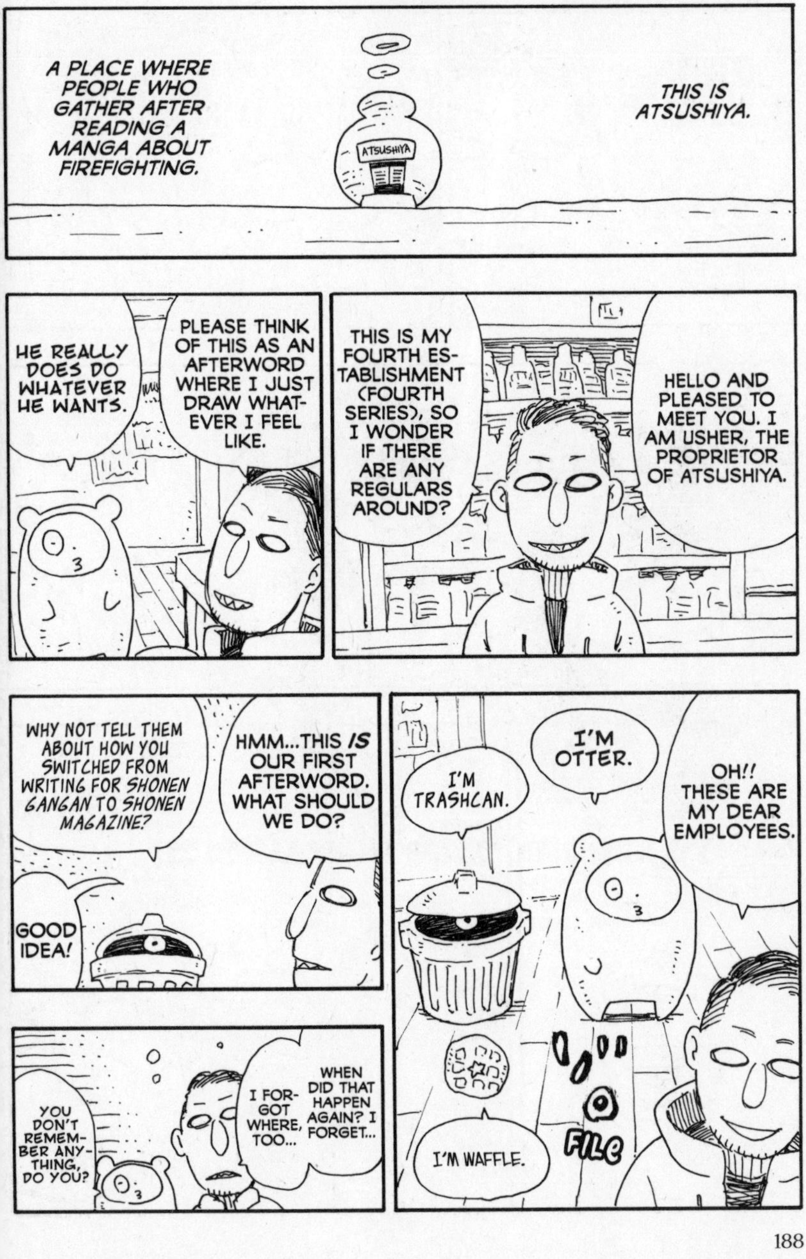
THIS IS ATSUSHIYA.
A PLACE WHERE PEOPLE WHO GATHER AFTER READING A MANGA ABOUT FIREFIGHTING.
ATSUSHIYA
HELLO AND PLEASED TO MEET YOU. I AM USHER, THE PROPRIETOR OF ATSUSHIYA.
THIS IS MY FOURTH ESTABLISHMENT (FOURTH SERIES), SO I WONDER IF THERE ARE ANY REGULARS AROUND?
PLEASE THINK OF THIS AS AN AFTERWORD WHERE I JUST DRAW WHATEVER I FEEL LIKE.
HE REALLY DOES DO WHATEVER HE WANTS.
OH!! THESE ARE MY DEAR EMPLOYEES.
I'M OTTER.
I'M TRASHCAN.
I'M WAFFLE.
FILE
HMM...THIS *IS* OUR FIRST AFTERWORD. WHAT SHOULD WE DO?
WHY NOT TELL THEM ABOUT HOW YOU SWITCHED FROM WRITING FOR *SHONEN GANGAN* TO *SHONEN MAGAZINE*?
GOOD IDEA!
WHEN DID THAT HAPPEN AGAIN? I FORGET...
I FORGOT WHERE, TOO...
YOU DON'T REMEMBER ANYTHING, DO YOU?

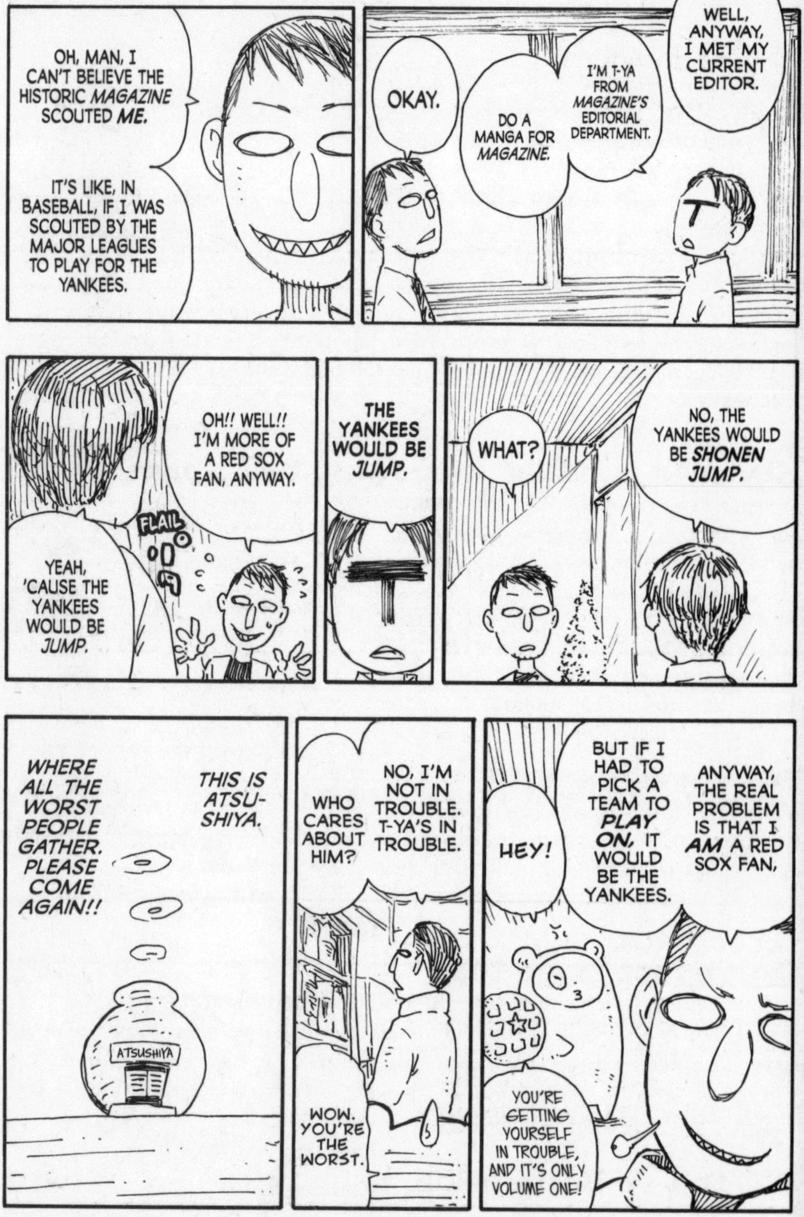
WELL, ANYWAY, I MET MY CURRENT EDITOR.
I'M T-YA FROM MAGAZINE'S EDITORIAL DEPARTMENT.
DO A MANGA FOR MAGAZINE.
OKAY.
OH, MAN, I CAN'T BELIEVE THE HISTORIC MAGAZINE SCOUTED ME.
IT'S LIKE, IN BASEBALL, IF I WAS SCOUTED BY THE MAJOR LEAGUES TO PLAY FOR THE YANKEES.
NO, THE YANKEES WOULD BE SHONEN JUMP.
WHAT?
THE YANKEES WOULD BE JUMP.
OH!! WELL!! I'M MORE OF A RED SOX FAN, ANYWAY.
FLAIL
YEAH, 'CAUSE THE YANKEES WOULD BE JUMP.
ANYWAY, THE REAL PROBLEM IS THAT I AM A RED SOX FAN,
BUT IF I HAD TO PICK A TEAM TO PLAY ON, IT WOULD BE THE YANKEES.
HEY!
YOU'RE GETTING YOURSELF IN TROUBLE, AND IT'S ONLY VOLUME ONE!
NO, I'M NOT IN TROUBLE. T-YA'S IN TROUBLE.
WHO CARES ABOUT HIM?
WOW. YOU'RE THE WORST.
THIS IS ATSUSHIYA.
WHERE ALL THE WORST PEOPLE GATHER. PLEASE COME AGAIN!!
ATSUSHIYA

Translation Notes:

Látom, page 27

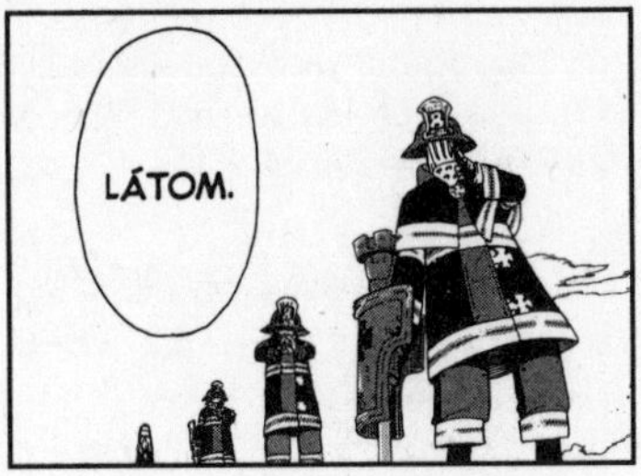
LÁTOM.

This is the word used by the Fire Force at the close of the prayer for the burning souls, sort of like "amen." Its origins are unclear, but there are many theories. It may have come from a Hungarian word meaning, "I see." There is also an Icelandic word, *lát*, which means "death." The religious organization affiliated with the Fire Force is the Holy Sol Temple, which honors the sun, so it's also possible that the L is meant to be an R, as a reference to the Egyptian sun god Ra. And finally, it may be an anagram of the Japanese word *tomurai*, which refers to mourning for the dead.

Her head is full of ... wedding bells, page 40

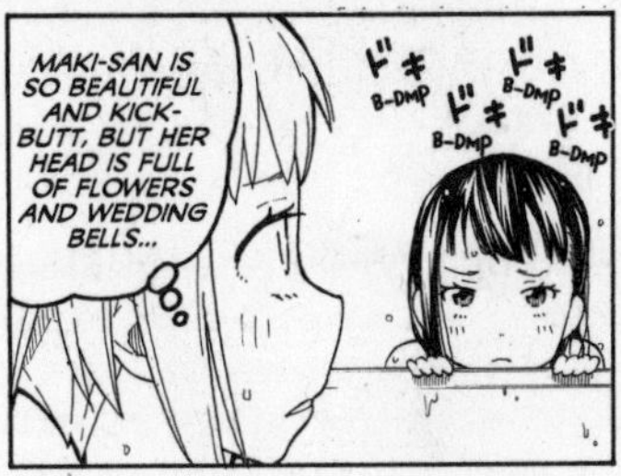
ドキ
B-DMP
ドキ
B-DMP
ドキ
B-DMP
ドキ
B-DMP
MAKI-SAN IS SO BEAUTIFUL AND KICK-BUTT, BUT HER HEAD IS FULL OF FLOWERS AND WEDDING BELLS...

In Japan, they have an idiom describing people who aren't always willing to face reality, usually meant as playful teasing. The phrase is *"atama ga ohana-batake,"* which literally means "his/her head is a field of flowers." In Maki's case, Iris can't help but upgrade it to *ohana-otome-batake*, making it a "field of flowers and girliness."

Flashover, page 68

A flashover is basically when an entire room explodes. What happens is the fire in the room causes everything to get hot, which in turn causes the exposed surfaces to release flammable gases. When those gases reach the right (or rather, wrong) temperature, they ignite and everything burns.

Onion face, page 103

In Japan, knights have been associated with onions since at least as far back as the 1990 release of *Final Fantasy III*, in which one of the jobs available to the playable characters is Onion Knight. Unfortunately, the origin of the association has been obscured through time, as not even the game developers can remember why they used that name.

Bobobo-bo Bo-bobwoh, page 129

Maki's familiars get their names from the onomatopoeia of the sounds created by the types of fires they represent. *Bo*, often rendered by the

translators as "bwoh," is usually the ignition of a fire, but can also be the roaring of a large fire such as this one. Of course, the name was likely also influenced by the hero of the manga *Bobobo-bo Bo-bobo*, although his powers are not fire-related.

Not polite to the captain, page 135

In the Japanese language, when speaking to other people, one would use either *teineigo* (polite speech) or *tameguchi* (plain speech). When talking to a superior, such as a captain or someone in authority, the proper thing to do is to at least use the minimum level of *teineigo*, and Arthur doesn't even bother to do that.

Blowing smoke, page 164

More accurately, our prankster friend says that the "Special Fire Force" is *kinakusai*, which means both "suspicious" and "smelling of smoke." The translators attempted to retain the smoky imagery with an English idiom, which we hope conveys a similar meaning. Ideally, the readers will also be put in mind of the phrase, "where there's smoke, there's fire," because *kinakusai* can also allude to imminent danger.

Wone Wone Nyine, page 171

The translators would like to apologize for the confusing spellings of these mascots' names. Their names come from a combination of the sounds dogs and cats make, and the numbers one-one-nine. In Japan, the emergency number to call the fire department is not 911, but 119. Because a Japanese dog says *wan* and a Japanese cat says *nyan*, this team of mascots can easily call for help. The old man, Mamoru-kun, is named for the Japanese word for "to protect."

Nekomata, page 183

According to Japanese folklore, if a cat lives long enough, its tail will split into two and it will become a supernatural creature known as a *nekomata*. While the full nature of Tamaki's powers has yet to be revealed, they do seem to give her cat-like reflexes.

Atsushiya and Usher, page 188

In Japan, an easy way to name a business you'd like to start would be to add *ya* ("room" or "shop") to the end of your name, for example. In this case, the Atsushiya was named after the creator of this manga, Atsushi Ohkubo. Another word that can be written with all the same characters as Atsushiya is the English word "usher," and thus the proprietor gets his name.

Fire Force volume 1 is a work of fiction. Names, characters, places, and incidents are the products of the author's imagination or are used fictitiously. Any resemblance to actual events, locales, or persons, living or dead, is entirely coincidental.

A Kodansha Comics Trade Paperback Original.

Fire Force volume 1 copyright © 2016 Atsushi Ohkubo
English translation copyright © 2016 Atsushi Ohkubo

All rights reserved.

Published in the United States by Kodansha Comics, an imprint of Kodansha USA Publishing, LLC, New York.

Publication rights for this English edition arranged through Kodansha Ltd., Tokyo.

First published in Japan in 2016 by Kodansha Ltd., Tokyo.

ISBN 978-1-63236-330-5

Printed in the United States of America.

www.kodanshacomics.com

9 8 7 6 5 4 3

Translation: Alethea Nibley & Athena Nibley
Lettering: AndWorld Design
Editing: Lauren Scanlan
Kodansha Comics edition cover design: Phil Balsman